The Churches in International Affairs

Reports 1999-2002

Edited by Dwain C. Epps

Commission of the Churches on International
Affairs of the World Council of Churches

Commission of the Churches on International Affairs of the World Council of Churches

Ecumenical Centre
P.O. Box 2100
150, route de Ferney
1211 Geneva 2
Switzerland

Tel. +41.22.791.61.11
Fax +41.22.791.03.61
E-mail: ccia@wcc-coe.org
Website: http://www.wcc-coe.org/what/international

Commission of the Churches on International Affairs of the World Council of Churches Liaison Office at the UN Headquarters

Church Centre
777 United Nations Plaza, Suite 9D
New York, NY 10017
U.S.A.

Tel. +1.212.867.58.90
Fax +1.212.867.74.62
E-mail: unlo@wcc-coe.org

ISBN: 2-8254-1418-2

Printed in Switzerland

For

Christiane Hoeffel

1941-2004

Administrative Assistant to
four Directors of the CCIA

Dear friend of the Commission and its staff

IN MEMORIAM

The Rev. Norbert Kenne

1960 – 2001

Devoted servant of the Lord Jesus Christ,
the Prince of Peace

Director of the Ecumenical Peace Service
(Service œcuménique pour la paix)
Yaoundé, Cameroun

Member of the
Commission of the Churches on International Affairs

TABLE OF CONTENTS

FOREWORD 1
ABBREVIATIONS 2
MODERATOR'S INTRODUCTION 3
DIRECTOR'S INTRODUCTION 5
Memorandum and Recommendations on Response to Armed Conflict
and International Law 7
*Recommendations adopted by the Central Committee and memorandum received
and commended to the churches, Geneva, 26 August-3 September 1999.*
The protection of endangered populations in situations of armed
violence: toward an ecumenical ethical approach.............................15
*Received by the Central Committee and commended to the churches for further
study, reflection and use, Potsdam, 29 January-6 February 2001.*
ENVIRONMENTAL JUSTICE 34
Message on the occasion of "Earth Day" 34
Sent by the General Secretary to North American churches, 22 April 1999.
A call to action in solidarity with those most affected by climate change......35
*Appeal issued on the occasion of the 8th session of the Conference of Parties
(COP8) to the UN Framework Convention on Climate Change, New Delhi,
October - November 2002.*
GLOBAL ECONOMY..38
Statement on the debt crisis 38
Issued in Geneva, 9 June 1999.
HUMAN RIGHTS..40
PEACE AND DISARMAMENT 41
ECUMENICAL POLICY 41
The Evolution of World Council of Churches Policy on Nuclear Arms
and Disarmament, 1948-2000 41
*Presentation to the Consultation with Churches on Nuclear Issues: Creation
at Risk, organized by the WCC, CEC, the NCCCUSA and the Canadian
Council of Churches, Brussels, 5-6 October 2000.*
Policy framework and guidelines on small arms and light weapons..............54
*Adopted by the CCIA at its 44th meeting, Crans Montana, Switzerland,
18 May 2001.*
PEACE CONCERNS...59
Easter Appeal for a Cessation of Armed Conflicts....................................59
*Issued by Konrad Raiser (WCC), Keith Clements (CEC), Ishmael Noko (LWF),
Milan Opocensky (WARC), Joe Hale (WMC), Denton Lotz (BWA), and
John L. Peterson of the Anglican Communion, 31 March 1999.*
The Decade to Overcome Violence (DOV), Churches Seeking
Reconciliation and Peace 60
*Message adopted by the Central Committee, Geneva,
26 August - 3 September 1999.*

A Basic Framework For The Decade To Overcome Violence...................... 62
Working document adopted by the Central Committee of the World Council of
Churches, Geneva, 26 August - 3 September 1999.
General Secretary's Christmas Message, 2000.. 66
Issued in Geneva, 17 November 2000.
Expression of concern about threats of retaliation following the
September 11th attacks in the U.S.A. 68
Letter to H.E. Kofi Annan, Secretary-General of the United Nations, 1 October
2001.
Letter to the heads of Muslim religious communities throughout the
world on the beginning of Ramadan 70
Sent to Muslim leaders and dialogue partners, 17 November 2001.
Pastoral letter to the churches and Christians in the United States
following the terrorist attacks of 11 September.. 72
Sent by the ecumenical "Living Letters" team at the conclusion of its ten-day visit,
Oakland, California, 16 November 2001.
Beyond 11 September: Assessing Global Implications................................. 75
Summary of the consultation convened in Geneva, 29 November-2 December 2001.
Beyond 11 September: Implications for US Churches and the World......... 88
Message to the WCC Central Committee from participants in the meeting
convened by the WCC in consultation with the NCCCUSA and CWS in
Washington, D.C., 5-6 August 2002.
Beyond 11 September: Implications for US Churches and the World......... 89
Draft Guide for Reflection from the Consultation with US church leaders,
Washington, D.C., 5-6 August 2002.
Minute on the tragedy of September 11th 2001 and the implications
of the US government's response 96
Adopted by the Central Committee, Geneva, 26 August-3 September 2002.
SMALL ARMS AND LIGHT WEAPONS (MICRODISARMAMENT)........................... 99
Ecumenical Consultation on Small Arms in Latin America......................... 100
Report of the WCC Consultation oraganized in collaboration with the Latin
American Council of Churches (CLAI) and in partnership with Viva Rio,
Rio de Janeiro, Brazil, 25-28 July 2000.
United Nations Conference on the Illicit Trade in Small Arms and Light
Weapons in All Its Aspects... 105
Oral intervention to the plenary, New York, 16 July 2001.................... 105
Humanitarian Statement of Concern addressed to the Conference by the CCIA
and other members of IANSA (International Action Network on Small Arms),
New York, 9-20 July 2001. 106
NUCLEAR WEAPONS 108
Call for the dismantling of nuclear weapons 108
Press release issued 23 April 1999.
Statement on nuclear disarmament, NATO policy and the churches 109
Adopted by the Executive Committee, Berlin, Germany, 26-27 January 2001.

Appeal on the occasion of the NATO Summit in Prague 114
Letter to foreign ministers of the non-nuclear member states of NATO,
14 November 2002.
UNITED NATIONS RELATIONS 117
ECUMENICAL POLICY 117
Resolution on United Nations Relations 117
Adopted by the CCIA at its meeting in Crans-Montana, Switzerland,
14-18 May 2001.
Statement on the Fiftieth Anniversary of the Creation of the Office of
the United Nations High Commissioner for Refugees (UNHCR) 118
Adopted by the Executive Committee, Geneva, 26-29 September 2000.
CONSULTATIVE RELATIONS 119
CCIA granted General Consultative Status with ECOSOC 119
New York, 3 May 2000.
SPECIAL SESSIONS OF THE UN GENERAL ASSEMBLY 120
Special Session of the General Assembly on the Implementation of the
Outcome of the World Summit for Social Development and Further
Initiatives ("Geneva 2000") 120
Contributions to the preparatory process, 1999-2000. 120
"A Call for a Change of Heart: Some Ethical Reflections to be considered for
the UN Draft Declaration," written statement submitted to the second
intersessional meeting for Geneva 2000, New York, 7-25 February 2000. 121
"Now is the time," oral statement to the Committee of the Whole, Geneva,
26 June 2000. 123
Letter from Konrad Raiser to UN Secretary-General Kofi Annan expressing
concerns about the role of UN-related International Financial Institutions at
"Geneva 2000", Geneva, 28 June 2000. 124
Response from the UN Secretary-General, 3 July 2000. 126
Reply to the UN Secretary-General, 7 July 2000. 128
UN General Assembly Special Session on HIV/AIDS (UNGASS),
New York, 25-27 June 2001 129
Statement by Faith-Based Organizations
UN WORLD SUMMITS 134
Millennium World Peace Summit of Religious and Spiritual Leaders 134
A Call to Dialogue, address by Konrad Raiser, United Nations, New York,
28-31 August 2000.
World Summit on Sustainable Development (WSSD), Johannesburg,
South Africa, 26 August-4 September 2002 136
"Seeking Sustainable Communities in a Globalizing World," statement of the
Ecumenical Team to the 8th Session of the Commission on Sustainable
Development, 1 May 2000. 136
"Justice - the Heart of Sustainability," contribution of the Ecumenical Team to
the Political Declaration, at the Ministerial Preparatory Committee meeting,
Bali, Indonesia, June 2002 139

iii

Written submissions issued by the Ecumenical Team at the World Summit: 139
*"Justice - The Heart of Sustainability," written contribution by the Ecumenical
Team for the Political Declaration.* 139
WORLD CONFERENCES 141
United Nations Conference on the Illicit Trade in Small Arms and
Light Weapons in All Its Aspects, New York, 9-20 July 2001 141
Oral intervention to the Conference, New York, 16 July 2001 141
*Humanitarian Statement of Concern addressed to the Conference by the CCIA
and other members of IANSA (International Action Network on Small Arms)* .. 141
World Conference Against Racism, Racial Discrimination, Xenophobia
and Related Intolerance, Durban, South Africa, 26 August -
7 September 2001 141
*Statement on the occasion of the International Day for the Elimination of Racial
Discrimination, 21 March 2001, issued by Konrad Raiser, 8 March 2001.* 141
*Background paper on the draft declaration and programme of action, submitted
to the UN High Commissioner for Human Rights, 15 August 2001* 143
*Oral statement of the Ecumenical Caucus to the plenary session on behalf of the
Ecumenical Caucus, 5 September 2001.* 151
*Statement presented to the media by Archbishop Desmond Tutu on behalf of the
Ecumenical Caucus, 5 September 2001.* 152
*Concluding statement issued by the World Council of Churches delegation,
Durban, 7 September 2001* 154
International Conference on Financing for Development (FfD),
Monterrey, Mexico, 18-22 March 2002 156
*Letter from Konrad Raiser to H.E. Ernesto Zedillo Ponce de León, President of
Mexico, April 2001* 156
*"Staying Engaged - For Justice," statement of the Ecumenical Team to the 4th
Preparatory Committee, New York, January 2002.* 157
*"Engagement with Commitment…?", press release issued by the Ecumenical
Team, Monterrey, Mexico, 19 March 2002.* 158
*Statement on the proposed "Monterrey Consensus Document" issued by the
Ecumenical Team, 18-22 March 2002.* 160
WRITTEN AND ORAL SUBMISSIONS TO OTHER UN BODIES 162
Commission and Subcommission on Human Rights 162
Review of Developments pertaining to the promotion and protection
of human rights and fundamental freedoms of Indigenous Peoples 164
*Intervention at the UN Working Group on Indigenous Populations, Geneva,
23-27 July 2001.*
Special Committee on the Situation with regard to the Implementation
of the Declaration on the Granting of Independence to Colonial
Countries and Peoples 165
*Statement to the United Nations Seminar on Assistance to the Palestinian
People, Division for Palestinian Rights, Vienna, 20-21 February 2001.* 165
Appeal for self-determination for Puerto Rico, New York, 6 July 1999. 165

Appeal for justice for residents of the island of Vieques, press release on the statement presented on behalf of the CCIA, New York, 12 July 2000. 169
RECOGNITIONS.. 171
Congratulations on the award of the Nobel Peace Prize 171
Letter to H.E. Kofi Annan, Secretary-General and to Ms. Rosemarie Waters, President of the UN Staff Committee, 16 October 2001.
UPROOTED PEOPLE.. 173
ECUMENICAL POLICY 173
Statement on the Fiftieth Anniversary of the Creation of the Office of the United Nations High Commissioner for Refugees (UNHCR) 173
Adopted by the Executive Committee, Geneva, 26-29 September 2000. (cf p. 118)
Resolution on uprooted people 173
Adopted by the Executive Committee, Berlin, Germany, 26-27 January 2001.
ASYLUM.. 177
Expression of concern about treatment of asylum seekers 177
Letter to WCC Member Churches in Australia and the National Council of Churches in Australia, 29 August 2001. (cf p. 279)
MIGRATION AND MIGRANTS' RIGHTS 177
Call for investigation into abuses of human rights of migrants in the countries of the Persian Gulf.. 177
Letter to Ms Gabriela Rodriguez, UN special rapporteur on the Human Rights of Migrants, 24 November 2000.
REGIONAL CONCERNS 179
AFRICA.. 179
ANGOLA... 179
Statement on Peace in Angola 179
Sent to the WCC Central Committee from the Executive Committee of the Council of Christian Churches in Angola, August 1999.
Affirmation of ecumenical efforts for peace and justice 181
Letter to the Rev. Gaspar Domingos, Council of Christian Churches in Angola (SICA), 3 September 1999.
Expression of thanks and invitation from the Council of Christian Churches in Angola, Luanda, 29 September 1999. 183
CONGO (REPUBLIC) 184
Appeals for international efforts for peace 184
Letter to UN Secretary-General Kofi Annan, 2 February 1999. 184
Letter to H.E. Jacques Chirac, President of France, 2 February 1999. 186
Message to the Ecumenical Council of Christian Churches of Congo (COECC) 188
Sent in February 1999.
Appeal for Peace and Humanitarian Action in Congo-Brazzaville............. 190
Statement issued at the conclusion of a consultation of concerned church leaders, Paris, 29-30 November 1999.
CONGO (DEMOCRATIC REPUBLIC) 191
Message of solidarity 191

Letter to the member churches in the Democratic Republic of Congo,
5 February 2001.
ETHIOPIAN-ERITREAN CONFLICT 192
Communication to religious leaders in Ethiopia 192
Letter to the members of the Interfaith Committee in Ethiopia via the Rev.
Yadessa Daba, General Secretary of the Mekane Jesu Church and member of
the WCC Executive Committee, 13 May 1999.
Minute on Peace and Reconciliation between Ethiopia and Eritrea 193
Adopted by the Central Committee, Geneva, 26 August-3 September 1999.
Message to the Participants in the Oslo Gathering of Religious Leaders 194
Letter conveying the minute of the Central Committee, 2 September 1999.
Congratulations to H.H. Patriarch Abuna Paulos on the award of the
Nansen Medal 194
Letter sent to the head of the Ethiopian Orthodox Tewahedo Church,
15 November 2000.
Appeal for the release of Ethiopian human rights defender 195
Letter to H.E. Prime Minister Meles Zenawi, 10 May 2001.
IVORY COAST 196
Expressions of concern about internal conflict 196
Letter to WCC member churches in the Ivory Coast, 10 October 2002. 196
Letter to the Executive Secretary of ECOWAS (Economic Community of West
African States), 10 October 2002. 199
LIBERIA 200
Appeal for the release of human rights defender 200
Letter to Mr Jeff Gongoer Dowana Sr, Head of Mission, Embassy of the
Republic of Liberia in London, 22 November 2002.
MADAGASCAR 200
Expression of concern about the post-election crisis 200
Open letter to the leaders of member churches in Madagascar, 24 January 2002 200
Letter to the churches of Madagascar, 22 February 2002 202
MOZAMBIQUE 203
Appeal for Debt Cancellation for Mozambique 203
Letter to WCC member churches in "Group of Eight" nations, 13 March 2000.
NIGERIA 205
Minute on Nigeria 205
Adopted by the Central Committee, Geneva, 26 August-3 September 1999.
Expression of condolences on the death of Bola Ige 206
Letter to H.E. Olusegun Obasanjo, President of Nigeria, 10 January 2002. 206
RWANDA 207
Unresolved questions related to the genocidal killings in Rwanda 207
Background information and suggestions for advocacy, issued in Geneva,
June 1999.
SIERRA LEONE 212
Support for UN peace efforts 212
Letter to H.E. Kofi Annan, Secretary-General, 11 May 2000.

SUDAN.. 21.

Appeal of the Sudan Ecumenical Forum on Sudan peace negotiations...... 215
Issued in Genera, 7 July 1999.

Statement on the situation in the Sudan.. 216
Adopted by the Central Committee, Potsdam, Germany, 28 January-
6 February 2001.

Minute on the peace process in Sudan.. 219
Adopted by the Central Committee, Geneva, 26 August-3 September 2002.

Call for respect for the Machakos Protocol and revival of the peace
process.. 220
Letter to H.E. President Omar Hassan al-Bashir, 7 October 2002.

ZIMBABWE.. 221

Expression of concern about pre-election repression and violence........... 221
Letter sent to Mr Densen Mafinyani, General Secretary, Zimbabwe Council of
Churches, 13 April 2000.

Pastoral letter to the churches.. 222
Joint letter to Mr Densen Mafinyani, General Secretary of the Zimbabwe
Council of Churches, 25 April 2000.

Planned visit to Zimbabwe in view of forthcoming elections...................... 225
Letter to Mr Densen Mafinyani, General Secretary of the ZCC, 9 May 2000.

WCC team recommends deployment of ecumenical peace observers for
Zimbabwe elections... 226
Press Statement issued in Harare, 29 May 2000.

Pastoral letter to the church leaders gathered at Victoria Falls.................. 228
Sent to Bishop Dr Ambrose Moyo, President of the ZCC, 19 July 2001.

Congratulations to church leaders on Victoria Falls communiqué.............. 229
Letter to Bishop Dr Ambrose Moyo of the Evangelical Lutheran Church in
Zimbabwe, President of Zimbabwe Council of Churches, 2 August 2001.

Statement on Zimbabwe.. 230
Adopted by the Executive Committee, Geneva, 11-14 September 2001.

Statement of the international ecumenical peace observer mission on the
Zimbabwe presidential election 232
Presented to the press in Harare, 13 March 2002.

ASIA... 235

ECUMENICAL POLICY 235

Justice, Peace and People's Security in North East Asia............................ 235
Report of the Ecumenical Consultation held in Kyoto, Japan, 26 February-3 March 2001.

Statement on South Asia... 240
Adopted by the Central Committee, Geneva, 26 August-3 September 2002.

AFGHANISTAN 246

Statement on the initiation of bombing in Afghanistan............................ 246
Issued by Mr Georges Lemopoulos, Acting General Secretary, Geneva,
8 October 2001.

BANGLADESH.. 247

Expression of condolences after church bombing 247

Letter to H.E. Mr Iftekhar Ahmed Chowdhury, Ambassador of Bangladesh to the United Nations Office in Geneva, 12 June 2001.

CHINA, PEOPLES REPUBLIC 248

Message to the seventh national conference of the China Christian Council 248

Conveyed from Geneva, 16 May 2002.

EAST TIMOR 249

Message on the extension of the mandate of UNAMET 249

Letter to UN Secretary-General Kofi Annan, 3 September 1999.

INDIA 250

Expression of solidarity with Christian leaders 250

Letter to the Rev. Dr Ipe Joseph, General Secretary of the National Council of Churches in India, 1 February 1999.

Condemnation of inter-communal violence in Gujarat 251

Letter to member churches and the National Council of Churches in India, 5 March 2002.

INDIA-PAKISTAN DISPUTE 252

Expression of hope for the success of India-Pakistan summit 252

Letter to member churches and councils of churches in India and Pakistan, 11 July 2001.

Appeal to the Governments of India and Pakistan for normalization of relations with Pakistan 253

Identical letters to H.E. Mr Atal Bihari Vajpayee, Prime Minister of India, and H.E. General Pervez Musharraf, President of Pakistan, 7 October 2002.

INDONESIA 254

Ecumenical delegation visit on request of the WCC eighth assembly 254

Press release issued at the conclusion of the visit to Indonesia, 27 January- 3 February 1999.

Appeal for decided action to stop inter-communal violence 256

Letter to H.E. President Bacharuddin Jusuf Habibie, 1 March 1999.

Minute on Indonesia 257

Adopted by the Central Committee, Geneva, 26 August-3 September 1999.

Protest of travel ban imposed on Central Committee member 258

Letter to H.E. M. N. Hassan Wirajuda, Ambassador of Indonesia to the United Nations in Geneva, 3 September 1999.

Appeal to Indonesian Government to end impunity 259

Letter sent to H.E. President Abdurrahman Wahid, 12 January 2000.

Minute on Indonesia 260

Adopted by the Executive Committee, Geneva, 29 February-3 March 2000.

Appeal for the restoration of law and order in the Malukus 261

Letter to H.E. Dr N. Hassan Wirajuda, Ambassador of Indonesia to the United Nations in Geneva, 27 June 2000.

Appeal on the situation in the Malukus 263

Letter to H.E. Mrs Mary Robinson, UN High Commissioner for Human Rights, 13 July 2000.

Appeal on sectarian violence in Central Sulawesi..264
Letter to H.E. Mrs. Mary Robinson, UN High Commissioner for Human
Rights, 10 December 2001.
Minute on Indonesia 265
Adopted by the Central Committee, Potsdam, Germany, 29 January-
6 February 2001.
Note on Indonesia...266
Minuted by the Central Committee, Geneva, Geneva, 26 August-
3 September 2002.
Expression of concern and condolences to the families of victims of
the bombing in Bali 266
Letter to member churches and national councils in Indonesia and Australia,
16 October 2002.
Appeal for protection of human rights in West Papua.................................267
Letter to H.E. Mme Megawati Soekarnoputri, President of the Republic,
20 September 2002.
KOREA 268
Congratulations to President Kim Dae-jung on the award of the
Nobel Peace Prize...268
Letter from the General Secretary, 13 October 2000.
PAKISTAN 269
Appeal for the release of blasphemy law protestors 269
Letter to H.E. General Pervaiz Musharraf, Chief Executive of Pakistan,
15 January 2001.
Expression of deep concern about the safety and security of the
Christian minority in Pakistan...271
Letter to H.E. General Pervaiz Musharraf, President of the Republic,
29 October 2001.
Condemnation of the assassination of human rights defenders..................272
Letter to H.E. General Pervaiz Musharraf, President of the Republic,
1 October 2002. 272
Open letter to member churches and the National Council of Churches in
Pakistan, 1 October 2002. 273
PHILIPPINES 274
Expression of concern about developments in the Philippines...................274
Letter to the National Council of Churches and WCC member churches in the
Philippines, January 2001.
SRI LANKA 275
Message to Member Churches and the National Christian Council...........275
Sent by the General Secretary, August 1999.
Statement on the situation in Sri Lanka...276
Issued by the CCIA and communicated to the parties to the conflict on
9 May 2000.

Message of congratulation on the signing of the Memorandum of
Agreement between the government of Sri Lanka and the Liberation
Tigers of Tamil Eelam (LTTE) 277
   Letter to H.E. President Chandrika Bandaranaike Kumaratunga,
   7 October 2002.
AUSTRALASIA 279
   AUSTRALIA 279
   Expression of concern about treatment of asylum seekers 279
      Letter to WCC Member Churches in Australia and the National Council of
      Churches in Australia, 29 August 2001.
   Expression of concern and condolences to the families of victims of
   the bombing in Bali 280
      Letter to member churches and national councils in Indonesia and Australia.
      16 October 2002 (cf p. 266).
CARIBBEAN 281
   HAITI 281
   Appeal to the government and leaders of the ruling Lavalas political
   party to put an end to violence and injustice 281
      Open letter addressed to the Haitian Protestant Federation, 19 December 2001.
   Support for the joint appeal by the Roman Catholic Church and the
   Protestant Federation of Haiti for prayer for peace, justice and integrity ... 283
      Letter to the churches and Christian communities in Haiti, 6 May 2002.
   Report of ecumenical election observers 285
      Issued in Port-au-Prince, 27 May 2001.
   PUERTO RICO 287
   Appeal for the cessation of US military exercises on the Island of
   Vieques 287
      Letter to U.S. President Bill Clinton, 30 November 1999.
   Appeal for protection of non-violent protesters on the Island of
   Vieques 288
      Letter to H.E. President Bill Clinton of the U.S.A., 2 May 2000.
EUROPE 290
   CYPRUS 290
   Minute on Cyprus 290
      Adopted by the Executive Committee, Geneva, 29 February-3 March 2000.
   Minute on Cyprus 290
      Adopted by the Central Committee, Potsdam, Germany,. 29 January -
      6 February 2001.
   ROMANIA 291
   Appeal for continued dialogue on church-state legislation 291
      Letter to President Emile Constaninescu, 4 February 2000.
   RUSSIAN FEDERATION 291
   Expression of condolences to victims of the bombings in Moscow 291
      Letter to H.H. Alexei II, Patriarch of Moscow and All Russia,
      15 September 1999.

Expression of profound concern about the continuing intervention in
Chechnya by Russian armed forces.. 292
Joint letter to His Holiness Alexei II, Patriarch of Moscow and All Russia,
15 November 1999.
Reiterated appeal to stop indiscriminate Russian military actions in
Chechnya... 293
Joint letter to His Holiness Alexei II, Patriarch of Moscow and All Russia,
10 December 1999.
Statement on Chechnya 295
Adopted by the Executive Committee, Geneva, 29 February-3 March 2000.
TURKEY.. 297
Statement on the situation of the Kurdish People and the arrest of
Abdullah Ocalan 297
Statement by Ms Kristine Greenaway, Director of Communication at a press
conference held jointly with representatives of the Kurdish community in
Switzerland at WCC headquarters in Geneva, 19 February 1999.
Expression of concern about the abduction, detention and trial in
Turkey of Mr Abdullah Ocalan... 297
Letter to Mr Daniel Tarschys, Secretary-General of the Council of Europe,
11 March 1999.
Appeal to commute the death sentence of Abdullah Ocalan....................... 299
Letter to H.E. Süleyman Demirel, President of the Republic, 2 July 1999.
Expression of condolences to earthquake victims....................................... 299
Letter to H.E. Süleyman Demirel, President of the Republic, 20 August 1999..... 299
YUGOSLAVIA (FORMER) 300
Message to the Conference on Peace and Tolerance in Kosovo 300
Conveyed to the conference held in Vienna, 16-18 March 1999.
Pastoral letter to WCC member churches in the Federal Republic of
Yugoslavia.. 301
Letter to leaders of the three WCC member churches in Yugoslavia,
25 March 1999.
Appeal for an immediate moratorium on the NATO military
intervention... 302
Letter to H.E. Kofi Annan, Secretary-General of the United Nations, from
the general secretaries of the WCC, CEC, and LWF and endorsed by the
general secretary of WARC, 29 March 1999.
Easter appeal for a cessation of armed conflicts 303
Issued from Geneva, 31 March 1999.
Statement on Protection of Humanitarian Principles in Kosovo
Refugee Response... 304
Issued jointly by the WCC, CEC, LWF and WARC, Geneva, 15 April 1999.
Yugoslavia's double tragedy.. 305
Ecumenical delegation Report, Novi Sad, Belgrade, 16-18 April 1999.
Church leaders consultation on the churches and the crisis in the
Balkans 314

Report of the consultation convened by the WCC and CEC in collaboration with the LWF, WARC and the Ecumenical Council of Hungary, Budapest, Hungary, 26-27 May 1999.

Ecumenical delegation visit to the FYR Macedonia and Albania.................316
Conclusions from the report of the joint delegation sent by the WCC, CEC and the LWF, 18-25 May 1999.

Ecumenical statement on the peace agreement for Kosovo.........................318
Issued jointly by the WCC, CEC, LWF and WARC, Geneva, 11 June 1999.

Pastoral letter to the Holy Synod of the Serbian Orthodox Church...........320
Letter to H.H. Patriarch Pavle, 24 June 1999.

Ecumenical delegation visit to Kosovo..321
Findings of the delegation sent by the WCC and CEC, 29 June -2 July 1999.

The crisis is not over ! Europe, the Kosovo Crisis and the Churches........324
Report of the consultation convened by CEC in cooperation with the WCC and the Serbian Orthodox Church, Oslo, 14-16 November 1999.

Condemnation of the destruction of churches 327
Joint letter to H.H. Patriarch Pavle of the Serbian Orthodox Church, 3 December 1999.

Expression of solidarity with the churches in Yugoslavia.............................328
Joint letter sent 6 October 2000.

Appeal for religious tolerance...329
Letter to His Holiness Pavle, Patriarch of the Serbian Orthodox Church, 16 August 2002..329
Letter to H.E. Mr Michael Steiner, Special Representative of the Secretary General, United Nations Interim Administration in Kosovo, 16 August 2002.

LATIN AMERICA...332

ARGENTINA 332

Congratulations on the granting of the World Methodist Council's Peace Prize to the Grandmothers of the Plaza de Mayo 332
Conveyed by letter to Bishop Aldo M. Etchegoyen of the Evangelical Methodist Church of Argentina, 13 August 1999.

Appeal on behalf of the "Prisoners of La Tablada".......................................333
Letter to H.E. President Fernando De La Rua, 7 July 2000.

Follow-up to the appeal on behalf of the "Prisoners of La Tablada" 336
Letter to H.E. President Fernando De La Rua, 13 November 2000.

Expression of appreciation for action to overcome impunity.....................337
Letter to the Hon Dr Gabriel Cavallo, 29 March 2001.

Expression of solidarity with the churches and people of Argentina.........339
Letter to member churches in Argentina, 10 January 2002.

BRAZIL...343

Expression of indignation at court decision to absolve officials charged with responsibility for the massacres of landless peasants 343
Letter to H.E. Dr Fernando Henrique Cardoso, President of the Republic, with copies to the president of the court of the State of Para, José Alberto Soares Maia, and to the minister of justice, 25 August 1999.

.CHILE 344
  Expression of concern about police intervention in FASIC headquarters. 344
  Letter to Amb. Javier Illanes Fernández, Permanent Representative of Chile
  to the UN in Geneva, 26 May 1999.
COLOMBIA 346
  Ecumenical Cooperation Forum with Colombia 346
  Report of meeting held in Geneva, 25-26 September 2001.
  Minute on Colombia 349
  Adopted by the Central Committee, Potsdam, Germany, 9 January-
  6 February 2001.
  Message on the massacre in the church of Bellavista 350
  Letter to the churches of Colombia, 10 May 2002.
  Statement on violence in Colombia 352
  Adopted by the Central Committee, Geneva, 2 September 2002.
GUATEMALA.. 354
  Oral interventions at the UN Commission on Human Rights.................... 354
  See p. 163.
MIDDLE EAST 355
  IRAQ 355
  Appeal to the UN Security Council to lift sanctions with direct and
  indiscriminate effect on the civilian population............................... 355
  Letter to H.E. Kofi Annan, Secretary-General of the UN, 18 February 2000.
  Statement on the threats of military action against Iraq.................... 357
  Adopted by the Central Committee, Geneva, 26 August - 3 September, 2002.
  Appeal to Iraq to respect the resolutions of the UN Security Council 358
  Letter to H.E. Saddam Hussein, President of Iraq, 19 September 2002.
  Appeal to the US Government... 359
  Letter to Amb. Kevin Edward Moley, Permanent Mission of the USA to the
  UN in Geneva, 19 September 2002.
  Appeal to the governments of China, France, Russia and the UK.............. 360
  Letters to the Permanent Representatives to the UN in Geneva,
  19 September 2002.
  Appeal against military action in Iraq.. 360
  Individual letters to Members States of the Security Council and to the Secretary
  General of the UN, 15th October, 2002.
  Appeal to church leaders in member states of the UN Security Council.... 362
  Letter to WCC member churches and Central Committee members, specialized
  ecumenical agencies, national and regional councils of churches, 24 October 2002.
ISRAEL... 363
  Expression of condolences to victims of suicide bombing 363
  Letter to H.E. Mr Yaakov Levy, Ambassador of Israel to the United Nations
  in Geneva, 6 June 2001.
ISRAELI-PALESTINIAN CONFLICT 364
  Letter of encouragement to the UN Secretary-General for his initiative

for a resumption of negotiations..364
Letter to H.E. Kofi Annan, Secretary-General of the UN, 10 October 2000.
Sharing the land, the truth and the peace..366
Written submission by the CCIA to the Fifth Special Session of the United
Nations Commission on Human Rights devoted to grave and massive violations
of the human rights of the Palestinian people by Israel, Geneva, 17 October 2000.
In Pursuit of Lasting Peace with Justice..369
Oral intervention by the CCIA to the Fifth Special Session of the United
Nations Commission on Human Rights, Geneva, 17 October 2000.
Minute on the situation in the Holy Land after the outbreak of the
second Palestinian uprising..372
Adopted by the Central Committee, Potsdam, Germany, 29 January-
6 February 2001.
Background Document on the Situation in the Middle East........................374
Commended to the churches for their study and urgent action by the Central
Committee, Potsdam, Germany, 29 January-6 February 2001.
Resolution on ecumenical response to the Palestinian-Israeli conflict........378
Adopted by the Executive Committee, Geneva, 11-14 September 2001.
Statement on Israel's obligations as occupying power..................................380
Issued by the CCIA on the occasion of the Conference of the High Contracting
Parties to the Fourth Geneva Convention, Geneva, 5 December 2001.
Appeal for urgent action 382
Open letter to the member churches, regional and national councils of churches
and ecumenical partner organizations, 15 March 2002.
Appeal to the European Union to take a leading role in seeking a just
and sustainable peace in the Middle East...384
Letter to foreign ministers of EU countries on the eve of their meeting in
Luxembourg, 12 April 2002.
Statement on the ecumenical response to the Israeli-Palestinian conflict
in the Holy Land 386
Adopted by the Central Committee, Geneva, 26 August-3 September 2002.
JERUSALEM..389
Minute on Jerusalem..389
Adopted by the Central Committee, Geneva, 26 August-3 September 1999.
Resolution on Jerusalem Final Status Negotiations.....................................391
Adopted by the Executive Committee, Geneva, 26-29 September 2000.
Advent message to the churches and Christian communities of
Jerusalem 392
Letter from the General Secretary to the patriarchs and heads of Christian
communities in Jerusalem, 12 December 2000.
LEBANON 393
Statement on the Israeli withdrawal from South Lebanon..........................393
Issued by the General Secretary in Geneva, 26 May 2000.
PALESTINE 395
Statement of support at the Bethlehem 2000 International Conference.....395

Presentation by the Director of the CCIA to the conference convened at FAO
headquarters by the UN Special Committee on Palestine, Rome,
18-19 February 1999.
Message of condolences on the death of Faissal Husseini 397
Letter to H.E. Mr Nabil Ramlawi, Permanent Observer of Palestine to the
United Nations in Geneva, 6 June 2001.
NORTH AMERICA 398
CANADA 398
Legal claims against the federal government and the churches arising
from past practices in residential schools for children of native peoples ... 398
Letter from the General Secretary to member churches in Canada: Anglican
Church of Canada, Presbyterian Church of Canada, United Church of Canada,
5 July 2000.
UNITED STATES OF AMERICA 399
Message to the churches after the bombing attacks of September 11th 399
Sent from the meeting of the Executive Committee, Geneva, 11 September 2001.
Open letter to the member churches in the United States 399
Geneva, September 20, 2001.
Congratulations to Jimmy Carter on the award of the Nobel Peace Prize . 402
Letter to the former president of the U.S.A., 16 October 2002.
PACIFIC 403
FEDERATED STATES OF MICRONESIA AND THE MARSHALL ISLANDS 403
Minute on the renegotiation of the Compacts of Free Association
between the U.S.A. and the Federated States of Micronesia and the
Republic of the Marshall Islands 403
Adopted by the Central Committee, Geneva, 26 August-3 September 2002.
FIJI 404
Message on the internal crisis 404
Message to the member churches in Fiji, 26 May 2000
BY-LAWS OF THE COMMISSION OF THE CHURCHES ON
INTERNATIONAL AFFAIRS (CCIA) 406
CCIA MEMBERSHIP 411
CCIA MEETINGS 412
Report of the XLIII Meeting of the Commission of the Churches on
International Affairs 412
La Longeraie, Morges, Switzerland, 22-28 January 2000.
Report of the XLIV Meeting of the Commission of the Churches on
International Affairs 415
Crans-Montana, Switzerland, 14-18 May 2001.
Report of the XLV meeting of the Commission of the Churches on
International Affairs 421
La Tour-de-Peilz, Switzerland, 3-7 June 2002.
CCIA STAFF 431

FOREWORD

This eighth volume of *The Churches in International Affairs* continues the annual reports to the churches produced in the first 22 years of the Commission of the Churches on International Affairs.

The WCC is a fellowship of 347 member churches in more than 120 countries in all continents and from nearly all Christian traditions. It Constitution and Rules notes, with respect to the authority of statements issued by the Council, that

While such statements may have great significance and influence as the expression of the judgment or concern of so widely representative a Christian body, ...their authority will consist only in the weight they carry by their own truth and wisdom.

As the first WCC Assembly (Amsterdam, 1948) said, these statements

will not be binding on any church unless that church has confirmed them, and made them its own.

A primary task of the CCIA is to assist the churches in forming a consensus on pressing international concerns on the basis of which the WCC's Central and Executive Committees establish policies that guide the day-to-day actions of the Council in consultation with its member churches.

As has happened periodically in the life of the WCC since it was founded in 1948, the Council established a new structure at the beginning of this period in response to diminishing financial resources and to adjust to the contemporary priorities of the ecumenical movement as identified at the Eighth Assembly in Harare (1998). This new configuration was built on the foundations of the five historical streams of ecumenical endeavor that flowed together after 1948 in the WCC, one being the CCIA. It included the merging of Refugee and Migrant Services with International Affairs, restoring a connection that existed in the earliest years. Reports on the meetings of the Commission held during these four years are included towards the end of this book.

This quadrennial report includes major studies undertaken; conclusions of major international consultations on specific areas of concern; policy statements, resolutions and decisions adopted by the governing bodies; and actions taken by the Council in the field of international affairs.

Unless otherwise indicated, all the documents reproduced here are from the WCC.

The editor owes a debt of gratitude to the CCIA staff and Commission members listed at the end of this volume for their work that is reflected in these pages. Special thanks are due to Libby Visinand for her painstaking proofreading of the final text.

ABBREVIATIONS

AACC   All Africa Council of Churches

ACT   Action by Churches Together (ACT) is a global alliance of churches of the World Council of Churches and the Lutheran World Federation and their related aid agencies working to save lives and support communities during emergencies

BWA   Baptist World Alliance

CCA   Christian Conference of Asia

CCC   Caribbean Conference of Churches

CCEE   Council of European Bishops Conferences

CCIA   Commission of the Churches on International Affairs of the World Council of Churches

CEC   Conference of European Churches

CLAI   Latin American Council of Churches

CWS   Church World Service

DOV   Decade to Overcome Violence

ECOSOC   UN Economic and Social Council

FfD   Financing for Development

LWF   Lutheran World Federation

MECC   Middle East Council of Churches

NCCCUSA   National Council of the Churches of Christ in the USA

PCC   Pacific Conference of Churches

POV   Program to Overcome Violence

WARC   World Alliance of Reformed Churches

WMC   World Methodist Council

MODERATOR'S INTRODUCTION

In the seven years that have elapsed since the World Council of Churches' 8th Assembly in Harare there has been a period of remarkable change in the world and in the WCC. The leadership has changed both for the Council with the election of a new General Secretary and for the Commission of the Churches on International Affairs with the departure of Dwain Epps, who was its Director since 1993, and the election of his successor, Peter Weiderud. Dwain Epps has left his footprints in the history of the work of the CCIA. During his tenure, he presided over the launching of the Decade to Overcome Violence – a very successful programme of the WCC, now being implemented by the churches around the world; the Ecumenical Accompaniment Programme in Palestine and Israel; and the Sudan Ecumenical Forum which supported the churches of Sudan in their peace efforts that culminated in the signing of a Peace Accord on the 9th of January 2005. We wish Dwain Epps our best for a well-deserved retirement albeit a busy one.

Peter Weiderud has assumed the mantle of Director of the Commission with energy. Since he took over, UN reforms have been looming large on the horizon with countries jostling for a place on the Security Council. The nuclear issue is disturbing. The prospects for the future of the Non-Proliferation Treaty are worrying to say the least. The number of nuclear bombs stands at upwards of thirty thousand. There has not been any significant change for decades. If anything, more countries are aspiring to become nuclear states. It seems that the world has been lulled to sleep with the demise of the Soviet Bloc, which ushered in a mono-polar world led by the United States of America, obsessed, after the 11th September 2001 attacks, with a military approach to global security. Afghanistan and Iraq were the first to feel the impact of US military might. North Korea and Iran have been put under pressure to renounce their nuclear programmes while the USA and their allies continue with theirs, contributing to the debacle of the recent UN Non-Proliferation Treaty Review Conference. Let us hope that the WCC's 9th Assembly in Porto Alegre, Brazil, in February 2006, will renew the First Assembly's call for active engagement of Christians in a new global campaign for the total elimination of nuclear weapons from the face of the earth. One nuclear bomb is a threat to the human race.

Given the present world situation, where globalization is becoming a reality that impinges on every aspect of life, the WCC must continue ever more aggressively to assist the member churches in articulating their positions and thus minimize the more negative and destructive aspects of globalization. Perhaps more than ever before it is necessary for Christians and their churches to pool resources together

3

rather than to fly their individual flags. Recent initiatives in the field of ecumenical advocacy where churches and specialized agencies are moving together provide a hopeful sign and deserve support and encouragement. Only thus can churches make a significant impact in the political, economic, financial and commercial arenas of our globalizing world. Let us hope that this effort will bear fruit and give hope to the millions who are being marginalized and left behind.

Amb. Bethuel A. Kiplagat

Nairobi, June 2005

DIRECTOR'S INTRODUCTION

The Commission of the Churches on International Affairs was created in 1946 by the International Missionary Council and the Provisional Committee of the World Council of Churches as a specialized instrument to serve its parent bodies and other international Christian bodies "as a source of information and guidance in their approach to international problems, as a medium of common counsel and action, and as an organ in formulating the Christian mind on world issues and in keeping that mind effectively to bear on such issues."

The first two of its "Aims" called for the promotion of education and action at the national and denominational level, reflecting the conviction that "witness that is truly ecumenical must spring from local conviction and determination."

The next three mandated the CCIA to study "selected problems of international justice and world order, including economic and social questions" through sub-committees, special groups and international study conferences.

Three remaining aims dealt with the realm of action: to call attention to urgent international problems; to suggest effective Christian action, to advise the parent bodies – or to speak in its own name – on "Christian principles" with direct bearing on immediate issues; and to represent the WCC at the United Nations, its related agencies and other relevant international organizations.*

The By-Laws of the CCIA have been reviewed and updated by WCC Assemblies and Central Committee over the past fifty years, most recently after the Eighth Assembly in Harare (1988). Yet the governing bodies have always considered the original aims still to be valid, and they are maintained virtually verbatim in the latest version reproduced towards the end of this volume.

This quadrennial report provides a measure of how the Commission has sought to serve the WCC and its member churches in the fulfillment of those aims in the face of nearly unprecedented challenges in international affairs. During these four years the local and regional conflicts that exploded around the world after 1991 in the wake of the Cold War continued to proliferate and become more complex. The new configuration of world affairs, dominated by the U.S.A. as the single world super-power, posed unprecedented new threats to the framework of international law and the role and authority of the United Nations.

Midway through this period, the tragic terrorist attacks of 11 September 2001 sent shockwaves around the globe, evoking virtually universal sympathy and solidarity with the government and people of the U.S.A., from friend and foe alike. Regretably, the decision of the U.S. government to respond with a global "war on

---

* Drawn from Richard M. Fagley, "The First Twenty Years," in *The Churches in International Affairs 1970-1973*, WCC, Geneva, 1973.

terror." Its virtually unilateral decision to respond with massive armed force first in Afghanistan and then again in Iraq, and the expansion of its military deployment to the four corners of the world squandered that outpouring of good will. It brought nearly universal condemnation, dividing and destabilizing the global political climate.

The WCC responded promptly to international, regional and national conflicts at the behest of the churches most directly affected or threatened, seeking to mobilize actions of solidarity from the global ecumenical movement, and on their behalf to bring influence to bear on governments and policy-makers at national and international levels in efforts either to avoid or to stop armed confrontations.

Several significant policy studies reported here sought to give theological, moral and ethical guidance on such complex areas of international controversy as whether armed intervention is acceptable as a means to protect non-combatants. The CCIA led the effort to express international ecumenical solidarity with the U.S.A. after the September 11th attacks, and organized major consultations with experts to consider the implications of the US global response. In the process it sought to bring new insights into the continuing debate in and among the churches between those who hold to strict pacifism and those who hold the use of armed force as a last resort to be justifiable or even necessary.

The consistent concern of the WCC for disarmament with respect to nuclear weapons was renewed and the impact of the growing trade in and use of small arms and light weapons was addressed as an issue effecting rich and poor alike.

In May 2000 the UN Economic and Social Council acknowledged the significant role the CCIA/WCC has played over the years as one of the first NGOs officially recognized, raising its consultative status to the highest level. This report shows the broad scope of the CCIA's impact, in cooperation with other specialized staff of the Council, in the UN's deliberations on global economic justice, peace, disarmament, human rights, racism and environmental concerns.

The task is the same as it was in 1946: education and action; theological reflection and technical studies; and the pursuit of church unity in mission, service and witness. The results of this work often show themselves only long after the fact, but they are sometimes dramatic, as was the signing as this report was concluded of a new peace agreement in the Sudan after more than three decades of ecumenical and diplomatic efforts. The key to success, as always, is consistent, coherent ecumenical action over the years, rooted in a manifest concern for the victims of war and injustice and careful study of the root causes. Undergirding all is shared faith in the biblical assurance that the loving God is the sovereign Lord of history, the source of boundless hope for a just and peaceful world.

Dwain C. Epps
Montbovon, Switzerland
January 2005

INTERNATIONAL ISSUES AND TRENDS

Memorandum and Recommendations on Response to Armed Conflict and International Law

Recommendations adopted by the Central Committee and memorandum received and commended to the churches, Geneva, 26 August - 3 September 1999.

The nine months since the WCC Harare Assembly have yet again been marked by costly international and internal armed conflicts in virtually all of the regions of the world, and by growing threats to international peace and security. Very many of them have had disastrous consequences for the human rights of affected populations, have resulted in massive loss of life and displacement of populations, and have damaged respect for democracy and the international rule of law. In response to some, major world or regional powers have intervened in the name of international security and humanitarian concern, sometimes with tragic unforeseen consequences. This was especially the case in the response to the Kosovo crisis. Many other conflicts, however, have been substantially ignored by the international media and received little effective attention by the international community.

The nature of the international response, the rationale offered for intervention, and the failure to respond in certain notable crises raise serious questions which require the attention of the churches. They are of particular concern for the ecumenical movement and for the World Council of Churches, which was formed in response to appeals like that made in 1920 by the Ecumenical Patriarchate, which urged the churches to join together to give a witness to the nations with respect to the need for a just, peaceful world order and effective international institutions to promote and sustain it. Thus, from the earliest beginnings the ecumenical movement's commitments to church unity, human rights, peace and justice, and the international rule of law have been bound together. In these interests, and out of a desire to remain faithful to the Gospel and to make Christian witness and mission credible to the world, the WCC has repeatedly sought to offer constructive critique and guidance to the nations.

Moreover, as the General Secretary has noted in his report to this meeting of the Central Committee, held in Geneva 26 August - 3 September 1999, the Vancouver Assembly's 1983 Statement on Peace with Justice, which said that without justice for all everywhere we shall never have peace anywhere, must be reconsidered in the light of the experience of the last decade. This affirmation is certainly true with respect to the lasting, comprehensive peace Christians receive from God. The Church can be satisfied with nothing less. Yet the conflicts of the past decade have shown that action for peace in the more limited sense of controlling armed conflict becomes an unavoidable priority in the face of today's massive threats to justice and life itself. The churches and the international system need to consider more deeply in the present context how the complementary and interrelated needs of people for both peace and justice can be more effectively related.

Once again, the Central Committee of the World Council of Churches feels compelled to address churches and nations in the light of the international response in recent months to armed conflicts in the Balkans, Africa, Asia, Latin America and the Middle East which have highlighted trends addressed by the WCC particularly since the Canberra Assembly in 1991:

- the erosion of the authority and capacity of the United Nations and its institutions created to develop, codify and guarantee respect for the international rule of law;
- the unwillingness, especially of influential states, especially in the West, to revise appropriately their policies and actions on international peace and security in the light of the new needs and opportunities created by the end of the Cold War;
- the tension between principles in the United Nations Charter of non-intervention in the affairs of sovereign states, and the obligation of the international community to intervene on humanitarian grounds when states fail to respect the human rights of people within their borders;
- the complex interrelationship between the need for justice as the essential basis of peace, and the need for peace as essential to the pursuit of justice; and
- the ever more pressing challenges confronting churches in particular national or international conflicts, and the ecumenical movement as a whole, in efforts to promote non-violent approaches to conflict transformation and resolution, and post-conflict healing and reconciliation.

The erosion of the authority of the United Nations

As the World Council of Churches has stated on many occasions, the United Nations plays a unique role in the world as the sole body where universally accepted standards of human rights are developed. Churches and other advocates of human rights depend on the impartiality and universality of the United Nations in seeking to hold governments of many different political persuasions accountable to international standards. Thus, a stronger and more effective United Nations is crucial to assure respect for the international rule of law, a measured collective approach to the maintenance of international peace and security, the enforcement of international human rights standards, and the promotion of justice in the world.

The dominant conflict in the period since the Harare Assembly has been the crisis in Kosovo. The decision of NATO powers to intervene there on humanitarian and national security grounds without effective reference to the UN Charter and the Security Council gave rise to heated international debate. The international response to Kosovo is a compelling example of the erosion of the authority of the United Nations and is thus worth examining in some detail. The decision to intervene militarily in Kosovo was defended in different ways by the NATO governments. Overriding considerations of national security were cited yet again by the United States and some other NATO powers to justify intervention in their own national security interests. The intervention was also justified on human rights and humanitarian grounds, with governments maintaining that the urgency of the humanitarian crisis demanded a more rapid response than the Security Council was capable of authorizing. Some governments cited previous decisions of the Security Council as having justified NATO acting on its own within the provisions of the Charter, noting that UN involvement in the Kosovo crisis stopped short - for political reasons - of authorizing force, but that it was moving in that direction.

In retrospect, many have felt that political and geopolitical interests of major powers prevailed over the intention of the Charter that all member states have equal rights under and obligations to international law. NATO decisions and actions with respect to Kosovo sidelined and undercut the authority of the United Nations, its Security Council and its specialized agencies, which have been constituted with the mandate to guide and conduct humanitarian operations, and led to violations of fundamental principles of international humanitarian law, especially with respect to the treatment of refugees. They effectively barred the Secretary-General from exercising his impartial mediating role, and blocked him from pursuing negotiations for a non-violent resolution. He and the UN as a whole were virtually excluded from the NATO-led Rambouillet negotiations held under the imminent threat of military intervention. Moreover, questions have been raised about the precedents set in Kosovo for the further development of a new NATO strategy and role in the world.

In the process, NATO powers subjected themselves to the charge of having applied a double-standard in assessing and responding to humanitarian needs. Few denied the legitimacy of the urgent humanitarian need created by increasing acts of ethnic cleansing against the ethnic Albanian population of Kosovo, but many raised serious questions about the failure of the same nations to respond with similar energy and decisiveness to crises in Africa and elsewhere, whose humanitarian dimensions were equally serious and often more dramatic in terms of the threats they posed to the life, peace and security of masses of people. It is hard to avoid the impression that racist attitudes have influenced such decisions.

The need for new approaches to international peace and security

The collapse of Communism in Eastern Europe, and the brief period of global entente which occurred after 1991, created new opportunities within the framework of the United Nations for powers from East and West to join together to help resolve a series of long-standing conflicts in parts of the world where they had previously confronted one another in proxy wars. Many held out the hope that this new-found cooperation would lead to rapid reductions of nuclear and conventional arsenals built up during decades of military stand-off between the two great military alliances. They expected this would lead to a thorough-going review of approaches to international security based on military alliances, building

9

on the experience of the Conference on Security and Cooperation in Europe (CSCE). Ecumenical bodies and others in North America and Europe, whose nations were parties to the CSCE Final Act, sought to help shape the new Organization for Security and Cooperation in Europe (OSCE). The hope was to strengthen international security within this regional sphere through adopting a more comprehensive approach to addressing the underlying causes of conflict and to create new, non-military regional and sub-regional alliances for peace based on respect for human rights.

The churches have supported the development of such regional civilian alliances as constructive alternatives to a Cold War ideology which divided reality into opposing enemy camps associated with good and evil, right and wrong, and which proved incapable of addressing the more complex historical, cultural, political and economic realities revealed by the conflicts which broke out in the immediate post-Cold War period.

The decision of the UN Security Council to invite the OSCE to deploy a large, unarmed civilian observation contingent in Kosovo was therefore welcomed in many quarters as a constructive, non-military approach to the protection of threatened civilian populations and to addressing the causes of the conflict through inter-ethnic dialogue. Alone, the OSCE might not have been able to achieve the desired goals, but combined with UN-led negotiations it might have had a chance to succeed. Opinions differ. Some hold that this form of intervention came too late to reverse the course of events, and that the only remaining option was strong, decisive military action. Others believe that the persistent threats and apparent determination of NATO powers to pursue armed intervention cut short this innovative alternative approach.

Developments in Kosovo have underscored the fact that the OSCE, like other regional bodies, is far from realizing its potential as an alternative approach to international security within Europe. While much work remains to be done to make the OSCE a credible alternative to military alliances, the churches should continue to support the vision of civilian-based regional alliances seeking peace based on respect for human rights.

Principles related to humanitarian intervention

The tension between the principle of national sovereignty, on which the present international system is based, and the moral obligation members of the international community may feel to intervene in urgent situations of humanitarian emergency, was intensified in the early 1990s around such African crises as Somalia, Rwanda and Sudan. This tension has been exacerbated by the changing nature of warfare.

Today's conflicts are characterized by an increasing number of civilian casualties and are fuelled by an arms trade of unprecedented proportions. In fact, far from being the unintended victims of warfare, civilian populations have increasingly become the targets of military action. As UN Under-Secretary-General Olara Otunnu, Special Representative of the Secretary-General on Children and Armed Conflicts, has reminded this Central Committee, in conflicts in which enemies are demonized, villages and entire populations have become the targets of military action in which children and women suffer disproportionately. Millions of children have been killed, maimed, uprooted, sexually abused and traumatized by today's wars. The UN Security Council Resolution 1261 (1999) of 25 August demonstrated that the international community is becoming aware of the tremendous impact of war on children and concrete suggestions have been made on ways to reduce the damage inflicted on them. But these measures need the support of churches, non-governmental organizations, governments and inter-governmental organizations. Concrete initiatives are needed to address the needs of children and women particularly in conflict situations; the issue of the protection of children must be placed on the agenda during peace negotiations; and the needs of children in post-conflict situations must be addressed. Children represent the future of their countries and our world. The international community needs to demonstrate flexibility and creativity to ensure that their needs are met and, most of all, that the conflicts which wreak havoc with their lives are prevented or resolved quickly.

The tension between the perceived need for the international community to take action to stem a tide of civilian deaths and the principle of non-intervention was brought into sharp focus by the discussions around humanitarian intervention in Kosovo.

We note that there is as yet no consensus among the churches about either the meaning of the term humanitarian intervention or about its justification in certain cases. For some, humanitarian intervention refers to a range of actions, short of the use of armed military force, which the international community can take to respond to situations where there are massive violations of human rights. For others, humanitarian intervention involves the use of force. For some churches, the use of military force can never be justified while others believe that in certain situations, when other non-military means have been exhausted, military action may be justifiable.

In recent years, Chapter VII of the UN Charter (Action with Respect to Threats to the Peace, Breaches of the Peace and Acts of Aggression) has often been cited as a justification for intervention in Iraq by the Gulf War coalition forces, in Somalia by the United States and some of its allies, and now again in Kosovo by NATO. It is necessary to recall that the clear preference of the Charter, in general, is for pacific resolution of disputes, and in Chapter VII, in particular, the preference is for measures not involving the use of armed force. Only when the Security Council considers such actions to be inadequate, or when these actions have proved to be inadequate, may other measures be taken to maintain or restore international peace and security by military or other forms of coercion (Art. 42). In such a case, a special agreement is required with the Security Council, including

11

specification of the numbers and types of forces, ...and the nature of the facilities and assistance to be provided (Art 43).

The NATO intervention took another direction. Not only did it ignore these provisions of the Charter, it used levels of force equivalent to those used in war. Since no declaration of war was issued, it could be argued that NATO powers also placed themselves outside the framework of international humanitarian law applicable in war. The UN Charter remains essentially silent with respect to intervention on humanitarian grounds, though the debate on this issue has included arguments that massive violations of the rights of citizens within a sovereign state constitute a threat to international peace and security, and thus fall within the terms of Chapter VII. Even in this case, no single power, nor a group of powers is authorized to take action outside specific decisions of and regular consultation with the Security Council. Laws are established both in the national and international sphere not primarily to authorize the use of force, but to limit it.

The moral obligation of the international community to protect groups and individuals when their rights are massively violated by the state, or when the state refuses or fails to protect them, still remains. It may well be that new standards of international conduct need to be established in this respect. In this debate, the churches need to be involved, seeking answers to such questions as: Have all other avenues of non-violent action been exhausted before military intervention is considered? Who determines that the violation of human rights has reached a level to warrant armed intervention? How can people be protected from mass violations of human rights? How are sovereign nations to be protected against politically-motivated intervention? What measures are necessary to prevent individual powers or groups of nations from taking the law into their own hands and engaging in actions guided less by international law than by their own particular interpretations of peace, democracy and human rights? If the legitimate international authority were to take a decision to intervene on humanitarian grounds as a last resort, what limits need to be placed on the use of armed force? Who sets the long-range goals and strategies to ensure that an effective long-term solution is achieved through intervention? How is the expertise of competent UN humanitarian agencies to be drawn upon in the setting and implementation of such goals? How can the roles of military and civilian components of such intervention forces be distinguished in a way which increases confidence in their impartiality and effectiveness? As the intervention in Kosovo and Yugoslavia as a whole showed, failure to have clear guidelines on these questions can lead to flagrant violations of basic international standards related to the protection of refugees, and of established international norms with respect to access and the delivery of humanitarian assistance.

The role of the churches and the ecumenical movement in times of conflict

Throughout history those who choose to go to war have sought religious support and justification for their actions. Conflicts during the past decade especially have often been cloaked in religious garb. It is also true that religious groups, including the churches, have for their own reasons increasingly complicated or reinforced national, ethnic and other tensions which underlie and sustain conflict. The Eighth Assembly has renewed the call for churches to build new, more effective interfaith alliances to transform and mediate conflict. This is especially urgent today when so many groups in society who feel marginalized or discriminated against seek to reaffirm their particular identities and have them recognized. Debates within the WCC in recent years have also shown the degree to which conflict, and the perceived role of churches within it, can be divisive of the ecumenical fellowship. The international approach to the conflict in Kosovo has highlighted this tension and revealed new dimensions of the historical, cultural, theological and ecclesiological questions involved. The Council began to address aspects of this more intensively through activities related to the Programme to Overcome Violence. Programmes on ecclesiology and ethics, the role of the churches in situations of ethnic and national tensions, and theological approaches to violence in society continue now within the context of the Ecumenical Decade to Overcome Violence.

Because of their shared commitment to Christ the peacemaker and to the universality of the Gospel, the churches are called to be agents of reconciliation in a troubled world. Reconciliation is not an easy task, particularly after many lives have been lost, people have been maimed or injured and lost their property and livelihood. Nor is reconciliation accomplished overnight; rather the steady, sustained commitment of religious communities is needed to heal the wounds of war and create conditions where peace can be maintained. It is also important that the churches commit themselves at an early stage to prevent the escalation of conflicts. In some places, churches are already working on the local level in peace-making and peace-building activities in their communities and those examples need to be held up and affirmed. But the ecumenical fellowship needs, in dialogue and cooperation with people of other faiths, to expand and intensify its efforts in the broader dimensions of peace-making for the sake of peace and justice in the world.

As Christians, we take inspiration from the words of the Apostle Paul:

So, if anyone is in Christ, there is a new creation: everything old has passed away; see, everything has become new! All this is from God, who reconciled us to himself through Christ, and has given us the ministry of reconciliation: that is, in Christ God was reconciling the world to himself, not counting their trespasses against them, and entrusting the message of reconciliation to us. So we are ambassadors for Christ, since God is making his appeal through us: we entreat you on behalf of Christ, be reconciled to God. (II Corinthians 5: 17-20)

In light of these considerations, the Central Committee of the World Council of Churches, meeting in Geneva, 26 August – 3 September 1999:

1. *Reaffirms* the long-standing support of the World Council of Churches for the United Nations as the unique instrument of the peoples of the world for guaranteeing respect for the international rule of law; for guiding and governing international actions for international peace and security; for providing leadership in response to humanitarian need in times of conflict; and for developing an approach to peace which holds together early-warning and prevention of armed conflict, peace-making and peace-keeping, and post-conflict reconstruction and peace-building.

2. *Encourages the United Nations* in its continuing efforts to find new and appropriate ways of responding to civil conflicts and other situations in which human rights are violated on a mass scale, including measures to overcome the culture of impunity.

3. *Reiterates its call on member churches* to raise awareness in their societies and impress upon their governments the need and obligation of all states to respect the obligations they have assumed under the UN Charter, and to support the United Nations and its specialized agencies so that they may more effectively fulfill the roles they have been assigned by the international community.

4. *Calls on the United Nations, churches and church-related institutions* to continue to raise awareness about the impact of war on children and women, to address the needs of children and women in conflict situations, to advocate for the inclusion of children's and women's issues during peace negotiations, to respond to the needs of children and women in post-conflict situations, and to support efforts by all organizations to advocate on behalf of children and women in situations of violence and armed conflict. In this context, the Central Committee welcomes UN Security Council resolution 1261 (1999) on Children and Armed Conflict, and urges the Security Council to apply these provisions whenever it considers responses to specific situations.

5. *Renews its call for* effective controls to be placed on research, production, use, sale or transfers of weapons of war, in the light of massive military actions such as that conducted by NATO in Kosovo and other parts of Yugoslavia, which serve the purpose of testing new, ever more sophisticated weapons in attacks on heavily populated areas, and which glorify such weapons.

6. *Recommends that the General Secretary* facilitate a study, in consultation and cooperation with church-related and other humanitarian agencies, and with competent research institutes, to be presented to the Central Committee on the ethics of so-called humanitarian intervention, taking into account the legitimate right of states to be free of undue interference in their internal

affairs and the moral obligation of the international community to respond when states are unwilling or incapable of guaranteeing respect for human rights and peace within their own borders.

7. *Calls on churches and church-related institutions* to reflect on the churches' unique contributions in facilitating reconciliation and encouraging peaceful means of resolving conflicts and to urge their governments to devote increased attention to non-violent means of conflict resolution and to develop and support institutions for training in alternative, non-military approaches to international peace and security consistent with the new demands and opportunities offered in the post-Cold War period.

8. *Calls on churches* to give expression to an ecumenism of the heart, to remain open to one another, and to engage in both bilateral and multilateral dialogue on issues related to their shared obligation to manifest the universality of the gospel at all times, particularly in times of religious, ethnic, national or international conflict, supporting and encouraging one another, and giving witness to their unity in Christ for the sake of the world.

9. *Calls on churches and church-related institutions* to participate actively in the Ecumenical Decade to Overcome Violence (2001-2010), to recover and uphold traditional means of non-violent conflict resolution, to develop creative approaches to prevention and responses to conflicts within their own contexts, and to share information about their activities with churches and church-related networks.

The protection of endangered populations in situations of armed violence: toward an ecumenical ethical approach
Received by the Central Committee and commended to the churches for further study, reflection and use, Potsdam, 29 January – 6 February 2001.

The Central Committee of the World Council of Churches, meeting in Potsdam, 29 January – 6 February 2001:

Notes and conveys to the churches that on the substance of the concern to protect populations caught in situations of armed violence described in the following background document there was broad agreement, but that some differences remain with respect to the use of armed force for the protection of endangered populations in situations of armed violence;

Receives and commends the document to the churches for further study, reflection and use – as they may deem appropriate – in their continuing dialogues with policy-makers, governments, international organizations, research bodies, groups advocating large-scale non-violent civilian intervention and other peace initiatives and with civil society at large.

Requests the churches to share the results of these studies, reflections and dialogues with the Commission of the Churches on International Affairs (CCIA); and

Requests the CCIA, in consultation with the Decade to Overcome Violence Reference Group, to report back to the Central Committee at a later date.

Church and ecumenical debates on these questions during the last decade of the 20th century risked being divisive of the fellowship, frequently along the lines of theological perspectives about the degree to which Christians can accept the use of armed force in any circumstance. Yet churches were being sought as partners in dialogue by government and international policy-makers seeking accompaniment as they too wrestled with the moral, ethical and even theological questions involved.

These issues are complicated, reflecting the new moral and ethical dilemmas with which the world and the ecumenical movement have increasingly been confronted since the end of the Cold War. The Commission of the Churches on International Affairs (CCIA), that was charged with carrying out the study requested by the Central Committee, immersed itself in these complexities and produced a draft of the attached document. This was significantly revised by the Central Committee at its meeting in Potsdam, Germany (January-February 2001), where the Decade to Overcome Violence was also launched. It understood that efforts to overcome violence are made in a violent world where populations are endangered even as these discussions are going on. The debate on the draft again revealed clearly the different theological perspectives among member churches with respect to violence and non-violence.

Members of the Central Committee were invited to submit this draft to the responsible policy bodies of their churches for further dialogue and reflection before the meeting and to submit their reactions and those of their churches to the Central Committee in the hope that a formulation might be found which could be adopted by consensus.

Such a consensus could not be found, however. The differences of perspectives among Christians with respect to the use of armed force – described in more detail below – continue. On the substance of the concern to protect populations caught in situations of armed violence described in the following background document there was broad agreement. The Central Committee reviewed and refined further a set of proposed criteria and guidelines for the protection of endangered populations in situations of armed violence. On these, some differences remain.

Background to the Ecumenical Concern

1. The moral obligation of the international community to protect the lives of civilian populations that are at risk in situations where their government is unable or unwilling to act has long been widely accepted in and beyond the ecumenical

movement, and questions of Christian responsibility in humanitarian crises have often been the subject of reflection, discussion, and prayer among churches. However, since the end of the Cold War, the practice of what was called "humanitarian intervention" has given rise to an often-heated international debate. The WCC Eighth Assembly (Harare 1998) affirmed

the emphasis of the Gospel on the value of all human beings in the sight of God, on the atoning and redeeming work of Christ that has given every person true dignity, on love as the motive for action, and on love for one's neighbors as the practical expression of active faith in Christ. We are members one of another, and when one suffers all are hurt. This is the responsibility Christians bear to ensure the human rights of every person.

2. The Central Committee agreed in 1992 "that active non-violent action be affirmed as a clear emphasis in programmes and projects related to conflict resolution." It called upon the WCC, "through a study and reflection process, (to) clarify to what extent the fellowship (*koinonia*) of the World Council is called into question when churches fail to categorically condemn any systematic violation of human rights that takes place in their country."

3. A study document entitled "Overcoming the Spirit, Logic and Practice of War," responding to this request was presented to the Central Committee at its meeting in Johannesburg, 1994.[1] It noted that the 1992 decision, reached following a Central Committee debate on the conflict in the former Yugoslavia,

... restated one of the oldest concerns of the ecumenical movement, one which has been formulated in different ways according to changing historical contexts.

The most often quoted version is the affirmation by the First Assembly (Amsterdam 1948), which held that

War as a method of settling disputes is incompatible with the teaching and example of our Lord Jesus Christ. The part which war plays in our present international life is a sin against God and a degradation of man.

A decade earlier, the Oxford Conference on Church, Community and State (1937) had said, on the eve of the Second World War,

If war breaks out, then pre-eminently the Church must manifestly be the Church, still united as the one Body of Christ, though the nations wherein it is planted fight each other, consciously offering the same prayers that God's name be hallowed, His Kingdom come, and His Will be done, in both, or all, the warring nations.

---

[1] Doc. C-11, Unit III Committee, WCC Central Committee, Johannesburg, 1994

4. The perspectives of Christians on matters of war and the use of armed force differ radically, and have time and again threatened the unity of the Church. The document cited above described the dilemma.

In 1948, no agreement was possible on how to answer this question. The most the Assembly could do was to restate the opposing positions as they had been outlined at Oxford:

(1) There are those who hold that, even though entering a war may be a Christian's duty in particular circumstances, modern warfare, with its mass destruction, can never be an act of justice.

(2) In the absence of impartial supranational institutions, there are those who hold that military action is the ultimate sanction of the rule of law, and that citizens must be distinctly taught that it is their duty to defend the law by force if necessary.

(3) Others, again, refuse military service of all kinds, convinced that an absolute witness against war and for peace is for them the will of God, and they desire that the Church should speak to the same effect.

The (First) Assembly went on to describe the dilemma in terms which apply to the debate as much today as it they did at the founding of the WCC:

We must frankly acknowledge our deep sense of perplexity in the face of these conflicting opinions, and urge upon all Christians the duty of wrestling continuously with the difficulties they raise and of praying humbly for God's guidance. We believe there is a special call to theologians to consider the theological problems involved. In the meantime, the churches must continue to hold within their full fellowship all who sincerely profess such viewpoints as those set out above and are prepared to submit themselves to the will of God in the light of such guidance as may be vouchsafed to them.

5. Against this background, the Central Committee created the Program to Overcome Violence in 1994 as a way for Christians and churches with such varied theological views to join together to seek to counter the rising tide of violence at all levels of contemporary society and promote a global culture of peace.

6. During the decade of the 1990s WCC Assemblies and the Central Committee repeatedly debated the appropriate Christian response to violent conflicts, and they condemned both the use of disproportionate armed force intended to control some such conflicts and the failure of the international community in others, like Rwanda, to protect populations in the face of predictable massive violence. It has drawn attention to the need to respond to emerging crisis at the earliest possible stages when non-violent action can be most effective in addressing the root causes of conflict.

7. In response to questions raised at the Central Committee in 1994 about whether, and under what conditions, the use of coercion is an acceptable tool to enforce human rights and the international rule of law in violent or potentially violent situations, the CCIA prepared for the Central Committee in 1995 a

"Memorandum and Recommendations on the Application of Sanctions" and the Central Committee adopted a set of "Criteria for Determining the Applicability and Effectiveness of Sanctions."

8. In September 1999 the Central Committee adopted a "Memorandum and Recommendations on International Security and Response to Armed Conflict" that called for new approaches to international peace and security in the post-Cold War world and highlighted some of the dilemmas around "humanitarian intervention" raised especially by the Kosovo experience. The Central Committee called on the WCC General Secretary to:

> Facilitate a study, in consultation and cooperation with church-related and other humanitarian agencies, and with competent research institutes, to be presented to the central committee on the ethics of so-called "humanitarian intervention," taking into account the legitimate right of states to be free of undue interference in their internal affairs and the moral obligation of the international community to respond when states are unwilling or incapable of guaranteeing respect for human rights and peace within their own borders.

9. A study process was initiated to clarify the issues and to develop guidelines to assist the churches. A background paper was prepared and widely circulated for comment. It was discussed by the Commission of the Churches on International Affairs (CCIA) in January 2000, and in a revised form it served as the basis for discussions in an ecumenical seminar hosted by the Ecumenical Institute at Bossey in April 2000. Participants in the seminar came from all regions and included specialists in humanitarian response, international law, human rights, ethics and theology, including representatives of churches whose countries have been affected in one way or another by recent interventions. Together with staff of the WCC and the Lutheran World Federation, participants reflected from an ethical perspective on the responsibility of the international community to protect populations at risk within the borders of sovereign states. The extensive report of that consultation was again widely circulated for response and comment to member churches and WCC-related agencies. Finally, the document was refined by a specialized CCIA reference group for presentation to the Central Committee for consideration as a companion document to the one adopted on sanctions in 1995.

10. Almost simultaneously with the completion of this document, the report of the Panel on United Nations Peace Operations (popularly known as the "Brahimi Report")[2] was presented to the UN Security Council and was considered in the 2000 Millennium General Assembly in New York. This landmark study offered not only a serious critique of UN peacekeeping, but made innovative suggestions

---

[2] Report of the Panel on United Nations Peace Operations ("Brahimi Report"), United Nations, Doc. A/55/305 or S/2000/809

for improvements that closely paralleled the conclusions of the WCC document. Subsequently, Canadian Minister of Foreign Affairs, Lloyd Axworthy, took the initiative to form a high-level panel to study further these issues, and invited the WCC to cooperate with it, providing its particular moral and ethical perspectives.

Re-shaping the debate

11. In calling for the present study, the Central Committee expressed its skepticism about the term by referring to "so-called 'humanitarian intervention'." The consultative process showed that others are equally wary of this term. Many participants in the study process were hesitant to discuss the "ethics of 'humanitarian intervention'." For them, the most important contribution of the churches was to help re-shape and clarify the terms of the debate in a way that would emphasize the fundamental ethical issues at stake.

12. Historically, and especially since 1991, intervening powers have often used the term *humanitarian* to characterize their motivations and to justify their actions. In fact, as repeated WCC Central Committee documents have argued, the motives for most interventions are at best mixed and often more in the self-interests of the intervening powers than of the endangered populations they purport to rescue.

13. The decision of Gulf Coalition Forces led by the USA to extend their operations to the Kurdish areas of Northern Iraq for "humanitarian reasons" raised doubts about the distinction between military strategic interests and the legitimate needs of the population at risk. This was followed almost immediately by the "humanitarian intervention" in Somalia that cut short UN-sponsored mediation efforts. The debate became more critical still when the UN peacekeeping force in Rwanda was withdrawn in 1994, abandoning the population to the forces of genocide. The often unequal protection offered civilians during the war in Bosnia-Herzegovina, and the spectacular NATO intervention in the case of Kosovo added fuel to the fire.

14. The word "humanitarian" has a special place in international humanitarian law which conveys the attributes of universality, independence, impartiality, and humanity. It is important to recall that the evolution of the humanitarian ideal did not happen overnight. In fact, over a hundred years passed since Henri Dunant saw the need for an impartial humanitarian response on the battlefields of Solferino and subsequently founded the Red Cross that codified basic principles of humanitarian action. Humanitarian assistance is to be extended to people solely on the basis of need, irrespective of religion, ethnicity, class, nationality or political opinion. Especially in today's world of highly politicized actions, the idea that meeting humanitarian needs should be a priority is an ideal which needs to be preserved and protected from casual or self-serving usage.

15. The term *intervention* also has varying connotations. In some contexts when people think of "intervention" they have in mind the actions of international financial institutions, transnational corporations and powerful states that intervene

at will in the internal affairs of weaker sovereign nations, often against the interests of the people. Others think of the military "interventions" of dominant foreign powers which overthrow elected governments or interrupt popular democratic processes. In some other contexts, "intervention" has the positive connotation of liberation or national salvation for civilian populations under siege or caught in brutal civil conflicts.

16. Thus for most churches the juxtaposition of the words "humanitarian" and "intervention" provokes unease, since in practice it too often represents a contradiction between humanitarian principles of compassion and the use of lethal military force.

17. What is the appropriate response of the international community to conflict situations in which whole populations are at risk and their governments are either unable or unwilling to protect them? For the churches in the ecumenical movement, the international community has a responsibility for conflict-prevention, peace-building, conflict-resolution and reconciliation. The decision to use armed force to respond to situations in which large numbers of people are endangered very often signals a failure of the international community to take necessary preventive actions in response to early warnings of crisis.

18. Rather than using the term "humanitarian intervention," discussions within the World Council of Churches suggest the alternative: "the protection of endangered populations in situations of armed violence."

19. Actions to this end must be planned and carried out as part of a long-range strategy that moves from local conflict transformation efforts to the use of diplomatic pressure, economic sanctions, and the deployment of an international protection force. The "Brahimi Report" represents a significant corrective to much of current peacekeeping practice, highlighting preventive action and peace-building and "a doctrinal shift in the use of civilian police and related rule of law elements in peace operations that emphasizes a team approach to upholding the rule of law and respect for human rights and helping communities coming out of a conflict to achieve national reconciliation; ... disarmament, demobilization, and reintegration programmes." The report identifies the need, however, for a peacekeeping doctrine and well-defined mandates in which the "consent of the local parties, impartiality and the use of force only in self-defense should remain the bedrock principles." The report recommends that forces deployed should "be capable of defending themselves, other mission components and the mission's mandate. Rules of engagement should be sufficiently robust and not force United Nations contingents to cede the initiative to their attackers."

20. The protection of endangered populations in situations of armed violence often requires "robust" action to stop atrocities and restore the rule of law, but then moves beyond this to rehabilitate the physical, political and civil infrastructures of the country, set up peace-building and conflict-resolution mechanisms and make provisions for the reconciliation of society. It must also be

21

understood that different organizations and personnel will be required to implement the different phases of the process.

The responsibility of the international community for prevention of violent conflict

21. First and foremost, the international community (governments, intergovernmental organizations, international financial institutions, transnational corporations, the mass media and civil society) has a responsibility to address the causes which lead to violent conflict. It must take timely, effective action when conflicts do emerge in order to prevent their escalation. Churches are often particularly well placed to read the danger signals in their communities and to call for appropriate action before conflicts become violent. In some cases, these early warnings lead to effective preventive action by the churches or the broader international community. Too often, however, the international community – and the churches – fail to take effective action during the period in which conflicts are most susceptible to transformation through non-violent means. Churches often speak therefore of *kairos* – the recognition that a particular historical moment has come when faith compels Christians to action.

22. Through the World Council of Churches' Programme to Overcome Violence, churches have developed a greater awareness that conflict-prevention goes hand in hand with building cultures of peace in which *metanoia* – a change of heart – and reconciliation efforts contribute to conflict transformation, the Christian's preferred alternative to the *lex talionis* – an eye for an eye, a tooth for a tooth. This approach involves long-term commitments to things like community-building, peace education, civic education, election monitoring, inter-faith dialogue and human rights awareness-raising where the churches can and must play a particularly active role.

Impunity, truth and reconciliation

23. Post-conflict responsibilities of the international community include efforts to prevent the resurgence of conflicts and to ensure peace and stability in countries which have experienced the trauma of war. Again here, churches are often well placed to monitor the implementation of peace accords and to alert the wider international community when problems arise.

24. In the post-conflict period, the challenge remains of overcoming impunity by bringing perpetrators of violence to justice. Not only is there a need to hold individual leaders accountable, but also to develop structures, such as the International Criminal Court, to uphold the principle and practice of accountability. The churches, together with other members of civil society, can play major roles in this complex and often painful process, as shown by the pioneering work of South Africa's Truth and Reconciliation Commission and efforts to hold Chilean General Augusto Pinochet accountable for the crimes committed under his leadership. The churches have a pastoral responsibility to help the healing processes in their communities by encouraging people to share

their memories, by working to build a collective history of a conflict and by preaching forgiveness and reconciliation. WCC studies in recent years have shown how essential this work is to the process leading to reconciliation. This is reflected in the priority the Central Committee has given to the role of the churches in reconciliation in making it one of the major emphases of the Decade to Overcome Violence.

25. Once a peace agreement has been signed and once the television cameras have moved on to other crises, there is a tendency for the international community – and the churches – to pay less attention to post-conflict situations. Yet, peace is a fragile process which requires sustained attention and nurturing to flourish and grow. When there are inequities in the implementation of peace accords and when genuine reconciliation does not take place, the seeds of future conflicts are sown. Reconciliation is thus both a means of preventing further violence and the basis for the construction of societies in which only non-violent means are used to resolve the inevitable conflicts which arise between social groups.

When prevention fails

26. However, in a sinful world with a propensity to violence, even the best efforts of the churches and the international community are likely to be inadequate to prevent some violent crises. In such cases, a range of non-violent responses to armed conflict are available and need to be tried:

> fact-finding missions, diplomacy and offering their good offices; provision of humanitarian assistance in a way that can build confidence between parties; protection of human rights through a variety of mechanisms including the appointment of special reporters and the provision of technical services;

> pastoral delegations, information sharing from the affected regions, public statements to clarify the nature of the conflict, maintaining an international presence to help protect populations at risk, advocating at various levels for peaceful resolution, and bringing churches and other religious communities from different sides of a conflict together to provide a common witness for peace.

27. When a government rejects all efforts of help to assist in the resolution of a conflict or refuses to comply with decisions of the competent international bodies like the UN Security Council, sanctions may be appropriately applied under Art. 41 of the United Nations Charter that "may include complete or partial interruption of economic relations and of rail, sea, air, postal, telegraphic, radio and other means of communication, and the severance of diplomatic relations." In its 1995 document on sanctions to which reference was made above, the Central Committee said:

> Sanctions are a valuable tool available to enforce international law and to bring about the peaceful resolution of disputes...

... diplomatic sanctions (have) a long tradition in the history of international relations. They include the recognition or non-recognition of another sovereign state, or the suspension of such diplomatic relations as a means of expressing displeasure with the behavior of the other. Diplomatic measures may include a strong inducement for a state to correct its behavior through the offer of recognition or the extension of greater privileges...

Economic sanctions are generally taken to include such things as restrictions on international travel and communication; trade, commerce, foreign investment, and other areas of finance; restrictions on access to certain goods, like arms and strategic materials; and cultural exchange. Diplomatic sanctions themselves also frequently have an economic effect.

28. Consistently applied, this range of non-violent actions moving from the least intrusive to the most coercive should be sufficient to deal with most situations which threaten the lives or well being of the civilian population. In practice, however, the international community has seldom been capable of such consistency. Early warning indicators sometimes fail to convey the urgency of the situation, but more often, early warning signs are either ignored or unheeded by an international community already over-burdened by an unprecedented number of complex internal conflicts. Many governments refuse to engage in negotiations to end a conflict and are unwilling to allow the international community to assist populations at risk within their borders. In a growing number of cases, states have collapsed and are no longer capable of offering protection. Too often, a failure to reconcile differences in post-conflict situations leads to renewed outbreaks of violence. In such cases, the international community has a right – or even a duty – to take decided steps to protect and assist people at risk.

Sovereignty and international law

29. This may require intervention in the internal affairs of a sovereign nation. Basic principles of international law and human rights strictly limit this.

30. The principle of national sovereignty has been the cornerstone of the international system since the Treaty of Westphalia in 1648. Nevertheless, there is a long history of military powers justifying their military intervention in the internal affairs of other countries on the grounds of "humanitarian" concern. Conscious of this and against the background of two devastating world wars, the framers of the United Nations Charter sought to protect weaker states from aggression by including the principle of non-intervention in the internal affairs of a sovereign state. Newly independent states jealously guarded this principle as a safeguard to reduce the possibilities of further interventions by former colonial or neo-colonial powers.

31. Article 2 (7) of the Charter precludes any intervention by the United Nations "in matters which are essentially within the jurisdiction of any state." The only exceptions are the one included in Article 51 which allows for the use of force in individual or collective self-defense, and those listed under Chapter VII that allow

the use of force under strictly limited conditions to maintain or restore international peace and security.

32. The ecumenical movement has consistently defended these principles over the years, believing that the integrity of states and their territory is essential to peace and security. The fundamental right of states to preserve their integrity and defend themselves is an essential bedrock of the international legal system which must be preserved. This right is being challenged today by one of the negative impacts of globalization, namely the weakening of the capacity of many states to resist undue external intervention in the internal affairs of their peoples.

33. There have been several cases in the past decade where the UN Security Council has justified intervention based on the argument that serious breaches of human rights committed by a state against its own citizens constituted a threat to peace (Res. 688/91). In Resolution 794 of 3 December 1992, it held that "the magnitude of the human tragedy caused by the conflict" in Somalia constituted a threat to peace within the meaning of Article 39 of the Charter. Again in Resolution 841 of 16 June 1993 the Security Council ruled in the case of Haiti that a form of government irreconcilable with democratic principles represented a threat to peace under Article 39.

34. Though the Security Council twice found that the situation in Kosovo constituted a threat to peace, it did not authorize military action. Nevertheless, NATO used military force against the Federal Republic of Yugoslavia in 1999 and justified its use on "humanitarian" grounds as necessary to protect the rights of threatened minorities in the province of Kosovo. The WCC and many of its member churches and related Christian World Communion bodies vigorously protested these actions that they regarded to be in violation of the intention of the UN Charter.

35. Recent responses to humanitarian crises – both action and inaction – raise many questions, both for international law and for the broader moral imperative. UN Secretary-General Kofi Annan underlined this central dilemma, using concrete examples, in his address to the UN General Assembly in September 1999:

> To those for whom the greatest threat to the future of international order is the use of force in the absence of a Security Council mandate, one might ask – not in the context of Kosovo, but in the context of Rwanda: If, in those dark days and hours leading up to the genocide, a coalition of States had been prepared to act in defense of the Tutsi population, but did not receive prompt Council authorization, should such a coalition have stood aside and allowed the horror to unfold?

> To those for whom the Kosovo action heralded a new era when States and groups of States can take military action outside the established mechanisms for enforcing international law, one might ask: Is there not a danger of such interventions undermining the imperfect, yet resilient, security system created

25

after the Second World War, and of setting dangerous precedents for future interventions without a clear criterion to decide who might invoke these precedents, and in what circumstances?[3]

36. While the UN Charter severely limits the ability of the organization to intervene unless there is a breach of international peace and security, the Charter also affirms the universality of human rights. Legal scholars point out that international law is not static, but in a constant process of evolution. Some of these developments could shed new light on the absolute character of the principle of non-intervention. Indeed, the evolution of human rights law and thinking over the past century has been marked by development and acceptance of universal standards of human rights, even if procedures to hold governments accountable for such violations have not yet been universally accepted. In its 2000 Human Development Report, the United Nations Development Program says that "Human rights – in an integrated world – requires global justice. The state-centered model of accountability must be extended to the obligations of non-state actors and to the state obligations beyond national borders."[4]

37. The churches have a long history of engagement in the development of these international human rights standards. As the *Statement on Human Rights*, adopted by the WCC Eighth Assembly in Harare, Zimbabwe in December 1998, says:

We reaffirm the universality of human rights as enunciated in the International Bill of Human Rights, and the duty of all states, irrespective of national culture or economic and political system, to promote and defend them. These rights are rooted in the histories of cultures, religions, and traditions, not just those whose role in the UN was dominant when the Universal Declaration was adopted. We recognize that this Declaration was accepted as a "standard of achievement," and the application of its principles needs to take into account different historical, cultural, and economic interests. At the same time we reject any attempt by states, national or ethnic groups, to justify the abrogation of, or derogation from, the full range of human rights on the basis of culture, religion, tradition, special socio-economic or security interests.

38. Even here, however, there are no absolute principles. Governments in some regions, notably Asia, have questioned the concept of the universality of human rights, arguing that they are based on Western concepts of individual rights rather than on peoples' rights. Some within the Orthodox tradition of Christianity question the exclusive concern for earthly life as the supreme value, emphasizing the primacy of salvation. While all life is sacred, they argue, holy places, objects of adoration and even land are also considered by the community of faith to be

---

[3] UN Press Release SG/SM/7136 GA/9596, 20 September 1999.

[4] *Human Development Report 2000*, United Nations Development Program, New York, Oxford Press, p. 9.

sacred, and their protection may take precedence in some situations. There are also questions about what kinds of human rights violations are so grave as to justify intervention. Is action by the international community to be used only in response to violations of civil and political rights? Or do violations of economic, social, and cultural rights also call for an international response?

39. The Convention on Genocide is a specific case where the international community has recognized that there are limits on national sovereignty and that the international community has a responsibility to act to prevent genocide. The question of intervention thus stands at the nexus between national sovereignty and evolving understandings of the global nature of human rights. It is important to underline that these are not only questions of international law; they are also moral issues in which the churches' theological perspectives have much to contribute.

Just Peacemaking: A Christian Approach

40. Before considering some of the ethical dimensions of actions to protect endangered populations in situations of armed violence, it is worth recalling the biblical imperatives of just peacemaking, along the lines expressed in the Central Committee's *Memorandum and Recommendations on the Application of Sanctions.*

41. Christian imperatives of justice and peace are especially grounded in the prophetic heritage of the scriptures and the ministry of reconciliation in Jesus Christ.

42. The vision of a world of justice and peace is central to the Gospel of Jesus Christ. While the perfecting of a just peace is beyond the possibility of human achievement, it is within the power of the Sovereign God of Love who has created one whole, indivisible human family in a covenant of peace. Before our Sovereign God, the nations rise and fall; but the promise of *shalom*, of love binding peace with justice, is eternal.

43. Every member of God's family bears God's sacred image and is entitled to an abundant life of freedom, security and well being. To be so endowed is to enjoy God-given dignity from which flow principles of human rights which it is the responsibility of all persons and governments to respect and protect. The ultimate justification for intervention must be such a concept of justice for the sake of authentic peace and security.

44. God has set our common life in human communities which have in turn established institutions necessary to govern them. Governments are responsible not only for justice and peace within their borders, and for security against aggression and other threats to their people. They are rightly called to policies of initiative and cooperation in the quest for a just peace among all nations. The indivisibility of political liberty, common security, civil equity, economic welfare and ecological integrity requires effective instruments of global governance and transnational action. Such instruments must promote the development of peoples, the resolution of conflicts, and the overcoming of violence.

45. The policies and actions of all human institutions, including government, must guarantee the protection of the innocent, the poor, the weak, the minorities and the oppressed; not only within domestic societies, but within any other society affected by these policies and actions.

46. Under the sovereignty of God, no nation or group of nations is entitled to prosecute vengeance against another. Nor is any nation entitled to make unilateral judgments and take unilateral actions that lead to the devastation of another nation and the massive suffering of its people. Whenever aggression or massive and flagrant abuses of human rights by one nation call for preventive or punitive action under international law, a concerted multilateral response authorized by the United Nations or other competent international body is most likely to meet the requirements of just peacemaking.

47. Recent international military engagements undertaken in some situations in the name of "humanitarian intervention" and the failure to intervene in others have raised serious moral and ethical questions: How can the international community come to the aid of people in crisis in a proportionate and consistent manner which gives equal value to all human life?

48. That it is ever necessary to consider the use of armed force in international relations is a reflection of the failure of the international community to have responded in a timely and appropriate fashion to prevent a conflict or to resolve a conflict during its early stages. An inadequate or inconsistent response to human suffering compounds the moral failure. Recent decisions to intervene with massive armed force have often been influenced by globalized public media that tend to report crises in a selective way, exaggerating some and ignoring others where equal or greater numbers of people were at imminent risk. For example, while the crisis in Kosovo was reported to be escalating to dangerous proportions, simultaneous crises in Africa, Asia, Latin America and the Middle East that continued to claim far higher numbers of lives received comparatively little media coverage in the North. Media have also often exaggerated the losses and suffering of some ethnic groups and almost ignored those of other groups. Some critics have charged that such media selectivity is rooted in racial, ethnic or political bias and that this has contributed to the situation in which the international community responds with disproportionate armed force in situations where some Europeans suffer, while refusing to intervene to save others, and ignores altogether many crises in the South where much larger populations are in clear danger.

49. For Christians, just peacemaking must always be shaped by our commitment to the ministry and message of reconciliation. The Gospel's promise of reconciliation is based on our faith in the triune God, incarnate in Jesus Christ who is our peace, breaking down the dividing walls of hostility, making us one new humanity. Such a faith obliges us to love even our enemies. Just peacemaking requires that Christians not endorse any coercive policy, whether economic or military, before seeking positive incentives to promote peace among aggrieved

adversaries. For Christians, the aim must always be the building or restoration of just, peaceful and humane relationships.

50. Just peacemaking also calls Christians to consider fundamental moral, ethical and theological questions in a world full of ambiguities. The question arises whether, from an ecumenical Christian perspective, the international community should refrain from taking up arms even to protect endangered populations in situations of armed violence or to defend those deployed by competent international authority for this purpose. Here competing moral and ethical values must be considered. Some Christians say yes, believing that the teachings of Jesus require us to oppose any use of armed force. Others say no, considering that the protection of human life may require it to do so in extreme situations, and recognizing that any such decision should be approached with great humility. In either case, responsibility for unintended consequences must be accepted both by those who choose to use armed force and by those who do not.

Against this background, and conscious of the fact that Christians must cooperate with peoples of other faiths and convictions in pursuit of answers to these complex questions, the Central Committee believes that in the context of the Decade to Overcome Violence the following considerations and criteria deserve further study and dialogue in and among the churches and with those currently engaged in efforts to establish clear and effective international frameworks within which masses of peoples in today's conflictive world can be provided with timely and essential protection to save lives and enable them to contribute to the building of truly just and peaceful societies.

Considerations and Criteria for discussion related to the Protection of Endangered Populations in Situations of Armed Violence

1. *Considerations*

   1.1. Intervention to protect endangered populations in situations of armed violence risks provoking additional violence that could inflict additional suffering on affected populations.

   1.2. The failure to take prompt and timely action, however, including the use of arms in self-defense in certain serious crises may also result in the further massive loss of human life and irreparable injury.

   1.3. Even for the protection of endangered populations in situations of armed violence, overriding the principles of sovereignty is a very serious action that should be undertaken only in the most grave and extraordinary circumstances. It is not a practice to be used in cases where human rights are routinely violated. There, the international community has a wide range of human rights instruments available under which to act, short of physical intervention that should be used only in the most grave and extraordinary circumstances when it is necessary to rescue and protect people in grave peril.

1.4. Actions to protect endangered populations must be applied within the framework of international law. The World Council of Churches has repeatedly reaffirmed its support for the principle of the international rule of law and for the United Nations Charter as the essential framework for its defense and further development.

1.5 According to the Charter, "All members shall refrain in their international relations from the threat or use of force against the territorial integrity or independence of any state;" (Art. 2.4) however the Security Council may decide to ask member states to take actions involving the use of armed force to obtain compliance with its decisions. Intervention needs to be clearly restricted in order to protect nations and peoples from undue interference, and decisions to intervene must be consistent with need wherever it occurs without distinction and consistent with the Charter.

1.6 The Charter also holds, however, that "universal respect for, and observance of, human rights and fundamental freedoms for all" is essential for international peace. (Art. 55.c)

1.7 In practice, the Security Council – given its present structure that gives veto power to its permanent members – has only rarely authorized a state, group of states or "regional agencies" to intervene, and this has given rise to intervention by regional bodies or groups of states in violation or on the margins of the requirements of the Charter.

1.8 While some of these armed interventions have brought effective relief to endangered populations, others have led to disproportionate destruction and questionable results.

1.9 Various proposals have been made for Security Council reform to make it more responsive to the changing character of threats to international peace and security, and taking into account the evolution of international law. It is clearly necessary today to develop a more effective basis for Security Council action, and/or to create additional mechanisms within the framework of the Charter that would have the agreement of the General Assembly and, in so far as possible, remove decisions on the protection of endangered populations in situations of armed violence from partisan political debate, and provide for timely and rapid intervention in the interest of populations at risk of massive loss of human life.

1.10 Given the present limitations of the international system and the reality of intervention, and in anticipation of the creation of new, more effective mechanisms, the following criteria could guide this aspect of UN reform and be respected in the interim whenever armed intervention for humanitarian purposes is undertaken.

2. *Criteria*

2.1. When may action to protect endangered populations in situations of armed violence be authorized?

The protection of endangered populations that involves intervention in the territory of a sovereign state should be limited to situations in which:

2.1.1 There are well-attested immediate or long-standing threats to life to a level amounting to crimes against humanity, carried out by governmental authorities or other organized forces, or with their connivance and support, or because of the inability or unwillingness of authorities to impede such atrocities.

2.1.2 Crimes against humanity result from anarchy in a sovereign state whose government or authorities are incapable of putting an end to such crimes and refuse to call upon or refuse offers by the international community to assist in doing so.

2.1.3 The more urgent and massive the threat or the open atrocities, the more intensive and immediate may be the need for intervention. Conversely, intervention would not be warranted in the case of a slowly unfolding crisis in which non-violent resolution methods can be effective.

2.2 Even when there is a well-founded and massive threat to human life, the decision to use arms in self-defense requires careful deliberation and balanced reflection. In particular, the following essential questions must be carefully considered by decision-makers:

2.2.1 who decides that their use is needed?

2.2.2 who provides the forces?

2.2.3 who oversees compliance?

2.2.4 what are the appropriate means, type, and conduct of forces?

2.2.5 what are the foreseeable side effects?

2.3 Who may intervene?

2.3.1 Actions to protect endangered populations in situations of armed violence should in principle be taken by an appropriate UN body or by a group of states authorized to act on its behalf and all such actions should be under the strict oversight of the Security Council or other multilateral international instance agreed to by the UN General Assembly.

2.3.2 Intervening protection forces should be clearly neutral with respect to the state in which intervention occurs and a decision to intervene should in no event serve as the pretext for the pursuit of narrow self-interests of foreign powers.

2.4 What forms of intervention are justified?

2.4.1 The specific aims and limits of intervention should be mutually agreed and clearly stated by the competent authorizing body before action is taken, and clear indications given of what is required for these aims to be met and forces withdrawn.

2.4.2 Actions to protect endangered populations in situations of armed violence must be viewed as part of a multi-faceted approach and of a continuum of actions related to a given crisis situation including: the restoration of the rule of law and respect for basic human rights, rehabilitation and reconstruction, and post-conflict peace-building and reconciliation to be carried out by civilian organizations. Thus planning and monitoring should be not just for an immediate emergency, but should have longer-range goals and contemplate the mobilization of resources needed to meet them.

2.4.3 Since action to protect endangered populations in situations of armed violence is distinct from war, specific training in new concepts and techniques related to the concept of "human security" should be undertaken for police and military forces at both national and international levels. This should include training in non-violent intervention techniques that take full advantage of the organizational, logistical and command skills of the military.

2.4.4 While intervention is by definition coercive, only that defensive force may be applied that is proportionate to the aims and is required to protect endangered populations and to equip and/or oblige the state concerned to fulfill its own responsibilities in their regard.

2.4.5 The deployment of armed police forces is often sufficient to offer the required protection. If the use of the military is deemed necessary to accomplish the aims, its role should be restricted to only that absolutely required to restore order or to provide safe humanitarian space.

2.4.6 The rules of engagement of forces to protect endangered populations must be consistent with international humanitarian law, respecting the immunity of non-combatants and the obligation to protect them.

2.4.7 When protection is required to guarantee the security of recognized intergovernmental and non-governmental humanitarian agencies' personnel engaged in the delivery of essential supplies to endangered populations clear distinctions need to be made between the roles of civilians in delivering humanitarian aid and the support roles of police or the military. Each must have clearly defined and agreed functions and command and management roles, and the police or military component should be removed as soon as conditions are established for the effective functioning of the strictly humanitarian component. Humanitarian agencies, including those related to the churches, should adhere strictly to established international codes of conduct.

2.5 Who oversees compliance?

Action to protect endangered populations should in principle be under UN auspices and overseen by the Security Council with the support of the Secretary-General. This oversight involves the conduct of operations, evaluation of progress toward stated goals, and the determination of the duration of phases and when operations should either be terminated or moved into longer-term programmatic involvement. The International Court of Justice (World Court) and other mechanisms of international jurisprudence could consider and rule upon the legitimacy of intervention and its compliance with international law.

3 *The role of the churches*

3.2 In the continuum of actions related to actions to protect endangered populations in situations of armed violence the churches have essential roles to play in all phases from early warning of potential danger to civilian populations, as agents of peace and reconciliation in efforts to avoid crises through mediation, as bodies to be consulted in decisions related to the rules of engagement in pastoral accompaniment of endangered women, men and children, in the delivery of humanitarian assistance, and in the post-conflict tasks of rehabilitation, reconstruction, peace-building and continuing reassessment of these criteria with all parties involved.

3.3 Churches within the situation are the key partners and should be consulted by churches and church-related agencies abroad at all stages in determining what ecumenical advocacy actions are necessary and as principal agents in the delivery of humanitarian assistance and post-conflict efforts.

3.4 Broad international ecumenical solidarity actions are essential to efforts to limit the use of force and to monitor it when it is necessary.

3.5 In all these efforts every opportunity should be pursued to maintain contact among the churches, both nationally, regionally and globally, and to ensure wherever appropriate and possible cooperation with other communities of faith and civil society actors caught up with Christian communities in situations of crisis with respect to actions to be taken.

ENVIRONMENTAL JUSTICE

Message on the occasion of "Earth Day"
Sent by the General Secretary to North American churches, 22 April 1999.

I greet you warmly in the name of the World Council of Churches on the occasion of Earth Day, 1999.

Caring for the well-being of God's creation has become a significant dimension of Christian discipleship in our times. Our eyes have been opened to the biblical imperatives to live in just relationships with all life and our spirits have been enlivened by the witness of many indigenous peoples and women who often are the ones living with the closest connections to the Earth.

Threats to the health of the planet are inter-related with sources of injustice against many members of the human community. Global economic forces and gross inequities in consumption levels leave vast numbers of humanity without the basics for a decent quality of life while enriching the privileged minority far beyond their needs. The challenge is to find ways in which human communities can live in a sustainable relationship with creation with all people enjoying the fullness of life.

At the global level, we are concerned by the apparent erosion of momentum for the spirit and agreements that emerged from the 1992 Earth Summit in Rio de Janeiro. Churches can play an important role in reinvigorating public support and protesting against the trend toward giving greater precedence to economic and trade interests over environment and development priorities.

The WCC commends your efforts as churches to strive toward individual and collective lifestyles which will be in closer harmony with creation and your participation in broader societal efforts to counter the sources of injustice against the Earth and the poor. Particularly encouraging for us in the World Council of Churches is to see how many of these initiatives are ecumenical and increasingly inter-faith. It is my prayer that the energy you bring to Earth Day be sustained throughout the year.

A call to action in solidarity with those most affected by climate change
Appeal issued on the occasion of the 8th session of the Conference of Parties (COP8) to the UN Framework Convention on Climate Change, New Delhi, October - November 2002.*

The overwhelming world scientific consensus is that human activities are causing observable changes to the global climate which are already having a significant environmental, social and economic impact, and are likely to have increasingly serious disruptive consequences as the century progresses.

There is growing evidence that weather extremes have become more frequent. Floods and droughts intensify. The mean global sea levels are rising. In the coming decades, according to the scientists of the Intergovernmental Panel on Climate Change, even a medium scenario predicts that changing climate conditions may turn 150 million people into refugees. A recent study, conducted by a renowned re-insurance company, speaks of an annual damage of up to US$ 300 billion. This pattern of climate events is consistent with what scientists predict would happen as a result of human-induced global warming.

For us these prospects are cause for deep concern. We represent people and churches in poor communities who will be especially hit by the adverse effects of climate change, and also concerned people and churches in materially rich

---

• Issued by the following eumenical development and relief agencies in collaboration with the WCC:

All Africa Council of Churches
Alt Katholische Diakonie, Germany
Anglican Diocese of Colombo, Church of Ceylon, Sri Lanka
Association of Protestant Churches and Missions (EMW), Germany,
Bread for all and HEKS, Switzerland
Brot für die Welt, Germany
Christian Aid, United Kingdom
Christian Conference of Asia
Christian World Service, New Zealand
Church of Sweden Aid, Sweden
Church of the Brethren (General Board), USA
Church World Service, USA
Church's Auxiliary for Social Action (CASA), India
Conference of European Churches

DanChurchAid, Denmark
European Christian Environmental Network
Evangelical Lutheran Church in America, USA
Global Ministries, The Netherlands,
Interchurch Organisation for Development Cooperation (ICCO), The Netherlands,
Norwegian Church Aid, Norway
Oikos, The Netherlands
Pacific Conference of Churches
Presbyterian Church (USA)
Presbyterian Church in Canada (National Committee of World Service and Development), Canada
United Church of Canada (Justice, Global and Ecumenical Relations Unit), Canada
World YWCA
WEED, Germany

countries who wish to bear witness that global actions to combat climate change are too slow. In addition we speak for the churches' international network of relief and development agencies, which has more than 50 years of experience in working in response to natural disasters and in addressing issues of poverty and injustice. We are committed both to alleviating suffering when catastrophes occur, and also to participating in efforts to promote economic justice. Over the years we have been engaged in numerous development projects, but now relief and development agencies are faced with a new situation. Firstly, the increasing need for emergency aid may considerably exceed the moral and economic capacities available in society to respond. Secondly, we will see increasingly situations where many years of careful and engaged development are put at risk, or even wiped out, by sudden extreme weather hazards.

The consequences of climate change further accentuate the deep injustices, which exist between industrialised and developing countries. Developing countries, where the majority of the world's population live, are more likely to be hit by weather anomalies, and lack the means to protect themselves against the impacts brought about by climate change. At the same time, the poor in these countries make only marginal contributions to global greenhouse gas emissions, while rich countries continue to be the prime producers. Moreover, there is a lack of commitment by leaders in the most powerful countries to take the necessary political and financial responsibility.

The overwhelming magnitude of the task can easily lead to indifference or to despair. Instead, there is an urgent need for action. Every effort must be undertaken to reduce greenhouse gas concentrations in the atmosphere.

The Kyoto Protocol is a first step in the global effort to combat climate change. The legal character and the compliance system are new elements in global institutional life. We call on all parties that have not yet ratified the Kyoto Protocol to do so, in particular the USA.

However, in the light of the Third Assessment Report of the Intergovernmental Panel on Climate Change (IPCC, 2000), we must be under no illusions. The impact of the Kyoto targets will only be very small. The Protocol needs to be followed up by much stronger efforts.

The Kyoto Protocol must indeed be ratified, but at the same we urge governments to proceed without delay with a new round of negotiations whose targets must be determined in the light of the long-term perspective. Two basic requirements must be met:

1. Stabilisation of greenhouse gases in the atmosphere at a level in accordance with the overall objective of the Climate Change Convention.

2. A fair distribution of rights and obligations, by establishing the concept of *per capita* emission rights for all countries, as proposed in the "Contraction and Convergence" scheme.

In order to achieve these requirements, strong actions must be taken in order to make possible the necessary transformation from fossil fuel to renewable energy. Developed countries must put a high priority to setting up steering mechanisms and incentives that favour renewable energy and non-fossil fuel based transportation. In developing countries, investment and development aid need to be directed towards ways of producing and using energy and systems of transport that are environmentally and socially sustainable.

The benefits of all these efforts to reduce the causes of global warming will take a long time to show their effects. In the meantime the climate will continue to warm because emissions are still rising and greenhouse gases have a long life. Weather anomalies are therefore projected to increase in the coming years and decades. Consequently there is an urgent need for increased mutual assistance and help. To maintain a minimum of justice in our world, a new sense of solidarity is called for.

We appeal therefore to all people not only to persevere in the struggle for a more just and peaceful world, but also to contribute to this goal in new ways. Only on the basis of such a new commitment will relief and development agencies be able to carry out their task in the future.

This task requires a response from each one of us. Through our own lifestyles we can contribute to the reduction of greenhouse gas emissions. Through our witness we can encourage governments to advance on the road towards responsible reduction targets.

GLOBAL ECONOMY

Statement on the debt crisis
Issued in Geneva, 9 June 1999.

The World Council of Churches is of the view that proposals made by G8 governments for solving the debt crisis are insufficient and calls on G8 leaders to adopt a more radical approach at their meeting next week in Cologne. The Council believes that it is lack of political will rather than financial resources that has made it difficult to find a lasting solution to the debt problem.

Experiences with the Highest Indebted Poor Country Initiative (HIPC) indicate that it does not adequately address the problems of the countries that qualify for debt reduction under HIPC conditions. The outcome of the meeting at Cologne is likely to be a broadened HIPC initiative with only slightly better conditions. This adds little to the original proposal as it links debt cancellation with stabilisation and structural adjustments imposed by the IMF.

Christians and Churches in the South and the North are increasingly concerned that major actors in the global economy have stipulated and reordered economic relationships and trade rules in their favour to maximise profits, growth and influence. An insufficient response to the call for cancellation of foreign debt will only motivate and provoke further critique of the global financial and trade systems by an increasing number of people. This will increase the number of voices pointing to the devastating consequences of unfettered and uncontrolled speculation and transnational flow of financial capital.

The G8 governments and the Bretton Woods institutions (World Bank and International Monetary Fund, IMF) have primary responsibility for the root causes of the debt crisis. They initially encouraged irresponsible lending and then compounded the problem by raising interest rates. This resulted in indebted countries being caught in endless cycles of borrowing, losing control of their financial, economic and social affairs, and being forced to implement IMF Stabilisation and Structural Adjustment Programmes. Moreover, debtor governments have also been obliged to give priority to their debt repayments rather than spending on health, sanitation, clean water, education, and other social needs. This has often led to the erosion of local democratic institutions and has built an environment for corruption.

If the G8 governments are genuinely concerned about poverty and impoverishment, they should accompany initiatives for debt cancellation with reforms of the financial and trading systems and also respond positively to the demand for greater control of the transnational flow of capital by governments and civil society. However, their response to the recent Asian financial crisis, which revealed the volatility of the global financial system, points in the opposite direction. Their response has supported the Multilateral Agreement on

Investments and increased power for the World Bank, IMF and WTO and, through them, for Transnational Corporations.

The Eighth Assembly of the World Council of Churches, which met in Harare last December, affirmed the importance of the biblical jubilee vision, which offers a critical mandate for periodically overcoming structural injustice and poverty, including release from debt and slavery, and restoration of right relationships. The Harare Assembly not only lent its support to the goals of the jubilee 2000 coalitions, but also appealed to the leaders of the G8 nations to recognize the urgent need to:

a. cancel the debts of the poorest countries to enable them to enter the new millennium with a fresh start;

b. substantially reduce the debts of the middle income countries within the same time frame;

c. accept that debt cancellation cannot wait until conditions set by creditors are met;

d. introduce a new, independent and transparent arbitration process for negotiating and agreeing upon international debt cancellation;

e. implement measures to promote accountability of debtor countries when debts are relieved. These measures must be determined and monitored by local community organisations, including churches and other representative organisations of civil society, to ensure that debt cancellation leads to a just distribution of wealth;

f. use their powers to ensure that funds illegitimately transferred to secret foreign bank accounts are returned to debtor nations;

g. engage, in consultation with civil society, in a process of global economic reform toward a just distribution of wealth and preventing new cycles of debt.

The WCC will continue to support and co-operate with member churches, ecumenical organizations and groups in their search for just and sustainable alternatives. The biblical vision of the jubilee encompasses and embraces more than a single campaign. It gives hope to people, struggling for economic justice and the affirmation of life.

HUMAN RIGHTS

[SEE CHAPTER ON UNITED NATIONS RELATION, pp. 117 ff]

PEACE AND DISARMAMENT

The Evolution of World Council of Churches Policy on Nuclear Arms and Disarmament, 1948-2000*

Presentation by Dwain C. Epps to the Consultation with Churches on Nuclear Issues: Creation at Risk, organized by the WCC, CEC, the NCCCUSA and the Canadian Council of Churches, Brussels, 5-6 October 2000.

The question of atomic, hydrogen and nuclear weapons has been at the heart of concerns of the World Council of Churches since its first Assembly in 1948. It was a logical focus of an ecumenical movement whose roots were in Christian peace movements going back to the late 19th century. The Amsterdam statement laid the foundations for ecumenical concern in the second half of the 20th century:

War as a method of settling disputes is incompatible with the teaching and example of our Lord Jesus Christ. The part which war plays in our present international life is a sin against God and a degradation of man. We recognise that the problem of war raises especially acute issues for Christians today. Warfare has greatly changed. War is now total and every man and woman is called for mobilisation in war service. Moreover, the immense use of air forces and the discovery of atomic and other new weapons render widespread and indiscriminate destruction inherent in the whole conduct of modern war in a sense never experienced in past conflicts...

The churches must also attack the causes of war by promoting peaceful change and the pursuit of justice. They must stand for the maintenance of good faith and the honouring of the pledged word, resist the pretensions of imperialist power, promote the multilateral reduction of armaments, and combat indifference and despair in the face of the futility of war...

[Report of Section IV, The Church and the International Disorder, *Official Report of the First Assembly*, Amsterdam, 1948, WCC, Geneva. p 89.]

The II. Assembly responded to developments beyond the atomic bomb:

The development of nuclear weapons makes this an age of fear. True peace cannot rest on fear. It is vain to think that the hydrogen bomb or its development has guaranteed peace because men will be afraid to go to war, nor can fear provide an effective restraint against the temptation to use a decisive weapon either in hope of total victory or in the desperation of total defeat.

---

* Excerpts from selected statements or actions that formed WCC policy.

The thought of all-out nuclear warfare is indeed horrifying. Such warfare introduces a new moral challenge. It has served to quicken public concern, and has intensified awareness of the urgency of finding means of prevention....

An international order of truth and peace would require:

a) effective international inspection and control and in such a way that no state would have cause to fear that its security was endangered, the elimination and prohibition of atomic, hydrogen and all other weapons of mass destruction, as well as the reduction of all armaments to a minimum...

We must also see that experimental tests of hydrogen bombs have raised issues of human rights, caused suffering and imposed an additional strain on human relations between nations. Among safeguards against the aggravation of these international tensions is the insistence that nations carry on tests only within their respective territories, or if elsewhere, only by international clearance and agreement.

[Report of Section IV, International Affairs: Christians in the Struggle for World Community, *Official Report of the Second Assembly*, Evanston, 1954, WCC, Geneva, pp. 131-134. The resolutions on International Affairs adopted by the Assembly did not include specific reference to nuclear weapons or disarmament.]

Between 1954 and 1961, the WCC's Commission of the Churches on International Affairs (CCIA) spoke and worked intensively on the need for an international instrument to control nuclear testing. The III. Assembly further underscored the dangers of nuclear weapons developments, and for the first time officially expressed concerns about the use of outer space.

The most serious problem facing the world today is that of disarmament. General and complete disarmament is widely recognized to be the desired goal...

The recent violations of the moratorium on nuclear bomb testing have shocked the nations into a new realization of the acute danger and horror of modern warfare. Churches must protest against the accelerating arms race and the mounting terror which it portends. The First Assembly...clearly recognized that war is contrary to the will of God. War in its newer forms is understood not only by Christians but the general conscience of the nations as an offense against both the world of nature and the race of man, threatening annihilation and laying on mankind an unbearable burden of cost and terror. The use of indiscriminate weapons must now be condemned by the churches as an affront to the Creator and a denial of the very purposes of the Creation. Christians must refuse to place their ultimate trust in war and nuclear weapons. In this situation the churches must never cease warning governments of the dangers, and they must repudiate absolutely the growing conviction in some quarters that the use of mass destruction weapons has become inevitable.

Christians must press most urgently upon their governments, as a first step towards the elimination of nuclear weapons, never to get themselves into a position in which they contemplate the first use of nuclear weapons. Christians must also maintain that the use of nuclear weapons, or other forms of major violence, against centers of population is in no circumstances reconcilable with the demands of the Christian Gospel.

Total disarmament is the goal, but it is a complex and long-term process in which the churches must not underestimate the importance of first steps. There may be possibilities of experimenting with limited geographical areas of controlled and inspected disarmament, of neutralizing certain zones, of devising security against surprise attack which would reduce tension, of controlling the use of outer space....

[*New Delhi Speaks*, Third WCC Assembly, New Delhi, 1961, Association Press, New York, 1962, pp. 79ff.]

The landmark 1966 Church and Society Conference in Geneva is most often recalled as having brought Third World perspectives and theologies of liberation onto the stage of the global ecumenical movement. However it too devoted particular attention to nuclear war, based again on the Amsterdam affirmation.

...(The) First Assembly...declared, 'War is contrary to the will of God'... We now say to all governments and peoples that nuclear war is against God's will and the greatest of evils. Therefore we affirm that it is the first duty of governments and their officials to prevent nuclear war. ...

The real problem is how the supreme task, to avoid nuclear war, can be carried out... (There is) an increasing role for the smaller powers in depolarizing international affairs...

The churches should add that they have [a] common...duty to preserve the life of the peoples of this world, and to work for a world order which will transcend the present uneasy peace of the equilibrium of power. It is intolerable for the peace of the world to depend on a precarious nuclear balance...

[*Official Report, World Conference on Church and Society*, WCC, Geneva 1966, pp. 123ff.]

That Conference deeply influenced the agenda of the IV. Assembly held two years later. That agenda was heavily devoted to the timely issues of racism and economic development and others stimulated by the global revolutionary fervor of the year 1968. But it too spoke out on the question of nuclear weapons, beginning once more with the Amsterdam declaration.

The WCC reaffirms its declaration at the (First Assembly): War as a method of settling disputes is incompatible with the teachings and example of our Lord Jesus Christ. Of all forms of war, nuclear war presents the gravest affront to the conscience of man. The avoidance of atomic, biological or chemical war has become a condition of human survival...The churches must insist that it is the first duty of governments to prevent such a war: to halt the present arms race, agree never to initiate the use of nuclear weapons, stop experiments concerned with and the production of weapons of mass human destruction by chemical and biological means and move away from the balance of terror towards disarmament. ...

The concentration of nuclear weapons in the hands of a few nations presents the world with serious problems: a) how to guarantee the security of the non-nuclear nations; b) how to enable these nations to play their part in preventing war, and; c) how to prevent the nuclear powers from freezing the existing order at the expense of changes needed for social and political justice....

[*Uppsala Speaks,* Fourth WCC Assembly, Uppsala, 1998, Geneva, 1968, pp. 62 ff.]

The V. Assembly in Nairobi was marked especially by the global concern for human rights and East-West tensions. In its Section on Structures of Injustice and Struggles for Liberation, it shifted the nature of Christian responsibility very significantly, based on ideas provided by the Federation of Churches in the German Democratic Republic:

Christians must resist the temptation to resign themselves to a false sense of impotence or security, The churches should emphasize their readiness to live without the protection of armaments, and take a significant initiative in pressing for effective disarmament. Churches, individual Christians, and members of the public in all countries should press their governments to ensure national security without resorting to the use of weapons of mass destruction...

We appeal to Christians to think, work and pray for a disarmed world.

[*Breaking Barriers,* The Official Report of the Fifth Assembly of the WCC, Nairobi, 1995, WCC, Geneva, p. 182.]

The nuclear arms race accelerated rapidly in the late 1970s, and the CCIA was asked by the Central Committee to organize a consultation to consider it and the proliferation of conventional weapons of mass destruction. Its 1978 report noted:

We are living in the shadow of an arms race more intense, more costly, more widespread and more dangerous than the world has ever known. Never before has the arms race been as close as it is now to total self-destruction. Today's arms race is an unparalleled waste of human and material resources; it aids repression and violates human rights; it promotes violence and insecurity in place of the security in whose name it is undertaken; it frustrates humanity's aspirations for justice and peace; it has no part in God's design for His world; it is demonic.... To hope in Christ is neither to be complacent about survival nor powerless in the fear of annihilation by the forces of evil but to open our eyes to the transcendent reality of Christ in history.

[Report of the WCC Consultation on Disarmament, Glion, Switzerland, 1978, in *The Churches in International Affairs 1974-1978,* WCC, Geneva 1979, p. 72]

That same year, Dr Philip Potter, WCC General Secretary, brought the concerns highlighted in the consultation to the attention of the United Nations in a plenary address to the General Assembly in which he addressed several of the underlying causes of the global arms race:

We must challenge the idol of a distorted concept of national security which is directed to encouraging fear and mistrust resulting in greater insecurity. The only security worthy of its name lies in enabling people to participate fully in the life of their nations and to establish relations of trust between peoples of different nations. It is only when there is a real dialogue – a sharing of life with life in mutual trust and respect – that there can be true security.

[Address of Dr Philip Potter, WCC General Secretary, to the First Special Session of the UN General Assembly devoted to Disarmament, N.Y., 1978. *op. cit.* pp. 70f.]

This concern for national security arose not only as a causal factor in the super-power nuclear arms race, but also as a justification for massive violations of human rights, especially by military dictatorships around the world. The Central Committee linked these concerns at its meeting in 1979:

...given the need not only to denounce militarism and the arms race, but to develop positive alternatives to the present destructive system...and as a matter of highest priority for the WCC...(the Central Committee establishes the) Programme for Disarmament and against Militarism and the Arms Race.

[*Minutes of the WCC Central Committee,* Kingston, Jamaica, 1979; also contained in *The Churches in International Affairs, 1970-82,* WCC, Geneva, 1983, p 35.]

The WCC Sub-Unit on Church and Society organized in 1979 a major World Conference on Faith, Science and the Future in Boston, Massachusetts. It adopted the following declaration which was subsequently endorsed by the Executive Committee and commended to the churches:

We, scientists, engineers, theologians and members of Christian churches from all parts of the world, participants in the WCC Conference on Faith, Science and the Future, now meeting at the Massachusetts Institute of Technology (USA), acknowledge with penitence the part played by science in the development of weapons of mass destruction and the failure of the churches to oppose it, and now plead with the nations of the world for the reduction and eventual abolition of such weapons.

Whereas:

- the arsenals of tens of thousands of nuclear weapons already constitute a grave peril to humankind;
- sharp changes by the super-powers towards a counterforce strategy are so destabilizing that sober scientists estimate a nuclear holocaust is probable before the end of the century;
- there is widespread ignorance of the horrible experience of Hiroshima and Nagasaki, and the even greater implications of limited or global nuclear war with current and projected nuclear weapons;
- we are profoundly disturbed by the willingness of some scientists, engineers and corporations, with the backing of governments, to pursue profit and prestige in weapons development at the risk of an unparalleled destruction of human life;
- the waste of the increasingly scarce materials and energy resources of the world on the instruments of war means further deprivation of the poor whom we are commanded to serve;
- we grieve that so many of the most able scientists, especially the young ones, are seduced away from the nobler aspirations of science into the unwitting service of mutual destruction;
- in a time of radical readjustment of the world economy the intolerable burden of the nuclear arms race creates worldwide economic problems;

And because we believe:

- that God made us and all creation;
- that He requires us to seek peace, justice and freedom, creating a world where none need fear and every life is sacred;
- that with His grace no work of faith, hope and love need seem too hard for those who trust him;

We now call upon:

- all member communions of the WCC and all sister churches sending official observers, and through them each individual church and congregation;
- our fellow religionists and believers in other cultures, whether Hindu, Jewish, Buddhist or Muslim, and our Marxist colleagues;
- the science and engineering community, especially those engaged in research and development, together with professional scientific associations and trade unions;
- the governments of all nations and especially the nuclear powers;
- all concerned citizens of the world;

To embark immediately on the following tasks:

- to support and implement the WCC Program on Disarmament and against Militarism and the Arms Race, and give special emphasis to issues related to military technology and its conversion to peaceful uses; ...

- to stop the development and production of new forms and systems of nuclear weapons...
- to educate and raise the consciousness of every constituency to the realities of nuclear war in such a way that people cease to avoid it as an issue too big to handle; ...
- to prepare local and national programs for the conversion to civilian use of laboratories and factories related to military research and production, and to provide for the retraining and re-employment of those who work on them;
- to resolve never again to allow science and technology to threaten the destruction of human life, and to accept the God-given task of using science for peace.

[*Minutes of the WCC Executive Committee*, Bossey, Switzerland, 1979, *op. cit.* pp. 40ff.]

That year, 1979, marked a major turning point in the mobilization of world public opinion about the nuclear arms race. The announcement by the USA of its intention to produce a neutron bomb and radically to escalate the number and quality of its nuclear arms based in Europe created a massive public outcry. The Central Committee echoed the demands of the anti-nuclear movement the following year:

The Central Committee urges all nuclear powers to:

a) freeze immediately all further testing, production and deployment of nuclear weapons and of missiles and new aircraft designed primarily to deliver nuclear weapons;
b) start immediately discussions with a view to making agreements not to enhance the existing nuclear potentials and progressively reducing the overall number of nuclear weapons and a speedy conclusion of a comprehensive test ban treaty.

[*Minutes of the WCC Central Committee*, Geneva, 1980, in *op. cit.* pp. 43f.]

The following year, in Dresden (GDR), it received a report from the Program for Disarmament and against Militarism and the Arms Race, and said:

The Central Committee...calls upon the churches now to:

1) challenge the military and militaristic policies that lead to disastrous distortions of foreign policy sapping the capacity of the nations of the world to deal with pressing economic and social priorities which have become a paramount political issue of our times;
2) counter the trend to characterize those of other nations and ideologies as the enemy through the promotion of hatred and prejudice;
3) assist in de-mythologizing current doctrines of national security and elaborate new concepts of security based on justice and the rights of peoples;...

Commends the work of a large number of peace and disarmament groups and movements, old and new, around the world, in several of which large numbers of Christians actively participate in obedience to the demands of the Gospel...

Urges the churches, in the context of the preparations for the Sixth Assembly, whose theme is Jesus Christ, the Life of the World, to make commitment to peace-making a special concern and to give emphasis to studies on issues related to pee, paying special attention to the underlying theological issues.

[*Minutes of the WCC Central Committee*, Dresden, 1981, in *op. cit.* pp 45ff.]

In November 1981, the WCC convened an International Public Hearing on Nuclear Weapons and Disarmament at the Free University in Amsterdam. A hearing panel of 17 church leaders, theologians and ethicists from all the world's regions heard testimony from 38 expert witnesses, including former US national security advisors, USSR foreign policy experts, senior diplomats in the field of disarmament, political leaders including Swedish Prime Minister Olof Palme, leading nuclear scientists and leaders of anti-nuclear peace movements in several parts of the world. Its extensive report was submitted to the WCC Central Committee and widely distributed. It contained, *inter alia*, the following affirmations:

We believe the time has come when the churches must unequivocally declare that the production and deployment as well as the use of nuclear weapons are a crime against humanity and that such activities must be condemned on ethical and theological grounds. ... We recognize that nuclear weapons will not disappear because of such an affirmation by the churches. But it will involve the churches and their members in a fundamental examination of their own implicit or explicit support of policies which, implicitly or explicitly, are based on the possession and use of those weapons.

[*Before It's Too Late: The Challenge of Nuclear Disarmament*, WCC, Geneva, 1983, pp. 3ff.]

Dr Philip Potter took these affirmations and the rising concern of the ecumenical movement back to the United Nations the following year when he addressed the plenary session of the Second Special Session of the General Assembly devoted to Disarmament.

... Compared with the public mood in 1978 when you last met, the growing massive strength of movements of people of every walk of life and ideological position gives us hope that the political will to take concrete steps to disarmament will emerge, and that governments will respect and act on this will. ...

During the last four years since the First Special Session on Disarmament the economic crisis has worsened throughout the world with grave consequences for the poor nations resulting in tensions within and among nations. The continuing stalemate in the North-South discussions on global issues has been accompanied by policies of confrontation and an attempt to divide the South. The present global military order is inextricably tied up with the economic and social system and therefore the quest for disarmament can in no way be isolated from the struggle for justice and human dignity. Consequently, there is deep distrust among the peoples of the Third World about the postures of the nuclear weapon states on deterrence and non-proliferation. Their struggles for social and political change are often distorted by the security considerations and economic interests of the major powers. ...

Choose Life! (Deut.30:15,19) Choose what is good, that is, what expresses our inner being as made in God's image to be shared with others. Choose the blessing, that is, what communicates our vitality to others, what enables us to put what we are and have at the disposal of others that they might become their true selves and share their lives also with others. That is God's purpose revealed in creation and in men and women made in his image to participate in his life and communicate that life to one another according to his commandments and promises of good. That is life. That is true security and peace.

> [Statement by WCC General Secretary Philip Potter to the Second Special Session of the UN General Assembly devoted to Disarmament, N.Y., June 1982, in *The Churches in International Affairs 1979-82*, pp. 49ff.]

At this same meeting of the UN General Assembly, Patriarch Pimen of the Russian Orthodox Church presented the report of the World Conference of Religious Workers for Saving the Sacred Gift of Life from Nuclear Catastrophe he convened in Moscow in May 1982.

The Central Committee in July 1982 commended the report of the International Public Hearings, highlighting its recommendations and calling upon the churches to take clear positions on them. It also issued a statement lamenting the lack of progress at the UN Special Session and renewed its call to the churches and governments to promote peace and disarmament.

In this same period, two volumes were published by the CCIA in the context of the Programme for Disarmament and against Militarism and the Arms Race, entitled *The Security Trap* I and II (WCC, Geneva, and IDOC, Rome, 1979 and 1982) that provided in-depth analysis and theological perspectives on militarism and the nuclear arms race. *Peace and Disarmament*, A compendium of major documents of the WCC and the Roman Catholic Church, was also published jointly by the CCIA and the Pontifical Commission Justitia et Pax (Rome and Geneva, 1982).

The Sixth WCC Assembly in Vancouver, 1983, was held at a time when massive public protests were being held around the world against the nuclear arms race, many of them inspired or led by the churches. This Assembly was particularly marked by this concern. It said:

Humanity is now living in the dark shadow of an arms race more intense, and of systems of injustice more widespread, more dangerous and more costly than the world has ever known. Never before has the human race been as close as it is now to total self-destruction. Never before have so many lived in the grip of deprivation and oppression.

Under that shadow we have gathered here...to proclaim our common faith in Jesus Christ, the Life of the Word, and to say to the world:

- fear not, for Christ has overcome the forces of evil; in him are all things made new;
- fear not; for the love of God, rise up for justice and for peace;
- trust in the power of Christ who reigns over all; give witness to him in word and in deed, regardless of the cost...

The churches today are called to confess anew their faith, and to repent for the times when Christians have remained silent in the face of injustice or threats to peace. The biblical vision of peace with justice for all, of wholeness, of unity for all God's people is not one of several options for the followers of Christ. It is an imperative in our time...

We call upon the churches, especially those in Europe, both East and West, and in North America, to redouble their efforts to convince their governments to reach a negotiated settlement and to turn away now, before it is too late, from plans to deploy additional or new nuclear weapons in Europe, and to begin immediately to reduce and then eliminate altogether present nuclear forces.

We urge the churches as well to intensify their efforts to stop the rapidly growing deployment of nuclear weapons and support systems in the Indian and Pacific Oceans, and to press their governments to withdraw from or refuse to base or service ships or airplanes bearing nuclear weapons in their regions...

...[I]n the spirit of the Fifth Assembly's appeal to the churches to emphasize their readiness to live without the protection of armaments, we believe that Christians should give witness to their unwillingness to participate in any conflict involving weapons of mass destruction or indiscriminate effect.

[*Gathered for Life*, Official Report of the VI. Assembly of the WCC, Vancouver, 1983, WCC, Geneva, pp. 131ff.]

The Vancouver Assembly also called on the churches to engage in a conciliar process of mutual commitment (covenant) to justice, peace and the integrity of all creation and to make this a priority for all WCC programs.

The period following the Vancouver Assembly provided no new policy statements on nuclear weapons, but was one in which the WCC encouraged a number of international disarmament initiatives and pressed on the major nuclear powers their responsibilities to disarm. WCC General Secretaries encouraged the initiatives of the Middle Power Coalition, the signatories of the Delhi Declaration, the Groupe Bellerive and others. Letters were written to President Reagan and General Secretary Gorbachev on the occasions of their summit meetings in Geneva and Iceland, encouraging them to take more rapid steps toward nuclear disarmament. On the eve of the meeting of the same leaders in Geneva in January 1987, the Central Committee welcomed the resumption of the earlier talks and appealed to the two nations:

- to declare a moratorium on nuclear tests as a provisional measure that would enable negotiations toward a comprehensive test ban treaty;
- to negotiate agreements on substantial reduction of strategic weapons and elimination of medium range missiles, with a definite time-table;
- to take all necessary steps to present the development of space weapons and to strengthen the terms of the Anti-Ballistic Missiles Treaty.

The WCC specially appeals to the US government to respond positively to the initiatives of the USSR on a moratorium on nuclear testing, to review its decision to exceed the SALT II ceilings and to reconsider its Strategic Defense Initiative. The WCC also appeals to the USSR government to reinstate and continue its moratorium on nuclear testing.

The Central Committee renews its appeal to the French government to stop forthwith nuclear weapon testing in Polynesia…

We urge the churches in the context of the call to strengthen their commitment to justice, peace and the integrity of creation:

- to intensify their engagement in efforts for peace by specifically working for an end to nuclear testing as an immediate priority;
- to engage in bilateral and multilateral discussions among churches with a view to promoting common understandings and developing common strategies;
- to join other forces of peace for public education and efforts to influence policies of governments and inter-governmental bodies;
- to support the Six Nations Initiative and that of the South Pacific Forum.

[*Minutes of the Central Committee*, Geneva, January 1987, in *The Churches in International Affairs, 1987-1990*, WCC, Geneva, 1990, pp. 44ff.]

Later that year, the WCC Officers welcomed the conclusion of the agreements at the USA-USSR Summit in Washington D.C., saying that

The agreement to eliminate intermediate nuclear forces and thus an entire class of nuclear weapons is a significant achievement especially with the elaborate system of verification which augurs well for further steps in nuclear disarmament. The initiative already taken for making proposals for reducing strategic nuclear weapons is reassuring.

[WCC Officers' Statement on the Washington Summit, 14 December 1987, *op. cit.*, p. 47.]

In a statement presented by Dr Lamar Gibble, a CCIA Commissioner, the WCC told the Third Session of the UN General Assembly devoted to Disarmament (1988):

In the limited time given for this testimony, among many concerns, we choose the following for emphasis. Firstly, even in the aura of a historic agreement to reduce intermediate range nuclear weapons, the awful risk of nuclear war remains. We are painfully aware that this agreement can only reduce the nuclear arsenal by 3%. We would, therefore, urge the pursuit of every possible effort to further reduce and ultimately eliminate these weapons of mass destruction. We reiterate the declaration of our most recent Assembly that the production and deployment of nuclear weapons as well as their use constitute a crime against humanity, and therefore there should be a complete halt in the production of nuclear weapons and in weapons research and development in all nations, to be expeditiously enforced through a treaty... Only if such a comprehensive approach is taken to nuclear disarmament and complemented and reinforced by mutually accepted verification procedures and by the new technology available for verification can the possibility of nuclear holocaust be significantly reduced. We would encourage this session to establish a multilateral mechanism under the auspices of the United Nations to perform such verification functions for our global community.

Secondly, while we recognize the possibility of significant steps in the reduction of nuclear weapons, we cannot overlook the significant new dynamics in the arms race. We view with alarm the development of star wars technology, chemical weapons, and the ever more deadly capacity of conventional weapons which blur the distinction between conventional and nuclear, and defensive and offensive weapons. Only through multilateral agreements banning the research, development and testing of these new weapons can we effectively end this process ... [*op. cit.* pp. 48ff.]

The WCC addressed a letter in 1987 to President Bush and General Secretary Gorbachev on the occasion of their summit meeting in Malta, reiterating appeals addressed earlier. But this was the last initiative on nuclear weapons before the VII. Assembly in Canberra (1991).

In Canberra the agenda was radically shifted in the direction of post Cold War armed interventions and internal conflicts. That assembly, meeting as the Gulf War was raging, gave strong clues that this would be a period of divided views and sometimes contentious relationships among the churches as they wrestled with new challenges. The VII. Assembly adopted a major policy statement on the implications of the use of armed force by the Gulf Coalition led by the USA, and another on internal conflicts. The attention of the Central Committee was fixed for most of the ensuing decade on the implications of such challenges and by renewed debates and efforts to address the churches' positions on violence.

The war in Bosnia/Herzegovina again led to contentious debates in the Central Committee on the old tension between the Christian traditions of pacifism and the just war. In 1994, on the basis of a background document, Overcoming the Spirit, Logic and Practice of War, the Central Committee created the Programme to Overcome Violence. In the course of the international campaign, Peace to the City, carried out in the context of the POV, the focus turned especially to the issue of small arms and light weapons, and this has continued as a part of the new ecumenical Decade to Overcome Violence established by the VIII. Assembly in Harare (1998).

The disarmament agenda shifted more to the area of conventional arms, following the line traced earlier in consultations on militarism and disarmament. The CCIA Commission held a consultation in 1993 on the conventional arms trade (cf. *The Arms Trade Today,* CCIA Background Information, 1993/1, WCC, Geneva, 1993) and adopted a statement on the subject.

Soon after the Harare Assembly, the following document was issued, and it was the last major policy statement devoted particularly to nuclear weapons to date.

Nuclear weapons, whether used or threatened, are grossly evil and therefore morally wrong. As an instrument of mass destruction, nuclear weapons slaughter the innocent and ravage the environment...

(Therefore) we ask the delegates to call resolutely upon the nuclear weapons states to embark upon a series of steps along the road leading to nuclear abolition. There is broad consensus...on what these steps should be. They include:

- declare a policy of no first use among themselves and non-use in relation to non-nuclear weapons states;
- cease all research, development, production, and deployment of new nuclear weapons;
- refrain from modernizing the existing nuclear arsenal and increasing the number of deployed nuclear weapons;
- take all nuclear forces off alert and remove warheads from delivery vehicles;
- achieve faster and deeper bilateral reduction of nuclear weapons by the United States and Russia.

...We ask the delegates to take the lead in commencing the process of developing a nuclear weapons convention to outlaw and abolish all nuclear weapons...We appeal to the delegates...to consider what is best for the whole Earth and its inhabitants when they vote on issues of nuclear non-proliferation and disarmament. Loyalty to all humankind exceeds that of loyalty within political blocs of nations. We urge delegates to act now, decisively and courageously for the benefit of all the peoples of the Earth.

[Joint statement of WCC General Secretary Konrad Raiser and Cardinal Daneels, President of Pax Christi International to the NPT Review Conference Preparatory Committee, Geneva, April 1998.]

At its first meeting (Morges, Switzerland, January 2000), the newly elected Commission of the Churches on International Affairs adopted guidelines for programmatic work in the field of disarmament which stressed the need for the WCC and its member churches to turn their attention back to the continuing threat of nuclear weapons. So, concern about nuclear weapons has not disappeared from the WCC agenda. However, it has been dropped to the lowest levels of priority of many churches, including those in nuclear weapons states. There is an urgent need for the ecumenical movement to remember its history and to reassert leadership at what is in fact a very critical moment of new challenges to the international disarmament regime and the ever more dangerous legacy of the decaying products of the decades-long US-USSR nuclear arms race. Statements alone will not be enough. The statements reviewed here were often backed by movements in the churches working to bring official church assemblies with them in action and conviction. If we are to be effective again, attention will have to be paid during the forthcoming ecumenical Decade to Overcome Violence to the strengthening, regeneration and re-connection of such movements.

Policy framework and guidelines on small arms and light weapons
Adopted by the CCIA at its 44th meeting, Crans Montana, Switzerland, 18 May 2001.

Background

Small Arms and Violence
Small arms and light weapons are the primary instruments through which persistent and deeply rooted political conflicts are transformed with alarming frequency into armed violence and war. Through war, crime, domestic violence and suicides, more than 10,000 lives are lost each week to small arms violence. The easy availability of small arms and light weapons exacerbates and prolongs armed conflicts, defers economic and social development, promotes crime, nurtures cultures of violence, and produces an extraordinary worldwide burden of cumulative personal tragedies and public crises.

The most devastating impact of small arms affects the vulnerable, especially teen-agers. The light weight, transportability and ease of use of small arms and light weapons has facilitated one of the most abusive elements of contemporary armed conflict, notably the engagement of children as armed combatants.

It is a matter of urgent public responsibility that the international community now act to address the problems of the proliferation, accumulation and misuse of small arms and light weapons, and to address their debilitating social, economic, political and humanitarian impacts.

The Role of the Churches
In response to the small arms crisis, and in the context of the international campaign, "Peace to the City," carried out in the context of the World Council of Churches' (WCC) Programme to Overcome Violence, the WCC Central Committee called in 1997 for "special attention to the concern for microdisarmament." Subsequently, international and regional consultations on micro-disarmament were held in Rio de Janeiro (May 1998 and July 2000) and Nairobi (October 2000); a Micro-disarmament Fund has been created to support local and regional initiatives; and an Ecumenical Network on Small Arms (ENSA) is in formation.

The July 2000 consultation in Rio declared that "the problem of armed violence and the diffusion of small arms...cannot be effectively addressed without the involvement of the Churches in the region." The Latin American declaration went on to say that "churches have deep roots in local communities and thus are especially well positioned to address the issues of micro-conflict. Churches know the people's needs, and can understand the insecurities that lead some to seek security through guns."

The churches are well placed to acknowledge and testify to the impact of small arms, since they minister to the victims and their families all around the world, in rich and poor nations. Churches see people's needs and are in a unique position to address the small arms epidemic, identifying its material, moral, ethical and spiritual dimensions. Churches can inform, mobilize and guide the community, offering a specific and holistic contribution to the international small arms campaign.

Churches also have a policy role to play, bringing theological insights and moral and ethical perspectives to bear upon the social and political pursuit of small arms control and demand reduction.

The Emerging Small Arms Agenda
Through a wide range of UN expert studies, UN resolutions, and civil society research and analysis, a broadly recognized international small arms agenda is emerging. The churches are challenged to support and advance that emerging small arms action agenda designed to control the supply and availability of small arms and light weapons, to promote social, economic and political conditions to reduce the demand for small arms and light weapons, and to facilitate and ensure effective implementation of and compliance with small arms control and reduction measures.

While individual states exercise varying degrees of control over small arms and light weapons, there exist no universal laws or standards by which to regulate the production, transfer, possession or use of small arms, and to protect individuals, families and communities from small arms abuse.

Nevertheless, a series of significant international initiatives by states have been taken that deserve the study of the churches, including:

a) The ECOWAS "Declaration of a Moratorium on Importation, Exportation and Manufacture of Light Weapons in West Africa" (November 1998);

b) The "Nairobi Declaration on the Problem of the Proliferation of Illicit Small Arms and Light Weapons in the Great Lakes Region and the Horn of Africa" (March 2000);

c) The "Bamako Declaration on an African Common Position on the Illicit Proliferation, Circulation and Trafficking of Small Arms and Light Weapons" (December 2000);

d) The OAS "Inter-American Convention against the Illicit Manufacturing of and Trafficking in Firearms, Ammunition, Explosives, and other Related Materials" (November 1997);

e) The Brasilia Declaration for the 2001 *United Nations Conference on the Illicit Arms Trade in Small Arms and All Its Aspects*, Regional Preparatory Meeting of the Latin American and Caribbean States for the UN Conference (November 2000);

f) European Union joint action on "Combating the Destabilising Accumulation and Spread of Small Arms and Light Weapons" (December 1998);

g) The UN "Protocol against the Illicit Manufacturing of and Trafficking in Firearms, Their Parts and Components and Ammunition," supplementing the "United Nations Convention against Transnational Organized Crime" (March 2001).

The UN 2001 Conference

The forthcoming (July 2001) *United Nations Conference on the Illicit Trade in Small Arms and Light Weapons in All Its Aspects* offers a significant opportunity to advance the three-fold small arms agenda, to recognize the humanitarian consequences of the proliferation of small arms, and to mobilize support for timely measures and commitments to mitigate their damaging impact.

It is vitally important that the UN conference commit States to measures that will have a real and beneficial impact on the lives of the people who now suffer the devastating and debilitating consequences of the presence and misuse of small arms in their communities. The conference could be a critically important step toward addressing the small arms crisis, but it will only be an early step on the way to developing the international measures, norms, and laws needed to reduce the demand for and enhance the control of small arms and light weapons.

A Call to Action on Small Arms and Light Weapons

Against the background of the work already undertaken on small arms and light weapons by the WCC International Relations staff and the CCIA Peacebuilding and Disarmament Reference Group, the Commission of the Churches on International Affairs of the World Council of Churches, at its forty-fourth meeting in Crans-Montana, Switzerland, 14-18 May 2001:

Renews the appeal to the churches of the Fifth WCC Assembly (Nairobi 1975) "to emphasize their readiness to live without the protection of armaments;" and urges Christians to do those things that make for peace with justice; and to foster the development of social and political institutions that provide security and physical and spiritual well-being for all without resort to weapons;

Renews its commitment to sustained participation in the emerging global effort to address the excessive and unregulated accumulations and proliferation of small arms that foment conflicts around the world, make them extraordinarily destructive, and render them more resistant to peaceful resolution;

Welcomes the convening of the UN Conference on small arms in 2001 and urges the churches to commit it and the broader small arms disarmament effort to God in prayer;

Emphasizes the urgent need for resolute international action through the 2001 conference and beyond to encourage the international community to put in place a sustained program of action to address the small arms crisis;

Welcomes the formation and work of the International NGO Action Network on Small Arms (IANSA), of which the WCC is a founding member;

Affirms the importance of church action and encourages the Ecumenical Network on Small Arms (ENSA) in its continuing work in collaboration with other members of IANSA;

Calls upon states to use the occasion of the 2001 UN Conference to agree and commit to the following measures, and to put in place policies and resources to ensure their effective follow-up and implementation:

a) to exercise restraint in the accumulation and transfer of small arms and light weapons, and to pursue a global "code of conduct" to control arms transfers in the context of and consistent with the obligations of states, including the obligation not to acquire arms for purposes other than or beyond levels needed for self-defence, to ensure the least possible diversion of resources to armaments, and to the obligation to respect and protect the welfare and rights of its citizens;

b) to implement strict domestic controls on the manufacture, possession and use of small arms, including consideration of the feasibility of adopting a legally binding instrument for a universal ban on civilian possession and use of military assault rifles;

c) to address social, political and economic conditions that tend to generate demand for small arms and light weapons (including a focus on human safety and protection, peaceful resolution of conflict, promoting cultures of peace, an urgent attention to reform of the security sector);

d) to cooperate, notably within and between regions, in support of more effective and consistent compliance with controls and regulations, including the pursuit of universal legally binding instruments to regulate brokering, and to adopt universal standards for marking, tracing, and record keeping of small arms and light weapons;

e) to adopt international standards for stockpile management, for post-conflict disarmament, demobilization, and reintegration of ex-combatants, for weapons collection, and for the destruction of surplus and collected weapons;

f) to promote the conversion of weapons manufacturing capacity into socially constructive production;

g) to practice maximum transparency in transactions and policies and regulations related to small arms and light weapons;

h) to provide increased international support and resources for programs and initiatives to promote social justice and advance human security as conditions essential to development, and to promote social, economic and political conditions conducive to long-term peace, stability and development;

i) to provide financial, technical, and political support for the effective implementation of the above measures and policies;

j) to put in place effective follow-up and accountability processes.

Urges the churches, in the context of the Decade to Overcome Violence, to join with other faiths and civil society partners in their own countries to obtain their governments' agreement to these goals;

Commits itself to continue to give special attention to ameliorating the social, political and economic conditions that tend to generate demand to violence-reduction efforts;

Commits itself to continuing active consultation with member churches and regional and national councils of churches to promote education and awareness raising, to develop and refine ecumenical policy on the issue, to contribute to the development of national, regional international plans of action to address armed violence and the proliferation of small arms and light weapons, and assist the churches in developing their own effective programs and actions to control and mitigate the effects of small arms and light weapons.

Easter Appeal for a Cessation of Armed Conflicts
Issued by Konrad Raiser (WCC), Keith Clements (CEC), Ishmael Noko (LWF), Milan Opocensky (WARC), Joe Hale (WMC), Denton Lotz (BWA), and John L. Peterson of the Anglican Communion, 31 March 1999.

In this season of Easter, Christians around the world share the profound pain of all those caught up in tragedies such as Kosovo. Our hearts go out to all those who are suffering the terrible consequences of the violence being inflicted on God's children in this region and in many other parts of the world. We lament the failure of imagination, collective will and human spirit made manifest in the incapacity to address the causes of conflict through peaceful means. As we remember again the sacrifice of Jesus Christ, the one proclaimed by the prophets as the Messiah, the Prince of Peace, our hearts are heavy for we recognize that we have not yet been able to overcome our inclination to turn to the sword in moments of doubt and fear.

Kosovo is but one of the many conflicts around the world today where people take up arms against one another out of fear, hate, greed or hopelessness. Many of these wars are largely hidden from the view of the wider world, and some of them have claimed an even more terrible toll than is now being inflicted in the Balkans. So we pray this Easter for all of those in Yugoslavia and elsewhere whose lives are shattered by war.

Leaders of Christian churches in both East and West, and leaders of other religious faiths have appealed in recent days for a cessation of such acts of violence and for the settlement of conflict by negotiation. Regrettably, such voices have not yet been heard over the clamour of charges and countercharges, and the roar of bombs, landmines and guns.

One of these leaders, His All Holiness The Ecumenical Patriarch Bartholomew, has summarized many of these sentiments in his appeal of 29 March 1999, saying,

in the name of God who loves humankind, in the name of the human race, in the name of civilization, at this season of the religious feast of the Muslims, the Easter of Roman Catholics and Protestants, the Passover of the Jews and the Pascha of the Orthodox, on bended knees [I] fervently appeal from the

---

* See also: Statement on the initiation of bombing in Afghanistan, p. 246; Message and letter to the US churches after the bombing attacks of September 11th, pp. 399ff; Expression of concern about the safety and security of the Christian minority in Pakistan, p. 271.

tormented depths of my heart to all world government leaders, to military commanders and to those who bear arms throughout the world, that they cease fire immediately and permanently. We beseech them to use mutual understanding and mutual concession to resolve peacefully their regional, international and worldwide disputes, in order that the God of peace and mercy might bless them and all people.

In this same spirit, we appeal to Christians around the world in these high holy days to join their hearts and spirits in this prayer that the bombings may cease and that the guns may fall silent. May the Spirit descend among us and inspire in us the courage to sacrifice our individual wills in order that the peace of the Risen Christ may prevail.

The Decade to Overcome Violence (DOV), Churches Seeking Reconciliation and Peace

Message adopted by the Central Committee, Geneva, 26 August - 3 September 1999.

Seek peace and pursue it. (Psalm 34:14)

In response to a call by the Eighth Assembly of the World Council of Churches, we embark on a Decade to Overcome Violence in the years 2001-2010 and invite churches, ecumenical groups, individual Christians and people of good will to contribute to it.

We are gathered for the first Central Committee meeting after the Harare Assembly at the end of the most violent century in human history. We are convinced: the churches are called to provide to the world a clear witness to peace, to reconciliation and nonviolence, grounded in justice.

We remember the saints and martyrs who have given their lives as a witness for God against the powers of violence, destruction and war. We recall the witness of people who became signs of hope within and beyond their respective communities, opening up alternatives to the deadly cycle of violence. As representatives of member churches of the World Council of Churches, we are inspired by the Gospel message of the peace of Christ, of love and of reconciliation, and the rich biblical tradition of peace with justice. God's promise of life and peace for all humankind and creation calls us to make our lives consistent with our faith, as individuals and as communities of faith.

But we are also aware that Christians and churches have added, through words and actions, to growing violence and injustice in a world of oppression and graceless competition. We are yearning for a community of humankind, in which nobody is excluded and everybody can live in peace with human dignity. As we engage in constructive efforts to build a culture of peace, we know that we are required to embark upon a deep process of change, beginning with repentance and a renewed commitment to the very sources of our faith.

We must give up being spectators of violence or merely lamenting it and must act to overcome violence both within and outside the walls of the church. We remind ourselves and the churches of our common responsibility to speak out boldly against any defense of unjust and oppressive structures, of racism, of the use of violence, including especially violence against women and children, and of other gross violations of human rights committed in the name of any nation or ethnic group. If churches do not combine their witness for peace and reconciliation with the search for unity among themselves, they fail in their mission to the world. Leaving behind what separates us, responding ecumenically to the challenge, proving that nonviolence is an active approach to conflict resolution, and offering in all humility what Jesus Christ taught his disciples to do, the churches have a unique message to bring to the violence-ridden world.

There are a number of positive and encouraging examples from congregations and churches around the world. We recognize the steady witness of monastic traditions and of the "historic peace churches", and we want to receive anew their contribution through the Decade. There are congregations and churches that have become centers of reflection and training for active nonviolence in their own context. They show the kind of courage, skills and creativity that is necessary for active nonviolence and nonviolent resistance. They are sensitive to the destruction of nature and concentrate on the situation of the most vulnerable groups. Part of the contribution to building a culture of peace involves listening to the stories of those who are the primary victims of violence, including people who are poor, women, youth and children, people with disabilities, and Indigenous Peoples.

There are those who teach us through their example that presence in the situations of violence, on the streets and in the war torn areas, the active involvement with victims and perpetrators of violence, is the very key to every process of transformation and change. Prior to the Harare Assembly, the WCC Programme to Overcome Violence and the Peace to the City Campaign have shown: peace is practical, it grows at grassroots level and is nurtured by the creativity of the people. They cooperate locally with civil society and engage in dialogue and common action with people of other faiths. The groups from the seven cities participating in the campaign were strengthened and encouraged by each other, sharing their experiences across different contexts and gaining new insight from reflection and exchange at the global level.

The Decade to Overcome Violence will provide a platform to share stories and experiences, develop relationships and learn from each other. The Decade will build upon the initiatives that are already there; we recognize that our work is parallel to the work of the United Nations "Decade for a Culture of Peace and Nonviolence for the Children of the World". We hope to connect with such initiatives and help them to motivate and strengthen each other. It will facilitate the churches to assist and support each other in their ministry. We offer with the Decade to Overcome Violence a truly ecumenical space, a safe space for encounter, mutual recognition, and common action. We will strive together to overcome the spirit, logic and practice of violence. We will work together to be agents of reconciliation and peace with justice in homes, churches and communities as well as in the political, social and economic structures at national and international levels. We will co-operate to build a culture of peace that is based on just and sustainable communities.

The Gospel vision of peace is a source of hope for change and a new beginning. Let us not betray what has been given to us. People around the world wait with eager longing for Christians to become who we are: children of God embodying the message of love, peace with justice and reconciliation.

Peace is possible. Peace is practical. Seek peace and pursue it.

Blessed are the peacemakers for they shall be called children of God. (Matthew 5:9)

A Basic Framework For The Decade To Overcome Violence
Working document adopted by the Central Committee of the World Council of Churches, Geneva, 26 August - 3 September 1999.

Introduction

The Eighth Assembly of the World Council of Churches gathered together under an African cross, in Harare, Zimbabwe, to discern priorities and programmes for the next seven years. Around the Assembly theme, "Turn to God - Rejoice in Hope", delegates established the Decade to Overcome Violence (DOV). The Assembly stated that the WCC must "work strategically with the churches on these issues of nonviolence and reconciliation to create a culture of nonviolence, linking and interacting with other international partners and organizations, and examining and developing appropriate approaches to conflict transformation and just peace-making in the new globalized context." The WCC intends, therefore, to further its solidarity with Africa and grow together with the world communion of people who are building cultures of nonviolence and peace.

Faithful to the Assembly's mandate, the focus of the WCC's work during the Decade to Overcome Violence will be on the concept "overcome", rather than "violence". Therefore, the methodology will bring out the positive experiences of churches and groups working towards overcoming violence. The Decade to Overcome Violence must grow out of the experiences and work of local churches and community contexts. The WCC can facilitate the exchange, act as a switchboard, and highlight experiences of local peace-building, peacekeeping, and prevention of violence. The Decade to Overcome Violence, however, should move beyond WCC structures in Geneva to include all member churches, non-member churches, NGOs, and other organizations that are committed to peace.

The Decade to Overcome Violence, therefore, will highlight and network efforts by churches, ecumenical organizations, and civil society movements to overcome different types of violence. The WCC should seek to establish points of contact with the relevant aims, programmes, and architecture of the United Nations Decade for a Culture of Peace and Nonviolence for the Children of the World (2001-2010). It is important for the Decade to Overcome Violence to focus on the specific and unique contributions of both the individual member churches and the WCC as a whole.

Calling on the WCC's rich heritage of programmes for peace and justice, the organizers for the WCC's work on the Decade to Overcome Violence can build on, and create continuity with, models of coordinating a decade, campaigns, and programmes. Organizers will particularly consider the following methodologies: team visits and Living Letters (such as those of the Ecumenical Decade of Churches in Solidarity with Women (EDCSW)) to address concerns and perspectives from all over the world; World Wide Web, video, and print materials (Peace to the City campaign); exchanges and visits. The Decade to Overcome Violence should further these methodologies. The Decade to Overcome Violence should continue the work already done through the Programme to Overcome Violence and the Peace to the City campaign.

I. *Goals*

In order to move peace-building from the periphery to the centre of the life and witness of the church and to build stronger alliances and understanding among churches, networks, and movements which are working toward a culture of peace, the goals of the Decade to Overcome Violence are:

Addressing holistically the wide varieties of violence, both direct and structural, in homes, communities, and in international arenas and learning from the local and regional analyses of violence and ways to overcome violence.

Challenging the churches to overcome the spirit, logic, and practice of violence; to relinquish any theological justification of violence; and to affirm anew the spirituality of reconciliation and active nonviolence.

Creating a new understanding of security in terms of cooperation and community, instead of in terms of domination and competition.

Learning from the spirituality and resources for peace-building of other faiths to work with communities of other faiths in the pursuit of peace and to challenge the churches to reflect on the misuse of religious and ethnic identities in pluralistic societies.

Challenging the growing militarization of our world, especially the proliferation of small arms and light weapons.

II. *A basic framework for the Decade to Overcome Violence*

1. *Keys to designing and implementing the Decade to Overcome Violence*

Allowing multiple entry points through which churches, groups, and issues may join and find their voice

Ensuring and supporting creative, effective, professional communication as central to the process and success of the Decade to Overcome Violence

Sustaining momentum over the ten years;

Using different methodologies appropriate to specific goals;

Developing clearly defined goals for the mid-point of the Decade to Overcome Violence (2005 Assembly), as well as for the end of the Decade in 2010;

Involving all WCC clusters and teams in the Decade to Overcome Violence.

2. *Two stages of the Decade to Overcome Violence*

2001-2005, culminating in the WCC's Ninth Assembly (2005).

2006-2010, culminating in an end of the Decade celebration.

3. *Phases of the Decade to Overcome Violence*

Phase I: 1999-2000: Preparation for the Decade and Launch. The WCC Central Committee will invite member churches and ecumenical partners to join the Decade to Overcome Violence. The WCC Central Committee will ask regional ecumenical gatherings to outline their specific priorities and projects and thus to contribute to the development of the architecture; formulation of the main message; creation of an appropriate organizational framework and budget for coordination and planning; development and implementation of communication strategies; preparation for the launch.

Phase II: 2001-2004: Launch and Decade to Overcome Violence Actions. In January 2001, simultaneous launches would be organized around the world, involving local congregations and groups as well as highly visible, international events. Different issues and appropriate methodologies will be used in the Decade to Overcome Violence process which are coordinated with regard to planning, communication, joint events, and common goals.

Phase III: 2004: Synthesis through Cross-Contextual Analysis and Experience. As some issues and actions continue, the WCC will facilitate exchanges between creative models of peacemaking addressed in the first three years with the aim of strengthening networks and building new alliances.

Phase IV: 2005: Analysis/Evaluation/Preparation for the Assembly and the Next Five Years. Analysis and evaluation of the first stage of the Decade to Overcome Violence will reflect on the process and assess the following questions: What are the lessons learned this far? What are the challenges to the churches? What are the churches doing? What still needs to be done? Strategic exchanges and visits will help Decade to Overcome Violence participants to listen and learn from one another. These evaluations and exchanges will contribute to the Assembly preparation and build new impetus for the Decade's second stage.

Phase V: 2005-2010: WCC Ninth Assembly.
Lessons and challenges from the first part of the Decade will be shared. The focus
and plan of action for 2006-2010 are finalized and adopted.

4. *Possible Approaches and Methodologies*

Study processes
Continuing and expanding the theological reflections on violence and
nonviolence, from the perspectives of the dignity and human rights of human
beings and of the community; an ongoing and accessible Biblical study process
(contextual, cross-contextual, cross-cultural); study and analysis of the work of
truth and reconciliation commissions.

Engaging the churches and regional networks in reflection on violence and peace-
building in the midst of structural challenges such as racism, globalization,
violence against women, violence among youth, violence against children, etc.

Campaigns
Providing practical support and solidarity to churches and groups in their efforts
to mobilize campaigns on specific issues with defined goals to prevent, transform
and overcome violence in their own contexts. Encouraging churches and
organizations to network for specific international campaigns.

Education
Collecting, compiling, and sharing peace education curricula for children, youth,
and adults, by building on existing models, particularly from the Christian
perspective, networking educators and resource people, as well as theological
institutions, who are engaged in conflict resolution, transformation, and
mediation. Challenging present educational systems and media which perpetuate
competition, aggressive individualism and violence, especially among children.

Worship and Spirituality
Sharing resources and practices for worship and prayer across traditions and
cultures in order to focus on our common efforts of peace-making and
reconciliation. The concept of *metanoia* is particularly important as the churches
take responsibility for their part in violent actions from the past and in the present.
Metanoia encompasses confession, repentance, renewal, and celebration of faith
and is therefore a foundation of a culture of peace.

Telling the Story - Decade "Open Space"
Sharing stories of violence, initiatives to overcome violence, and sustaining
cultures of peace, churches, communities, groups, and individuals will create
"open space" through the World Wide Web, print, video, events and personal
exchanges. These stories will connect people and efforts, provide support and
solidarity, share resources and ideas, and provide constant input into the process
and focus of the Decade, particularly for the second stage, 2006-2010.

5. Issues

"Violence" is not only physical. "Violence" is also emotional, intellectual, and structural. Throughout the Decade to Overcome Violence, the focus will be on the response and prevention to forms of violence, such as:

Overcoming violence between nations
Overcoming violence within nations
Overcoming violence in local communities
Overcoming violence within the home and the family
Overcoming violence within the church
Overcoming sexual violence
Overcoming socio-economic violence
Overcoming violence as a result of economic and political blockades
Overcoming violence among youth
Overcoming violence associated with religious and cultural practices
Overcoming violence within legal systems
Overcoming violence against creation
Overcoming violence as a result of racism and ethnic hatred

III. Concluding remarks

The Ecumenical Decade to Overcome Violence is meant to capture the excitement and expectations of churches, ecumenical organizations, groups and movements around the world for the positive, practical, and unique contribution of the churches to building a culture of peace. The design and methodology of the Decade to Overcome Violence should be focused and yet open to allow creativity and to utilize the dynamic energy of the churches and different groups in society. The architecture for the Decade to Overcome Violence will depend on the suggestions, plans, and leadership of the WCC's member churches and ecumenical partners who will define the issues and the processes that will lead the Decade to Overcome Violence forward.

This document will serve as a framework for preparatory steps in the Decade to Overcome Violence. Throughout the Decade, the Executive and Programme Committees will monitor the process and will sharpen the goals and methodologies.

General Secretary's Christmas Message, 2000
Issued in Geneva, 17 November 2000.

It has been a centuries-old unwritten rule that at Christmas a cease-fire be observed in all situations of military conflict. Will this be the case this year as well? What do those warlords who force young people – and often enough children – to fight their dirty wars know and care about this rule? From Sierra Leone to Indonesia, from Israel and Palestine to Sri Lanka, from Colombia to Chechnya, our world seems to be engulfed in a deadly cycle of war, violence and destruction.

A real culture of violence has taken root and is spreading, in open contempt of all the rules of humanitarian law. It manifests itself not only in armed conflict. Violence has become omnipresent in the streets, in subways, in schools and sports stadiums, in families and homes. Its victims are most often those who are different: members of ethnic, racial or religious minorities; refugees; people with disabilities; or simply the poor and marginalized.

Can this dynamic be stopped? In many places, people have begun to stand up and to form alliances resisting the culture of violence. Through its "Programme to Overcome Violence", the World Council of Churches has tried since 1994 to support such initiatives and give them greater visibility. Now at the beginning of the year 2001, the WCC will reinforce its efforts and launch a "Decade to Overcome Violence". This Decade is rooted in the conviction that Christians and their churches are called "to provide to the world a clear witness to peace, to reconciliation and non-violence grounded in justice". It is the objective of the Decade to open the space where an alternative culture of peace and reconciliation can grow.

Building a culture of peace and non-violence is an urgent demand, not only for political reasons. Churches are called to articulate the protest of the gospel against the cult of force and greed, against unbridled competition and impunity where fundamental human rights are being violated. The culture of violence is the result of a perversion of basic values; it manifests the inability to sustain relationships. Overcoming violence therefore has to begin in the hearts and minds of people. A culture of peace cannot be imposed from above. It grows where space is provided for learning how to resolve conflicts peacefully, to sustain difficult relationships, to encounter the stranger without anxiety.

Each year at Christmas, we hear the message of the angels: "Glory to God in the highest heaven, and on earth peace to those whom he favours" (Luke 2:14). We celebrate the birth of the "Prince of Peace" (Isaiah 9:6), the one who reconciled us to God and with each other and thus proclaimed peace (Eph. 2:17) and a new relationship between those who had been separated by alienation and hostility.

As we celebrate Christmas this year, let us consider what we can contribute to overcoming violence and building a culture of peace. Living in a situation where violence has become omnipresent, those who have heard and accepted the gospel of the peace of Christ are entrusted with the message of reconciliation. They are made ambassadors for Christ and called into a ministry of reconciliation (2 Cor. 5:18-20).

This, then, is our mission today as Christians: wherever the walls of hostility are being broken down, wherever communal conflict is being resolved peacefully, wherever women and children are being saved from becoming victims of violence, the peace of Christ is being proclaimed to the glory of God.

Expression of concern about threats of retaliation following the September 11th attacks in the U.S.A.

Letter to H.E. Kofi Annan, Secretary-General of the United Nations, 1 October 2001.

Dear Mr Secretary-General,

I write to thank you for the wise and measured leadership you have given your staff, the United Nations and the peoples of the world in the difficult period since the tragic, heart-rending day of 11 September.

We were especially grateful for your address to the General Assembly on 24 September. Your words of encouragement in the face of widespread despair, your message of hope, and your call for the rejection of the path of violence were both poignant and timely.

As you have so clearly pointed out, these attacks have shown the extreme vulnerability of all nations, and indeed the fragility of the present global system. A world in which ever greater numbers of nations and peoples are being consigned to extreme poverty while great wealth accumulates in others is inherently unstable and vulnerable to acts of extreme violence. A world in which the spirit, logic and practice of war dominate the policies of powerful nations, and is reflected back to the peoples of the world through an increasingly monochrome global media, is a world that breeds violence.

The violence of terrorism – in all its many forms – is abhorrent to all who believe human life is a gift of God and therefore infinitely precious. Every attempt to intimidate others by inflicting indiscriminate death and injury upon them is to be universally condemned. The answer to terrorism, however, cannot be to respond in kind, for this can lead only to more violence and terror. Instead a concerted effort of all nations is needed to remove any possible justification for such acts.

So long as the cries of those humiliated by unremitting injustice, by the systematic deprivation of their rights, and by the arrogance of power of those who possess unchallenged military might are ignored or neglected by a seemingly uncaring world, terrorism will not be overcome. The answer to terrorism must be found in redressing these wrongs that breed violence between and within nations.

We hope and pray that the response to the terrible tragedies of 11 September will mark a turning point for a global reassessment of our collective responsibility to heal the wounds and offer new perspectives to our world. Certainly it is this, not the language of war, that would be the finest tribute to those who lost their lives in these terrible attacks.

In the context of the Decade to Overcome Violence launched by the World Council of Churches early this year, churches and individual Christians around the world are striving to break the rising spiral of retributive violence that has brought so much pain and suffering to people through the ages. In declaring this Decade, the WCC Assembly in Harare (1998) gave recognition to the UN "International Decade for a Culture of Peace and Non-Violence for the Children of the World." The assembly was acutely aware of the fact that Christians have often contributed to shaping a culture of violence. We have often blessed the war-makers and offered justification for violence. Thus the Decade represents a call to repentance and calls churches and individual Christians to reflect deeply on the violence we bear within us and seek to free ourselves from its bondage. It also calls us to pursue ever more vigorously a Dialogue among Civilizations, and to deepen inter-religious dialogue with all those who believe that God wills justice and peace for all peoples.

We hope that the nations and their leaders will now approach their responsibilities in a similar way. This is not a time for the building of coalitions of states that accede to or agree to participate in further acts of retaliation or aggression. It is rather an opportunity to rally the peoples and the nations to a renewed universal commitment to the aims of the Charter of the United Nations and to forge a new global force for justice. As you have so rightly put it, the most effective international coalition to overcome the threat of terrorism is the United Nations itself, and it is, as you put it, "the natural forum" that "alone can give global legitimacy" to this effort. Only together can the nations and their peoples hope to achieve true peace and security. The messages of compassion that have been sent from the four corners of the world to the government and people of the United States need to be embodied in policies and acts of compassion for all those who languish now in abject poverty and armed conflict.

The reaction to these acts must not be greater isolationism, but rather should lead all nations to join fully in the efforts of the international community to face common challenges, and there to assume their full share of obligations under the Charter, financial and other, to the United Nations.

The reaction to these acts must not be a global retreat back into militarism, doctrines of national security or states of emergency that suspend guarantees and protection of fundamental human rights. Democracy has been purchased at too high a price for its freedoms again to be sacrificed. Reliance on notions of security based on superior military power must give way to new approaches that seek human security based on justice for all.

Respect for and the strengthening of the rule of law at both national and international levels is the basis of common security and true justice. It must not be allowed to erode further. Such justice must also extend to those alleged to be responsible for these and similar acts of terrorism who should be brought before impartial courts to answer to charges. Vigilante justice under any guise is another form of terrorism and cannot be condoned.

At this session of the General Assembly intensive debates will be held on strengthening measures to combat international terrorism. In this connection we hope that all nations will now see the urgency of ratifying the Rome Statutes of the International Criminal Court in order that it can be established as soon as possible.

The reaction to these acts must not be to close all doors to those seeking asylum from terror, to migrants driven from their homes by extreme poverty, to refugees fleeing from war and internal conflict. The international protection regimes must not now be weakened, but strengthened to comprehend those for whom international protections are still inadequate or not scrupulously respected.

Finally, the response to these inhuman acts must not be to stigmatize any national, ethnic or religious group. The hypothesis of a "clash of civilizations" must not be allowed to become a self-fulfilling prophecy. This is the time for universal dialogue, tolerance and acts of compassion.

We are grateful for your leadership in the realization of these goals, and reassure you and your staff of our continued prayers that God guide and sustain you in your efforts on behalf of a needy world.

Respectfully yours,

Konrad Raiser
General Secretary

Letter to the heads of Muslim religious communities throughout the world on the beginning of Ramadan
Sent to Muslim leaders and dialogue partners, 17 November 2001.

Your Eminences,
Your Excellencies,
Dear friends,

The blessed month of Ramadan and the Christian Holy time of Advent during which the faithful prepare themselves in fasting and recollection for the Nativity of Jesus Christ coincide this year. Thus, they become one among many signs that make us "nearest in affection" and draw us together in common obedience to God. The spiritual bonds that unite us need to be rediscovered anew in these trying times.

Fasting is indeed a reminder of God's presence. It invites believers, in their personal lives as well as in community, to turn to God in humility and love, seeking forgiveness and strength. Fasting is a time of mercy. We receive anew God's mercy upon us but also that which we beseech for each other. It is a time of piety, deepened devotion and generous alms-giving. The special endurance of believers, asserting that human beings have other needs than bread and that their bodies are their servants not their masters, reminds us that to have is to share. It is a call to render justice; for dealing justly with others is inseparable from true piety.

The abominable acts of September 11 were condemned by the authoritative voices throughout the Islamic community and among the churches. The Quranic principle that no soul shall bear another's burden was widely echoed by Muslims. We have heard many Muslim friends reminding themselves and all of us of the Quranic injunction not to let the hatred of others make us swerve to wrong and depart from justice. Muslims and Christians are standing up forcefully for justice, and have warned against the temptation of blind vengeance and indiscriminate retaliation. Churches, in the USA and beyond, have opened themselves in humility to the call of the apostle not to repay anyone evil for evil. Many Christians have affirmed that the answer to terrorism must not reinforce the cycle of violence. All acts which destroy life, whether through terrorism or in war, are contrary to the will of God.

The recent tragic events have shown the vulnerability of all nations and the fragility of the international order. A world in which more and more people and even whole nations are being consigned to extreme poverty while others accumulate great wealth is inherently unstable. The tendency to impose one's will - if need be, even by force - which is manifesting itself in the policies of powerful nations provokes resentment among the weaker ones. The language of threat and the logic of war breeds violence. As long as the cries of those who are humiliated by unremitting injustice, by the systematic deprivation of their rights as persons and as peoples and by the arrogance of power based on military might are ignored or neglected, terrorism will not be overcome. The answer is to be found in redressing the wrongs that breed violence between and within nations.

The violence of terrorism - in its various forms - is abhorrent, particularly to all those who believe that human life is a gift of God and therefore infinitely precious. Every attempt to intimidate others and inflict indiscriminate death and injury upon them is to be universally condemned, whoever are the perpetrators. The response to these inhuman acts, however, must not lead to stigmatizing Muslims, Arabs and any other ethnic groups. Churches are called to let the voices of fraternity and compassion drown those of hostility, racism and intolerance. The voice of faith, which has been expressed through the many initiatives of friendship and solidarity, needs to defeat those of bigotry, fear and nihilism.

As Christians we reject the tendency, not uncommon in many Western countries, to perceive Muslims as a threat and portray Islam in negative terms while projecting a positive self-image. Christians live under the divine commandment not to bear false witness against their neighbours. The encounter of Christians with Islam and with Muslims requires intellectual honesty and integrity. They need to be present with their Muslim neighbours in the spirit of love, sensitive to their deepest faith commitments, and recognizing what God has done and is doing among them. Here the dialogue between Muslims and Christians, to which the World Council of Churches remains strongly committed, finds its authentic meaning. Many today call for an intensification of the dialogue of religions and cultures. However, such dialogue cannot bear fruits unless it is built on trust, on an unequivocal respect for the identity and integrity of others, an openness to understand them on their own terms and a willingness to question one's self-understanding, history and present reality.

In the dialogue of life and the encounter of commitments between Christians and Muslims in various parts of the world, we have learned that our religious communities are not two monolithic blocks confronting or competing with each other. We have learned that tensions and conflicts, when they arise, do not and should not define bloody borders between Muslims and Christians. We recognize that religion speaks for the deepest feelings and sensitivities of individuals and communities, carries deep historical memories and often appeals to universal loyalties. But this does not justify uncritical responses that draw people into each other's conflicts instead of joining efforts, across religious loyalties, to apply common principles of justice and reconciliation. Islam and Christianity need to be released from the burden of sectional interests and self-serving interpretations of beliefs and convictions. Their beliefs should rather constitute a basis for critical engagement in the face of human weakness and defective social, economic and political orders.

This is the time for giving signs of genuine cooperation, particularly by engaging in joint efforts to provide assistance to the victims and to defend human rights and humanitarian law. This area of cooperation is critical at a time when humanitarian work suffers from restrictions and suspicions and is being used for political and propaganda purposes, to the point of being linked with the war operations. It is the time to deepen our encounter, share our pains, mutual expectations and hopes.

Dear friends,

The prayer for God's peace is at the heart of the spirituality of Muslims and Christians. At the beginning of the month of Ramadan we greet you with a word of peace and friendship.

May your fast, and ours, be pleasant to God.

Konrad Raiser
General Secretary

Pastoral letter to the churches and Christians in the United States following the terrorist attacks of 11 September
Sent by the ecumenical "Living Letters" team at the conclusion of its ten-day visit, Oakland, California, 16 November 2001.

Dear Sisters and Brothers in Christ,

We have come as "living letters" to your country. Shocked at the tragic events of 11 September, we have come as representatives of member churches of the World Council of Churches, committed to the Decade to Overcome Violence:

Churches seeking peace and reconciliation. We have come to be with you as a sign of compassion and solidarity in your suffering. We have come out of our wounded contexts to share with you in your woundedness. We have not come with answers; we have come to love you.

We have stood at Ground Zero and experienced it as death. We were profoundly moved by the terrible silence, the colourlessness, the sense of loss. In that emptiness, we grasped hands and offered our prayers; we reclaimed life in the midst of death.

It is always difficult to walk into a house of grief. But you have received us with gracious hospitality in this time of sorrow, and we are grateful. In South Africa, there is a saying used at the time of mourning: "What has happened to you has happened to others as well." We are witnesses that God makes it possible for life to continue. Many American churches have visited us in our difficult times to help us find a way when we have been overwhelmed with our grief. We now say to you, take courage. We have come to you as living letters, signs of hope in the suffering and pain of the cross.

During our visit, in New York, Chicago, Washington, D.C. and Oakland, California, we have had the privilege to listen to different voices and words. We have listened to words of hurt and anger from a pastor on the front lines: "We are not ready to be lectured. We still smell the smoke; there are too many funerals each day to be objective. A new consciousness will arise, but if it is forced, it will only stoke the anger." There is the need for space to grieve. And we are ready to wait with you, in your mourning and in your healing.

We have heard voices of deep sadness. We have been moved by the ways in which you have expressed this sadness. This sea of sorrow also engulfs those who minister, who are now exhausted. "Who will heal the healers?" someone has asked.

We have heard persons speak of "joining the world": "I didn't just see my congregation weeping, I saw a weeping world." A pastor spoke of the interconnectedness of pain and suffering as he ministered to wounded and orphaned children in New York. "I would have liked to embrace also the children of Iraq, who have been wounded and orphaned. Maybe this experience of suffering will help us to embrace all others who suffer."

We have heard people speak of fear and insecurity, from immigrants who came to the US for safety and freedom to peace workers who feel intimidated and accused of being unpatriotic.

We have not heard words of bitterness or of revenge. We have been moved to humility and encouraged to hear church leaders battling with questions that are broader than their own concerns, that take in the larger context of the world. The discussion is just beginning.

We have heard some asking: "What things have been done by us and in our name that have made people feel such hatred for us?"

We have heard people speak of their ignorance and fear of Islam, but we also heard expressions of solidarity with Muslim neighbours.

We have heard people relating their suffering to the sufferings of people in Afghanistan and Palestine.

We have heard people explaining how difficult it is for some Christian communities to be engaged by ethical issues of the response to 11 September.

We have listened to a pastor in tears ask: "How can the bombing of Afghanistan be the way of Christ?"

These words did not call for answers from us. We have cried and prayed with you; now, together with you, we ask the questions that have accompanied our conversations:

1. Where do we find the basis to be together? What can be our common search in the days ahead? We have in common to reject terrorism. We can affirm that military response will never bring security and peace. What kind of relationships with neighbours, across geographical and faith borders, need urgently to be built?

2. How can churches be at the front line of the struggle against injustice? The churches have responsibility to reflect together and to name together the major injustices in the world. In our encounter we have spoken of the destructive economic imbalances, oppression in places like Palestine, gender and racial discrimination, support of totalitarian regimes.

3. How can we communicate the imperatives of the Gospel where there is a struggle for the hearts and minds of people? What kind of communication, what images, will bind us together in community, rather than increase the gulf between people, as dominant media images do? As Christians, we have been given the stories and invited into a community that speaks truth to power. We say to our churches: listen carefully to other Christians around the world. By allowing the churches to tell their stories, you give them voice.

4. Do we wait to speak until there is unanimity? How do we encourage the prophetic voices in our midst? Love unites us. You are our sisters and brothers. Together we are the body of Christ. Let us hold hands and seek to overcome all forms of violence, direct and structural, in order to build a culture of peace.

Bishop Mvumelwano Dandala of the Methodist Church of Southern Africa, and president of the South Africa Council of Churches, led the "Living Letters" delegation.

Other members were:
Rev. Jean-Arnold de Clermont, president of the French Protestant Federation
Bishop Samuel Azariah of the Church of Pakistan
Rev. Father Nicholas Balachov, Russian Orthodox Church
Ms Septemmy Lakawa, Indonesian theologian and WCC Executive Committee member
Metropolitan Elias Audi, Greek Orthodox Patriarchate of Antioch and All the East, Lebanon
Jean Zaru, presiding clerk, Religious Society of Friends, Ramallah, Palestine.
Accompanying the team were:
Rev. Kathryn Bannister, moderator of the US Conference for the WCC and WCC president for North America;
Georges Lemopoulos, acting general secretary of the WCC
Jean S. Stromberg, executive director, US Office of the WCC

Beyond 11 September: Assessing Global Implications
Summary of the consultation convened in Geneva, 29 November - 2 December 2001.

Introduction

This was an unusual meeting to respond to an urgent situation. Convened by the World Council of Churches, some 20 participants from all regions gathered in Geneva at short notice to reflect, together with WCC staff, on the consequences of the 11 September attacks and the subsequent military retaliation. Because of the short notice, many of those originally invited were unable to attend and many of those who did attend had to re-arrange busy schedules to do so. Rather than seeking to produce a statement or to arrive at consensus on recommendations for churches, the meeting was intended as a privileged opportunity to reflect, to analyze, to brainstorm and to try to discern together the meaning of these events. Discussion was lively and far ranging. Questions about the possible consequences of 11 September led, perhaps inevitably, into reflections on theology, globalization, power, and many other subjects.

In terms of methodology, a few individuals were asked to lead off the discussion of particular issues by posing questions to the participants. Those presentations, as well as a background paper prepared by Dwain Epps and closing reflections by Konrad Raiser, are included as annexes to this report.

Rather than summarizing the proceedings, this report seeks to bring together comments and insights by participants around certain themes. In a few cases, individual speakers have been identified. For the most part, individual contributions have been grouped together.

Most of the participants felt that this meeting had been a particularly rich opportunity to come together to analyze, reflect and discern together the impact of recent events on the course of the world. They urged WCC to convene similar types of meetings in the future, recognizing the need for critical new thinking on major global issues. While political leaders often have to act quickly in responding to world events, churches can offer space for quiet reflection to discern the "signs of the times" which are not immediately apparent. In the words of Isaiah "In quietness will be your strength."

How do we understand what's happening?

Initial discussions revealed important differences in perceptions of both the attacks of 11 September and the military actions which began on 7 October. Bishop Mano Rumalshah's reports of conversations in the bazaars of Peshawar revealed a different perception of reality to those experienced by a Scottish congregation or a senior United Nations official.

A central theme of the meeting was the inadequacy of traditional analytical tools and categories comprehensive enough to make sense of what was happening. One participant suggested that it is too early – less than 3 months – since the 11 September attacks and we probably will not be able to grasp the full dimensions of their meaning for some time. At a global level, participants asked "how can we divide economics from global governance, peace from security, human rights from theology?" At a more down to earth level, participants from Asia and the Middle East compared mainstream and marginal discourses on the events, noting that while Asian governments, for example, were quick to become US allies in the war against terrorism, there was a different perception and reaction from those marginalized from political power.

One participant referred to television newscasters occasionally apologizing for blurred images coming from Afghanistan by commenting that "clear images blur our perception of reality." The danger of over-simplifying reality in the search for clear and simple answers was a constant thread in the discussion. In particular, use of the word "terrorism" came under particular criticism (and is further discussed in the following section.)

Konrad Raiser stressed that one's perception of what happened determines what response is seen as appropriate. For some this was an act of terrorism which is understood as the most irrational evil act which in turn legitimizes an irrational response. But the problem with responding to terrorism is that "you are in danger of becoming what you fight against." A second perception of the 11 September attacks is that they were a "declaration of war against civilization." If this is one's understanding of the conflict, then the appropriate response is one of self-defense which in turns leads to a military response and consideration of the action as a "just war." But he argued that none of the traditional features of war seem to apply in this case and that response with traditional military strategic measures is inappropriate. A third perception of the attacks is that they were a criminal act and that they constituted crimes against humanity. This category is clearly established in international law and there are judicial means to respond which have been used in other cases of crimes against humanity. In other words, the way in which the initial attack is defined determines the appropriate response and the justification for this response.

Participants noted the lack of adequate political analysis on the consequences of the attacks on US domestic and international politics, the need to address the global project of Al Qaida and the psychological dimensions of the conflict, and to deepen analysis of the symbolic level of conflict. One participant noted the use of masculine imagery by both US President George Bush and Pakistani President Musharref and the need to further consider the relationship between nation, state and religion in construction of this kind of virile identity. The extraordinary role played by the media in this conflict and the need for further critical thinking about the media were underlined.

Need for new thinking and alternatives

Participants agreed not only that there is a need for deeper analysis of the events associated with 11 September, but a need to invest more energy and resources in developing creative thinking on the range of issues discussed at the meeting. Dr Patricia Lewis noted that Institutes for Strategic Studies are well funded and disproportionately influential in shaping governmental policies while think tanks devoted to alternative perceptions of security tend to be poorly funded. There is a need to put more resources into supporting the development of progressive ideas. Non-Eurocentric models for development of such ideas need to be developed where the voices of the grassroots can be heard.

"Who is to be included in the world we talk about?" asked Jean Manipon, from the Philippines, urging that more attention be given to questions of cultural identity and to the inclusiveness of the concepts we use. Glenda Wildschut noted the important developments, growing out of the South African experience, in conceptual thinking about justice with the movement from retributive to restorative justice. She asked whether similar developments could be expected from supporting alternative centres for creative thinking. Bertrand Ramcharan reviewed the important role which churches had played in creating the UN Charter and Universal Declaration of Human Rights and later in creative thinking about development. He urged churches and particularly the WCC to reclaim this role of developing important new thinking on current issues. We not only need to develop new thinking, but also to be creative in exploring how to move new concepts to the top of the international agenda.

What is terrorism?

The issue of the meaning and use of the word "terrorism" generated considerable debate and participants urged further analysis of the definition, anatomy and genealogy of terrorism. Several participants commented on the paucity of statements by churches on the nature of terrorism although, as the discussion revealed, the issue is complex.

"The word terrorism doesn't exist in Pakistan and Afghanistan," Bishop Rumalshah reported. "Terrorism is a response by people who have no other alternatives." Several participants commented on the relationship between poverty, injustice and fanaticism. They also commented on the popularity of Osama bin Laden as the one who dared – and succeeded – in defying the world's superpower, and the brisk sale of t-shirts adorned with his likeness in some parts of the world. However, many cautioned that "Osama bin Laden is not the spokesperson for the world's poor" and that we should be careful in drawing simple connections between poverty and injustice and terrorist actions.

Many participants pointed to the contradictions in the use of the label "terrorist". "At one time," Glenda Wildschut reported, "Nelson Mandela was seen as a terrorist." Soritua Nababan recalled that Indonesian freedom fighters against Dutch colonization were called "terrorists." Konrad Raiser noted that terrorism is a word used more by the powerful than by the weak, perhaps because the powerful sense that their power is illegitimate and call terrorism those who attack their legitimacy. Several participants pointed out that the current anti-terrorism campaign could become a kind of continuation of the West's earlier campaign against communism.

While churches condemn terrorism as a perversion, Pablo Richard pointed out that "Latin America is facing the effects of US state terrorism." He pointed out that the first "11 September" took place in Chile in 1973 when the US intervened to overthrow a democratically elected government. He also questioned why we use the word terrorism to refer only to the acts of a few individuals while "for the poor each day is a day of terror."

The theme of US involvement in terrorism was a pervasive one throughout the meeting. Professor Rudolf El Kareh asked why in the past 10-12 years America's "friends" have become its enemies. Saddam Hussein, Slobodan Milosevic, and Osama bin Laden were all supported by the United States but were later labeled as terrorists when US political interests changed. Many participants pointed out the connections between bin Laden and the US government, noting the US's role in creating and arming his fighters in the early 1980s.

"Beware of simple explanations for terrorism," warned Patricia Lewis. "It is a more complex situation than a struggle between the haves and the have-nots."

What's new in the world as a result of 11 September?

Another theme running throughout the meeting was the struggle to define what has changed as a result of 11 September. Does 11 September signify a radical re-definition of the world, does it mark the intensification of certain previously identifiable trends, or is its significance the result of media attention?

Patricia Lewis reminded participants that the world and the US have had terrorist attacks before. Even the World Trade Center itself had been the object of a terrorist attack and most countries in the world have experienced or been parties to various terrorist acts. This isn't new. Rather, we treat this as a new phenomenon because of the scale of the attacks (the largest by a non-state actor), the audacity and symbolic importance of the attacks, and the scale of the response.

Participants agreed, however, that a genuinely new element in the world is the realization of US vulnerability. "Before 11 September," Bishop Stephen reported, "Nigerians had seen the United States as the most secure country in the world. That perception was shattered by the attacks in New York and Washington." This seemingly invincible superpower suddenly became vulnerable.

And in the United States, this feeling of vulnerability and related trauma is a new experience for most Americans. Victor Hsu commented that "this loss of innocence has created a suspension of rationality. There is paranoia about bioterrorism, security breakdowns at airports, and two national alerts – a paranoia fueled by 24-hour newscasts. The US is now imbued with a sacred mission to save the world with a vengeance." Some observers noted their earlier hopes that this feeling of US vulnerability would lead to increased identification and solidarity with people who are vulnerable in other countries, but that the US had moved in a different direction since 11 September. "Will a perceived US victory in Afghanistan quench the thirst for revenge and punishment," one participant asked, "or will it lead to more wars?"

According to Bernice Powell-Jackson, "this may be a kairos moment for US churches." But the US churches, like the US people, are divided and uncertain. US peace activists feel threatened and isolated for not being patriotic at a time like this. "Can US churches speak to the people rather than for them?" asked Margaret Thomas.

Another major change resulting from 11 September is the increasing polarization between people, between North and South and between Christians and Muslims. In spite of efforts by political and religious leaders to prevent it, the polarization is being manifest as the Western world versus Islam.

It is often said that September 11th marks a fundamental change in the political system, but most of the discussion at this meeting emphasized that the signs of a crisis were there before 11 September. Konrad Raiser noted that a dramatic interpretation of the changes occurring as a result of 11 September leads us to think in terms of a war (a long war) between good and evil, of maximum sacrifice, of unconditional solidarity, and of being prepared for the final confrontation. The use of "secularized apocalyptic language" on both sides of the conflict contributes to the sense that life on the planet has dramatically and irrevocably changed. But the reality may be different.

What isn't new?

The US military actions in Afghanistan need to be understood in a historical context. Dwain Epps' paper "War without End," prepared for this meeting, highlights the long-term US policy of projecting its power in other regions. This paper traces long-standing efforts of the US military, strategic and political plans to render Afghanistan friendly and accessible to Western interests. The paper also details the global reach of US military power, highlighting the actions of the US Special Forces Command which has deployed large numbers of forces to almost 100 countries in recent years. It is likely that the global reach of US military policies will continue – and intensify -- as a result of the 11 September attacks.

Many participants noted that the basic asymmetries of power in the world existed long before 11 September and will continue in the future. The US will remain the world's "hyperpower" and the prime engine of globalization. While many have deplored the current economic recession, the fact is that the signs of an economic downturn were present long before 11 September. Bertrand Ramcharan noted that the international rules of the game won't change as a result of the attacks, that poverty will continue to increase, and that international conflicts will continue to claim many lives. Poor governance will probably be exacerbated by the events of 11 September, but he noted that it was hard to uphold human rights before then and will continue to be hard in the future.

What role does religion play in this conflict?

In introducing the issue, Bishop Mano Rumalshah stated that "Western leadership, both political and religious, has been in a denial mode, at least in public, about seeing the place of religions in this complex cobweb... To deny the place of religious potency in human conflicts is being absurdly naïve."

This triggered considerable discussion as participants grappled with the extent to which religion is a factor in the present conflict. Soritua Nababan reported that "the initial sympathy and grief felt by Indonesians at the 11 September attacks lasted only a few hours. When US President Bush used the term "Crusade" it became a religious war."

Keith Clements asked how do we give due attention to the real religious dimension to the conflict without exaggerating or discounting it? The tendency in Europe is to discount religious motivations and to emphasize that the real factors are socio-economic. The question of how we identify religious elements is particularly difficult for Islam and Christianity which coexisted in the past because they occupied different parts of the planet, but today they increasingly share the same lands. Different faiths have different worldviews which must be considered. Soritua Nababan asked how do we free ourselves from identification of churches with the West and globalization and at the same time remain faithful to the universal church?

Christians presently own 60% of the world's resources and this basic inequality shapes relationships. Konrad Raiser highlighted the mirror image of Islam and Christianity, where both have experienced imperial rule and the memory of humiliation of being exposed to domination by infidels.

Both sides have sought to use religion to justify their position. Osama bin Laden, quoted in the paper by Bishop Rumalshah, said "Every Muslim, the minute he can start differentiating, carries hate towards Americans, Jews and Christians. This is part of our ideology." US President George Bush has repeatedly characterized the conflict as a struggle between good and evil.

What is the role of churches in understanding the role of religion in conflict and in increasing inter-faith dialogue?

What does this mean for inter-faith relations?

Inter-faith dialogue has become more difficult in some countries as a result of the 11 September attacks and aftermath. In both South Africa and Kenya, there has been an apparent reluctance by Islamic groups to join in inter-faith events on issues such as domestic violence since the 11 September attacks. In other countries, such as Scotland and Germany, interest in inter-faith dialogue has increased. For example, there had been a run on Korans in Germany and more people than ever before were interested in learning about Islam. Many Americans hadn't realized that there are 5-7 million Muslims in the United States until the events of 11 September.

"Could 11 September mark a new beginning between Islam and Christianity?" Bishop Rumalshah asked. He went on to argue that "the challenge to religions will therefore have to be that they not only cleanse their bloody past, by promoting peace and harmonious living in our time, but also by actively engaging in issues of advocacy and justice." He pointed the way toward developing our common humanity, affirming our common God, developing our common values, and understanding our common mission.

Konrad Raiser noted the tendency in both Christianity and Islam to see power as total domination and to appeal to power in terms of total obedience. Both religions are deeply rooted in monotheistic and patriarchal cultures which have used exclusive language to draw lines of distinction against those worshipping other gods. But we have to learn to communicate with each other at a symbolic level. And we need to join forces with those in the Muslim community who also don't want to be part of the self-perpetuating cycle of violence.

Global governance, multilateralism and how to hold the US accountable

Peter Weiderud introduced the issue of global governance by noting three approaches to international response:

1. The need to meet the immediate threat – destroy the Al Qaida network and stop further activities. This has basically been a military response, with the legal framework relating to UN Security Council Resolution 1368 of 12 September.

2. The need to deal with the threat of terrorism – coordinate efforts to stop terrorist activities – money, space, support, information-sharing, etc. This

has been undertaken from a criminal law perspective and the legal framework relates primarily to UN Security Council Resolution 1373.

3. The need to address the root causes and breeding grounds of international terrorism – social injustice, cultural arrogance, lack of coherence and illegitimacy in global governance. This needs to be undertaken within a perspective of conflict prevention and demands a comprehensive approach, including UN reforms.

The issue of global governance led immediately to discussion of the unequal distribution of power in the world. In spite of US efforts to build an international coalition against terrorism, US foreign policy remains essentially unilateralist in nature. The central issue of foreign relations for all countries in the world has become how to relate to the United States. Specifically, how can the United States be held accountable to international law? What levers are available to the rest of the world to constrain the US sense of divine mission? How can the internationalization of US foreign policy be prevented?

While some emphasized the need to exploit the new vulnerability of the United States to encourage a more multilateralist approach, others pointed out that there are many examples of continuing unilateral actions being undertaken by the USA.

The dependency of the UN on major powers and the influence that these major powers have over the UN is central to discussions about the future of multilateralism. While the United Nations principle of "one nation, one vote" is still valid, the reality is that asymmetry in power is the dominant practice. Or as one participant put it, "While the UN Charter begins 'we the peoples,' in fact the UN represents 'we the States, we the elites'."

Many emphasized the need for fundamental reform of the international institutions: "we have talked about re-structuring multilateral institutions, but if that change doesn't take place, we'll be strengthening institutions that exclude many people." While several participants referred to impressive proposals to reform global governance, the lack of political will has impeded their progress.

International law is not neutral as evidenced in discussions about the Nuclear Nonproliferation Treaty which makes it legal for five nations to have nuclear weapons and illegal for other countries to have them. While this isn't "fair," Peter Weiderud argued that this isn't reason to abandon the treaty. Rather we need to find ways to persuade the five nuclear nations to live up to their end of the bargain and move to reduce them. "A world without international law would be fully shaped by powerful states."

Participants called for a public debate about the meaning of the rule of law in today's world and how to ensure that relations between nations are governed by law rather than by the policies of the world's most powerful states.

Patricia Lewis introduced the issue of global security by reviewing the present insecurity of the world situation. She emphasized that disarmament was going badly before 11 September and that on several occasions the US government had blocked further progress on specific disarmament instruments since the 11 September attacks. The basic security architecture dates back to the Cold War and has yet to be replaced with more appropriate measures. While there are many reasons to criticize the United States, she argued, critics also have a responsibility to put forward alternative proposals.

Much of the ensuing discussion focused on the need for new paradigms and understandings of security. The fact that individuals bearing knives could attack the world's mightiest military power raises serious questions about the relationship between military strength and fundamental security.

"How can we talk about disarmament without talking about sustainable development?" "We need to re-imagine the concept of security which is based on the paradigm that security rests on nation-states and that there is always a threat to be confronted." National security is an illusion and self-destructive; more conceptual work is required on human security, collective security and cooperative security.

Global governance and security are needed for all the world's people, including the 60% of people who are presently living on the margins of the system. Security is more than military security and must be analyzed in the context of globalization.

Konrad Raiser argued that US vulnerability is an inevitable consequence of globalization. The belief in the US that its population was invulnerable to the effects of globalization has been challenged. While the immediate response was to think in military terms and the hasty development of new security laws, our discernment should lead us to conclude that there is no security against this kind of attack. You become more secure only in accepting your own vulnerability. Maximum security is possible only for people in total isolation. We need a new understanding of security and vulnerability. God became vulnerable to the utmost extent which was ultimately an act of liberation. Understanding the relationship between vulnerability and security leads to a different understanding of power – power not as the ability to protect yourself or to provide maximum security, but rather power in the energy of life in relatedness.

Victor Hsu asked "how will people with political aspirations – people wanting to claim their heritage and identity – hear this message? What is in it for them? If we shouldn't confront power with power, how will the disenfranchised understand their role?" Similarly Bishop Stephen of Nigeria argued that "when faced with the reality of evil – when church buildings are burned down, for example – you can't be analytical. How can people respond? They feel powerless and helpless. There is no other language for that than evil." Jean Manipon raised the question about the relationship between victimhood and vulnerability, noting that victimization is also experienced in the individual and collective consciousness.

These questions generated considerable discussion about the meaning of national identity in a context of globalization, about how to transform the energy and anger in the face of evil into power to change the community, and the need to understand the dynamic of victimhood. Not all victims become Osama bin Ladens and 11 September was, in a sense, an experience of collective victimhood. The identification of an individual as a victim is a way to state a claim for countervailing power. But by claiming victimhood a person doesn't escape from the struggle for power. In fact, the superior power needs a victim to accept being a victim in order to legitimize its power. To break this cycle, proponents of non-violent action insist that when an individual refuses to be degraded to a victim, that is when weakness and vulnerability are discovered in what appears to be overwhelming power.

How has 11 September affected the economy?

John Langmore reviewed the economic implications of the 11 September attacks, noting that in the short-term, there was the destruction of US property in the attacks and the still-unknown destruction of infrastructure in Afghanistan. In addition, there was disruption of economic activities (in sectors such as airlines, travel, tourism, insurance, etc.) and a fall in consumer confidence which led to declines in profits and layoffs. He noted that the argument that war comes along to relieve economic depression is simplistic; rather military spending is a diversion of economic resources from both consumers and from investment in productive capacity. In the longer term, state involvement in the economy has been strengthened as a result of the attacks and within Europe there is a willingness to contemplate substantial increases to overseas development assistance. He emphasized that military planners never, ever, take into the account the long-term effects of post-traumatic stress syndrome on future generations.

In the discussion participants focused on the underlying economic inequalities of the globalized world. The role of transnational corporations and their relationship to both governments and international institutions needs to be more clearly understood. Both macro- and microeconomic analyses are needed in order to understand what these changes mean for people living on the margins of society.

"Africans are already suffering. Now African governments are told to brace themselves for even harder times," Agnes Abuom commented. She went on to lament the disproportionate use of economic resources. "It's hard to see the money being poured into anti-anthrax medications given the lack of drugs to combat HIV/AIDS." Similarly, participants noted the discrepancy between the money raised to support the victims of the 11 September attacks and funds available to support both the reconstruction of Afghanistan and "forgotten" emergencies in other parts of the world.

Glenda Wildschut affirmed that post-traumatic stress syndrome will clearly affect generations traumatized by the events and aftermath of 11 September. She explained that post-traumatic stress syndrome requires a clearly identified stressor which was certainly the case with the US attacks. But many people are suffering "continuous post-traumatic stress syndrome" where there isn't a single event which is a stressor but rather continuing acute stress caused by poverty, disease, death, etc. There is no agreement of the importance of this continuous stress syndrome or consensus on how it can be addressed.

What does 11 September mean for human rights?

Dr Bertrand Ramcharan began by challenging participants to think about what they would have done had they been president of the United States on 11 September, noting that the idea of going after the perpetrators of the attacks is not a shocking idea. Mary Robinson, UN High Commissioner for Human Rights, had stated that anti-terrorism measures should not restrict human rights. In his past experience of working with the government of Algeria during a time of terrorist attacks, the United Nations had insisted that terrorism must be confronted within the law in full respect of human rights and principles of sovereignty. He went on to establish criteria for evaluating countries' performance on human rights, with particular emphasis on the difficulties for Southern governments of meeting internationally accepted standards. In terms of the impact of the 11 September attacks on civil liberties and the conflict between freedom and security, he suggested that the effect will be felt mostly by non-citizens in Northern countries.

Several US participants remarked on the decline of civil liberties in the US since the 11 September attacks, particularly evident in the militarization of society, the silencing of dissent, the extensive use of national guards, the decision that suspects in the attacks would be tried by a military tribunal, and public debate on the justification of torture to extract information from detained suspects.

Participants remarked that while human rights violations haven't become much worse since 11 September, the possibilities for legitimizing human rights abuses have increased. Thus, the Sharon government labels the Palestinian leadership as "terrorist" and the Russian government seeks broader understanding of its struggle to subdue Chechen "terrorists." Tarek Mitri commented that the labeling of certain Islamic non-governmental organizations as "terrorist" had contributed to creating a climate of suspicion.

Guillermo Kerber asked how a just trial could be guaranteed for the perpetrators of the acts. Like others, he raised particular concerns about the demand by the US government to have the trial in a US military court. In the discussion, questions were raised about what it means to bring people to justice and whether our legal institutions are capable of bringing about justice.

85

Elizabeth Ferris presented an overview of some of the dilemmas involved in providing humanitarian assistance to Afghanistan, highlighting the problems of involvement of the military in humanitarian operations, difficulties of access and security, and the impact of closed borders on the international refugee protection regime. Given the media-driven nature of emergency response, she noted that it is likely that other emergencies will be "forgotten" as international assistance is mobilized for Afghanistan. The cruel irony is that Afghanistan itself was a largely "forgotten emergency" until 11 September.

Several participants noted that military involvement takes various forms, from UN peacekeepers to policing functions to military forces. While it may be appropriate for UN peacekeeping forces to provide security to humanitarian workers, when such security is provided by a combatant force, it takes on a different meaning.

The mixing of humanitarian and military operations gives rise to such contradictory terms as "humanitarian bombing" and some participants reacted strongly to the diminution of the term "humanitarian." Geneviève Jacques suggested that it is important to reclaim the term "humanitarian" by focusing on the needs of the victims. Others suggested the need for a forum to discuss the ethical questions arising from the distribution of humanitarian assistance.

In discussing pressures for the 3.5 million refugees presently in Pakistan and Iran to return to Afghanistan, participants expressed concern that such a repatriation could be a de-stabilizing factor for the country. Participants also linked the humanitarian issues to security concerns discussed earlier, particularly the devastating impact of the proliferation of small arms.

A symbolic conflict?

In his closing reflections, Konrad Raiser argued that what is fundamentally different about this conflict is its symbolic nature. The targets of the attacks were symbolic in nature, the claims of Osama bin Laden are about symbols and the military response is being justified in symbolic terms. Unlike previous conflicts, this is not a struggle for resources, trade routes, or territory but for symbolic hegemony. This is one of the reasons that our traditional analytical models are inadequate to understand the conflict and why theology and religious insights are needed. All power is legitimized through symbols and religion is the strongest carrier of the symbolic. Religious communities are the trustees of basic values and the symbols that hold societies together. Moreover, all forms of human power are mirrors of how divine power is understood. Neither side can win in a conflict about symbolic hegemony. Rather, we need to reaffirm the alternative view of power as power shared in community and in recognition of the other.

While we have been trained to deal with religion as a separate category from politics, economics, and psychology, in fact religion is an inescapable component of this conflict. It is impossible to understand the nature of this conflict for symbolic hegemony without incorporating religious insights and theology. But neither our theology nor our tools for political-social-economic analysis are adequate. For example, economic statistical analysis doesn't tell us anything about people's lives and feelings. But religion brings one closer to the 'feeling' dimension of the conflict and may move us to insights beyond those obtained through detached statistical analysis.

For churches, the fight between good and evil has already been decided; for Christians, the final event has already taken place in the life, death and resurrection of Jesus Christ. An eschatological realism thus leads us away from the idea that we must defend a particular nation or ideology and leads us into a process of discernment. From the perspective of the churches, we have reasons to refresh our hope.

What happens next?

A number of suggestions were made on how to follow up the many issues discussed at this meeting. On the programmatic level, participants urged WCC staff to continue their important on-going work on theological, economic, political and social issues. The crisis since 11 September has affirmed the Council's long-term priorities. WCC was also encouraged to continue its advocacy work at the United Nations. UN representatives participating in this meeting affirmed the important role that the religious community plays in international policy debates. "Churches can say things that governments cannot," John Langmore remarked, "don't underestimate your potential to bring about meaningful change." Konrad Raiser, speaking on a broader level, said that "we need to overcome our hesitancy to use our religious symbols and to re-open the political energy for life that they contain."

Participants affirmed that now, more than ever, churches need to speak up about the present conflict and about the long-term political and economic inequities at the global level. The need for providing an ecumenical space for reflection, analysis and discernment was particularly emphasized.

Participants agreed that they would report on this meeting in their own congregations and churches and they encouraged WCC to facilitate the convening of similar international discussions at the regional level. WCC staff indicated that the reflections from this meeting would feed into on-going programmatic work in a number of areas, including the Decade to Overcome Violence and plans for a consultative process on the role of the churches in international affairs. Participants suggested that the report of this meeting be shared with the WCC Executive Committee and that it be widely disseminated among the churches.

Thanks were extended to WCC International Relations staff, and particularly to Dwain Epps, for convening the meeting; to Geneviève Jacques and Clement John for moderating the meeting; to Bishop Rumalshah, Pablo Richard, Agnes Abuom, and Bishop Stephen for offering prayers during the course of the meeting; to

Isabel Csupor for providing administrative support; to Elizabeth Ferris for writing this report; and to all the participants whose contributions provided much food for thought.

Beyond 11 September: Implications for US Churches and the World

Message to the WCC Central Committee from participants in the meeting convened by the WCC in consultation with the NCCCUSA and CWS in Washington, D.C., 5-6 August 2002.

As the anniversary of 11 September 2001 approaches, we came together as Christians from the United States and other parts of the world to discern together the challenges which we now face as a result of the horrific events of 11 September and the US response. Our prayers are with all those who suffered loss in the events of September 11 and acts of terror around the world. While much of our discussion focused on peace and security, as Christians we affirmed that true security comes only from Jesus Christ who is "the way, the truth and the life" (John 14:6)

We have come to understand that ongoing dialogue, with churches worldwide and other faith communities, is essential to formulating a constructive Christian response to the insecurities and vulnerabilities that we and other people around the world experience. We encourage our churches – from the global to the congregational levels – to engage in sustained study and reflection on the meaning and sources of true peace and security in the present age.

In looking at threats to peace and security, we particularly lift up the concerns in the Middle East. We call on US churches to press their government to work for a just resolution of the Palestine-Israeli conflict, without delay, which will result in a viable and secure Palestinian state and a secure Israel at peace with its neighbors. Furthermore, at this particular moment in history, US churches are called to *speak out against the threat of a military attack by their government against Iraq.*

Our discussions affirmed certain fundamental principles:

- Security must be grounded in respect for human rights, due process, and international law. Security does not result from military actions.
- Moreover, human security and national security depend on economic justice and peace, in our own countries and throughout the world. We fear that the military response to terrorism will further divert needed resources away from meeting human needs.
- Peaceful relations among nations and peoples are achieved through multilateral decision-making, not by the unilateral economic and military actions of one country. The current US-led "war on terrorism" undermines these principles and threatens genuine peace and justice.
- As Christians we put our security in the hands of Jesus Christ and the biblical witness, which says, "perfect love casts out fear." (I John 4:18a)

Beyond 11 September: Implications for US Churches and the World
Draft Guide for Reflection from the Consultation with US church leaders, Washington, D.C., 5-6 August 2002.

Beyond 11 September: Implications for US Churches and the World
Orthodox Feast of the Transfiguration of Our Lord
Anniversary of the Dropping of the Atom Bomb on Hiroshima

6 August 2002

The Prophetic Voice of the Churches

For from the least to the greatest of them, everyone is greedy for unjust gain; and from prophet to priest, everyone deals falsely. They have treated the wound of my people carelessly, saying, "Peace, peace," when there is no peace. Jeremiah: 6: 13-15.

Across the ages, the prophets of the Hebrew Scriptures warned their people to turn from their wicked ways, to speak out against injustice and to put their faith in God. Sometimes, prophets, such as Ezekiel, resist delivering God's message to their errant people. But God tells Ezekiel that he will be held responsible if the message is not delivered and if people perish because they did not hear the prophecy (Ezekiel 3:17-24). Speaking out against the prevailing powers is often uncomfortable. But the experience of the prophets compels us to speak even when it is uncomfortable to do so.

Introduction

A group of Christians from various churches gathered in Washington, D.C. from 5-6 August 2002 at the invitation of the World Council of Churches (WCC) in consultation with the National Council of Churches of Christ USA (NCCCUSA) and Church World Service (CWS) to discern together the implications of the 11 September attacks for the US churches and the world. Participants at the two-day meeting included representatives of churches in the United States and from churches located in other parts of the world, as well as staff from the WCC, NCCCUSA and CWS. It was an intense meeting as participants struggled to understand what is happening in our world and to discern God's will for themselves and for their churches. With the approach of the anniversary of the 11 September attacks, participants expressed their continuing grief and solidarity with those who lost family members and friends in the attacks. At the same time, participants felt called to extend their solidarity to the many who are suffering from the consequences of US policies in the aftermath of the 11 September attacks.*

---

* A number of initiatives were organized by the WCC, including letters to the US churches and the UN Secretary-General; inter-faith meetings; the November 2001 visit to the United States of an international delegation of religious leaders as

There have been many efforts by ecumenical organizations to express solidarity and to discern the meaning of these events and this meeting sought to build on these previous efforts.

There was a sense among those gathered at the meeting that immediately following the attack, a window of time opened during which people from every corner of the world stood with the people of the United States, sharing their horror, outrage and grief. And there was a moment in time when the people of the United States stood with the rest of the world with a new understanding of the horrors of vulnerability many others had been experiencing long before September 11. The sense of global community deepened. The window seemed to provide an opportunity for people to listen to one another and for Americans to recognize US interdependence with the rest of the world. The sense of global community deepened with the possibility that a US response to these horrific attacks could lead to a more just world where all would be more secure. Now this window seems to have closed.

US policy internationally – particularly in Afghanistan, the Middle East, and Iraq – and also domestically has eroded the goodwill born of the tragedy of September 11 and has alienated many who were predisposed to stand in solidarity with the United States. In considering military response, many in the United States feel so violated by the events of 11 September that no response by the United States would have seemed too severe. Others are horrified by the intensity of the response and a perception that undisclosed motives underlie both the choice of aggressive action abroad and the undermining of constitutional principles at home. The United States government is seen as embracing a policy of "America first and foremost" and pursuing unilateral policies based on its own self-interest rather than working to support multilateral efforts to promote the common good.

US churches are still responding to grief, to broken communities and to the shock of unfamiliar vulnerability, but some are also beginning to raise larger questions about the meaning of these events and about US policies in the world. They are grappling with these many issues without clear consensus within their own

---

"Living Letters" to the churches and people of the United States; the November 2001 meeting whose report is entitled "Beyond 11 September: Assessing Global Implications," and an alternative news service known as "Behind the News: Visions for Peace, Voices of Faith." The National Council of Churches of Christ in the USA has issued a number of statements and collected resources, including a liturgy to mark the anniversary of the 11 September attacks. Churches in other parts of the world have also organized initiatives to express solidarity with US churches and to try to understand the consequences of the changing world. See for example: "Bridging the Gaps: Report on an ecumenical visit to the U.S.A. March 2002 – six months after 9/11 by Churches Together in Britain and Ireland," May 2002.

countries or among their leadership. There is also a sense that the influence of US church leaders has not been felt or, in some cases, sufficiently exercised.

At the meeting, the international participants expressed their solidarity and support for the pastoral responsibility of the US churches. However, they also expressed their concern that US policies intended to respond to terrorism may undermine fundamental responsibilities in the global system, such as commitment to multilateral actions, respect for human rights, acceptance of cultural diversity, national sovereignty and social justice.

Those gathered at this meeting have chosen to offer the following questions for further reflection by the churches of the United States and by churches throughout the world through the ecumenical fellowship of churches. They do so in the conviction that all people of faith are called to live their lives in a manner consistent with that faith.

Reflections on the situation of the churches of the United States

Many people in the United States continue to grieve, both for those lost directly in the attacks and for the loss of their sense of security.

- How do churches help people to heal from grief, hurt and trauma so that they can move towards reconciliation and forgiveness?
- Can individual experience of fear and vulnerability move us to greater compassion towards all those whose lives have long been characterized by fear and vulnerability?
- How can the churches help define the difference between justice and vengeance?
- What is the responsibility of Christians in the United States to learn about US policies abroad and their consequences?
- In thinking about forgiveness, whom should we forgive and from whom should we seek forgiveness?

The people killed on September 11, 2001 included citizens of nations from every corner of the globe and adherents of many different faiths. The US population includes people from nearly every religion, and race. As the people of the world gathered in prayer, faith communities were challenged to recognize in one another a common humanity and kindred spiritual quest. The search for restoration of a sense of security challenges assumptions about "we" and "they." God's love extends to the whole world.

- How do US churches witness to the Christian understanding that each and every human being is made in the image and likeness of God?
- How do Christian churches maintain the full integrity of faith in Jesus Christ while embracing people of other faith traditions?
- What can the churches do to promote inter-religious dialogue as a vehicle to protect and promote human rights of all people?
- How can churches work together to overcome the fear of the "other"?
- How should the churches of the United States engage in dialogue on these issues with other Christian churches and ecumenical partners?

What can churches contribute to the public debate about the use of political discourse to classify some nations or peoples as "evil" and to classify ourselves as "good"?

◆ What does the response of the United States to September 11 show us about racism, both domestically and in US foreign policy?

Soon after September 11, the genuine sense of national unity experienced by many Americans was directed into the expectation that patriotic citizens would acquiesce to all decisions by the country's political leaders. Criticism of the government, its actions, direction or motivation, whether by elected officials, public figures, church leaders or anyone else, was portrayed as disloyal and unpatriotic.

"Oh Lord, open my lips, and my mouth will declare your praise." Psalm 51:15.

- How can churches find their prophetic voice in critiquing policies of the US government during times of uncertainty and fear?
- Is there danger that "worship of nation" has replaced worship of God?
- Has use of the language of religion and moral authority been manipulated by governmental officials? Does this affect the authentic voice and moral authority of the churches?
- How can Christians honestly confront the causes of terrorism without justifying its use?
- What should be the role of the church when statutory violence is used by government to counter "terrorism" that may have political, social, religious or economic roots?

The United States embarked on a war against Afghanistan described as a justified response to the September 11 attacks and is threatening unilateral war against Iraq without consultation with other countries through the UN Security Council. The United States spends more on its military than do all of the other nations of the world combined. Many Americans are questioning the influence of economic and corporate interests in their political system and their military policies. The international community fears the unilateral exercise of military power by the world's most powerful country.

- Do Christians need to re-examine the long-standing debates on "pacifism" and "just war" in light of the continuing development of new weapons of mass destruction and the preponderance of bombing campaigns from the air in recent US military attacks?
- What does "just war" mean in the context of the present situation? Do US military actions fulfill the criteria of just war theory? For example, was the military campaign in Afghanistan a proportionate and just response to the attacks of September 11?
- What is the role of the churches in responding to current discussions about increasing US security? What are the tradeoffs for Americans of trying to enhance security?

- What are the consequences for other countries of US efforts to achieve greater security? What has it meant in places like the Philippines, Puerto Rico, and the Middle East?
- What is the role of US churches in speaking to military engagement and intervention by the US government?
- To what extent is US foreign policy driven by the desire to preserve the wealth of its citizens? What is the relationship between policies to assure the comfort and well being of US citizens and poverty elsewhere?
- Are Christians called to be peacemakers? What does Christian peacemaking mean in today's world? How can churches do more to lift up peacemaking as an alternative to military action?

The United States sees itself as having been uniquely injured by "terrorism" on September 11 and thus as uniquely entitled to retaliate globally and preemptively against terrorism. Many countries have lived for decades with uncertainty in an atmosphere constantly at risk from terror. In the United States, September 11, 2001 is seen as a turning point in international affairs; but in other countries, there are other turning points, e.g. HIV/AIDS, poverty. The terms "terrorism" and "war on terrorism" have often been used in other countries and contexts to justify heightened military activities, violations of human rights and repression of political dissent.

- How can churches contribute to the effort to counter terrorism without condoning the brutalization of civil societies?
- What are the similarities between the actions of 11 September 1973 – when the CIA supported a military coup in Chile – and the attacks of 11 September 2001? Are there other dates which mark turning points in our understandings of international events and the exercise of power?
- How can churches provide a historical memory of events which have marked turning points in regions without the massive media coverage which marked the events of 11 September 2001?
- How do churches in areas of the world that have endured violence and terrorism for decades or generations support the churches of the United States in their pastoral work with Americans?
- How can churches help to ensure that all victims of violence are given a voice?
- How should the churches support and protect non-violent movements for justice and freedom?

The United States is the richest nation in the world, although there are significant inequalities in the distribution of that wealth. The ethical and moral justification for policies of the United States that place the United States and its citizens first as an individual nation rather than as part of the global community have been called into question by the international community.

"Truly I tell you, just as you did it to one of the least of these who are members of my family, you did it to me." Matthew 25:40.

- What is the relationship of the US churches to the parable of the rich man and Lazarus? Is it wealth or the indifference to the suffering of poverty that condemns the rich man in the parable?
- What does the separation of church and state mean in the current crisis?
- What is the responsibility of the church in the development and preservation of international law and cooperation?
- How do we find the words and actions that can change the agendas of politicians?
- Is the United States' self-interest equivalent to the public good?

Conclusion

This is an extraordinary time in the history of the United States. It is a time that calls the religious community to articulate a faithful response and to speak truth to power. Christian churches have a particular message rooted in their understandings of the Gospel and must not be silent. The power of the churches is not solely in its human institutions but in the presence, inspiration and grace of God. It is the power of the Holy Spirit which brings peace and speaks the truth.

This meeting encourages the churches in the United States to give attention to these and related questions and concerns as they assess the ongoing response of their government, not only to the events of September 11, 2001 but also to the exercise of US power in the world. The way in which this power is exercised has major consequences for all people living on earth.

Among many such challenges, the discussions identified a number of areas where further discussion and reflection are needed, including:

1. The impact of the "war on terrorism" for human rights and security in the US and abroad.
   - The erosion of constitutional principles and civil liberties at home, including the treatment of detainees.
   - The impact of US policies on human rights in other countries.
   - US policies towards states it has identified as supporters of terrorism, with particular emphasis on Iraq.
   - The contrast between national security and global security.

2. US policies toward specific countries directly impacted by the US response to the attacks of 11 September.
   - Israel and Palestine.
   - Pakistan and India.
   - Afghanistan and its efforts to recover from war.

3. National defense and arms control.
   - The impact of the US assertion of a right to make preemptive strikes, including with nuclear weapons.
   - The consequences of US resumption of nuclear testing.
   - The effects of US policies toward the sales of small arms, including to non-state actors.
   - The impact of diversion of scarce resources to military forces.
   - The need to develop alternatives to war.

4. The United States as a member of the Global Community.
   - The impact of US unilateral actions in areas such as the environment, UN conferences, UN peacekeeping operations, and disarmament for global peace and security.
   - The effects of US opposition to the International Criminal Court and weakening of other international treaties.
   - The extent to which US actions are undermining international law and global governance.
   - The perception that the US has abrogated its moral authority to mercantile interests.

Those gathered at this meeting urge the churches of the United States and the leadership of the churches to engage in dialogue on these issues and to take the opportunity to consult with and listen to their ecumenical partners from the international community.

Is this not the fast that I choose: to loose the bonds of injustice, to undo the thongs of the yoke, to let the oppressed go free, and to break every yoke?

Is it not to share your bread with the hungry, and bring the homeless poor into your house; when you see the naked, to cover them, and not to hide yourself from your own kin?

Then your light shall break forth like the dawn, and your healing shall spring up quickly; your vindicator shall go before you, the glory of the Lord shall be your rear guard.

Then you shall call, and the Lord will answer; you shall cry for help, and he will say, Here I am. If you remove the yoke from among you, the pointing of the finger, the speaking of evil,

If you offer your food to the hungry and satisfy the needs of the afflicted, then your light shall rise in the darkness and your gloom be like the noonday.

The Lord will guide you continually and satisfy your needs in parched places, and make your bones strong; and you shall be like a watered garden, like a spring of water, whose waters never fail.

Your ancient ruins shall be rebuilt; you shall raise up the foundations of many generations; you shall be called the repairer of the breach, the restorer of streets to live in.
Isaiah 58: 6-12.

Minute on the tragedy of September 11th 2001 and the implications of the US government's response
Adopted by the Central Committee, Geneva, 26 August – 3 September 2002.

The Central Committee expresses its deep appreciation for the report it has received on the extensive efforts undertaken by the Executive Committee, the General Secretary and the staff of the Council in response to the terrorist attacks on the USA on 11 September 2001. It endorses the brief message sent to the US churches by the General Secretary on behalf of the Executive Committee that was in session in Geneva on that day, and his subsequent pastoral letter to them of 20 September. As the letter of 11 September said: "We pray especially for the victims of these tragedies and for their families and loved ones…We fervently pray that this is the end of terror, and implore those responsible to desist from any further such acts of inhumanity." Those prayers continue.

By the sending of a "living letters" pastoral delegation to the churches in the USA, the Council embodied the outpouring of solidarity and sympathy – and also the forebodings – of churches and related councils around the world. As the team expressed, "we have come out of our wounded contexts to share with you in your woundedness. We have been moved to humility and encouraged to hear church leaders battling with questions that are broader than their own concerns, that take in the larger context of the world." US churches have been encouraged and uplifted by the expressions of support and sympathy from every corner of the globe, including from those who have experienced the devastating effects of terrorism and war.

In adopting this minute, the Central Committee recognizes that it has been just one year since the attacks, that the wounds are still deep and that the resulting and pervasive sense of vulnerability remains in the people of the United States and people elsewhere. We also recognize that these attacks were orchestrated by a well-financed and dispersed terrorist network. Further, we recognize that many members of the US churches are still engaged in the spiritual struggle to resolve the tension between a heightened patriotism evoked by these attacks against US symbols and citizens on the one hand and a renewed spirituality that calls for them to embrace unfamiliar vulnerability and to reflect on the moral complexities of these events on the other.

The US churches responded and continue to respond to grief, to broken communities and to the shock of unfamiliar vulnerability. Many US churches have spoken publicly about the negative consequences of their government's response to the terrorist attacks. At its November 2001 Assembly, the National Council of the Churches of Christ in the USA (NCCCUSA) stated "We believe that the tragedy of the September 11th attacks and the ensuing war on terrorism … provide a *kairos* moment, a place within God's time – a time for the Church to bear witness to the fullness of God, our creator, redeemer and comforter." In that statement, NCCCUSA also expressed grave concern about the violation of human rights and the civil liberties of those being detained by the US government and expressed a concern that the US government work with the community of nations in responding to the threat of terrorism and working for justice and peace. But the space for open public discussion of the current US response to terrorism is limited and critics are often portrayed as disloyal and unpatriotic.

The US military response to the attacks led the WCC to take a series of clear and appropriate public issues actions. Through *Behind the News: Voices of Faith, Visions of Hope*, produced jointly with Action by Churches Together (ACT) and the Ecumenical Advocacy Alliance, the Council provided essential information and analysis that was not otherwise generally available, helping member communions and others to better understand developments. The two "discernment" consultations convened in Geneva (November 2001) and Washington, D.C. (August 2002) by the Commission of the Churches on International Affairs have helped churches around the world to think through the issues and challenges and to begin to develop their responses in a concerted way.

The background paper on Public Issues prepared for this meeting by the International Relations staff seeks to provide a cogent analysis of the implications of the US government's response to the events of 11 September. In solidarity with those who suffer in the USA and around the world because of the events since 11 September, we share the following concerns in hope and prayer for a more just and peaceful world:

1. *The impact on international peace and security.* The US government has responded to the events of 11 September through military means and has pressed all the nations of the world to align themselves with US policies by threatening serious repercussions if they do not. This "war on terrorism" has reinforced the concept of military "solutions" to complex issues, thus giving licence for the continuation and escalation of civil wars and other armed conflicts, including the Israel-Palestine conflict. Further, governments in all regions have used the "war on terrorism" to justify repression of political dissent. By dividing the world into the "good and the evil", US leadership has encouraged dangerously simplistic approaches to complex realities. The churches have a particular responsibility to resist oversimplification of complex realities.

2. *The impact on human rights and international law.* In its response to the attacks, the US government has implemented a series of measures which threaten human rights and civil liberties in both the United States and elsewhere. The US government has demanded decisive measures by other nations to adopt legislation and practices that mirror those of the US. In doing so, the USA has contributed to the adoption of policies in many countries reminiscent of the 1970s and 1980s when repressive military governments applied the doctrine of "national security" through declarations of states of emergency that set aside constitutional protections for human rights and civil liberties. Both the

immediate and long-term implications of this are deeply troubling and challenge Christians to continue to speak and to support strong human rights standards which churches themselves have had a preeminent role in developing.

Similarly, the US government has indicated on many occasions that it will bypass the United Nations. By so doing, and by its opposition to the newly established International Criminal Court, the USA has seriously undercut international law and standards. It has thus put in severe jeopardy efforts of more than half a century to establish a just world order. The churches' own long-standing commitment to the development of international law and cooperation is at stake.

3. *The practice of unilateralism.* The determination of the US government to act alone wherever it deems necessary, and to claim for itself immunity both under the UN Charter and its own treaty obligations sows the seeds of serious international confrontations in the future. It has already abrogated several treaty obligations entered into by previous Administrations, several of them ratified by the US Congress (for example the Anti-Ballistic Missile Treaty and the Comprehensive Test Ban Treaty). In UN gatherings before and since 11 September, the US has often stood virtually alone against the world on matters ranging from disarmament to environmental policies to racism. This too is troubling. As participants in the August 2002 Washington meeting said in their message to the WCC Central Committee, "peaceful relations among nations and peoples are achieved through multilateral decision-making, not by the unilateral economic and military actions of one country".

4. *The global rise of militarism and new military doctrines.* Already before 11 September, the USA had strengthened its own military presence around the world. This presence has been growing since 11 September so that it is reported that US military forces are today stationed in more than 100 countries. Beyond this extension of its global military reach, the Bush administration advocates unilateral pre-emptive military strikes in response to perceived threats to US security. This runs counter to the UN Charter and creates a pattern that could seriously undermine international security. This implied equation of security with military force is in stark contrast to the commitment of churches to human security, which can be achieved only through economic justice, peace, and respect for human rights and international law.

As the world faces the real and ongoing threat of terrorism, we reaffirm that the most effective ways of combating terrorism are to be found in building a more just world order in which the rights and dignity of all human beings are upheld and affirmed. Powerful as it is – politically, economically and militarily – the USA is only one nation within the world community. It is earnestly hoped that the US government will again work with other nations to strengthen the framework of world order that it was itself instrumental in shaping at the Founding Conference of the United Nations in San Francisco.

The churches of all nations have a critical moral and ethical responsibility to speak truth to power. The fulfillment of this responsibility requires thoughtful discussion of these issues and prayerful discernment of Christian responses. Within the framework of the Decade to Overcome Violence, the churches are challenged to promote reconciliation and healing, to intensify efforts at interfaith dialogue, and to strengthen their relations with each other in responding to this new and dangerous world order. We are called to address these issues taking account of Christ's words to his disciples:

You have heard that it was said, "You shall love your neighbour and hate your enemy." But I say to you, Love your enemies and pray for those who persecute you, so that you may be children of your Father in heaven; for he makes his sun rise on the evil and on the good, and sends rain on the righteous and on the unrighteous. Matt. 5:43-45

SMALL ARMS AND LIGHT WEAPONS (MICRODISARMAMENT)

The WCC uses the following definitions:

The term "microdisarmament" refers to initiatives that seek to reduce the availability of small arms and light weapons especially in post-conflict situations and violence-ridden urban areas. Such initiatives also seek to reduce the demand for small arms by offering alternative ways to ensure personal and community security.

Small Arms and Light Weapons
While there are a variety of definitions of "small arms", they are generally defined as including all weapons that are person-portable. In addition to guns and rifles of all calibers, this includes shoulder-fired rockets and missile launchers as well as anti-personnel landmines.

small arms
revolvers and self-loading pistols
rifles and carbines
assault rifles
sub-machine guns
machine guns

light weapons
hand-held under-barrel and mounted grenade launchers
portable anti-aircraft guns
portable anti-tank guns, recoilless rifles
mortars of calibre up to 82 mm inclusively
ammunition for the above-mentioned weapons
portable launchers of anti-tank missile and rocket systems, including missiles

portable launchers of anti-aircraft missile systems, including missiles
mobile containers with missiles or shells for single action anti-aircraft and anti-tank
anti-personnel and anti-tank hand grenades
anti-personnel and anti-tank mines
ammunition and explosives
cartridges (rounds) for small arms
shells, missiles, and mines for light weapons
mobile containers with missiles or shells for single-action anti-aircraft and anti-tank systems
anti-personnel and anti-tank mines
anti-personnel and anti-tank hand grenades

Ecumenical Consultation on Small Arms in Latin America

Report of the WCC Consultation oraganized in collaboration with the Latin American Council of Churches (CLAI) and in partnership with Viva Rio, Rio de Janeiro, Brazil, 25-28 July 2000.

The Latin American ecumenical consultation on small arms calls on churches to renew their commitment to addressing, as a matter of urgency, the problems of violence in Latin American society and, in particular, to addressing issues of armed violence and the diffusion and misuse of small arms in their societies.

The meeting, involving representatives of churches throughout Latin America, as well as representatives of the churches and civil society in Latin America and beyond, noted with gratitude the increased international attention to the global small arms problem. Participants called on the international community, including governments, civil society and churches, also to address the conditions that lead to violence, especially the global diffusion of small arms and light weapons. Participants pledged to work within local, national, regional and international contexts, ecumenically and in cooperation with other elements of civil society, to build awareness of the United Nations Conference on Small Arms in 2001 and to promote measures designed to advance international commitment and cooperation towards the effective control of firearms, small arms and light weapons.

The meeting was organized by the World Council of Churches (WCC) in cooperation with the Latin American Council of Churches (CLAI) and Viva Rio, a local NGO, as part of their joint effort to give priority to issues of micro-disarmament within the context of the Decade to Overcome Violence: Churches Seeking Reconciliation and Peace (2001-2010) and to facilitate and encourage the churches' ongoing attention to the small arms problem. Participants noted with appreciation the leadership of the World Council of Churches in the efforts of international civil society to curb the supply and misuse of small arms and to reinvigorate efforts to build the kinds of social, economic, and political conditions conducive to sustainable human security and to reducing the demand for small arms.

The consultation welcomed the Antigua Declaration of June 29, 2000 on the proliferation of light weapons in Central America and commends it, including the policy recommendations, to governments and civil society throughout Latin America. Churches are encouraged to refer to the Antigua Declaration in the context of developing policy proposals relevant to the 2001 UN Conference.

Small Arms and Violence in the Latin American Context

The consultation heard from scholars and researchers from all of the subregions of Latin America (the Southern Cone, the Andean sub-region, and Central America and Mexico). The information and analyses presented on small arms issues in Latin America indicate the profoundly disturbing presence, spread and impact of armed violence in Latin American societies. Small arms diffusion affects regional and sub-regional stability as well as national crime rates. Latin America, the gathering was told, is burdened with extraordinarily high rates of homicide by international standards. As one participant put it, "Crimes that once shocked us are now only statistics."

While parts of the region, notably Colombia, have high rates of crime that are closely linked to entrenched political conflict, in Latin America generally the small arms problem is very closely linked to, and manifest in, drug trafficking, other crimes and desperate local social and economic conditions.

Arms production facilities within the region contribute to the diffusion of small arms and, in addition, the region has a legacy of large stocks of weapons, accumulated during the Cold War period, which now circulate within countries and throughout the region. Peace agreements in Central America for the most part failed to make effective provision for the collection of surplus guns, and the current lack of coordination of national gun control policies mean that illicit trafficking is widespread.

The consultation addressed the wide variety of factors that contribute to current high levels of armed violence, noting particularly the process of rapid urbanization as well as social and economic marginalization. Economic inequality in and exclusion from the international economy are also significant in producing the desperate social and economic conditions in urban communities that provoke a demand for guns in Latin America.

While the demand for small arms is generated through a broad range of social, economic and political circumstances, it is in local communities that it finds its most immediate expression – on the streets of urban slums, where guns are all too often viewed as a personal solution to endemic and systemic social and economic disintegration. The consultation emphasized that in Latin America, as elsewhere, the reduction of armed violence and especially the reduction of the availability of guns requires a reduction in the demand for guns, which in turn requires real social and economic transformation, in local communities and beyond.

Responding to the Small Arms Crisis

A first step towards mobilizing an effective response to the small arms crisis in Latin America must be a two-fold acknowledgement: first, that the crisis exists and that, while it has complex roots, it has deep local manifestations that must be addressed at the local level; and second, that effective attention to the problem at the local level is aided by international initiatives designed to address the small arms problem at a global level.

The consultation noted that while the solutions must be local, attempts to forge international norms and standards for restricting weapons transfers, possession and use are essential to setting a constructive context for local efforts. Thus the consultation welcomed in particular the adoption by the Organization of American States (OAS) in 1997 of the *Inter-American Convention against the Illicit Manufacturing of and Trafficking in Firearms, Ammunition, Explosives, and other Related Materials*. The convention commits states in the region to introduce a wide range of gun-control measures and to pursue regional cooperation towards more effective controls on the transfer, possession and use of small arms.

Similarly, the consultation welcomed current efforts to broaden and extend key provisions of the OAS convention through negotiations within the United Nations towards a *Protocol against the Illicit Manufacturing of and Trafficking in Firearms, Their Parts and Components and Ammunition, supplementing the United Nations Convention Against Transnational Organized Crime*. Once agreed, this Firearms Protocol will establish common international standards and promote international cooperation in their application with regard to weapons transfers. As such, it will facilitate more effective tracing of firearms.

The consultation also welcomed the forthcoming (in 2001) *United Nations Conference on the Illicit Trade in Small Arms and Light Weapons in all its Aspects*. This conference promises to be a major opportunity for the international community to further advance international norms and standards for effective control on the transfer, possession and use of firearms.

The consultation endorsed the initiative of the Nobel peace laureates to promote an International Code of Conduct on international arms transfers as a key element in the effort to restrict weapons flows and to encourage and establish international norms and standards against firearms possession and use.

In welcoming these international initiatives as well as initiatives in other regions, the consultation affirmed the importance of encouraging international values and norms in support of the effective control of small arms, and called for the prominent engagement of civil society and especially the churches in efforts to support and strengthen these initiatives. The churches in Latin America are urged to encourage their governments to ratify and implement the OAS convention, to support negotiations on the UN Protocol to promote the most effective controls possible, and to participate in the 2001 conference.

The consultation emphasized that, despite welcoming regional and international efforts, much more needs to be done to implement genuine hemispheric cooperation in support of gun control. Policy coordination in response to the small arms crisis has lagged far behind economic coordination and integration in the region.

The consultation identified a range of additional policy measures that should be taken by governments within regional and national contexts. Three sub-regional working groups developed policy measures relevant to each of the sub-regions, with the Southern Cone group paying particular attention to legislative measures, including current efforts to ban the possession and commerce of firearms in Brazil, as well as the need to strengthen inter-state cooperation in law enforcement measures on the sub-regional level within the *Mercosur* integration context. The Central American group focused on public education and advocacy measures, while the Andean group addressed national policy and legislative issues as well as public awareness-raising programmes.

Prominent among the measures discussed is the need for reform of security sectors. The consultation expressed concern about the "re-militarization" and the "para-militarization" of security and security forces. Of particular concern is rapid growth in the use of private security firms, with serious implications for national sovereignty in some instances, and with far-reaching consequences for states' and citizens' full enjoyment of natural resources, human rights, and self-determination. The consultation called for the reassertion of publicly accountable security institutions under the direct authority of states. In addition, states are called on to address problems of corruption within police forces, and to encourage the modernization of police training and procedures, including the establishment of special units within police forces to deal more effectively with domestic and family violence.

While the consultation acknowledged that addressing the root causes of the social and micro-conflicts that generate the demand for firearms in Latin American societies is a slow and arduous process, it recognized that such efforts are necessary and central to effective and long-term firearms control and to the reduction of armed violence. At the same time, the pursuit of gun control cannot wait until entrenched social and economic problems are successfully dealt with. Gun control must be pursued immediately and urgently, even in the context of ongoing social and economic disintegration. Indeed, the consultation asserted that measures to control firearms are themselves important for social reconstruction and creating cultures of peace.

The consultation urged that in all measures to control firearms and promote social and economic conditions conducive to peaceful communities, human security values, community empowerment, mechanisms for the peaceful resolution of conflict, and post-conflict peacebuilding must become central strategies and commitments.

The Role of Churches

The problem of armed violence and the diffusion of small arms in Latin America cannot be effectively addressed without the involvement of the churches of the region. The consultation encouraged the churches to acknowledge their responsibility to engage directly in public policy dialogue and advocacy. In that engagement the church must also work with other sectors of society. Churches have a special responsibility to bring central moral and ethical perspectives to bear on the social and political pursuit of microdisarmament.

In the course of addressing issues of armed violence, peacebuilding must become a central, active and strategic focus of the mission of the church. And within that mission, small arms control must be held up as an urgent objective requiring the active witness of the church.

The church was urged to train leaders within the community to give prominence to small arms issues and to build a broad capacity within the church to enable it sustain its presence both in policy development (at local, national, and international levels) and in direct community action and peace-building.

The consultation pointed to the Decade to Overcome Violence: Churches Seeking Reconciliation and Peace (2001-2010) as providing the churches with an essential framework for coordinated action, at local to international levels. In this context, a broad range of church action was discussed and recommended.

Churches have deep roots in local communities and thus are especially well positioned to address the issues of micro-conflict. Churches know the people's needs, and can understand the insecurities that lead some to seek security through guns. It is important that the churches directly connect their work to communities' needs, seeking to create gun-free zones in which the resolution of conflicts can be more constructively pursued. The consultation learned about the WCC "Peace to the City" Network, and envisioned participation in networks of cities where churches are active in addressing issues of armed violence and gun control.

The church has a calling to stand in solidarity with persons and communities which are subject to ongoing violence. Solidarity action includes the development of campaigns that mobilize citizen participation and promote the entrenchment of cultures of peace.

The churches are also well positioned to give leadership in efforts to raise awareness of the nature and extent of the small arms problem and of the urgent need for gun control measures. The gathering and dissemination of reliable information is essential, and churches were encouraged to support research efforts within civil society and the academic community, including research on issues such as the magnitude of gun availability and the physical and psychological consequences of gun proliferation. The consultation emphasized the role of the media in shaping public knowledge and attitudes and encouraged engagement with the media in explorations of responsible media coverage of violence and small arms issues.

Churches belong to a major international fellowship, and churches in Latin America are encouraged to become part of the already initiated Ecumenical Network on Small Arms (ENSA). ENSA links to the International Action Network on Small Arms (IANSA) and through these and other relationships, the churches of Latin America are urged to work ecumenically and cooperatively with civil society organizations and research institutions.

Consultation participants were moved by the tragic realities of gun violence, and yet they concluded the Rio meeting energized by the knowledge that their work to address the small arms problem is carried out in the context of a growing international community of concern and action. In summing up the consultation's call for decisive and sustained church action, participants decided the call could be boiled down to one clear assertion: "IT'S TIME FOR THE CHURCHES TO SAY NO TO GUNS."

United Nations Conference on the Illicit Trade in Small Arms and Light Weapons in All Its Aspects
Oral intervention by Salpy Eskidjian to the plenary, New York, 16 July 2001.

Thank you Mr. Chairman. I am pleased to address you from the perspective of a worldwide faith community. Like others of the world's many faith groups woven into the fabric of human societies, the World Council of Churches speaks out of local and global realities. On a daily basis local churches, as well as mosques, synagogues, temples and other local religious ministries, attend to the victims of gun violence. We witness first-hand the impact of endemic poverty, human rights abuses, and political exclusion on people in their homes and communities, and we understand why some are driven to seek security through guns.

In our global role, speaking on behalf of a worldwide fellowship of churches, we put before you one primary and urgent appeal – that the final document of this conference acknowledge that unless the overwhelming insecurities of people are effectively addressed, the heavy demand for small arms and light weapons will continue to frustrate even the best efforts to control them.

As the UN Experts Groups noted in its 1997 report, when states lose control over essential security functions and fail to maintain the basic human security of their citizens, the subsequent growth of armed violence, banditry and organized crime increases the demand for weapons by citizens seeking to protect themselves and their property (see A/52/298, para. 42). Such demand is obviously and especially strong in the world's many ongoing armed conflicts, but it is also disturbingly present in urban communities of the global north, as well as the south. And the only means of reducing that demand for weapons is through social, political, and economic change that creates other options and offers genuine protection to people. The pursuit of such change must engage a range of peacebuilding, development, governance, and social justice imperatives.

The centrality of demand reduction to the prevention of illicit gun use and trading is inadequately reflected in the draft Program of Action in L 4 (Rev. 1). paragraph 20 of the Preamble outlines broadly the means by which states intend to "prevent, combat and eradicate the illicit trade in small arms and light weapons," and it would be significantly strengthened by the addition of a sub-paragraph on demand reduction. We offer the following formulation, drawing in part on the Bamako Declaration of 2000, for your consideration:

"Recognizing that to address the problem of the illicit trade in SALW (Small Arms and Light Weapons) in all its aspects in a comprehensive, integrated, and sustainable manner, it is necessary to reduce the demand for weapons through measures that promote the strengthening of democracy, respect for human rights, the rule of law and good governance, as well as economic recovery and equitable growth, and other measures such as reform of the security sector and programmes to reverse cultures of violence and to create cultures of peace."

We also urge that the Programme of Action emerging from this conference specifically acknowledge that demand reduction efforts require new and extensive infusions of resources, and here we urge that the commitment of states to render assistance (contained in Section III, paragraph 3) be strengthened by including the appeal, contained in the Nairobi Declaration of 2000, for: "increased international support for programmes and initiatives that advance human security and promote conditions conducive to long-term peace, stability and development".

Churches and other faith communities are especially aware that the extraordinary humanitarian problems posed by small arms and light weapons cannot be solved by states on their own. We stand ready to work in partnership with governments and other elements of civil society to reduce demand for, and enhance control of, small arms and light weapons as one key step toward achieving true human security.

Humanitarian Statement of Concern addressed to the Conference by the CCIA and other members of IANSA (International Action Network on Small Arms), New York, 9-20 July 2001.

1. Humanitarian, human rights, health and development workers witness the devastating effects of small arms proliferation on civilians all over the world. Providing relief to refugees and civilians displaced by war, facilitating development projects and the provision of medical services, mediating for humanitarian access and ensuring respect for human rights often place our organisations at the frontlines. These experiences have led us to believe that the uncontrolled

proliferation and misuse of small arms and light weapons have contributed to a global humanitarian crisis – a crisis which results in approximately 500,000 deaths a year.

2. The proliferation of small arms and light weapons adds another unpredictable and lethal dimension to the activities of organisations dedicated to human rights, humanitarian, health and development work. The ability of workers to undertake their duties is increasingly constrained due to the threat and use of small arms, as many are kidnapped, assaulted and deprived of their liberty under the threat of a gun.

"More and more I am frightened to travel to the field. By air we go - small aircraft... by road, the risk of death and rape is very high. The worries before and during travel will leave a permanent impact on my health - long after I have left organisation X. I can't cope anymore."
Humanitarian worker, Uganda, 2000

3. The UN Conference on the Illicit Trade in Small Arms and Light Weapons in All Its Aspects provides governments with an historic opportunity to set high common standards and policies to address this scourge.

4. The right of states to buy and sell weapons for purposes of self-defence brings with it important responsibilities, including to respect and ensure respect for international human rights and humanitarian law. All too often in the past, the transfer of weapons to abusive military, paramilitary, security and police forces, whether arranged by arms brokers or directly by governments, has violated this obligation. The consequences have been devastating for millions of civilians around the world.

"There were about 12 of them all carrying Kalashnikov rifles with their faces covered. They asked us to give them our daughter. We refused to give her to them... One of them lifted his Kalashnikov and shot my daughter in front of our eyes. She was only 20 and was just about to finish high school."
Abbas Fiaz, "Afghanistan: Atrocities against civilians", in *Common Grounds: Violence Against Women in War and Armed Conflict Situations*, 1998

5. Factors leading to the demand for small arms are multiple and complex and are related to problems of poverty, underdevelopment, human rights abuse, insecurity and injustice. Our organisations have long committed themselves to alleviating these realities. However, this work is undermined by the easy availability and violent misuse of small arms and light weapons.

6. Small arms and light weapons are almost all produced legally, often then moving through a series of legal or illegal hands. The UN Conference must examine all aspects of this flow, and governments must agree to create control mechanisms that meet their responsibilities – to their own citizens, to civilians around the world and to the international community.

7. We therefore call on all governments to take assertive and coordinated action to:

- stop the supply of small arms and light weapons to those who use them to violate recognised standards of international human rights and humanitarian law; and
- address the human suffering caused by the millions of weapons in circulation.

The results of this Conference will be judged by the degree to which they contribute to the safety, dignity and well-being of those who live under the shadow of armed violence.

NUCLEAR WEAPONS

Call for the dismantling of nuclear weapons
Press release issued 23 April 1999.

The World Council of Churches (WCC) has called on non-NATO nuclear weapon states to join in efforts for the rapid elimination of nuclear weapons. The WCC's appeal supports an initiative by the Conference of European Churches (CEC), the Canadian Council of Churches (CCC) and the National Council of the Churches of Christ in the USA (NCCCUSA) on the occasion of NATO's fiftieth anniversary and the summit to be held in Washington, D.C., on 24-25 April. During the summit, NATO will review its strategic concept.

CEC, CCC and NCCCUSA wrote to the ministers of Foreign Affairs in March and early April, urgently requesting them to revise "NATO's present assertion that nuclear weapons 'fulfil an essential role' and are the 'supreme guarantee of the security of the allies'." The WCC endorses this appeal and has now extended it to include non-NATO nuclear weapon states.

In letters to diplomatic missions in Geneva, the WCC calls on the Russian Federation, the Islamic Republic of Pakistan, the People's Republic of China, and India, which are not members of NATO, likewise to adopt the three recommendations addressed to NATO.

The appeal issued by CEC, CCC and NCCCUSA, and supported by the WCC, calls on NATO "to ensure that the new NATO strategic concept:

affirms NATO's support for the rapid global elimination of nuclear weapons and commits the Alliance to take programmatic action to advance this goal;

commits NATO to reducing the alert status of nuclear weapons possessed by NATO members, and to pursuing effective arrangements for the rapid de-alerting of all nuclear weapons possessed by member states; and *renounces* the first-use of nuclear weapons by any NATO members under any circumstances, and commits NATO to the pursuit of equivalent commitments from other states possessing nuclear weapons."

The WCC has also written to the National Council of Churches in Pakistan, the National Council of Churches in India, the Hong Kong Christian Council and the Russian Orthodox Church, encouraging them to take appropriate steps in their countries to support the appeal.

Statement on nuclear disarmament, NATO policy and the churches
Adopted by the Executive Committee, Berlin, Germany, 26-27 January 2001.

The global threat posed by the existence of nuclear weapons did not disappear with the end of the Cold War. The May 2000 nuclear Non-Proliferation Treaty Review Conference ended with an "unequivocal undertaking by the nuclear weapon states to accomplish the total elimination of their nuclear arsenals." Many other developments of recent years however – the defeat of the Comprehensive Test Ban Treaty in the US Senate, the nuclearization of South Asia, the retention of Cold War-era nuclear postures by the United States and Russia – have tended in the opposite direction: towards the indefinite retention and even the spread of nuclear capabilities. The looming prospect of missile defence deployment threatens further damage to nuclear arms control and disarmament efforts. The opportunity that now exists to make dramatic advances toward the elimination of nuclear weapons is at risk of being lost. Partly due to the significant new agreements on nuclear disarmament after 1987, but more particularly as a result of pressing new challenges posed by non-nuclear conflicts since 1991, nuclear arms have been given comparatively low priority on the churches' disarmament priorities in the last decade of the twentieth century. It is again important that the voice of the churches be heard on this question at a decisive moment.

The nuclear disarmament agenda

Among the most positive disarmament developments of recent years has been the renewed attention given to the desirability and feasibility of abolishing nuclear weapons. The debate over the future of nuclear weapons is far from resolved, and the Nuclear Weapon States are still far from committed to immediate action towards abolition. But the broad outlines of the global nuclear disarmament agenda are now widely accepted.

The Final Document of the recent NPT Review Conference, adopted by consensus, incorporated a substantive set of principles and measures to guide future nuclear disarmament activities. These included "an unequivocal undertaking by the nuclear weapon states to accomplish the total elimination of their nuclear arsenals" (though without specifying when that might be accomplished), and support for a number of interim steps such as "concrete agreed measures to further reduce the operational status of nuclear weapons systems" (commonly known as "de-alerting"), and "a diminishing role for nuclear weapons in security policies to minimize the risk that these weapons ever be used and to facilitate the process of their total elimination."

The "New Agenda" resolution adopted by an overwhelming majority at the last session of the UN General Assembly (2000) was directly based on the NPT Final Document. Countries that voted in favour of the resolution included China, the United States, the United Kingdom, and every NATO member except France, which abstained. Only three countries, Israel, India, and Pakistan – the three nuclear-armed countries that are not signatories of the NPT – voted against the resolution. A handful of others abstained.

These decisions demonstrate that a near-consensus now exists on the outlines of the global nuclear disarmament agenda. It remains to be seen, however, how rapidly and completely that agenda will be translated into action.

NATO nuclear policy

Crucial decisions being taken individually and collectively by the member states of NATO will do much to determine the future success or failure of the nuclear disarmament agenda.

In its new Strategic Concept in 1999 NATO formally restated its position that nuclear weapons are "the supreme guarantee of the security of the Allies," pledging to retain them "for the foreseeable future." The Alliance also agreed, however, to conduct an internal review of its nuclear policies, including "options for confidence and security-building measures, verification, non-proliferation and arms control and disarmament."

The results of this review were presented to the North Atlantic Council in December 2000. The report maintained the status quo with respect to nuclear weapons policy, reiterating that NATO deems nuclear weapons to be "essential" to Alliance security, and asserting the need to retain them "for the foreseeable future." The report also says that "There is a clear rationale for a continued, though much more limited, presence of substrategic nuclear weapons in Europe." Significantly, however, the report states that "Alliance nations reaffirm their commitment under Art. VI of the NPT to pursue negotiations in good faith on effective measures relating to the cessation of the nuclear arms race at an early date and to nuclear disarmament and on a treaty on general and complete disarmament under strict and effective international control." It also declares NATO's support for the thirteen action items agreed during the 2000 NPT Review Conference and reiterated in the "New Agenda" resolution. These are positive steps.

Unfortunately, however, the report gives no indication of how NATO intends to go about implementing these commitments, or how the decision to retain its present nuclear policies can be reconciled with such steps. There is no specific provision for the review process to continue, yet it is crucial to the future of

110

nuclear disarmament and non-proliferation efforts that NATO's nuclear policies be revised to conform to the global nuclear disarmament agenda.

The report takes no position on the US National Missile Defense (NMD) programme, though other NATO members have protested vigorously against it and are known to be consulting now on its implications. President Clinton's decision in September 2000 to delay deployment of the system has been reversed by the new US Administration that has declared its intention to proceed with it. Such an action could inflict serious damage on the existing arms control, disarmament and non-proliferation regime.

Up to now NATO discussions on nuclear policy have been conducted mainly behind closed doors. The recent report now acknowledges that there is a need for greater openness and transparency, promising that "the Alliance will continue to broaden its engagement with interested non-governmental organizations, academic institutions and the general public and will contribute actively to discussion and debate regarding nuclear weapons and nuclear arms control and disarmament issues."

The voice of the churches

The churches have a long history of addressing nuclear weapons issues, and in recent years the European and North American churches have worked together on NATO nuclear policy questions. In April 1999 the Canadian Council of Churches, the Conference of European Churches, and the National Council of the Churches of Christ in the USA sent a joint letter to all NATO members declaring that "Contrary to NATO's current strategic concept, nuclear weapons do not, cannot guarantee security. They deliver only insecurity and peril through their promise to annihilate life itself and to ravage the global ecosystem upon which all life depends."

The Councils called on the governments of all NATO members to ensure that NATO policy:

- affirms NATO's support for the rapid global elimination of nuclear weapons and commits the Alliance to take programmatic action to advance this goal;
- commits NATO to reducing the alert status of nuclear weapons possessed by NATO members, and to pursuing effective arrangements for the rapid de-alerting of all nuclear weapons possessed by all states; and
- renounces the first-use of nuclear weapons by any NATO members under any circumstances, and commits NATO to the pursuit of equivalent commitments from other states possessing nuclear weapons.

As part of the same initiative, the World Council of Churches sent a similar letter to the governments of all non-NATO nuclear-weapons states.

Brussels Consultation

More recently, the WCC helped to organize an international gathering of church representatives to explore effective church responses to the NATO nuclear review. American, Canadian, and European church staff with responsibility for public policy issues, individuals from related denominational and ecumenical committees and institutions, and representatives of the Canadian Council of Churches, the Conference of European Churches, the National Council of the Churches of Christ in the U.S.A., and the WCC attended this event, which took place in Brussels on 5-6 October 2000. They were assisted by researchers in security and arms control, and benefited from a session with a senior NATO official. The consultation agreed:

- to recommend to the ecumenical community that it should engage directly with the current NATO review process with a view to encouraging NATO states and NATO itself to conform to the obligations undertaken in the Non-Proliferation Treaty; and
- to impress upon churches the need to re-energize their peace witness and, within the framework of the Decade to Overcome Violence, to undertake education, public awareness activity, and advocacy regarding the continuing threat of nuclear weapons.

Ecumenical action

Renewed debates on the future of nuclear power plants and on the health effects on civilian populations and military personnel of the use of depleted uranium weapons stir public opinion again, raising new, serious questions. The collective efforts of the churches are needed now, and could make an important contribution to raise public awareness of the crucial nuclear-related decisions facing NATO countries, to encourage greater transparency in NATO's decision-making processes, and to reinforce public demands for real progress towards the elimination of nuclear weapons.

One means for the ecumenical community to engage directly with the NATO review process would be to send a delegation of church leaders from representative WCC churches to meet with government ministers and officials in key non-nuclear NATO states. The purpose of these coordinated visits would be to encourage those states to work to ensure that NATO nuclear policies conform to the nuclear disarmament obligations undertaken in the Non-Proliferation Treaty and reaffirmed and elaborated upon in the Final Document of the 2000 NPT Review Conference and in the recent "New Agenda" resolution in the UN General Assembly. These meetings could also be used to encourage greater transparency and public access to NATO's decision-making processes on nuclear issues. In addition, such a tour could help to raise public consciousness of the continuing importance of nuclear disarmament both within the ecumenical community and beyond it.

Statement on Nuclear Weapons Disarmament

The Executive Committee of the World Council of Churches, meeting in Berlin, 26-27 January 2001,

Reiterates its deep and long-standing concern at the continued risk to creation posed by the existence of nuclear weapons,

Welcomes the successful outcome of the Sixth Review Conference of the Non-Proliferation Treaty in May 2000,

Welcomes the Final Document of the Review Conference, which established a new global agenda for nuclear disarmament,

Expresses its satisfaction at the overwhelming support received by the "New Agenda" resolution adopted by the United Nations General Assembly in its 55th Session (Millennium Assembly, 2000), which reaffirmed states' commitment to the pursuit of this disarmament agenda,

Notes the significance of continuing deliberations within and among the member states of NATO on NATO nuclear policy and the future of nuclear disarmament,

Stresses the vital importance of ensuring that the policies of NATO members and NATO itself conform to the obligations undertaken by states in the Non-Proliferation Treaty and are consistent with pursuit of the global nuclear disarmament agenda, and

In the light of the recommendations made at the international gathering of church representatives in Brussels in October 2000,

Calls upon the member states of NATO and NATO itself to ensure that their nuclear weapons policies conform to the obligations undertaken by states in the Non-Proliferation Treaty and are consistent with pursuit of the global nuclear disarmament agenda, and in particular:

♦ to affirm NATO's support for the rapid global elimination of nuclear weapons and to commit the Alliance to take programmatic action to advance this goal;

♦ to commit NATO to reducing the alert status of nuclear weapons possessed by NATO members, and to pursuing effective arrangements for the rapid de-alerting of all nuclear weapons possessed by all states; and

♦ to renounce the first-use of nuclear weapons by any NATO member under any circumstances, and to commit NATO to the pursuit of equivalent commitments from other states possessing nuclear weapons;

Encourages the member states of NATO and NATO itself to provide greater transparency and public access to NATO's decision-making processes on nuclear weapons issues;

Asks the WCC, in consultation with the Conference of European Churches, the National Council of the Churches of Christ in the USA and the Canadian Council of Churches, to organize a delegation of church leaders to meet with government

113

ministers and officials in key non-nuclear NATO states to encourage those states to support these policies;

Asks the WCC further to organize comparable processes on the role of nuclear arms and the ways towards nuclear disarmament in other regions of the World Council of Churches, like North East Asia or the Middle East, and

Calls upon member churches in the context of the Decade to Overcome Violence to renew their witness for peace and disarmament through education, public awareness building and advocacy to overcome the continuing threat of nuclear weapons.

Appeal on the occasion of the NATO Summit in Prague

Letter to foreign ministers of the non-nuclear member states of NATO, 14 November 2002.

I write on behalf of the World Council of Churches (WCC) on the occasion of the 2002 Prague Summit of NATO to encourage you and your colleagues to guide NATO and its member States on a course of irreversible nuclear disarmament in accordance with the requirements of the Nuclear Non-Proliferation Treaty (NPT).

Two years ago NATO Foreign Ministers approved the final report of the Alliance's Nuclear Policy Review, which had been mandated in Paragraph 32 of the 1999 Washington Summit, declaring support for the thirteen practical steps toward the nuclear disarmament as set out in the final document of the NPT Review Conference of 2000. While the WCC welcomed NATO's endorsement of the 13 steps, we regretted NATO's failure to offer any plans or measures towards the implementation of those steps. I must now point out that, since then, the gap between NATO policy and obligations under the NPT has widened.

Of particular concern is the continuing assertion in NATO's Strategic Concept that nuclear weapons are essential to Alliance security and that the Alliance and its Nuclear Weapon State (NWS) members intend to retain their nuclear arsenals for the foreseeable future. From its inception, it has been the testimony of the WCC that nuclear weapons promise insecurity rather than security. Already in 1966 the WCC declared that nuclear war is against God's will and is the greatest of evils. In 1983 the WCC world assembly in Vancouver confirmed that it is a core belief of the worldwide ecumenical community that the production and deployment as well as the use of nuclear weapons are a crime against humanity and that such activities must be condemned on ethical and theological grounds.

Complete nuclear disarmament is thus an urgent moral imperative. It is also a legal obligation. In 1996 the International Court of Justice advisory opinion issued a unanimous decision that, in accordance with Article VI of the NPT, there exists an obligation to ... bring to a conclusion negotiations leading to nuclear disarmament.

NATO's ongoing commitment to the indefinite retention of nuclear weapons violates both moral and legal responsibility and threatens global security. The Prague Summit offers the Alliance an important opportunity to begin planning for concrete disarmament action to implement NPT obligations. The WCC, on behalf of the global ecumenical community and according to the 2001 action of the Central Committee, urges you and your colleagues to adopt the following measures:

- to re-affirm NATO's support for early progress towards the global elimination of nuclear weapons and to commit the Alliance to take programmatic action to advance this goal;

- to commit NATO to reducing the alert status of nuclear weapons possessed by NATO members, and to pursuing effective arrangements for the rapid de-alerting of all nuclear weapons possessed by all states;

- to renounce the first-use of nuclear weapons by any NATO member under any circumstances, and to commit NATO to the pursuit of equivalent commitments from other states possessing nuclear weapons.

In addition, we urge NATO leaders to recommit, as agreed in the NPT practical steps (step 9), to implementing security policies that clearly involve a diminishing role for nuclear weapons. We are concerned that elements of the US Nuclear Posture Review, as reported earlier this year, indicate increased roles for nuclear weapons. We note in particular that the discussion of contributions of the new triad to defence policy goals indicates that US nuclear forces will continue to provide assurance to security partners, particularly in the presence of known or suspected threats of nuclear, biological or chemical attacks or in the event of surprising military developments. The implication that nuclear weapons would be used or threatened in such circumstances, even in response to surprising military developments, is a clear violation of the commitment to diminish the place of nuclear weapons in security policies.

We also encourage NATO to take immediate steps to remove all nuclear weapons within the Alliance from the territories of non-nuclear-weapon states. As evidence of NATO's commitment to non-proliferation, all nuclear weapons in the Alliance must be returned to the territory of the country owning them. An end to NATO's current nuclear sharing practices would bring NATO policy into line with the intent of Articles I and II of the Treaty. Article I states that each nuclear-weapon State Party to the Treaty undertakes not to transfer to any recipient whatsoever nuclear weapons or other nuclear explosives or devices directly or indirectly; and Article II states that each non-nuclear-weapon State Party ... undertakes not to receive the transfer from any state whatsoever of nuclear weapons...).

115

In addition, we are concerned that, according to the Final Communique of NATO Defence Ministers meeting in Reykjavik in May, steps are being taken for the development of vital new capabilities in NATO and that the Prague Summit will mark a decisive step forward in achieving this objective. This proposed action, which implies a radical makeover of NATO's mission, is being pursued without any public disclosure or consultation. We call on NATO leaders not to endorse any such plans without full debate in their respective Parliaments after appropriate public consultations. To do otherwise is to denigrate the very democratic values on which NATO was founded out of the ashes of the Second World War.

Nuclear weapons, regardless of where they are and who controls them, represent an unacceptable threat to all of humanity, and any use of such weapons would represent a heinous crime against humanity. There is no circumstance in which the use of nuclear weapons could be conceived of as contributing to human security or carrying out the purposes of a loving God. The prospect of such weapons spreading to additional states or to non-state actors only adds to our collective peril. The leaders of NATO, the world's pre-eminent nuclear weapons alliance, bear a grave responsibility to lead the world towards the rapid and early elimination of nuclear weapons and to support effective multilateral mechanisms to permanently prevent their re-emergence and spread.

I pray that God will guide you and grant you wisdom and courage in your deliberations towards that urgent end.

Sincerely,

Peter Weiderud
Director
Commission of the Churches on International Affairs
World Council of Churches

UNITED NATIONS RELATIONS

ECUMENICAL POLICY

Resolution on United Nations Relations
Adopted by the CCIA at its meeting in Crans-Montana, Switzerland, 14-18 May 2001.

Recalling and reaffirming the "Memorandum and Recommendations on the Occasion of the Fiftieth Anniversary of the United Nations," adopted by the Central Committee in September 1995, that states the policy of the WCC on UN relations;

Recalling the mandate of the CCIA and the team on International Relations
- to maintain and provide for the maintenance of contacts with international bodies and the coordination thereof before these international bodies, as may be specifically arranged;
- to represent, facilitate and help coordinate the representation of member churches, related international Christian organizations and non-member churches before such bodies;
- to seek and maintain on behalf of the World Council of Churches consultative status with the United Nations, its Specialized Agencies and other inter-governmental organizations;
- to be responsible for facilitating and arranging such direct contact with organs and specialized agencies of the United Nations as may be requested by other teams of the World Council or churches and related ecumenical organizations.

Noting with appreciation the innovative work done in recent years by the UN Headquarters Liaison Office in New York that has enhanced the visibility and effectiveness of the WCC, the member churches and other partners in bringing ecumenical perspectives to bear on key policy debates;

Noting with appreciation the work of the International Relations staff with the UN in Geneva, especially in relation to the UNHCR and the Commission on Human Rights, and in coordinating, facilitating and assisting other teams' direct relations with various UN bodies and agencies in the areas of their mandates;

Notes that both opportunities for and expectations of the WCC in the field of UN relations have risen considerably in recent years, but that the capacity of the WCC to respond has not kept pace;

Conveys to the Central Committee through the Programme Committee its conviction that his capacity must be strengthened as a matter of urgency;

Requests the staff of International Relations to develop immediately a proposal for designated funding for a minimum period of three years to allow for the addition of an experienced programme staff person and a technical staff person to the staff of the UN Liaison Office in New York;

Encourages funding partners to provide sufficient resources in time to engage the programme staff person by 1 January 2002 in order to assure continuity and a smooth transition in that office in view of the retirement of the current staff person in late 2002; and

Expresses the hope that the strengthening of the staff in the UN Headquarters Liaison Office in New York be done in a way that tightens the programmatic link of this office with Geneva headquarters and assures general oversight of UN relations, including maintenance of consultative status, and cooperation with NGO partners in promoting effective NGO relations with the UN and its related agencies.

Statement on the Fiftieth Anniversary of the Creation of the Office of the United Nations High Commissioner for Refugees (UNHCR)
Adopted by the Executive Committee, Geneva, 26-29 September 2000.

On 14 December 2000, the Office of the United Nations High Commissioner for Refugees (UNHCR) will commemorate its 50th anniversary. The UNHCR was created as a temporary instrument to respond to the needs of Europeans displaced as a result of World War II. Since then its mandate has not only been renewed every few years, but the scope of its work has expanded enormously. Today it is the primary instrument of the United Nations working with more than 22 million refugees, asylum seekers, returnees, and internally displaced people in 152 countries in all regions of the world.

The churches too have a long history of responding to the needs of uprooted people. Even before the formation of the World Council of Churches, churches were working together to meet the needs of those forced by war and economic circumstances to flee their homes. Working closely with UNHCR since it was created, the churches have provided assistance to uprooted people, facilitated their local integration, repatriation, and resettlement, and have advocated for their protection and for the respect of their human rights. In 1995, the World Council of Churches Central Committee issued a statement urging churches to address the needs of uprooted people in their own communities and in 1997 it adopted a major policy statement and called upon the churches to join in an "Ecumenical Year of Churches in Solidarity with Uprooted People."

Since then, the situation has deteriorated. Governments have devised more sophisticated ways of preventing would-be asylum-seekers and migrants from reaching their borders. Xenophobia, racism and hatred of the stranger are increasing in all regions of the world with increasing displays of hostility and even violence toward foreigners. The international community has yet to respond adequately to meet the needs of those who are displaced by violence but remain within their country's borders. Some governments have gone so far as to suggest that the 1951 Refugee Convention is outdated and needs to be revised to make it even more restrictive. The UNHCR is increasingly subject to contradictory pressures from its member governments and civil society: host governments call for adequate assistance to refugees on their territory; donor governments seek to reduce expenditures and urge repatriation as soon as possible; human rights groups press for more vigorous defense of the rights of uprooted people; and others, especially the churches call for the UNHCR to exercise more energetically the moral authority of its office.

The Executive Committee of the World Council of Churches, meeting in Geneva, 26-29 September 2000, therefore:

Extends its congratulations to the United Nations High Commissioner for Refugees and her staff for the dedicated work they have done for refugees, migrants and internally displaced people over the past fifty years;

Urges the UNHCR to remain a beacon of hope and an uncompromising defender of the rights of those who are forcibly displaced from their communities because of violence, persecution, human rights abuses, and war;

Assures UNHCR of the continuing support of the churches as it works to uphold and to strengthen its mandate to protect asylum-seekers and refugees;

Calls on governments to make available the necessary resources to enable UNHCR to fulfill its mandate and to provide leadership to the international community in this field;

Reaffirms its support for the principles of the 1951 Convention on Refugees and its 1967 protocol as the foundation stone of international refugee law;

Urges governments to adhere to the spirit and the letter of these laws in extending protection to those who are in need of it;

Calls upon the churches to use the occasion of the 50th anniversary of the creation of the UNHCR to raise awareness about the plight of uprooted people in their communities and to seek ways to ensure that their rights and dignity are respected, and their basic needs are met.

CONSULTATIVE RELATIONS

CCIA granted General Consultative Status with ECOSOC
New York, 3 May 2000.

In Decision 2000/214, adopted at its 7th plenary meeting on 3 May 2000, the United Nations Economic and Social Council (ECOSOC) approved the request of the Commission of the Churches on International Affairs of the World Council of Churches for reclassification from Special to General consultative status.

The CCIA was among the first international non-governmental organizations (NGOs) to be granted consultative status with the UN in 1947 under the provisions of Art 71 of the UN Charter. At that time the CCIA and other major world religious organizations agreed to remain in what was then called "category B" (from 1969 "category II") consultative status. Only a small number of widely representative international NGOs like the international trade union federations and the World Federation of UN Associations were granted "category A" (later "category I"). In the 1980s, and especially in the decade of the 1990s ECOSOC responded to the rapid proliferation of civil society organizations around the world by granting consultative status to an ever-greater number of national and international NGOs. In that context, the CCIA decided to seek reclassification to a category that better reflected the character of the WCC as one of the world's largest and most widely representative international NGOs.

ECOSOC Resolution 1996/31, the current basis for consultative relations with non-governmental organizations, divides NGOs into general, special and roster categories. Those in general and special consultative status may send representatives to observe all public meetings of ECOSOC and its subsidiary bodies (roster organizations are restricted to meetings in their specific fields of competence). Organizations in general consultative status may, in addition, request the inclusion of specific items on the ECOSOC agenda, have greater latitude in the presentation of written statements to UN bodies (2000 words rather than 500), and can request to make an oral presentation to ECOSOC on items listed on its agenda.

Organizations in consultative status receive documentation on the UN's work in the social and economic fields and are granted access to UN premises for consultation with the secretariat and to attend meetings.

SPECIAL SESSIONS OF THE UN GENERAL ASSEMBLY

Special Session of the General Assembly on the Implementation of the Outcome of the World Summit for Social Development and Further Initiatives ("Geneva 2000")
Contributions to the preparatory process, 1999-2000.

1999: 37th Session of the Commission for Social Development, New York, 9-19 February. Oral Intervention by the Ecumenical Team, "Promises to Keep – Miles to Go," assessing the achievements made toward implementing the Copenhagen World Social Summit Commitments.

Preparatory Committee meeting, New York, May, Ecumenical Team review of the Implementation of the World Summit for Social Development with an emphasis on globalized economy, jubilee and foreign debt.

2000: Preparatory Committee meeting, New York, February. Written submission, "A Call for a Change of Heart, Ethical Reflections to be considered for the Draft Declaration".

Preparatory Committee meeting, New York, April: Written submission, "For Clarity of Vision, A Sense of Urgency and a Change of Heart," calling for an alternative vision of a global community to be included in the Political Declaration. More than 50 NGOs supported the Ecumenical Team's appeal.

General Assembly Special Session for Social Development ("Geneva 2000"), June. The Ecumenical Team updated its lobbying positions in a document, "The Time to Act is Now".

"A Call for a Change of Heart: Some Ethical Reflections to be considered for the UN Draft Declaration," written statement submitted to the second intersessional meeting for Geneva 2000, New York, 7-25 February 2000.

At the World Summit on Social Development, delegates acknowledged that the inequity of the current market system has prevented many people from being able to share in the global common wealth. At a time when globalization was seen as inevitable, this important admission created a context for more honest conversations, clearer analysis of the roots of poverty, and more effective strategies for social development.

The rising levels of poverty, the growing disparity between rich and poor, the escalating number of armed conflicts, and a host of other symptoms point to the sad reality that the hopes of Copenhagen have not been furthered. In many ways, the international community has found itself mired in the turbulent currents of globalization. The inability to fulfill the hopes of the Social Summit leaves the human family facing the same profound moral and ethical crisis. Ironically, many continue to believe that the inequities of the market can be rectified by market remedies alone! The neo-liberal market cannot resolve the problems that globalization has created.

Poverty is not merely the inability to provide for material human needs. It is also a social and spiritual crisis that tests the very soul of the human family and its ultimate values. If Copenhagen identified the moral imperative for social development, the WSSD Review needs to unleash the moral energy and the political will to address the continuing crisis posed by the failure of the neo-liberal market prescription, especially the crushing burden of external debt. Recognizing that the resources are now available to eradicate extreme poverty, we call upon member states and the international community to fulfill the financial commitments they have already made, and to redouble their efforts to reduce and cancel the debt of developing countries.

121

One result of globalization that diminishes our collective capacity to achieve social development is the redefinition of many institutions of our common life. Globalization is redefining the nature and role of state and international governance bodies, subordinating democratic political processes to publicly unaccountable economic actors. Globalization thus undermines the ability of governments to serve as guarantors of the social, economic, political and cultural health of our communities. The corporate and finance sectors have exceeded their appropriate roles by claiming to provide a vision for all aspects of our common life. Such ceding and seizure of power has diminished the capacity of human communities to shape their own futures. Civil society, which should be, *inter alia*, a source of new ideas and a generating center for meaning and purpose in the lives of communities, is increasingly filling the gap as a service provider.

Five years after Copenhagen, we have failed to move toward a more just, peace-filled and sustainable world. What is required of us in this moment is the development of an economics of life and a politics of hope. As churches we urge all actors to foster sustainable communities. Sustainable community requires a just and moral economy where people are empowered to participate in decisions affecting their lives, where resources are equitably shared, and where public and private institutions are held accountable for the social and ecological consequences of their operations. In building sustainable communities, we would be wise to look to indigenous communities for concrete lessons in fostering and maintaining sustainability. We need to reassert the right of the people to make choices and the capacity of governments to safeguard the collective social health of our communities. The neo-liberal focus on "freeing" trade and investment from public oversight has diminished that ability.

The immense and complex problems confronting the global human community require a fresh vision and a change of heart. We call for an alternative vision of a global community whose interdependence is not reduced to trade and markets. We affirm our common destiny as co-inhabitants of the one earth for which we all share responsibility and from which we should all equitably benefit. We call for a change of heart which recognizes that real value cannot be expressed in monetary terms and that life – and that which is essential to sustain it – cannot be commodified. The role of the economy is to serve people, communities, and the health of the earth. A moral vision calls for economic actors to be accountable to poor and powerless people and for the voices that have been neglected to be lifted up. The aim of economic life should be to nurture sustainable, just and participatory communities. Building such communities will require nothing less than profound moral courage and the willingness to be open to new ways of living and working together.

"Now is the time," oral statement to the Committee of the Whole, Geneva, 26 June 2000.

I (Judy Williams, Grenada) speak to you on behalf of the Ecumenical Team which is co-ordinated by the World Council of Churches. In partnership with many others, we have made the journey from Copenhagen in 1995 to Geneva 2000. We have arrived at a critical moment in the process of implementing the commitments made by the world's governments at Copenhagen. From our faith-based perspective, poverty eradication, full employment and social integration are fundamental. Our Jubilee vision includes sustainable, just and participatory communities and an interdependent world in which we share responsibility for one another.

We come to Geneva 2000 with a sense of profound disappointment. Efforts to implement the Copenhagen Declaration and Programme of Action have neither reversed nor significantly improved the situation for millions of the world's people. In fact, the reality for many has dramatically worsened in spite of huge increases in wealth worldwide. In the past five years the few have continued to accumulate excessive wealth, while many still lack basic necessities and are constantly struggling to survive with human dignity and hope.

At this Special Session, we find the absence of a significant number of heads of states disturbing. Is this a sign that governments have abandoned their responsibilities? Does this reveal the extent to which the power of governments to act in the interests of their citizens has been usurped by the forces of globalization? Have governments been held hostage to market forces, and coerced into excluding social development from their central policy agendas?

People around the world are calling upon their governments and political leaders to stand up and to say "No!" – no to the imposition of globalization that allows markets to determine life and death for many; no to the privatization of goods and services necessary to sustain life; no to the illusion of "free" markets that lead to wealth concentration, weaken public accountability, and diminish social responsibility. Some significant voices in the global community are questioning a market system that widens the gap between rich and poor, disables democracy, undermines cultural diversity, and threatens biodiversity and the natural resources upon which life as we know and love it depends. People know the vital distinction between growth that nurtures just and sustainable communities, and growth that aggravates social inequity and environmental destruction.

Now is the time for people, their governments and the United Nations to claim a clear Jubilee vision and move boldly toward it, a vision of a global community whose interdependence is not reduced to trade and markets. This requires a change of heart, which recognizes that real value cannot be expressed in monetary terms, and that life in its many forms cannot be commodified. The economy should serve the well-being of people, rather than people being servants of the economy. This moral vision upholds the right of all people – particularly those excluded – to participate in the economic realities that impact their lives. The ultimate aim of economic life is to nurture sustainable and just communities. Building such communities requires nothing less than profound moral courage and political action.

The urgency of the situation, and the Jubilee vision for sustainable and just communities leads us to call yet again for fundamental changes. We call for new financial institutions and systems that include the concerns and participation of developing countries in determining the direction of international financial institutions and trade regimes. We call for a stronger United Nations governance role through the Economic and Social Council (ECOSOC) in establishing policy and accountability of international monetary, financial, and trade institutions and monitoring their practices. We support the implementation of currency transaction taxes. We reiterate the need for binding codes of conduct for transnational corporations, and financial and investment institutions to insure they are held accountable and responsible for the social and ecological consequences of their operations. Governments need to support fully the legitimate role of non-governmental organizations and people's movements in planning, fostering, and monitoring social development. Finally, we repeat our fundamental opposition to proposals for an Enhanced HIPC initiative. Debt cancellation is a Jubilee imperative. The governments of the world must take political action to cancel the debt ... and do it now!

Now is the time for governments to recognize their fundamental responsibility for social development, and to take political action to honour the promises made at Copenhagen. Now is the time for the governments represented at Geneva 2000 to have a change of heart, commit themselves to true global solidarity, and dare to address the pressing social concerns of our time with courage and determination. Now is the time for the United Nations to be accorded – and to claim – its legitimate role in building a world in which social justice and the social development of all people is secured. Now is the time for an economics of life and a politics of hope. Those who depend on you to act can wait no longer!

Letter from Konrad Raiser to UN Secretary-General Kofi Annan expressing concerns about the role of UN-related International Financial Institutions at "Geneva 2000", Geneva, 28 June 2000.

Dear Mr Secretary-General,

We were gratified by your presence at the Cathédrale Saint Pierre this past Sunday, and for your public words there and elsewhere in recent weeks about what is at stake in "Geneva 2000".

It is therefore with some regret that I feel compelled to write to you with respect to the report, A Better World for All, that you issued jointly with the senior officers of the OECD, the World Bank and the IMF as the Summit opened.

This report was received with great astonishment, disappointment and even anger by many representatives of civil society and of non-governmental organizations gathered in Geneva to support and encourage the Special Session on Social Development following your consistent injunction to move the world closer to placing controls on the negative features of globalization. Among these representatives are members of the Ecumenical Team coordinated by the World Council of Churches.

The consternation of these civil society representatives, and a good many of the government delegates as well, was aroused by your participation in what amounted to a propaganda exercise for international finance institutions whose policies are widely held to be at the root of many of the most grave social problems facing the poor all over the world and especially those in the poor nations. We and many other non-governmental organizations have consistently supported the United Nations and encouraged you in efforts to address the injustices embodied in these institutions. By identifying yourself with the goals and the vision promoted by this report in your address to the General Assembly on 26 June, you have cast doubt upon the will of the United Nations to reaffirm the Copenhagen commitments and translate them into effective strategies for the eradication of poverty and further significant progress towards the goals of a people-centered approach to social development.

The World Council of Churches addresses these concerns to you not as a simplistic criticism of the United Nations or of your role as its Secretary-General. The WCC has been with the UN as a supporter and cooperating body since the San Francisco Conference. While we have not hesitated to issue our critique when it was due, we have done so as an organization deeply committed to the aims of the Charter, and as one substantially involved in many of the aspects of the work of the Organization. You are well aware of our consistent efforts to sustain and support you personally in your enlightened approach to leadership of the world body in challenging and critical times. Thus we warmly welcomed the statement in your Millennium Report that the challenges of globalization need a functioning platform for States "working together on global issues - all pulling their weight and all having their say."

We have noted with dismay in recent years how the UN's development agenda has floundered as more and more responsibility for global economic and trade reform was ceded to the World Trade Organization and the Bretton Woods institutions controlled by a small number of highly industrialized countries. Their policies have not only failed to bridge the gap between rich and poor and achieve greater equality, but rather contributed to a widening gap, the virtual exclusion of an increasing number of the poor and widespread social disintegration. The OECD, comprised exclusively of rich countries can hardly be said to have the interests of the poor nations at the centre of its concerns.

By privileging these organizations as your partners in presenting a vision to UNGASS, considerable damage has been done to the credibility of the UN as the last real hope of the victims of globalization. It signals an acceptance of the logic of the market and could further limit space for governments and civil society to develop alternative goals and means to achieving social development through democratic and transparent processes. The question of how major international decisions are made has become one of pressing urgency in the world today. If the UN abdicates its independence and its authority, to whom are the peoples to turn?

I am deeply aware of the difficulties involved in the burdens you have been asked to carry. Repeatedly you have said that the change for which you and we have all hoped through this Special Session would come in large part through the imagination, technical skills and courage of civil society to press the case of the people. You have often appealed to these forces as your source of hope and support. The motto of our own ecumenical team which has participated actively since Copenhagen in the preparation of Geneva 2000 has been: "A Change of Heart." In this spirit, we remain with and stand behind you, encouraging you to hold steadfastly to your oft-stated goals for this Social Summit.

Respectfully,

Konrad Raiser
General Secretary

Response from the UN Secretary-General, 3 July 2000.

Dear Mr Raiser,

Thank you for your letter of 28 June 2000, which has been forwarded to me while on official travel. Because of the seriousness of the issues you address I wanted to respond without delay.

Let me say at the outset how much I appreciate the support the United Nations receives from the World Council of Churches, and from other civil society organizations. We would not succeed in most of our endeavors were it not for the selfless efforts by the non-governmental community, particularly on the ground in developing countries. As you know, I have been a steadfast advocate of having the UN reach out more extensively and effectively to civil society in all its dimensions.

But I believe that my consistent position in favor of civil society also entitles me to be absolutely frank with its representatives when we have occasion to disagree. The issuance of the report, *A Better World for All*, appears to be such an occasion.

Perhaps the most important point to make is that the report contains our targets and our objectives – these are the aims of the United Nations, as expressed at Copenhagen and elsewhere, for which our partner organizations now express their support as well. It would be truly ironic if, after years of trying to get them to do so, were we now not to accept their "yes" as an answer.

I should also add that all of our intergovernmental bodies – at the United Nations and the Bretton Woods institutions alike – have asked us to cooperate more effectively among ourselves, especially in development-related work. Indeed, some of our respective governing bodies have begun to convene regular joint meetings. We all serve the same people, and we all agree that the need for more effective cooperation and greater policy coherence is imperative if the needs of the people are to be best served. This report was a response to that demand – and to repeat, it enshrines UN objectives and UN targets.

Finally, I should note that the report is not a policy document but a compendium of desirable targets and objectives. And while all of the co-sponsoring organizations now agree on the objectives, there may well continue to be differences among them regarding how best to achieve them.

In fact, if I have one regret in retrospect, it is that we did not make a stronger and more e3xplicit case for the necessary contributions by the entire international community to meeting these targets and objectives. I did so in my Millennium Report, "We the Peoples: The Role of the United Nations in the 21st Century," a copy of which I enclose. There, I addressed the issue of debt relief, including offering some innovative proposals that were formulated with the help of Jubilee 2000: specific bench-mark dates for accdess to the markets of the industrialized countries by the least developed; and the need to increase official development assistancew. Meeting poverty targets, I concluded, "will be only a pipedream" unless these steps are taken.

It is my hope that the participation of the OECD in the *Better World for All* initiative represents a renewed commitment by the donor community to live up to its commitments and responsibilities.

Once again, thank you for raising these important issues.

With very best wishes.

Yours sincerely,

Kofi A. Annan

Dear Mr. Secretary-General,

I acknowledge with thanks your reply of 3 July to my letter expressing concern about the document, *A Better World for All.* I sincerely appreciate the prompt and serious attention you have paid to the points raised in my letter.

I welcome the restatement of the value you ascribe to the increasing role of NGOs and civil society in general in the process of global governance, and your support for the contributions they make within the UN system. I also share your view that different actors in the system of global governance may from time to time disagree. Your reply shows that these can be faced honestly through dialogue among those who strive and hope for a better world. It is therefore encouraging that you have made your response public.

In that same spirit, I would like to continue the dialogue now in a more personal way.

I do not deny that the institutions with whom you joined in issuing this document have adjusted their positions in recent times. It is to your credit that they have come to endorse many, if not all the objectives of the United Nations in the field of social development.

This change in attitude has resulted in part from their critical self-assessment of the negative results of past practices which failed to alleviate poverty or to meet basic human needs for the poorest of the world's people. It was hastened by growing popular resistance to policies imposed by the rich on the poor with little or no consultation with them. For many, however, this change is dangerously slow, and not all of it is in the right direction. A quarter-century ago the Club of Rome issued clear warnings about the implications of unlimited growth as an economic goal. Now OECD harmonises its policies with the Bretton Woods institutions' obsession with growth. I do not believe that this form of "greater policy coherence" best serves the needs of the people.

While I consider that the targets and objectives listed are too modest and incomplete, this is not the basis for my fundamental disagreement with the document. It is rather with regard to what the document proposes as actions required to meet even these comparatively limited goals. These remain committed to the goal of economic growth at any price. This has not only failed to reduce poverty, it has in fact increased it. They hold to the firm application of the principles of unrestricted free markets. This has served the rich, not the poor. What is needed is not an adaptation of these policies, but their radical change. This is what I had in mind when I called for "a change of paradigm" when I addressed the Copenhagen Social Summit.

I firmly believe that such change will not come from institutions that virtually exclude the voices of the poor and tend to serve first and foremost the interests of the rich countries of the "donor community" and the rich sectors of "client" states.

Because I believe so firmly in the promise offered by the United Nations Charter, I remain convinced that effective changes of approach to development and the goals of Copenhagen and Geneva 2000 can best be served by bringing international financial institutions under the mandate of the global forum of the Economic and Social Council. The world cannot afford to leave critical decisions on the shape and directions of the global economy only to those who control global capital and the flow of resources.

Thank you, too, for enclosing a copy of your Millennium Report. You may be assured that I read it carefully indeed the day it was issued. It was because I agree so much with your effort there to establish the UN as the legitimate authority in all matters relating to social development that I wrote to encourage and support you in that endeavour.

I should say again that the WCC's critical analysis of the international financial system is not a product simply of our reaction to the negative impact of present-day globalisation. It has characterised our work over decades of efforts to be faithful to the biblical mandate to place people and their interests at the centre of all our concern. We have long argued that persistent structural poverty is a violation of the basic human dignity invested by God in people, and that systems and institutions that perpetuate poverty must be transformed and made accountable.

To this end I reiterate my pledge of support to you personally and to the United Nations.

Thank you again for your letter. I look forward to opportunities to continue this exchange in an appropriate setting.

Sincerely yours,

Konrad Raiser
General Secretary

UN General Assembly Special Session on HIV/AIDS (UNGASS), New York, 25-27 June 2001

Statement by Faith-Based Organizations facilitated by the World Council of Churches for the UN Special General Assembly on HIV/AIDS, 25-27 June 2001.

HIV/AIDS has been correctly described as the greatest threat to human well-being and public health in modern times. Millions of people have already died from this disease and millions more are directly or indirectly affected. The Faith-Based Organisations (FBOs) presenting this statement wish to express our appreciation and respect to the United Nations for organising this timely and most important Special General Assembly. We are committing ourselves to support all efforts already undertaken by local communities, governments, non-governmental and inter-governmental organisations to alleviate the human suffering caused by this pandemic and to prevent its further spread.

FBOs are acutely aware of the complex nature of the infection and the root causes that have fuelled this pandemic, such as global socio-economic inequalities, marginalisation of vulnerable people, poverty and gender issues. It has become increasingly apparent that the prevalence of HIV/AIDS rises in association with poverty and indeed causes poverty. Women and girls are disproportionately represented among the poor. Women often bear a triple burden as a result of HIV/AIDS, and men carry a special responsibility to change these factors:

1. Women are particularly vulnerable to HIV infection due to biological and social factors including their lack of rights in regard to self-determination in sexual relationships.

2. HIV positive women often face a greater degree of discrimination when trying to obtain treatment, look after children, etc.

3. Women are the traditional caregivers to the sick and HIV/AIDS orphans.

FBOs are joining many other actors in the global fight against this devastating pandemic and can offer specific resources and strengths. At the same time we acknowledge that we have not always responded appropriately to the challenges posed by HIV/AIDS. We deeply regret instances where FBOs have contributed to stigma, fear and misinformation.

However, it is also fair to say that FBOs have often played a positive role in the global fight against HIV/AIDS. Countries such as Senegal, Uganda, and Thailand, which have involved religious leaders early on in the planning and implementation of national AIDS strategies, have seen dramatic changes in the course of the epidemic. For example, religious communities in Uganda, working hand-in-hand with AIDS service organisations and the government, have championed peer education, counselling and home care programmes. A church leader has led the National AIDS Commission in Uganda since 1995. In Uganda, Zambia and Tanzania, prevention efforts have resulted in changed sexual behaviour including delayed sexual activity among adolescents, and a reduction in the number of sexual partners. These modifications of behaviour have been part of the message of many FBOs. In Thailand, Buddhist and Christian groups have introduced home-based care services and greatly contributed to the destigmatisation of the disease.

Right from the beginning of the HIV/AIDS crisis, local communities have been at the very forefront of caring for those affected by HIV/AIDS. FBOs are rooted in local structures and are therefore in an excellent position to mobilise communities to respond to the HIV/AIDS crisis. In many cases, religious organisations and people of faith have been among the first to respond to the basic needs of people affected by the disease, and indeed have pioneered much of the community-based work. And yet these FBOs are often overlooked. More often than not, the capacity of FBOs has not been maximised because we have not received adequate levels of training or resources to address the impact of the disease.

We have learnt that prevention works provided there is openness and dialogue. Many HIV prevention strategies, such as promoting temporary abstinence leading, for example to delayed sexual activity in young people, voluntary testing and counselling, mutual faithfulness in sexual relationships, and the use of condoms, have contributed to the reduction of the risk of HIV transmission. These methods should be promoted jointly by governments and civil society including FBOs.

Resources that FBOs offer in the fight against HIV/AIDS

Reach. FBOs are present in communities all over the world. We have deep historical roots and are closely linked to the cultural and social environment of the people and have effective channels of communication that can be utilised.

Experience and capacity. FBOs have been seeking to serve the needs of people affected by HIV/AIDS since the beginning of the pandemic. We have developed pioneering innovative approaches such as home-based care, both for people living with HIV/AIDS and for affected children. In many countries, particularly in Africa, we provide a significant proportion of health and educational services. These institutions can and should be utilised in any extended programmes on care and treatment.

Spiritual Mandate. FBOs are in a unique position to address the spiritual needs of people affected by the disease. We provide a holistic ministry for those infected and affected by HIV/AIDS, addressing the physical, spiritual, and emotional well-being of the individual and the community.

Sustainability. It is not just the scale of the AIDS pandemic that presents a fundamental challenge to the world, but also its duration. Long-term commitments are necessary to control this disease. As FBOs, we have proven our sustainability through continuous presence in human communities for centuries. We have withstood conflict, natural disaster, political oppression and plagues. Members of religious organisations have demonstrated commitment to respond to human needs based on the moral teachings of their faith, and they do this voluntarily and over long periods of time. It is acknowledged that HIV/AIDS has decimated communities and fragmented families, resulting in the breakdown of traditional caring relationships; community-based FBOs are in a position to make sustained efforts to address this deficit.

Recommendations For Future Collaboration

We are asking the leaders of Faith-Based Organisations to consider:

1. Putting in place programmes that would eliminate traditional and cultural inequalities that exacerbate the vulnerability of women and children.

2. Using resources to ensure that all people living with or affected by HIV/AIDS are receiving the highest possible level of care, respect, love and solidarity.

3. Raising the consciousness of leaders and members of society at all levels and training them on HIV/AIDS prevention and care.

4. Strongly advocating fair and equal access to care and treatment according to need and not depending on economic affluence, ethnic background or gender.

We are asking governments to consider:

1. Providing extensive support to FBOs (access to information, training and financial resources) in order that we may fulfil our role effectively.

2. Acknowledging and promoting the importance of community involvement in prevention efforts, including community-based health care as the basis for effective care and treatment.

3. Continuing all efforts for debt relief of highly indebted countries to make sure that a significant proportion of the released funds are used for the fight against HIV/AIDS.

4. Governments of countries belonging to the Organisation of Economic Co-operation and Development (OECD) should re-intensify their efforts to meet the 0.7 % of Gross National Product (GNP) target for Official Development Aid (ODA). HIV/AIDS can only be controlled if serious efforts to overcome global economic inequalities are undertaken.

5. Ensuring access to life-saving drugs for the treatment of HIV/AIDS and its opportunistic infections, including antiretroviral drugs. This should include the reduction of prices of patented drugs and generic production in highly-affected countries where appropriate.

We are asking UNAIDS and other UN organisations to consider:

1. Involving FBOs in the planning, implementation and monitoring of HIV/AIDS programmes at local, national and international levels.

2. Calling on religious leaders wherever possible to make use of their moral and spiritual influence in all communities to decrease the vulnerability of people for responding to HIV/AIDS and to contribute to the highest level of care and support that is attainable.

The international community can take this opportunity offered by UNGASS to build on the unique resources offered by FBOs given our local community presence, influence, spirit of volunteerism and genuine compassion facilitated by our spiritual mandate. Governments alone will not be able to launch the broad-based approach that is required to address this problem decisively. This Special Session on HIV/AIDS should lead to a broad coalition between governments, UN organisations, civil society, and NGOs including faith-based organisations.

Given this joint co-operation and the necessary resources we can make a tremendous difference to the fight against AIDS in terms of prevention, care and treatment.

The FBOs represented at this Special General Assembly on HIV/AIDS realize that we cannot claim to speak for all world religions and religious organisations. But we wish to express our sincere commitment to continuing to work within our own communities for the dignity and rights of People Living with HIV/AIDS, for an attitude of care and solidarity that rejects all forms of stigma and discrimination, for an open atmosphere of dialogue in which the sensitive root causes of HIV/AIDS can be addressed and for a strong advocacy to mobilise all the necessary resources for an effective global response to the pandemic.

This statement has been endorsed and supported by:

Anglican Communion

Catholic Organization for Relief and Development Aid in the Netherlands

Christian Aid, UK

Church Women United, USA

Evangelical Church in Germany (EKD) - Office for Ecumenical Relations and Ministries Abroad

Family Life Movement of Zambia

Institute for Islamic Studies, Mumbai, India

International Christian AIDS Network

International Council of Jewish Women, UK

Lutheran World Relief

MAP International

Presbyterian Church USA - International Health Ministries Office

Religion Counts, interfaith organization based in Washington, D.C.

Salvation Army

United Evangelical Lutheran Church in India

Vivat International, New York

World Alliance of Young Men's Christian Association (YMCA)

World Alliance of Young Women's Christian Association (YWCA)

World Conference on Religion and Peace

World Council of Churches (WCC)

World Vision International.

Millennium World Peace Summit of Religious and Spiritual Leaders

A Call to Dialogue, address by Konrad Raiser, United Nations, New York, 28-31 August 2000.

Mr. Secretary-General, Mr. President of the General Assembly, Mr Secretary-General of the World Peace Summit, Excellencies, Eminences, fellow participants, friends.

We gather here in this Millennium World Peace Summit of Religious and Spiritual Leaders at a time when many millions of our sisters and brothers hunger and thirst for righteousness, for justice, for peace. We have come as those who bear responsibility for keeping alive hope for the least of these, our sisters and brothers. In an age of the cynical use of power, we come as religious leaders to assert the truth that it is God who reigns over all for the good of the whole Creation and those who dwell in it.

We meet in a time of great transition from an age of secularism which tended to despise religion. Today, peoples around the world are looking again to religion as a source of spiritual values which transcend earthly power. In religion people are finding new sources of community bonds, of human solidarity, of hope for a better future

As General Secretary of the World Council of Churches, a fellowship of 337 Christian member churches in over 100 countries in all the world's regions, I speak to you this morning out of the experience of more than fifty years of efforts to promote dialogue among Christian churches and between them and people of other faiths.

All true religion wills justice, peace and harmony. Yet, as we engage here in dialogue we are conscious of the fact that wars are being fought in many parts of the world appealing to the name of religion. Our own religious communities are being divided along lines of competing doctrines or as a result of alliances between religious and national, ethnic and other secular groupings which have assumed a holy character. As was the case in the age of secularism, religion continues to be misused by those controlling power whose interests have little to do with religion, faith or the spirituality of believers.

Mr Secretary-General,

Dialogue within and between religions requires not just tolerance but deep respect for the other in his or her authentic relationship with the Holy. True dialogue should enable each partner to deepen his or her own faith or belief, not to weaken or abandon it. We seek not an amalgam of spiritual truths, some sort of global set of minimum religious values or a shared code of behaviour comprised of eternal truths drawn from our various faiths. Rather we seek ways to create a global culture of mutual respect which will provide a model to those who bear responsibility for governance at all levels of society, be it in the private, communal or public spheres.

Most of us will agree, I think, that the spirit of secularism which either sought to abolish religion, or to restrict it to the sphere of personal spirituality has contributed to a breakdown in both public and private morality. But as religious and spiritual leaders we should be honest with ourselves and with the world and therefore admit that we have too often remained silent in the face of this breakdown in ethics and morality. Some of our own institutions have at times been complicit with or have even succumbed themselves to such abuses of public trust and responsibility to God.

Here in the Main Hall of the United Nations General Assembly where normally leaders of the world's governments meet, we who respond to a higher power must have something to say about dialogue in the sphere of global governance. The international community has failed to eradicate poverty, to provide for the general social welfare of all peoples, to resolve conflict short of the use of overwhelming military power and to rid the world of the scourge of weapons of mass destruction. We still do not have a truly democratic forum in which rich and poor, powerful and weak nations alike can share equitably and fully in responsibility for global affairs. All of this defies the spirit of the Charter of the United Nations and the lofty aims set out in its Preamble. We cannot blame the United Nations alone for these failures which have allowed the law of the most powerful to dominate over the international rule of law. We must assume collective responsibility. Yet there is reason to lament the lack of civil courage and statesmanship of many government leaders who have been more concerned about the preservation of national self-interests – and often their own personal privileges – than for the collective interest of the peoples of the United Nations.

Is it possible that we who are gathered here, without any pretense of assuming the responsibilities of governments, can provide a global free space within which accountability, public morality, ethical standards, and spiritual values can be fostered?

There is an emerging global civil society movement which seeks to hold global institutions and the instruments of global capital accountable to the peoples, especially the victims of globalization. Many of those involved in this movement do so out of their spiritual understandings and religious convictions. Is it possible that religions together can help widen a global free space for this new, vital expression of the global popular will?

Mr Secretary-General, Eminences and friends,

The last Assembly of the World Council of Churches, held in Harare, Zimbabwe, declared an ecumenical Decade to Overcome Violence. It will be launched next January in Berlin. It is based on our conviction that dialogue today must have at its centre the overcoming of violence in our world and the creation of a global culture of peace.

The dimensions of this task are manifold, and in all of them religions have a crucial role to play together. Nowhere, however, is our concerted effort more urgently needed as in the address to international and internal conflicts in which religions are involved, or that are being fought in the name of religion. It is my sincere prayer and hope that in the dialogue we shall pursue in these days, and in close collaboration with the United Nations, we can strengthen the commitment to a culture of peace and in particular deny the sanction of religion to those who seek to make it a tool of violence.

May God guide our deliberations in the paths of righteousness and of peace for God's sake, for the sake of God's world and for the sake of all God's people.

In the certainty that you all share this prayer, I bid you peace and thank you sincerely.

World Summit on Sustainable Development (WSSD), Johannesburg, South Africa, 26 August - 4 September 2002
"Seeking Sustainable Communities in a Globalizing World," statement of the Ecumenical Team to the 8th Session of the Commission on Sustainable Development, 1 May 2000.

Ethical Context

The challenge before us is to reverse the impact of a growth-driven development model that has brought about the worst environmental crisis and world poverty that we have ever witnessed and experienced.

The enormity of the task and the urgency of the situation call upon us to challenge our prevailing notion of development that puts more value on material wealth than people. We believe that the relentless pursuit of this type of development is not sustainable, and that ecological sustainability without social justice has no meaning. Rather, the focus should be that of ensuring a good quality of life for all people within a healthy environment.

The Ecumenical Team proposes that we work toward the building of sustainable communities. Our concept of *sustainable communities* requires a just and moral economy where people are empowered to participate in decisions affecting their lives, where public and private institutions are held accountable for the social and environmental consequences of their operations, and where the earth is nurtured rather than exploited and degraded. We speak increasingly of sustainable communities because it implies the nurturing of equitable relationships both within the human family and also between humans and the rest of the ecological community. We speak of justice within the whole of God's creation.

Our focus on sustainable communities necessarily leads us to a serious critique of the current trends toward economic globalization, including a concentration of

136

power in the hands of a minority, the widening gap between the rich and the poor, regional and global threats to the environment, and a weakening of political institutions and their legitimacy at the national and international level. We are particularly concerned about the impacts of economic globalization on the most vulnerable, including Indigenous Peoples, women and children.

Within this ethical context, we would like to address issues related to CSD8 agenda items on Finance, Trade and Investment.

Finance

On Debt Cancellation: The CSD should encourage the cancellation of 100% of the debts (both bilateral and multilateral) of Africa and the least developed countries without Structural Adjustment conditions attached, along with a process for the comprehensive write-down of middle-income country debts.

The CSD must call for deeper, faster, broader debt relief and cancellation processes that encompass:
- an effective, equitable, development-oriented, and durable debt relief and management strategy;
- breaking the link between debt cancellation and conditionalities;
- developing an international lending-borrowing mechanism which involves civil society in the process of debt relief and the prevention of future debt crises.

On Official Development Assistance: We reiterate the NGO caucus' call for the CSD to require governments to reaffirm commitments to 0.7% GNP or a substantially higher percentage for ODA, and to agree on target dates. There is also a need to ensure that ODA will go to the financing of sustainable development efforts and activities, and that a proper monitoring system is in place to track ODA financing for sustainable development.

Trade

We call on the CSD to help correct the imbalances and inequities in the world trading system. Because of these historic inequities, special and differential treatment needs to be accorded to developing countries with regard to agricultural subsidies. Subsidies for agricultural products need to be reduced in developed countries, in order to increase market access for products from developing countries. Conversely, developing countries may need to implement or increase agricultural subsidies in order to offset low commodity prices and dumping of developed country products in their countries. Developing countries should not be pressured to further open their markets to import food products, and should be encouraged to implement policies which support food production for the local market, with particular focus on small farmers.

Investment

On Foreign Direct Investments: Not all Foreign Direct Investments contribute to sustainable communities. In many cases, activities and operations of transnational corporations in developing countries have contributed to the degradation of the environment, and have resulted in the displacement of local communities and Indigenous Peoples. We therefore call for a shift from voluntary initiatives to binding codes of conduct in order for Transnational Corporations (TNCs) and Financial Investment Institutions to effectively fulfill their social responsibilities.

On Portfolio Investments and Currency Transaction Tax: Unfettered capital flows and excessive financial speculation are directly linked to the impoverishment, unemployment and social exclusion of millions of innocent people. We call on the CSD to work toward the establishment of a new global financial architecture, which will effectively curb excessive financial speculation and make resources available for poverty eradication and supporting sustainable communities.

Specifically, we urge the CSD to call for a Currency Transaction Tax, or a tax on international currency trades, that would discourage excessive speculation on world money markets, promote greater financial stability and could raise much needed revenue for our communities.

Alternative Models

In our search for alternatives, we only need to learn from the experiences of Indigenous Peoples to realize that there are in fact existing models of sustainable communities. Unfortunately, economic globalization is seriously undermining the ability of indigenous peoples to continue living their sustainable practices and lifestyles, just as colonization has, in the past, jeopardized these same practices and lifestyles. Perhaps the best proof of their sustainability, despite colonization and re-colonization, is that they have survived and persisted until now.

Change of Heart

We reiterate our vision for an alternative global community whose interdependence is not reduced to trade and markets. We call for a change of heart which recognizes that real value cannot be expressed in monetary terms; that life – and all that is essential to sustain it – cannot be commodified. The role of the economy is to serve people and communities, and to preserve the health of the earth. We affirm our common destiny as co-inhabitants of the one earth for which we all share responsibility and from which we should all equitably benefit. A moral vision calls for the full participation of diverse communities of poor and powerless people in the economic, social and political decisions which affect them. The aim of economic life should be to nurture sustainable, just and participatory communities. Building such communities will require nothing less than profound moral courage and the willingness to be open to new ways of living and working together.

"Justice - the Heart of Sustainability," contribution of the Ecumenical Team to the Political Declaration, at the Ministerial Preparatory Committee meeting, Bali, Indonesia, June 2002

Written submissions issued by the Ecumenical Team at the World Summit:

- "Water for Life -- Streams of Justice"
- "North Owes South Huge Ecological Debt"
- "Corporate Accountability -- A Matter of Sustainable Justice"
- "New Partnership for Africa's Development (NEPAD)"
- "Sustainable Communities -- People and Their Livelihoods"

"Justice - The Heart of Sustainability," written contribution by the Ecumenical Team for the Political Declaration.

"We share a common future...The neglect of longer-term concerns today will sow the seeds of future suffering, conflict and poverty." (UN Secretary General's Report: Implementing Agenda 21)

Our grounding vision

The members of the Ecumenical Team base their engagement in the WSSD process on recognition of the sacred nature of Creation and the spiritual interrelationship among all its parts. Inspired by this vision, we advocate a life-centred, life-defending and life-fulfilling ethic. Such an ethic involves respect for the integrity of the cosmos and commitment to respecting the dignity and promoting the wellbeing of all members of the Earth community.

Our hopes for the outcome of the WSSD process are linked to our commitment to building just and sustainable communities. This notion embodies the vision of an economic system based on equitable sharing of resources; a decent quality of life for all in a healthy environment; people's empowerment to participate at every level in decisions affecting their lives; accountability by public and private institutions for the social and environmental consequences of their operations; and a harmonious and just relationship between humans and the rest of the natural world. From this standpoint, we insist that an ethical approach to the WSSD process requires the integration of social justice and ecological sustainability, and includes:

- Respect for Diversity - recognizing and embracing the complementarity of, for example, cultures, species, religious traditions;

- Equity - sharing both the benefits of and responsibility for preserving the Global Commons for future generations;

- Full and meaningful participation - acknowledging and making space in decision-making for all stakeholders, especially the vulnerable and those most affected;

- Mutual accountability - ensuring full disclosure, monitoring, verification and compliance;
- Solidarity - rebuilding relationships and standing in particular with those who have been disempowered, marginalized and made voiceless;
- Sufficiency - meeting needs before wants and not allowing greed and abuse to outstrip the availability of resources;
- Subsidiarity - appropriately assessing roles and responsibilities at the level closest to where they are required, from local to global.

Our fundamental global concerns

In light of the above vision and ethical principles, we consider the following aspects of the state of global affairs to be of critical concern to the WSSD process and its outcomes:

- a globalization characterized by unprecedented and uncontrolled growth in the size, reach and scope of corporate actors and of their economic and political power, with a simultaneous erosion of the capacity of governments to guarantee the basic rights of all;
- the violence and alienation inflicted on people by the negative political, socio-economic, cultural and environmental impacts of globalization;
- the scandal of extreme poverty in the face of unprecedented wealth, especially over the last decade, enjoyed by a small minority of countries and privileged elites;
- constantly expanding over-consumption of Earth's non-renewable resources by the same minority, and the growing potential for conflict over scare resources;
- the development of a pattern worldwide whereby the pursuit of short-term political and economic gains undermines and destroys locally sustainable livelihoods;
- the threat and early warning of major environmental disasters linked to human activity, and their inevitable incommensurate impact on people already suffering impoverishment and marginalization;
- the devastating effects of war, militarism and escalating military activities on communities and the environment;
- a growing power imbalance in multilateral political and economic interactions, whereby the actions of certain member States undermine the United Nations Charter itself and the capacity of other States to exercise their sovereign rights;
- the ecological debts due to the peoples and countries of the South, not only in terms of money or political economy, but also in terms of the degradation and destruction of the sources of life and sustenance of affected communities.

Will Johannesburg make a difference?

To this question we answer: only if people in the townships of Alexandra and Soweto, and in townships and villages around the world, have their rights acknowledged and have access to the means for a sustainable future; only if it provides the opportunity for meaningful participation by the growing networks of people worldwide committed to working for a common sustainable future; and only if political leaders demonstrate their collective willingness to subscribe to a new set of values for shaping international relations in order to overcome the paralysis caused by the dynamics of domination. Blocks set in place by powerful self-interests and utilitarian compromise must be replaced by a culture of respect, solidarity and meaningful reciprocity. A culture of truth-telling and transparency must replace the tendency to cloak the issues or minimize the urgency of the decisions that must be made.

If the road to Johannesburg is not to be littered with more unfulfilled hopes, political leaders must demonstrate an unwavering determination to take concrete and timely steps to address the collective concerns vital to the future of the global community and its earthly home. No emphasis on "partnerships" can substitute for political responsibility. Any model of partnerships which does not address huge inequalities in power and wealth between prospective partners and widely divergent value systems will make no significant contribution towards the building and on-going viability of a sustainable earth community.

As members of the Ecumenical Team, we recommit ourselves to on-going mobilization of our own constituencies in the final preparatory stage towards Johannesburg, joining our efforts with others who seek a future in which sustainable communities can flourish.

WORLD CONFERENCES

United Nations Conference on the Illicit Trade in Small Arms and Light Weapons in All Its Aspects, New York, 9-20 July 2001
Oral intervention to the Conference, New York, 16 July 2001.

Humanitarian Statement of Concern addressed to the Conference by the CCIA and other members of IANSA (International Action Network on Small Arms)

(See texts in chapter on Disarmament and Peacemaking, pp. 105ff)

World Conference Against Racism, Racial Discrimination, Xenophobia and Related Intolerance, Durban, South Africa, 26 August – 7 September 2001
Statement on the occasion of the International Day for the Elimination of Racial Discrimination, 21 March 2001, issued by Konrad Raiser, 8 March 2001.

Christians believe that *Adam*, the human being, male and female, was created in God's own image, blessed and made co-responsible with God for creation (Genesis 1:26-28). In Jesus Christ, we believe, God humbled himself and became man in order that we may be reconciled to one another and with the Creator. God makes no distinction among us based on race, colour, nationality, ethnica belonging, religious or other belief, sex or any other difference. The Apostle Paul, writing to the Galatians, reminded us that, "There is neither Jew nor Greek, there is neither slave nor free, there is neither male nor female; for you are all one in Christ Jesus" (Gal. 4:28). To the Corinthians he wrote: "For just as the body is one and has many members, and all the members of the body, though many, are one body, so it is with Christ. God has so arranged the body, giving the greater honour to the inferior member, that there may be no dissension within the body, but the members may have the same care for one another. If one member suffers, all suffer together with it; if one member is honoured, all rejoice together with it" (I Cor. 12:12,26).

In a religio-cultural ethos where social hierarchies were legitimised with philosophical imagery, St. Paul re-interprets the image of the body to uphold the spiritual significance of respecting the value and worth of every human being. He presents this image to emphasise the need to recognise diversity as an expression of God's wisdom and love, and calls for the need to be led by a spirituality that recognises one's own worth in relation to the other. By drawing on the example of Christ, he offers a social vision embodied by the values of equality, justice and love.

The ecumenical movement, which has emerged out of this broader understanding of the Christian faith, views Christian vocation as seeking peace and justice in all human relationships at all levels. The World Council of Churches, as one of its organisational expressions at the global level, is driven by this vision of the world. The elimination of racism, sexism, and all other forms of discrimination and exclusion have been some of its major concerns right from its inception. Since the beginning of the last century major ecumenical meetings have devoted attention to the impact of racism and intolerance in society. Particularly since the decade of the 1960s, through its Programme to Combat Racism, the WCC has done much to raise such awareness through programmes of research and education and through concrete action to counter the impact of racism in international relations. "God wills a society in which all can exercise full human rights," the World Council of Churches Fifth Assembly said in 1975. "All human beings are created in God's image, equal, infinitely precious in God's sight and ours." In response, the churches gathered in the World Council of Churches have accelerated their efforts to foster tolerance. In January of this year we launched "The Decade to Overcome Violence: Churches Seeking Reconciliation and Peace."

On this first International Day for the Elimination of Racial Discrimination in the new millennium, people of all nations are called to rejoice in the God-given gift of human diversity, and to join together to build a world based on justice and peace.

142

It is our hope that Christians around the world will join with peoples of other faiths in seeking to create a world free of the poverty and forms of discrimination that are at the root of violence. As I put it at the Millennium World Peace Summit of Religious and Spiritual Leaders in New York last August, dialogue within and between religions must lead not only to tolerance but to deep respect for the other in his or her authentic relationship with the Holy. Together, we must seek ways to create a global culture of mutual respect which will provide a model to those who bear responsibility for governance at all levels of society, be it in the private, communal or public spheres.

Preparations for the forthcoming World Conference against Racism, Racial Discrimination, Xenophobia and Related Intolerance, to be held in Durban later this year, provide for not only governments, but also business and civil society to recommit themselves to its goals. In today's world, the biblical injunction that we be kind and tenderhearted with one another sounds pious indeed. World peace, and I dare say the future of humanity itself, depends on such commitments and on their realization in every place.

Background paper on the draft declaration and programme of action, submitted to the UN High Commissioner for Human Rights, 15 August 2001.

The Commission of the Churches on International Affairs, against the background of more than fifty years of work by the World Council of Churches against racism and its effects, notably through its Program to Combat Racism, has submitted earlier comments for consideration in the drafting of the Draft Declaration and Programme of Action.

This submission in its present form has been revised to integrate the comments and amendments presented by the participants of the Regional Preparatory Consultations organized by the World Council of Churches in Latin America, Asia/Pacific, Africa (two Consultations) and Gender, Religion and Racism for the Africa region.

These preliminary proposals reflect the experience of victims around the world who are members of or related to the 342 member churches of the WCC.

Sources, causes, forms and contemporary manifestations of racism, racial discrimination, xenophobia and related intolerance.

No country or society today is completely free of racism, racial discrimination, xenophobia and related intolerance. Thus it is appropriate that the Declaration and Programme of Action address all governments, non-state and private-sector actors and civil society organizations - including the churches and church-based organizations and religious institutions - that bear shared responsibility for the elimination of such violations of fundamental human rights in their own societies and for the application of universal standards in all countries.

Racism, racial discrimination, xenophobia and related intolerance are at the root of many contemporary internal and international armed conflicts, and efforts to eliminate these sources of injustice are integral to the global Agenda for Peace and to the building of a universal culture of peace and non-violent approaches to conflict transformation.

Racism, racial discrimination, xenophobia and related intolerance are barriers to development in poor countries and to equal economic opportunity in rich ones. The negative impact of economic globalization, which includes racial/ethnic inequities and the exclusion of large sectors from the benefits of the global economy, discriminates especially against former colonies and continuing territorial colonies of European powers in Africa, Asia, the Caribbean and the Pacific, against Indigenous Peoples in Latin America, and against native and Aboriginal and Indigenous Peoples in predominately-white industrialized nations. Colonization and slavery demonstrated the heinous nature of economic globalization driven by self-interest and devoid of compassion

The dominant source of this social ill is white racism against people of colour around the world. The rising tide of violence in internal conflicts in many regions, however, demonstrates that extreme manifestations of national identity and of ethnocentrism are forms of related intolerance that have similar impact upon peoples of the same or similar racial heritage in many societies. The relationship between internal conflict and colonial heritage cannot be overlooked

Caste is a prevalent form of discrimination affecting some 240 million people in South Asia and some parts of Africa, in violation of Art. 2 of the Universal Declaration of Human Rights. The sources of this discrimination lie deep in the cultures and religious formation of these societies, making it especially complex and resistant to purely legal remedies.

The role that Christianity has played in denigrating and devaluing Indigenous contributions to the understanding of Christianity in the context of non-Western traditions has to be acknowledged. Religious intolerance and the political manipulation of religion and religious affiliation are on the rise in many parts of the world, and are increasingly a factor in national and international conflict. As a religious institution we recognize that certain religious teachings and practices contribute to and aggravate religious intolerance, as well as perpetuate cultural and racial discrimination. Historically certain religious enterprises have been used as catalysts for colonization, slavery and apartheid. The efforts of the Special Rapporteur on Religious Intolerance, who has drawn attention to these questions, should be supported and strengthened.

Governments should be further encouraged to respect the right to religious freedom, and to acknowledge the spiritualities of Indigenous Peoples as authentic religion, as per the recommendations of the Special Rapporteur on Religious Intolerance. The perpetuation of state religion should be discouraged for it aggravates discrimination of those from other religious affiliation different from the state religion

Victims of racism, racial discrimination, xenophobia and related intolerance.

Women and children of colour often suffer first and most severely the effects of racism, sexism, caste and class discrimination. Societies and social systems dominated by patriarchal attitudes and use of power often favour racism, racial discrimination, xenophobia and related intolerance, making the oppression of women still more acute and complex. Racism, sexism and class frequently form a triangle of discrimination in which many women of colour are trapped in their daily lives. Women of color throughout the world are victims of this triangle of discrimination.

The poor are the most vulnerable to the impact of racism, racial discrimination, xenophobia and related intolerance. With the feminization of poverty it is again women who are most severely affected and rendered vulnerable to other violations of human rights through sex tourism and trafficking of women, discriminatory population control policies and sterilization, inequitable access to education and discrimination in employment which relegates them to the most poorly paid and demeaning jobs.

Victims of racism, racial discrimination, xenophobia and related intolerance, especially Indigenous and displaced peoples and those living in colonized territories, tend to be denied ownership of, control over, access to, and relationships with their ancestral lands. This has profound economic consequences for these peoples, and often constitutes a violation of religious liberty for those whose spirituality is profoundly linked to the land and the natural environment. Regardless of where they live, what their political or social culture, or their particular beliefs, Indigenous Peoples all view the land as sacred and the essential basis of their survival. Their identities, cultures, languages, philosophies of life and spiritualities are bound together in a balanced relationship with all creation.

Victims of caste discrimination suffer the imposition of separate habitation, exclusion due to prohibitions of inter-dining and inter-marriage, untouchability, discrimination and denial of equal opportunity in public life.

Examination of contemporary manifestations of racism should address issues of environmental racism. In many countries people of African-descent, Indigenous Peoples and ethnic minorities are those who are more likely than whites to live in environmentally hazardous conditions and near uncontrolled toxic waste sites. Indigenous Peoples' lands and sacred places are home to extensive mining operations and radioactive waste sites. A double standard exists as to what practices are acceptable in certain communities, villages or cities and not in others. As a consequence, the residents of these communities suffer shorter life spans; higher maternal, infant and adult mortality; poor health; poverty;

diminished economic opportunities and substandard housing. Their quality of life overall is degraded.

Expressions of xenophobia – the rejection of outsiders – are increasingly evident in all regions of the world. Governments are devising more sophisticated ways of preventing would-be migrants and asylum-seekers from reaching their territories. These policies made by such governments are designed to keep people of color out of these countries and to control their population growth. Politicians often use foreigners as a scapegoat for domestic political and economic problems. There are increasing incidents of hostility and violence towards foreigners, whether legal migrants, undocumented workers, refugees, or asylum-seekers. Undocumented migrants, particularly migrant women, are especially vulnerable. They have no recourse for redress of any form of violence to which they are subjected.

Governments should be encouraged to sign and to ratify the Convention on the Rights of All Migrant Workers and Members of their Families. Governments should commit themselves to addressing the causes which force people to leave their communities, such as political and religious persecution, human rights violations, war, poverty, and environmental degradation. Governments should refrain from keeping asylum seekers in prison for long periods of time while their case is being processed.

Governments should develop awareness-raising programmes about the reasons for migration, the contributions which migrants make to their societies, and the need to appreciate the rich variety of cultures in the world. The relationship between xenophobia and racism needs further study.

Governments should ensure that their asylum procedures provide maximum protection to those seeking protection from persecution and that they are in full accord with international refugee law.

Governments should consider adopting measures to legalize the undocumented status of migrants in their countries, to facilitate the integration of migrants into national life and to allow long-term migrants to become citizens.

Governments should acknowledge that the institutions of their societies have been built on the values, beliefs and traditions of white society, and as such deny the values, beliefs, and knowledge of Indigenous Peoples.

The Second Optional Protocol to the International Covenant on Civil and Political Rights aiming at the abolition of the death penalty and related decisions adopted by the United Nations have encouraged states to abolish or strictly limit the death penalty. Article 6(5) of the International Covenant on Civil and Political Rights (ICCPR) expressly prohibits the imposition of the death penalty for crimes committed by persons below eighteen years of age. In some countries which continue to apply the death penalty – including to juvenile offenders – statistics show a consistent pattern of racial discrimination and racial bias towards juvenile and adult offenders in law enforcement and the administration of criminal justice.

Governments that have made reservations to Article 6(5) which are incompatible with the object and purpose of the ICCPR should withdraw these reservations. Special measures should be adopted at the national level to address discriminatory attitudes and conduct within the juvenile and adult justice systems, including the police. Governments should also evaluate and dismantle any racist judicial structures/procedures that render people of colour vulnerable to judgement without proper legal representation or a fair trial.

Measures of prevention, education and protection aimed at the eradication of racism, racial discrimination, xenophobia and related intolerance at the national, regional and international levels.

Government ministries of education, those responsible for education at all levels of society, including through private and/or religious schools should review curriculum content at all levels of schooling and education, and revise all those which either explicitly or implicitly discriminate against social groups on the basis of race, ethnicity, nationality, caste or descent. New, innovative educational materials should be researched and developed to promote race, ethnic and national tolerance and a culture of inclusiveness and non-discrimination. Such an approach to education should include civic education with respect to anti-racist laws and forms of legal redress available to the victims of racism, racial discrimination, xenophobia and related intolerance. History text books and teaching materials need to be rewritten, to reflect the perspective of those who have suffered colonization, slavery, apartheid, genocide, religious conquest, etc.

Programmes promoting tolerance, language recovery, the recovery of truth in history and multi-culturalism should be encouraged in the schools and through public awareness-raising campaigns. Targets for equitable outcomes should be set, and monitoring mechanisms put in place.

Governments of countries where caste discrimination is widespread should put in place all necessary constitutional, legislative and administrative measures, including appropriate forms of affirmative action, to prohibit discrimination on the basis of caste-bound occupation and descent, and put in place effective legal standards at state and local levels.

Provision of effective remedies, recourse, redress, (compensatory) and other measures at the national, regional and international levels.

Impunity for past offenders responsible for massive crimes, including slavery, colonization, apartheid, genocide and indentured labour, committed against populations based on racism, racial discrimination, xenophobia and related intolerance should be abolished in international and national law. Victims are entitled to the truth, to have it recognized publicly, and to compensation for offenses committed. Living offenders should be charged and tried, preferably in national courts of justice, or in appropriate international courts or tribunals. Removing impunity and allowing formal public accounting for past offenses and compensation are important for increasing public awareness and essential to the process of social healing and reconciliation in order to break spirals of retribution and violence which pass from generation to generation. The removal of impunity for past offenders must be accompanied by the redistribution of national wealth, e.g. land and financial and industrial institutions.

The international community should establish international structures to prosecute those who benefit from armed conflict through their sale and supply of arms to warring parties, and the extortion of natural resources such as oil, diamonds and gold.

Governments of countries where caste discrimination continues should implement legislation, monitor compliance and provide accessible avenues of redress through instruments accessible to victims; ensure that persons or institutions responsible for discrimination based on caste, occupation or descent, or for the trafficking of women, do not remain immune from prosecution under the law; and assure that victims are fairly compensated. Degrading practices such as manual scavenging should be brought to an end and persons engaged in them rehabilitated and trained for occupations which respect human dignity. Their contribution to society must be recognized and adequately compensated.

The UN WCAR presents governments with the opportunity to right the wrongs of the past and design new ways of combating racism today. While the International Convention on the Elimination of All Forms of Racial Discrimination condemns racial discrimination, it does not provide strategies for remedies. These remedies may come in the form of reparations to victims and communities who have suffered racism, including the cancellation of debt for former colonized poor countries, which are highly indebted to financial and governmental institutions of former colonizers.

Strategies to achieve full and effective equality, including international cooperation and enhancement of the United Nations and other international mechanisms in combating racism, racial discrimination, xenophobia and related intolerance, and follow-up.

The consistency and political will exercised by the United Nations in support of those in South Africa who struggled for decades to abolish the apartheid system stands as a pertinent example of the capacity of the international community to address effectively the root causes of racism and racial discrimination. This international, multi-sectoral approach should be reflected in the Programme of Action of the World Conference, taking into account measures ranging from economic cooperation and practice in both public and private sectors, education and awareness-building campaigns, cooperation in the military and security spheres, and others tending to sanction and/or isolate governments of countries where there is a consistent pattern of gross violations of human rights based on racism, racial discrimination, xenophobia and related intolerance. The international community must refrain from declaring reconciliation without justice or without the establishment of mechanisms that would prevent further racial discrimination and violence.

The call of the Vienna World Conference on Human Rights for more effective coordination among United Nations bodies in the field of human rights should be reiterated and strengthened with respect to racism, racial discrimination, xenophobia and related intolerance.

At the national level, participatory mechanisms for assessment of the implementation of the Declaration and Programme of Action should be established, possibly within the national institutions for thepPromotion and protection of human rights. As provided in the Paris Principles of 1991, the composition of national institutions should ensure the pluralist representation of civil society, including representatives of organizations involved in efforts to combat racism, racial discrimination, xenophobia and related intolerance, as well as discrimination based on descent.

National mechanisms for redress, including the judiciary at all levels, should also comprise persons belonging to groups representing victims of racial discrimination, xenophobia and related intolerance, including discrimination based on descent.

At the international level, a thematic mechanism should be established within the United Nations human rights machinery to examine, monitor and publicly report on discriminatory practices related to occupation and descent, including caste.

The international community should institute a political and legal mechanism that will prevent the flow of resources from poor countries to rich countries through corruption and unequal trade policies, and begin the repatriation of such extorted resources back to poor countries.

A permanent follow-up mechanism should be established within the Office of the High Commissioner for Human Rights to monitor and evaluate programmes to combat racism and to coordinate the exchange of information. This mechanism would monitor and report on the implementation of the final outcome of the World Conference.

A time-defined review of the implementation of the Programme of Action under the auspices of the United Nations should be included.

In addition to the recommendations for action included under previous headings, the following should be considered for inclusion in the Draft Program of Action:

- To establish effective mechanisms for the eradication of poverty and equality on the distribution of wealth within States and basic conditions to improve the living conditions of women and children;
- To establish effective mechanisms within States to redress the inequalities of opportunities for formal education and employment;

- To put into place effective measures to prevent and to redress practices of sex tourism and trafficking of women and children in general, and women and children whose lives have been affected by racism and caste;
- To ensure that the health systems provide equal treatment to women = of racial/ethnic communities and women of descent related to caste, and that their reproductive rights are respected;
- To ensure accessibility of health facilities and medication to women of color.
- To institute compensatory measures to all victims of racial violence and discrimination, and establish programs to uplift the well-being of the victims;
- To affirm the economic, political, social, cultural and spiritual rights of Indigenous Peoples as coequals in the shaping of the world's historical, cultural and spiritual heritage;
- To establish effective policies for land redistribution in colonized countries where Indigenous Peoples have been displaced from their land;
- To foster the building of bridges between Indigenous Peoples and the wider community, and to help unite and strengthen Indigenous Peoples' experiences and their existing institutions so that they may play a full and active part in the elimination of racism. To encourage greater diffusion of information about the rights and values of Indigenous Peoples and their traditional cultures at national and international levels;
- To establish international policies to monitor and prosecute multinational corporations that are involved in the exploitation of communities of color, engaged in child labour and those that practice environmental racism;
- To reiterate the need for affirmative action to redress the injustices done to all victims of racism, racial discrimination, xenophobia or related intolerance;
- To conduct studies on toxic and hazardous waste facilities, threatening presence of poisons and pollutants and their impact on the health and livelihood of communities of African-descent, Indigenous Peoples and ethnic minorities; propose measures to control such abuse and punish offenders; and propose domestic and international remedies and compensation for victims of environmental racism;
- To establish mechanisms in which to monitor the role of media in perpetuating racial stereotypes and exacerbating racial violence.
- To establish legal systems free of racial prejudices and end the criminalization of people of color;
- To conduct in-depth analysis of the negative impact of racial and gender discrimination on women of color, and implement legislation, policies and educational strategies to protect their rights;
- To render visible the multiple forms of discrimination to which women of color are subjected, in order to establish effective measures to end these forms of multiple discrimination.

Oral statement of the Ecumenical Caucus to the plenary session on behalf of the Ecumenical Caucus,* 5 September 2001.

Madame chairperson, distinguished delegates, people of faith and goodwill, sisters and brothers. Racism is a sin. It is contrary to God's will and an affront to human dignity and human rights.

We believe that the churches must acknowledge their complicity with, and participation in, the perpetuation of racism, slavery and colonialism. This acknowledgement is critical because it can lead to the necessary acts of apology, confession and repentance. These elements form part of redress and reparations that are due to the victims of racism past and present.

On the issues of slavery, colonialism, apartheid and reparations, we believe that it is essential for our churches and governments to acknowledge that they have benefited from the exploitation of Africans and African descendants, Asians and Asian descendants and Indigenous Peoples through slavery and colonialism. We are clear that the trans-Atlantic, trans-Pacific and trans-Saharan slave trades, and all forms of slavery, constitute crimes against humanity.

On the issue of Palestine, we are calling for the end of Israeli occupation of the Occupied Palestinian Territories, the achievement of the right of self-determination by the Palestinian people, including the right of return, and for the establishment of a sovereign Palestinian State. We encourage dialogue between Jews, Muslims and Christians to promote peace, tolerance and harmonious relationships.

On the issue of Dalits and caste-based discrimination, we call for the recognition of Dalits among the victims of racial discrimination and for caste-based discrimination to be included in the list of sources of racism. Further mechanisms must be evolved by the United Nations, governments and civil society to prohibit and redress discrimination on the basis of work and descent.

---

* The Ecumenical Caucus included representatives of the World Council of Churches (WCC), United Methodist Church (General Board of Church and Society and General Board Global Ministries), United Church of Christ/Disciples of Christ, Lutheran World Federation (LWF), Church World Service and Witness/National Council of the Churches of Christ in the USA, Diakonia Council of Churches (Durban), Church of England, Sisters of Mercy, Canadian Council of Churches, Presbyterian Church USA, Church of Christ in Thailand, Medical Mission Sisters, Christian Reformed Church of Canada, and Uniting Reformed Church in Southern Africa. (Procedural difficulties at the Conference prevented the presentation of the more substantial statement given subsequently to the press by Archbishop Desmond Tutu.)

Finally, with regard to Indigenous Peoples, we are calling for joint efforts among all entities to stand in solidarity with Indigenous Peoples in their struggles for self-determination and in their efforts to build peaceful and sustainable communities; and to safeguard their Indigenous knowledge and resources, free from discrimination and based on respect, freedom and equality.

Statement presented to the media by Archbishop Desmond Tutu on behalf of the Ecumenical Caucus, 5 September 2001.

Racism is a sin. It is contrary to God's will for love, peace, equality, justice and compassion for all. It is an affront to human dignity and a gross violation of human rights.

Human dignity is God's gift to all humankind. It is the gift of God's image and likeness in every human being. Racism desecrates God's likeness in every person. Human rights are the protections we give to human dignity. We participate in the human rights struggle to restore wholeness that has been broken by racism. The struggle against racism, racial discrimination, xenophobia and related intolerance is the struggle to sanctify and affirm life in all its fullness.

Racism dehumanizes, disempowers, marginalizes and impoverishes human beings. Its systematic and institutional forms have resulted in the death of many peoples, the plunder of resources, and the decimation of communities and nations.

Racism, racial discrimination, xenophobia, and related intolerance all work, singularly and collectively, to diminish our common humanity. They thrive within the intersections of race, caste, colour, age, gender, sexual orientation, class, landlessness, ethnicity, nationality, language and disability. The dismantling and eradication of racism requires that we address all its manifestations and historical expressions, especially slavery and colonialism.

As people of faith, we call on all peoples, non-governmental organizations and governments to earnestly strive to break the cycles of racism and assist the oppressed to achieve self-determination and establish sustainable communities, without violating the rights of others.

The time to dismantle and eradicate racism is now. To be credible, it is urgent for us and our churches to acknowledge our complicity with and participation in the perpetuation of racism, slavery and colonialism. This acknowledgment is critical because it leads to the necessary acts of apology and confession, of repentance and reconciliation, and of healing and wholeness. All of these elements form part of redress and reparations that are due the victims of racism, past and present.

As a faith community we pledge to struggle against racism and all its manifestations in the hope that God's people fulfil today the Gospel mandate that we "may all be one" (John 17:21).

To the above ends we commit ourselves to put the following priorities before the World Conference Against Racism as well as to our churches and related ecumenical bodies and institutions

1. *Slavery, Colonialism, Apartheid and Reparations.* Our churches and governments should acknowledge that they have benefited from the exploitation of Africans and African descendants and Asians and Asian descendants, and Indigenous Peoples through slavery and colonialism. We further call upon our churches to address the issue of reparations as a way of redressing the wrongs done, and to be clear that the trans-Saharan and transoceanic - Atlantic, Pacific and Indian - slave trade and all forms of slavery constitute crimes against humanity.

2. *Palestine.* For the end of Israeli colonialist occupation in the occupied Palestinian territories, the achievement of the right to self-determination by the Palestinian people, including the right of return, and for the establishment of a sovereign Palestinian state. We encourage dialogue between and among Jews, Muslims and Christians to promote peace, tolerance and harmonious relationships.

3. *Dalits and Caste-based Discrimination.* Dalits must be recognized as among the victims of racial discrimination and caste-based discrimination must be included in the list of sources of racism. Further, mechanisms must be evolved by governments and the United Nations to prohibit and redress discrimination on the basis of work and descent.

4. *Roma, Sinti and Travellers.* For churches and governments to recognize that they have exploited Roma through slavery, ethnocide and assimilation. Governments should adopt immediate and concrete measures to eradicate the widespread discrimination, persecution, stigmatization and violence against the above peoples on the basis of their social origin and identity. They must be assured of public welfare, including accommodation, education, medical care, and employment, as well as citizenship and political participation. All these concerns must be addressed with the participation of Roma, Sinti and Travellers and their communities.

5. *Migrant Workers and Globalization.* To ensure that all migrant workers have the right to fair working conditions, decent wages and the right to organize, free from racism, racial discrimination, xenophobia and related intolerance, both in sending as well as receiving countries. We urge governments to legislate against and stop the trafficking of women and children for sexual exploitation and domestic labour. Poverty and landlessness breed racism. The relation between migration, poverty and landlessness must be analyzed especially under schemes of privatization and globalization.

6. *Migrants, Asylum-seekers, Refugees, and Internally Displaced Peoples.* To acknowledge that racism and all its manifestations are at the root of discrimination against refugees, migrants, asylum-seekers, displaced peoples, undocumented persons and internally displaced persons. We urge the United Nations to call on governments to take appropriate action to protect the rights of such individuals in both the

receiving as well as the sending countries, ensuring them freedom of movement, equitable access to education and health, housing and legal services.

7. *Indigenous Peoples.* We must join with others in efforts to stand in solidarity with Indigenous Peoples in their struggles for self-determination and in their efforts to build peaceful and sustainable communities and to safeguard their indigenous knowledge, resources, land and ancestral domains, free from discrimination and based on respect, freedom and equality. We also call on all of us to embrace the richness of the social, cultural, spiritual and linguistic diversities of Indigenous Peoples.

8. *Religious Liberty and Religious Intolerance.* We must promote religious freedom and religious liberty as human rights. Any intolerance, aggression towards, or denial of this freedom to anyone and any community or society is an attack on human dignity. Even as churches must examine their complicity in religious intolerance in the past and present, we call on churches and governments to respect the freedom of religion or belief and protect the act of religious worship. We must acknowledge the negative impacts of religion, including the uncritical use of sacred texts that unduly results in the assertion of superiority of one group over another, but especially so on women, and take immediate steps to address the violence that stems from such impacts.

9. *Children and Young People.* We must ensure and empower children and young people to have a voice and be included in anti-racism strategies. Non-governmental organizations and governments should develop programmes in consultation with children and young people on all matters aimed at educating them about their rights, involving them in cultural, political and economic decision-making, and assisting them in creating positive self-identity and confidence, ensuring that their ethnic, indigenous, linguistic and religious heritages are valued.

10. *Follow-Up and Monitoring Mechanisms.* To ensure that there are clear follow-up measures and monitoring mechanisms to both the implementation of and adherence to the aspirations contained in the Declaration and the concrete actions contained in the Programme of Action of the World Conference Against Racism. Considering the specificity of women's experiences of racism, the Programme of Action must incorporate gender analysis. National action plans must be developed and resources identified and allocated for the implementation of this Programme. The Programme of Action must be gender-sensitive on all levels - local, national and international.

Concluding statement issued by the World Council of Churches delegation, Durban, 7 September 2001.

The sin of racism has been a central concern for the ecumenical movement since the beginning of the last century, and at the heart of the life of the World

Council of Churches (WCC) since 1948. Out of this commitment, the WCC offered strong support to the UN Conference from its early planning stages onwards and itself contributed to the process by convening a number of regional ecumenical consultations. In August 2000, the WCC submitted a detailed submission to the High Commissioner for Human Rights, which was subsequently revised after the regional meetings. The final submission was delivered to the Durban Conference.

The NGO Forum was perhaps the largest civil society gathering devoted to racism that has ever assembled and certainly the most representative of those victimized by racism and racial discrimination. It provided the victims of racism with a place to speak of their experience and their pain and to make proposals for change. The WCC delegation celebrates that such a forum was held, because it falls within the WCC's long-cherished tradition of giving space, and supporting victims to speak publicly.

The WCC delegation considered the process adopted by the NGO Forum to be vitally important, worthy of affirmation and respect, and recognized that the NGO Forum document contains the aspirations and recommendations of many communities of marginalized peoples.

Many ideas and recommendations from the NGO Forum were incorporated into the document. The debate on that text was long and, at times, complex because of the huge numbers of people involved. The methodology used was to ask specific caucuses within the Forum to react, provide amendments and then vote. Members of the WCC delegation were part of the Ecumenical and other caucuses and did not vote as the WCC itself.

The focus of the NGO Forum and the World Conference was profoundly affected by current world affairs. The Durban meetings convened at a time when the situation in the Middle East was in the forefront of people's minds, and the issues this highlighted quickly gained prominence in the NGO Forum. The WCC delegation was greatly helped by the sensitive explanations and support of its Palestinian members.

During the NGO Forum, in keeping with WCC policy, the WCC delegation supported the right of self-determination for Palestinians, the right of return and the establishment of a Palestinian state. It also affirmed the right of the State of Israel to exist, and condemned anti-Semitism. There are some statements in the NGO Forum document which are outside the WCC's policy framework, and which the WCC cannot support, such as: equating Zionism with racism, describing Israel as an apartheid state, and the call for a general boycott of Israeli goods.

This does not detract from the WCC's support for the document as a whole.

The WCC delegation believes that to focus only on some sections of the NGO Forum document is disrespectful to all other sections, which cover a vast number

155

of issues significant to the victims of racism, racial discrimination and xenophobia. Those wide concerns are represented within the membership of the WCC delegation and cannot be ignored.

International Conference on Financing for Development (FfD), Monterrey, Mexico, 18-22 March 2002
Letter from Konrad Raiser to H.E. Ernesto Zedillo Ponce de León, President of Mexico, April 2001

Your Excellency,

On behalf of the World Council of Churches I wish to extend our best wishes to you and the other members of the United Nations Secretary-General's High-level Panel on Financing for Development (FfD) for every success in your efforts to address the need for increased and appropriate financing for sustainable development.

The World Council of Churches (WCC) has, for almost all of the 53 years of its existence, emphasized both the importance of global justice and equitable sharing of resources as essential prerequisites for human development. The WCC has also advocated appropriate public and non-governmental policies which will be of real benefit to the poor. In keeping with that tradition, the Council in collaboration with the Lutheran World Federation (LWF), other churches and church-related organizations have collaborated together as an Ecumenical Team to follow the preparations for the International Conference on Financing for Development to be held in Mexico next year. Other organizations which have joined the WCC and LWF on the Ecumenical Team include the Canadian Council of Churches, the General Board of Church and Society of the United Methodist Church, and Sisters of Mercy. Enclosed you will find a background paper which was prepared for the Financing for Development initiative. This document, entitled *"Justice: The Heart of the Matter - An Ecumenical Approach to Financing for Development"*, takes up the six areas identified by the UN Member States and the Secretariat as critical to the ecumenical community concerning financing for development and outlines areas for future commitments and common action.

Recognizing the importance of the panel in which you will serve as a moderator, we would appreciate your consideration of these proposals and welcome an opportunity to enter into dialogue with you and the high-level panel about them.

Our aim, which we know you share, is not just the reduction, but the elimination of poverty. In a world rife with conflicts, most of which have at their root poverty, economic inequity and competition for the control of resources, the work of your panel is urgent and essential to save precious human lives around the world.

Respectfully,

Konrad Raiser
General Secretary

"Staying Engaged - For Justice," statement of the Ecumenical Team to the 4th Preparatory Committee, New York, January 2002.

The ecumenical community welcomes the FfD process as an unprecedented opportunity for the global community to collectively – and with determination – address the urgent issues of global economic justice. The dominant neo-liberal economic model exacerbates poverty, inequality and exclusion and is an impediment to the implementation of the Millennium Development Goals. The global community cannot remain passive spectators of the relentless march of a globalizing economic system which allows a few unaccountable economic and financial actors to wield excessive power at the expense of the vast majority of the world's peoples.

Financing must not be an end in itself, but focused on people-centred development. The recent financial crises in Asia and the current hardships faced by the people of Argentina are two stark illustrations of failed economic models. The ecumenical community cannot endorse economic models that simply focus on increasing monetary wealth for the few without meaningful mechanisms to address poverty eradication and equitable development.

Justice is the heart of the matter. It is the key to the realization of human dignity and development within secure and sustainable communities. Such communities require a just and moral economy where people are empowered to participate in decisions affecting their lives, and where public and private institutions are held accountable for the social and environmental consequences of their operations. Justice demands the transformation of global economic governance and the international financial system so that their institutions are accountable to and serve all people, not simply the wealthy and powerful.

Staying engaged requires tangible commitments and actions. Engagement without demonstrated commitment is a waste of time. At the very least the Monterrey conference must make commitments to:

The principle of the primacy of fair trade, to include:
- Immediate market access for developing countries
- Elimination of the structural inequities in the global trading system

- Mutuality, transparency and public participation in future trade negotiations.

The Jubilee principle of a fresh start, to include:
- Immediate cancellation of the external debt of the poorest countries
- Substantial debt reduction for heavily indebted middle-income countries
- The establishment of an independent and fair debt arbitration mechanism for current and future loans, which will promote ethical lending and borrowing policies.

The principle of democratization of the international financial system, to include:
- Strengthening ECOSOC's capacity to exercise its responsibility in the domains of development, economics, finance, trade, and social policy
- Democratizing the decision-making processes within the Bretton Woods institutions and the WTO
- Establishing within the UN system a global forum on taxation to study and propose new forms of taxation and support national efforts to counteract excessive tax competition and tax evasion.

Real value cannot be expressed in monetary terms, nor can life – and that which is essential to sustain it – be commodified. To "remake the world" and tackle growing inequality, concentration of power, and social exclusion, a *people-centred approach* to financing for development is required. To the implementation of these principles and goals the ecumenical community stays engaged and committed.

"Engagement with Commitment...?", press release issued by the Ecumenical Team, Monterrey, Mexico, 19 March 2002.

To claim that an international economic and financial system based on "market forces" will address the fundamental challenges of financing for development is a form of "science fiction". The debt burden of the world's poorest countries must be acknowledged as an international scandal, and political goodwill be mobilised to eliminate it without delay.

"Market Forces" or Greed?

The economic and financial indicators published in the reports of all the relevant international multilateral institutions point incontrovertibly to the increasingly unconscionable inequities in the global human community. What stares us in the face is a world in which the material overabundance enjoyed by a small percentage of this community exists and continues to grow side by side with the deprivation and exclusion of many.

Even in the developed countries themselves, the free reign of "market forces" leads to glaring injustices and growing gaps. One only need take the common example of corporate practice, in which, in the name of such forces, thousands of workers are laid off, the already excessive remuneration of top executives is simultaneously increased, and the stock market value of the company automatically goes up. The growing power and reach of global financial markets pose an even greater threat to equitable development.

The engine driving these forces – from Enron to Argentina - must be named for what it is: outright greed. How can we rely on such a dysfunctional engine to take us toward sustainable development?

External Debt

The debt burden of developing countries remains a fundamental obstacle to poverty eradication and human development for all within just and sustainable communities. All the conventional debt relief initiatives proposed so far by bilateral and multilateral creditors, including HIPC, have failed to adequately address the moral and financial crisis faced by people in low-income countries. Likewise, the FfD process has failed to give due recognition to the urgency of finding a comprehensive and lasting solution to the debt crisis if any real progress is to be made in achieving the Millennium Development Goals.

Justice demands the outright cancellation of all illegitimate debts and the elimination of Structural Adjustment Programs. The root causes of injustice and inequality underlying the debt crisis must be addressed. The credibility of the Northern countries' commitment to financing for development in the post-Monterrey context hinges in a fundamental way on their willingness to take up this challenge.

The Ecumenical Team advocates the Jubilee principle of a fair start, to include:

- the outright cancellation of the bilateral and multilateral debts of the poorest countries within the next five years;
- substantial debt reduction for severely indebted middle-income countries;
- immediate repatriation to the countries concerned of funds held by foreign banks obtained from corrupt public officials;
- the elimination of structural adjustment programs (SAPs) imposed by of such programs to intense public scrutiny in the countries concerned;
- the establishment of an independent, fair and transparent arbitration mechanism between sovereign debtors and their creditors, which will, in addition, be responsible for promote ethical lending and borrowing policies. This mechanism should be under the guidance of the United Nations, with four key elements:
  - a neutral decision-making body;
  - the right of all stakeholders to be heard;
  - the protection of the debtor's basic needs, and
  - a guarantee of an automatic stay of debt servicing once the case is opened.

Statement on the proposed "Monterrey Consensus Document" issued by the Ecumenical Team, 18-22 March 2002.

Critique of the Monterrey Consensus Document

Financing cannot and must not be seen to be an end in itself. It must focus on people-centered development. But this is a concept which has been pushed to the margins of the FfD process. We should not forget that we live in a world in which the powerful 20% of the world's population consumes more than 83% of the global income; a world rife with conflicts, most with poverty at their root; a world characterized by economic inequity and competition for the control of resources.

The Monterrey Consensus Document offers too little to such a world. It is not explicit either on control of financial markets or on the promotion of equity and human rights as factors in world trade. There is not even an explicit time frame to meet the commitments set out in the document. We believe that this is what this world expects from the nations and global economic institutions related to financing for development.

It is also evident that the drastic financial liberalization that has so significantly shaped the results of the FfD process, harms developing countries rather than benefits them. Contrary to the views of those whose ideas have influenced the FfD process, it exposes economies with weak financial infrastructures to the speculative forces of world financial markets, shaking their socio-economic integrity to breaking point. It is the sovereign right of each nation to take discretionary capital control measures whenever necessary. It is the duty of every nation to promote the common goal of economic prosperity for all and to work to re-shape the future agendas of the International Financial Institutions in such a way as to prevent policy discussions from unilateralism when it comes to capital flows and investment.

Are not the lessons drawn from the financial crisis in Asia and the virtual social, political and economic collapse of Argentina not enough to demonstrate the failure of conventional economic models which ignore the development of the people in favour of the growth of financial capital?

The instrument of Poverty Reduction Strategy Papers (PRSPs) under the HIPC programme, has failed to solve the financial problems of the Highly Indebted Countries because it is tied to Structural Adjustment programmes (SAPs) which shift resources from the poor to the rich, nationally and globally. The WCC flatly rejects such economic models as being contrary to the notion of economic equity sought by Christians.

The Monterrey Consensus Document is notably uncritical especially of the neo-liberal economic model. This model holds out no real hope for eliminating or even reducing poverty, but rather continues to exacerbate it. It increases inequality and excludes communities around the world. This model was neither critiqued during the FfD preparation process nor mentioned in the final document. We are concerned that a United Nations conference will again be dominated by the neo-liberal economic policies of the World Trade Organization, the World Bank and the International Monetary Fund.

The policies of these institutions have not changed significantly from those our general secretary, Rev. Dr Konrad Raiser, criticised in his open letter to UN Secretary-General Kofi Annan, at the time of the World Summit on Social Development in June 2000. They have failed to bridge the gap between the rich and the poor or to achieve greater equality. Instead they have contributed to widening the gap to the virtual exclusion of an increasing number of people languishing in poverty, to widespread social disintegration and, by condoning economic crimes and contributing to wars, pose a present threat to peace and international security.

Tangible Commitments and Actions

We have all witnessed how the declarations pile up year after year without serious implementation. Like so many others the Monterrey Consensus Document does not propose any binding obligations. This leads us to the question about which, if any, countries actually intend to implement the six areas outlined for financing for development. We hope our doubts are unfounded, and that states will declare their intention to implement to the full these minimal norms. This will not be considered enough by people in poverty throughout the world. Thus we urge the UN to undertake a critical review of the neo-liberal economic paradigm and to attend to the following three major points: 1) the elimination of structural inequalities in the global trading system and the establishment of mutuality, transparency and public participation in future negotiations; 2) pursuit of a permanent solution to the debt problem both for poor countries and middle-income countries starting with an immediate cancellation of the external debt of poor countries and setting up, under UN auspices, an independent and fair debt arbitration mechanism for current and future loans which will promote ethical lending and borrowing policies; and 3) strengthen the UN's role in the fields of global economic, finance, trade and social policy through strengthening the capacity of ECOSOC and UNCTAD to deal effectively with these issues.

The WCC advocates a people-centred approach

The WCC has, for almost all of the 54 years of its existence, emphasized both the importance of global justice and equitable sharing of resources as essential prerequisites for human development. The WCC has also advocated appropriate public and non-governmental policies which will be of real benefit to people in poverty. In keeping with that tradition, the WCC and the Lutheran World Federation (LWF), together with other churches and church-related organizations, have cooperated as an Ecumenical Team to follow the preparations for the International Conference on Financing for Development to be held in Monterrey, Mexico, 18-22 March 2002. Other organizations which have joined the WCC on the Ecumenical Team include the Latin American Council of Churches (CLAI), the General Board of Church and Society of the United Methodist Church (USA), the United Church of Christ (USA), the Sisters of Mercy, the International Shinto Foundation and the Anglican Communion.

Based on a document entitled, *Justice: The Heart of the Matter - An Ecumenical Approach to Financing for Development*, the Ecumenical Team has taken up the six areas identified by the UN Member States and the UN Secretariat as critical in financing for development.

Real value, in the final instance, cannot be expressed in monetary terms. Life, and that which is essential to sustain it, cannot be commodified. We firmly believe, and reiterate now, that a people-centred approach to financing for development is essential to "remake the world" into a place where no one is excluded, no one is deprived of their social power to participate in decisions related to their lives.

The WCC will stay engaged to that end, working with all those who share such a goal. We hope that the "change of heart" for which our ecumenical teams have been calling over these past years, will happen for some in the Monterrey Conference and that we can join hands together for the sake of life, of human dignity and for the human security that justice alone can provide.

Written and Oral Submissions to other UN Bodies

Commission and Subcommission on Human Rights

1999: Oral intervention on human rights violations in Nigeria and Indonesia, Geneva, 7 April.

Oral intervention on religious intolerance presented to the Commission on behalf of the WCC, LWF, WARC and CEC noting violations in Uzbekistan and Pakistan, and supporting the work of the Special Rapporteur, Geneva, 9 April.

Oral intervention on impunity in Guatemala, 13 April.

Oral intervention calling for rapid progress on Indigenous Peoples' concerns, 19 April.

2000: "Sharing the land, the truth and the peace," oral intervention at the Fifth Special Session of the Commission devoted to the human rights situation in the occupied Palestinian territories, Geneva, 17 October.

Written submissions to the Commission on religious intolerance; discrimination against Dalits in India; and on human rights violations in Indonesia.

Oral intervention at the Commission on mass exoduses and displaced persons.

2001: Oral intervention to the Subcommission on measures to improve the situation and ensure the human rights and dignity of all migrant workers, February.

Written statements to the Commission on economic, social and cultural rights in the context of globalisation and on religious freedom, liberty and religious intolerance.

Oral intervention on violations of human rights in the occupied Arab territories, including Palestine to the Commission, Geneva, 28 March.

Oral intervention on the violation of human rights and fundamental freedom in West Papua/Irian Jaya, Indonesia and Cyprus, 2 April.

Oral intervention made on behalf of the CCIA by Monsignor Alvaro Ramazzini, Roman Catholic Bishop of the San Marcos Diocese, Interdiocesan Project for the Recovery of Historical Memory (REMHI), on the protection of freedom of opinion and expression in Guatemala, calling for the renewal of the UN mandate for oversight of the human rights aspects of the Guatemala peace accord, 6 April.

2002: Written Statement on civil and political rights, including the question of torture and detention.

Oral intervention on Israeli violations of human rights and international law, especially of the Fourth Geneva Convention, and endorsing the High Commissioner for Human Rights' call for an international presence to reduce violence, restore respect for human rights and create conditions propitious for negotiations, Geneva, 2 April.

Oral intervention on the urgent need for increased human rights protections for refugees and internally displaced persons, Geneva, 4 April.

Oral intervention on the increasing environment of repression in West Papua/Irian Jaya, urging the Commission to use its influence with the Government of Indonesia to cease human rights violations and repression in this territory, Geneva, 16 April.

Review of Developments pertaining to the promotion and protection of human rights and fundamental freedoms of Indigenous Peoples

Intervention at the UN Working Group on Indigenous Populations, Geneva, 23-27 July 2001.

Madam Chair, distinguished members of the Working Group, indigenous brothers and sisters,

Thank you for this opportunity to address the meeting. I am a Maori from Aotearoa New Zealand, representing the Commission of the Churches on International Affairs of the World Council of Churches (WCC).

Throughout the past two years the WCC has facilitated three significant meetings for Indigenous Peoples exploring issues of land and identity, environment and racism, and inter religious dialogue.

In each of these meetings, Indigenous Peoples said the same thing. "We continue in the struggle against oppression, against that which would make us less than who we are, against that which would seek to separate us from the core elements of our identity, that is - our land, language, culture, and self determination."

Madam Chair, the WCC remains committed to the struggle of Indigenous Peoples. We welcome the incremental progress of the establishment of a Permanent Forum and the recent creation of the post for a Special Rapporteur. We look forward to the adoption of the draft declaration on the rights of Indigenous Peoples and we view each of these mechanisms as vital to ensuring that basic human rights of Indigenous Peoples are upheld.

Of course, in tandem with these developments is the need for *full and meaningful participation* of Indigenous Peoples in these same processes. Indeed, the preceding interventions have also highlighted this same issue. Indigenous Peoples continue to call for consultation that is cognisant of their right of participation in processes which will impact upon them. The WCC takes seriously this challenge, and within its own limited means, continues to accompany Indigenous Peoples in the regional processes for the selection of indigenous representatives to the Permanent Forum. We would encourage member states and relevant UN representatives to do the same.

Madam Chair, the processes and forums of the United Nations are very much removed from the day-to-day realities of ordinary people who wish merely to enjoy a fullness of life that should be theirs by right. As we sit in meetings, children grow up in the midst of war; as we lobby delegates and other UN representatives, parents wonder how they will find the food to feed their families today; and as we argue over words and semantics, entire communities find themselves subjected to a jurisprudence of oppression that is overwhelming in its power.

I would like to end with the words of an indigenous woman from northern Ghana, shared in a WCC meeting, who faced with the onslaught of desertification on her tribal lands, as a result of poor development models says:

"If I had poisoned darts, I would shoot at this monster that dries up the streams, that drives dusty winds into my eyes and blows the topsoil away. The heartless monster that dictates what we eat, and that has enslaved me to work for it."

Madam Chair, there is an urgency to these words that we cannot ignore. There is a cry for help that we cannot turn away from. The responsibility is ours and the moment is now.

Special Committee on the Situation with regard to the Implementation of the Declaration on the Granting of Independence to Colonial Countries and Peoples
Statement to the United Nations Seminar on Assistance to the Palestinian People, Division for Palestinian Rights, Vienna, 20-21 February 2001.

Remarks were made to the meeting on behalf of the CCIA by Dr. Bernard Sabella, Executive Secretary, Department of Service to Palestine Refugees, Middle East Council of Churches

Appeal for self-determination for Puerto Rico delivered by the Rev. Eunice Santana, New York, 6 July 1999.

Una vez más comparecemos ante este distinguido Comité de Descolonización de la Organización de las Naciones Unidas en representación del Consejo Mundial de Iglesias. APRA reiterar nuestra posición en torno al caso de Puerto Rico y para solicitarles nuevamente que actúen, acorde con su mandato, asegurando que el pueblo de Puerto Rico ejerza su derecho a la autodeterminación con libertad de conciencia y libre de toda coerción.

Al hablar del pueblo puertorriqueño hablamos de un pueblo que anhela y lucha a favor de la paz y que ansia que se le haga justicia como queda evidenciado sobretodo por el caso de Vieques. Esta es la historia de un pueblo atrapado para el cual la Segunda Guerra Mundial aún no termina. Es la historia de un pueblo que está cansado de los juegos de guerra; cansado de ser cómplice de la agresión contra otros pueblos hermanos y la destrucción de la Creación de Dios. Un pueblo cansado de que se le impongan restricciones que le privan del derecho a moverse con libertad dentro de su propio territorio; de que el ruido de las explosiones les interrumpa su vida, los estudios, la hora de la cena y el recreo, el sueño y hasta los momentos de hacerse el amor. Es un pueblo cansado de vivir con el temor de que algún accidente les quite la vida y de que mientras tanto otros se la controlen. Un pueblo cansado de ver a sus hijos marcharse fuera del país en busca de mejores condiciones de vida, de no tener medios a través de los cuales ganarse su sustento

165

y de que aún los más elementales derechos humanos les sean pisoteados y negados como lo son el derecho al trabajo, a la seguridad, a la salud, al disfrute de los recursos naturales, al desarrollo social pleno que erradique la pobreza, a la felicidad – en fin – a la Vida misma.

Esta es una historia sobre el poder y el abuso del poder: de militarismo, injusticias, destrucción del medio ambiente, contaminación de todo tipo, cáncer, arrestos, encarcelamientos, y muerte. Es una historia comparable a la historia bíblica de David y Goliat en la cual un jovencito lucha contra un gigante.

El caso de Puerto Rico nos presenta la historia de un pueblo que no se da por vencido, que vive inmerso en la búsqueda de la paz, la justicia, la defensa de los derechos humanos y el sentido de la vida. Pero es también la historia de un pueblo latinoamericano y caribeño que está cansado de ser invisible, de sentir que nadie le escucha y de no poder ejercer su derecho a la autodeterminación.

Todo este cansancio es causa de preocupación para amplios sectores en Puerto Rico, incluyendo a las iglesias. El desbalance craso entre lo que la gente desea y pide y las respuestas que recibe, por ejemplo, de la Marina de Guerra y el gobierno de los Estados Unidos, van creando las condiciones para la desestabilización social. Mientras que en Puerto Rico se ha levantado un consenso en contra de la presencia militar en Vieques y amplios sectores del pueblo repudian la utilización militar que se le da al país, Estados Unidos insiste en continuar con las prácticas militares así como incrementar estos renglones con el traslado del Comando Sur a Puerto Rico y la construcción de un sistema de radares (Relocatable Over the Horizon Radar) que incluye la isla municipio de Vieques y otro lugar en la Isla Grande. Todo esto apunta hacia unas imposiciones violatorias de derechos y una determinación unilateral por parte de EE UU de no ceder su control sobre Puerto Rico y de imposibilitar el ejercicio a la libre determinación del pueble puertorriqueño.

Otro asunto sobre el cual existe un consenso en Puerto Rico, y que está relacionado con los procesos y los derechos de los pueblos, es a favor de la excarcelación de las mujeres y los hombres, presos políticos puertorriqueños, que actualmente están encarcelados en Estados Unidos. El Consejo Mundial de Iglesias, así como otros organismos ecuménicos e internacionales, ha unido su voz a la de las iglesias en Puerto Rico y de miles de personas, dentro y fuera de Puerto Rico, que le han solicitado al Presidente de Estados Unidos que actúe a su favor por entender que éste es un reclamo justo que le compete a toda la comunidad.

Abogamos a favor de un proceso válido de descolonización para Puerto Rico bajo de los cánones establecidos por la Organización de las Naciones Unidas y su escrutinio. Somos conscientes y concurrimos con la determinación de las Naciones Unidas de que la validez de cualquier referéndum requiere el retiro de la presencia militar del país interventor del territorio invadido por esta representar un impedimento contundente al principio y al proceso de autodeterminación mismo. Además, la presencia militar es de por sí violatoria de otros derechos fundamentales, controla la economía y la ecología, entre otros renglones, y sobretodo está en abierta oposición con el principio básico e inviolable de la soberanía.

Señoras y señores miembros de este distinguido cuerpo, al igual que hicimos el año pasado, le hacemos un llamado en nombre de las iglesias y del Consejo Mundial de Iglesias para que exijan la descolonización para Puerto Rico de acuerdo a la Resolución 1514 (XV) de este Comité. Renovamos nuestra invitación anterior a efectuar una visita sobre el terreno para ver con sus propios ojos lo que aquí les presentamos y para recibir información mas detallada.

Reiteramos nuestro requerimiento de que este Comité asuma su responsabilidad respecto a los territorios que aún no ejercen gobierno propio en relación con el caso de Puerto Rico. Es necesario que este Comité actúe creando las condiciones propias APRA que pronto se dé un proceso legítimo de auto determinación para el pueblo puertorriqueño. Es necesario que la Organización de las Naciones Unidas asuma el papel que le ha sido asignado de erradicar el colonialismo a través de procesos válidos asegurando que los pueblos puedan expresar su voluntad libremente. Mientras esto no suceda en Puerto Rico su agenda está inconclusa, la humanidad sufre y la justicia y la paz permanecen como meras aspiraciones imposibles de alcanzar.

Señoras y señores, ante Uds. dejamos este reto, que representa además una oportunidad magnífica para demostrarle al mundo que la esperanza no ha muerto, que aún es posible crear un mundo temor para todas y todos en el cual los derechos colectivos y de unos/as y otros/as sean reconocidos y respetados, permitiendo así una sana convivencia entre los pueblos, lo cual a nuestro entender, desde la fe, nos acerca mas a la voluntad de Dios.

Muchas gracias.

[TRANSLATION]

Once again we appear before this disinguished Decolonization Committee of the United Nations Organization on behalf of the World Council of Churches to reiterate our position with respect to the case of Puerto Rico and to solicit again your action, under your mandate, to assure that the people of Puerto Rico may exercize its right to self-determination with freedom of conscience and free from all coercion.

When we speak of the Puerto Rican people, we speak of a people that longs and struggles for peace and that hopes that justice will be done in the case of Vieques. This is the story of a captive people for whom the Second World War has not yet ended. It is the story of a people that is tired of the war games; tired of being made accomplices of aggression against other peoples and the destruction of God's Creation; tired of the restrictions imposed that deprive them of their right

167

to move freely within its own territory; for whom the noise of explosions disrupt their lives, their studies, mealtimes and recreation, their sleep and even their lovemaking. It is a people tired of living with the fear that some accident will take their lives while others are in control of the threat. A people tired of seeing its children leave the country in search of better living conditions, of not having the means to earn their own living and of having their most fundamental rights trampled upon and denied, rights like that to work, security, health, dispose of their own natural resources, full social development to eradicate poverty, to happiness, and – finally – to life itself.

This is a story of power and the abuse of power: of militarism, injustices, destruction of the environment, contamination of every sort: cancer, arrests, detentions and death. It is a story comparable to the bibilical story of David and Goliath where a youth struggles against a giant.

The case of Puerto Rico presents the story of a people that does not give up, that lives immersed in the pursuit of peace, justice, the defense of human rights and the meaning of life. It is also the story of a Latin American and Caribbean people that is tired of being invisible, of feeling that no one listens and of being unable to exercise its right to self-determination.

This weariness is a source of concern to broad sectors in Puerto Rico, including the churches. The crass imbalance between what the people desire and demand and the answers it receives, for example, from the Navy and the government of the United States, are creating conditions for social unrest.

While in Puerto Rico a consensus has arisen against the military presence in Vieques and broad sectors of the people repudiate the military use given to the country, the United States insists on continuing with its military exercise and has increased its forces on the ground through the moving of the Southern Command headquarters to PuertoRico and the construction of a new radar system (Relocatable Over the Horizon Radar) on the municipal island of Vieques and another site on the Isla Grande. All this points to further impositions in violation of rights and a unilateral determination on the part of the USA not to cede its control over Puerto Rico and to make impossible the free exercise of self-determination of the Puerto Rican people.

Another concern on which there exists a consensus in Puerto Rico, and that is related to the processes and the rights of peoples, is the demand for the release of the women and men, Puerto Rican political prisoners, presently incarcerated in the United States. The World Council of Churches, joined by other ecumenical and international organizations, has joined its voice with that of the churches in Puerto Rico and of thousands of persons in and beyond Puerto Rico that have asked the President of the United States, in his own interest, to respond to this appeal as a matter of justice for the whole community.

168

We call for a valid process of decolonization for Puerto Rico to be undertaken according to the established norms of the United Nations Organization and under its scrutiny. We are aware of and we agree with the determination of the United Nations that the validity of any referendum requires the prior withdrawal of the military presence of the intervening power from the invaded territory since this poses a serious impediment to the principle and process of self-determination. Beyond this, the military presence is in violation of other fundamental rights: it controls the economy and the ecology, among other things, and above all it violates the basic and inviolable principle of sovereignty.

Ladies and gentlemen, members of this distinguished body, as we did last year, we call upon you in the name of the churches and the World Council of Churches to demand the decolonization of Puerto Rico in accordance with Resolution 1514 (XV) of this Committee. We renew our invitation to you to visit the territory to see for yourselves what we have presented here and to receive more detailed information.

We reiterate our request that this Committee assume its responsibility with respect to non-self-governing territories in relation to the case of Puerto Rico. It is necessary for this Committee to create propitious conditions for a prompt and legitimate process of self-determination to be undertaken for the Puerto Rican people. It is necessary that the United Nations Organization assume the role it has been assigned to eradicate colonialism and through valid processes to assure that peoples may be able freely to express their will. So long as this does not occur in Puerto Rico your agenda is not concluded, humanity suffers and justice and peace remain mere hopes that are impossible to achieve.

Ladies and genetlemen, this challenge that we place before you represents a magnificent opportunity to demonstrate to the world that hope is not dead, that it is still possible to create a better world for all in which the collective rights of all are recognized and respected, thereby permitting healthy coexistence among the peoples, and to move in the direction that we believe, based on our faith, corresponds to the will of God.

Many thanks.

Appeal for justice for residents of the island of Vieques, press release on the statement presented on behalf of the CCIA, New York, 12 July 2000.

A statement delivered on behalf of the WCC's Commission of the Churches on International Affairs (CCIA) to the UN Committee on Granting of Independence to Colonial Countries and Peoples also asked for assistance to Puerto Ricans in securing justice for residents of Vieques, one of the smaller islands of Puerto Rico just east of the main island.

The statement was presented by Eunice Santana, a Disciples of Christ minister and former WCC president who directs the Caribbean Institute of Ecumenical Formation and Action in Arecibo, Puerto Rico.

Speaking in Spanish, Santana said the decade for the elimination of colonialism, launched by the UN in 1990, had ended without a solution for Puerto Rico, and left one of humanity's most disgraceful situations.

She reminded the Committee that she had drawn its attention to Vieques in delivering WCC statements in 1998 and 1999, and said actions of the United States Navy there in the past 15 months showed a continuing lack of regard for the rights of the Puerto Rican people.

Hundreds of Puerto Ricans camped out in the restricted part of Vieques used by the US Navy since 1941 for practice operations – risking their lives as human shields – and many of them, including a bishop and dozens of clergy, were arrested, she said. The protesters were inspired by the liberation experience revealed in the Bible, she told the UN.

Last November, CCIA director Dwain C. Epps wrote to President Bill Clinton in support of the protests. And on 2 May, when plans for the arrests had been announced, WCC general secretary Konrad Raiser said in a follow-up letter that such arrests will hardly be understood by the churches, and urged that Clinton call a halt to this intervention immediately. However, the protesters were arrested two days later.

Santana said a referendum proposed by the US Navy to let the people of Vieques decide whether to accept US Dollars 40 million for its use of the disputed area for three years or US Dollars 50 million for permanent use was a bad joke. She said this would require the people to sell their conscience, and excluded the option most people would prefer - immediate departure of the Navy.

She appealed for a legitimate process of self-determination by the Puerto Rican people. And she appealed for the UN Committee's help in getting the United States to end bombardment of Vieques, clean up the area, compensate the people of Vieques for the damages they have suffered and return the area to them.

As the UN Committee heard a series of speakers, it had before it a resolution introduced by Cuba asserting that initiatives previously taken had failed to set in motion the process of decolonization of Puerto Rico, and noting with satisfaction that proposals had been made for a sovereign Constituent Conference of the people of Puerto Rico.

Referring to Puerto Ricans convicted of violent protest actions in the United States, the resolution welcomed the release of 11 of them last year, and called on Clinton to release all Puerto Rican political prisoners.

Spain ceded Puerto Rico to the United States in 1898. Puerto Ricans were made citizens of the United States in 1917, and later gained the right to elect their own governor and legislature, and to send a non-voting representative to the US House of Representatives. But they do not vote in US elections or pay US taxes.

In a 1993 referendum, 48 per cent of Puerto Rican voters favoured retaining their current commonwealth status, 44 per cent becoming a state of the United States, and 4 per cent independence. However, some Puerto Ricans say the referendum did not resolve the Puerto Rican issue because of the way political parties were involved, and a new approach such as a Constituent Conference is needed.

The WCC statement to the UN Committee did not endorse the Cuban resolution, but Santana said afterwards it was compatible with the WCC position. And she reported that she was very happy when the committee approved the resolution by consensus at the end of the day's hearings. Similar resolutions were adopted in previous years, but always by divided votes, she said.

RECOGNITIONS

Congratulations on the award of the Nobel Peace Prize

Letter to H.E. Kofi Annan, Secretary-General and to Ms. Rosemarie Waters, President of the UN Staff Committee, 16 October 2001.

Dear Mr Secretary-General and Mme President,

The World Council of Churches sends its hearty congratulations for the award to you of the Nobel Peace Prize for 2001.

Mr Secretary-General, this prize justly recognizes the roles of global mediator, negotiator, peacemaker and guardian of the international rule of law that you have performed so brilliantly during your first term in office. Coming as it does when you have been elected to a new term of office this award is a welcome reflection of the broad international support you have for the wise leadership you have provided as the leader of the United Nations.

The purpose of this award was also to recognize the whole of the United Nations. Though the UN is not only its staff, we are especially delighted that this extraordinary body of far-flung, greatly talented, deeply committed international civil servants who provide leadership to the United Nations in every corner of the world has also been recognized. You have come up through these ranks. You know the qualities of these people. You are at one with them.

Mme President, through you we would like to address directly the members of the United Nations staff in New York and around the world, from the 38th floor to the sub-basements of UN Headquarters and from the chambers of the Security Council to the refugee camps and impoverished local villages. You are the too-often unsung heroes of the world. You are in the backrooms and on the frontlines of the efforts of the United Nations to address the most challenging and complex agenda ever confronted by humanity.

We have been with you from San Francisco to Lake Placid to Turtle Bay; at the Palais des Nations; and in Paris, Rome, Vienna and Nairobi. We have worked with you at the General Assembly and in commissions and committees for more than half a century. Perhaps more importantly, we have been alongside you as you have undertaken complex negotiations for peace and respect for human rights, and as you have sought to bring sanitation, health services and protection to the poorest and most vulnerable of the world's people. We are painfully aware of the human costs of this engagement, including the large number of UN staff who have given their lives in the pursuance of their duties.

The occasion of the granting of the Nobel Prize for peace to you offers us the opportunity to thank you all for your part in seeking to embody and give life to the aspirations of the Peoples of the United Nations expressed in the Preamble to the Charter. Our prayers are with you particularly in this, perhaps the most challenging moment in recent years, as you pursue your weighty responsibilities on behalf of us all.

Yours cordially,

Georges Lemopoùlos
Acting General Secretary

UPROOTED PEOPLE

Statement on the Fiftieth Anniversary of the Creation of the Office of the United Nations High Commissioner for Refugees (UNHCR)
Adopted by the Executive Committee, Geneva, 26-29 September 2000. (cf p. 117)

Resolution on uprooted people
Adopted by the Executive Committee, Berlin, Germany, 26-27 January 2001.

Background. The WCC Central Committee adopted a major policy statement on uprooted people in 1995, emphasizing the increasingly grave plight of refugees and migrants in a time of escalating conflicts around the world. Over the past five years the situation has become much worse still. The pressures of globalization and the persistence of intractable conflicts are leading ever more people to leave their communities or their countries. Of the 150 million people living outside their country of origin, only about 17 million are recognized as refugees by the United Nations High Commissioner for Refugees or by the UN Relief and Works Administration for Palestinian refugees. In fact, the number of recognized refugees has slightly declined in the past five years. However, the number of people displaced within the borders of their own countries has increased dramatically as governments make it more difficult for refugees to find safety in other countries. Presently they number close to 35 million.

In every region around the world, racism and xenophobia are on the rise. Refugees and migrants are viewed more as threats than as human beings in need and are used as scapegoats by political leaders under pressure to protect jobs and national economies. Uprooted people often find borders closed when they manage to get to them, and are frequently expelled if they succeed in crossing them. Governments in all regions are increasingly putting asylum-seekers into detention, or prison, as a way of deterring others from coming. People who are desperate to leave their countries are victimized by traffickers and migrants are increasingly treated as criminals.

Assistance to refugees. Uprooted people very often turn to the churches for assistance, as they have for centuries. For more than six decades the World Council of Churches has provided a focal point for the churches' response. Even before its formation in 1948 churches related to the WCC (in process of formation) worked together to help refugees escape German-occupied Europe. Later, they played leadership roles in seeking solutions for those displaced in the aftermath of World War II and the 1948 war in Palestine. They advocated for the creation of and cooperated closely with the office of the United Nations High Commissioner for Refugees (UNHCR). By the late 1960s, WCC member churches had responded to refugee crises throughout Africa as wars for independence and political conflicts generated new refugee flows. The 1970s and 1980s witnessed the globalization of the refugee phenomena, with massive refugee outflows from Afghanistan, Indochina, Sri Lanka, Latin America and the Caribbean. In the 1990s, conflicts in the former Yugoslavia, and later in Chechnya, made it clear that refugee issues in Europe were far from solved. In all of these cases, many churches responded generously and often courageously to the needs of refugees. In these cases, as it did from the beginning, WCC's service with uprooted people included a strong advocacy component.

Internally displaced people. At the same time, churches began to realize that the problems of displacement went far beyond traditional concerns for refugees. Growing numbers of people were uprooted because of violence but unable to leave their countries. They fled for the same reasons as refugees and often had greater protection and assistance needs, but there was no international institution like the United Nations High Commissioner for Refugees, to whom they could appeal for help. It was the WCC, in cooperation with the Friends World Committee for Consultation (FWCC), that first placed the issue of internally displaced people on the international agenda by documenting their needs to the UN Human Rights Commission.

Migrants. The needs of migrants, most leaving their countries for "voluntary" economic reasons, were always considered differently from those of refugees fleeing persecution. Yet in a globalizing world of increasing inequality, growing numbers of marginalized people simply can no longer survive in their home countries. While international law draws a clear distinction between refugees, migrants, internally displaced people and returnees, the churches' mandate is to reach out to all those in need. Thus in its 1995 statement the WCC referred to "uprooted people" to encompass everyone forced to leave their communities, regardless of the labels they are given by the international community.

Protection. At the international level, international protection standards are under attack on many fronts:

- Governments seeking to restrict the number of asylum-seekers arriving at their borders apply increasingly narrow interpretations of the 1951 Geneva convention on refugees and its 1967 protocol. Some maintain that asylum can only be granted to individuals who are persecuted by their own states, rejecting those persecuted by non-state actors or who live in a country without a functioning state.

- While some governments have found that women persecuted because of their gender have legitimate asylum claims, others do not acknowledge gender-based persecution as grounds for asylum. Under the 1951 Geneva Convention on Refugees, decisions on the granting of asylum should be made on a case-by-case basis, but many governments now routinely exclude whole classes of individuals from asylum procedures. Some governments have questioned the widely-accepted right to family reunification, the right of recognized refugees to be joined by their families.

- More and more governments argue that the Convention itself needs re-examination in light of increasing migration flows, leading to fears that international standards will be further weakened.

- The UNHCR is under mounting financial pressures that threaten its ability to fulfill its mandate, and some governments tend now to turn to other actors to perform lead roles in humanitarian emergencies resulting in massive displacement of persons.

- Despite more than 13 years of efforts, emerging international standards for the protection of internally displaced people do not yet have official UN sanction nor are they implemented in practice.

- Ten years after its adoption by the UN General Assembly, the number of ratifications necessary to bring the 1990 International Convention on the Rights of Migrant Workers and Their Families into force has not been achieved, and not a single country which hosts large numbers of migrants has even signed the Convention.

Other general trends regarding uprooted people are matters of serious concern:

- Growing expressions of xenophobic and racial violence against refugees and migrants in many countries.

- Increasing tendencies to consider migrants as criminals, rather than as victims of internationally organized traffickers in human beings.

- Declining financial assistance from government and church-related agencies to ecumenical and church-related ministries to uprooted people in the most affected regions of the world.

Convinced that the churches can and must support international initiatives underway to arrest these trends and to intensify their own ministries with uprooted people along the lines of the WCC 1995 policy statement:

The Executive Committee of the World Council of Churches, meeting in Berlin, Germany, 26-27 January 2001,

Recalling and reaffirming the 1995 Statement of the Central Committee, *A Moment to Choose: Risking to Be with Uprooted People;*

Recognizing the growing complexity and severity of the situation confronted by uprooted people and by the churches seeking to accompany them;

Mindful of the importance of international legal standards for the protection and assistance for all uprooted people in need;

Aware of the serious and growing unmet protection needs for refugees, internally displaced people and migrants

Conscious of the growing racist and xenophobic climate in many countries of the world, and

Commending the actions of churches in many countries in solidarity with victims of acts of aggression against foreigners and their efforts to create a climate of hospitality for uprooted people;

Reaffirms ministry to uprooted people as a central biblical mandate for the churches;

Renews its call upon the churches in all regions to offer support, solidarity and accompaniment to those who have been forced to leave their communities, and to strengthen their own churches' and ecumenical ministries with uprooted people;

Welcomes and reaffirms the Executive Committee's statement of September 2000 on the 50th Anniversary of UNHCR supporting its central mandate of protection;

Urges church and church-related agencies to review and increase their financial support for ecumenical work with uprooted people, especially in the most affected regions;

Encourages the churches to strengthen or to undertake advocacy with their own governments, with relevant regional inter-governmental bodies and with international bodies on behalf of refugees, migrants and internally displaced people, particularly with regard to:

• provision of adequate financial and political support to UNHCR and UNRWA;

• the Global Consultations on Refugee Protection organized by UNHCR, reaffirming the 1951 UN Convention on Refugees and an interpretation of the Convention which includes recognition of non-state actors as agents of persecution, gender-based persecution as grounds for asylum, strictly limited policies of exclusion, and the right of refugees to family reunification;

• international discussions on the protection and assistance of internally displaced people, urging the Inter-agency Standing Committee to develop effective coordinating mechanisms, and supporting the UN's Senior Inter-Agency Network on Internal Displacement;

• the 1990 International Convention on the Rights of All Migrant Workers and their Families, urging their governments to sign and ratify this convention as soon as possible and to use it to raise awareness about the particular needs of migrants in their communities;

• the World Conference on Racism, Racial Discrimination, Xenophobia, and Related Intolerance, advocating with their governments and in the UN preparatory process that the Conference address the particular abuses of migrants.

ASYLUM

Expression of concern about treatment of asylum seekers

Letter to WCC Member Churches in Australia and the National Council of Churches in Australia, 29 August 2001. (cf p. 279)

MIGRATION AND MIGRANTS' RIGHTS

Call for investigation into abuses of human rights of migrants in the countries of the Persian Gulf

Letter to Ms Gabriela Rodriguez, UN special rapporteur on the Human Rights of Migrants, 24 November 2000.

Dear Ms Rodriguez,

We are deeply concerned about the situation of migrant workers in the Persian Gulf countries and ask you to investigate their situation as part of your mandate.

The many reports of beatings, deaths and suicides of domestic migrant workers make such an investigation by your office necessary.

The International Catholic Migration Commission and the World Council of Churches have a long history of advocating for the rights of migrant workers. It is in that spirit that we ask your office to take up the challenge of examining the particular needs of migrant workers in the Gulf.

As you know, large numbers of migrant workers are present in the Gulf countries; although accurate statistics are not available, we understand that they number close to twelve million, with the majority coming from South Asia and Egypt.

We know from reports of human rights organizations, migrants' associations and other sources, that migrants in the Gulf face serious difficulties. Of particular concern to us are reports of serious abuse, the routine confiscation of passports by employers or sponsors, and the lack of adequate judicial recourse when conflicts arise between workers and employers.

We are especially troubled by the vulnerability of workers whose passports are taken by their employers. Moreover, the involvement of private recruitment and sponsoring agencies makes it difficult to assign responsibility when a migrant worker does not receive promised wages or benefits. When legal recourse does exist, it is often so time-consuming and expensive that migrants are unable to use such mechanisms.

Domestic workers are particularly vulnerable because they are not included in the labour laws of most Gulf countries. This means they have no legal recourse whatsoever when an employer requires them to work eighteen hours a day, seven days a week.

In a world where migrant workers face difficulties in every region, the situation in the Gulf countries is a particularly difficult one which requires further investigation. Unlike other parts of the world where migrant workers are present, there are no local organizations in the Gulf which can give migrants a voice.

We hope your office will be able to visit the region to collect first-hand accounts of the situation from both governments and migrants, and then to recommend appropriate actions to the UN Human Rights Commission.

Respectfully,

Dwain C. Epps	William Canny
Director	Secretary-General
Commission of the Churches	International Catholic
on International Affairs	Migration Commission

REGIONAL CONCERNS

AFRICA

ANGOLA

Statement on Peace in Angola
Sent to the WCC Central Committee from the Executive Committee of the Council of Christian Churches in Angola, August 1999.

Dirigentes das Igrejas que constituem o Conselho de Igrejas Cristãs em Angola, reunidos na 41ª sessão do Comité Executivo da organização de 5-6 de Agosto/99 no Centro de Formação e Cultura em Luianda; cientes e apreensivos da situação política, social, económica e cultural que se deteriora dia apois dia, havendo por conseguinte necessidade de que algo seja feito para se evitar um desastre humanitário piôr do que os anteriores.

Reconhecemos que Angola tem sido sacrificada por um longo cíclo de guerras que não tem conseguido trazer a paz pelo contraário o país tem sido cada vez mais destruido avolumando-se o número de mortos, pessoas deslocadas, refugiados, mutilados, crianças de ruas e uma cultura de violência que atinge proporções incontroláveis.

Nós Dirigentes de Igrejas reunidos neste magno Comité Executivo, reconhecemos a necessidade urgente de se chamar a nação a razão para se encontrar uma via racional para a solução de conflito.

Neste contexto, nós dirigentes de Igre3jas deste Conselho reconhecemos que Angola e a vida dos angolanos são um dom de Deus que a ninguém compete destruí-las.

O encontro de homens e mulheres de boa vontade previne qualquer violência e por isso, continuamos acreditar que só a consertação entre todos angolanos pode salvar Angola de um conflito eterno.

Para nós, sermos patriotas no nosso contexto deve significar tomar decisões sábias que poupam a vida de todos angolanos, cria um ambiente favorável a realização das suas aspriações, como povo criado por Deus e a sua imagem, e viabilize o desenvolvimento sócio-económico, religioso e cultural..

Para que essa possa ser a nossa sorte:

1. Reconhecemos que somos homens e mulheres de lábios impuros, e que vivemos no meio de um povo impuro, por isso, nos compremetemos a

2. confessar as nossas fraquezas e assumir atitudes que dignificam a vontade do Criador (Deus) para connosco.

3. Nos compremetemos a continuar a trabalhar para unidade e cooperação entre as Igrejas e as forças vivas da nação, interessadas a desenvolver um país pacifico, democrático e próspero.

4. Neste contexto, encorajamos as nossas comunidades e ao povo angolano em geral, aos Dirigentes políticos e religiosos, para terem como agenda prioritária o cessar da violência e a resolução pacífica dos nossos conflitos.

5. Apelamos a todos angolanos e a Comunidades Internacional, a reconhecerem a grave situação humanitária que o país vive e a conjugarmos esforços para que recursos suficientes sejam mobilizados e honestamente utilizados para as comunidades mais vulneráveis.

Finalmente, ao caminharmos para esse final do século, devemos celebrar o Jubileu, isto é o período da graça que nos é oferecido para que povos escravizados em todos os sentidos sejam libertos e capazes de entender a mensagem que diz: *"Deus falará de paz ao seu povo desde que3 os seus santos não voltem a loucura, certamente que a salvação está perto daqueles que o temem. A misericórdia e a verdade se encontram, a justiça e a paz se beijam, o Senhor dará o bem a nossa terra." (Salmos 85:8-13)*

[TRANSLATION]

The leaders of the member churches of the Council of Christian Churches in Angola, at the 41st meeting of its Executive Committee, 5-6 August 1999, at the Formation and Culture Center in Luanda were aware and fearful of the daily worsening political, social, economic and cultural situation. There is thus need for action to be taken to avoid a humanitarian catastrophe greater than previous ones.

We acknowledge that Angola has been the victim of a long series of wars which have not succeeded in bringing peace. On the contrary, the country has been progressively destroyed with increasing numbers of people dying, displaced persons, refugees, disabled people and street children, together with a culture of violence which is reaching uncontrollable levels.

We, the leaders of churches gathered in this Executive Committee, acknowledge the urgent need to call the nation to reason so that it can find a rational way to solve the conflict.

In this context we, the leaders of the churches of this council, acknowledge that Angola and the life of Angolans are a gift from God which no one has the right to destroy.

Encounter between men and women of goodwill is a defense against any form of violence and we thus continue to believe that only agreement between all Angolans can save Angola from permanent conflict.

For us to be patriotic in our context must mean taking wise decisions which will save the life of all Angolans, create an environment favorable to the achievement

180

of their hopes as a people created by God in God's image and make possible social, economic, religious and cultural development.

So that this can be our destiny:

1. We acknowledge that we are men and women of unclean lips and that we dwell in the midst of a people of unclean lips and we thus commit ourselves to:

2. Confess our weaknesses and develop attitudes which are worthy of the creator's (God's) will for us;

3. Continue to work for unity and cooperation between the churches and the vital forces in the nation which are concerned to develop a peaceful, democratic and prosperous country;

4. Encourage in this context our communities, the Angolan people in general and political and religious leaders to place at the top of their agenda the cessation of violence and the peaceful resolution of our conflicts;

5. Appeal to all Angolans and to the international community to recognize the grave humanitarian situation the country is experiencing and to join forces with us so that sufficient resources can be mobilized and honestly used for the most vulnerable communities.

Finally, as we move to the end of the century, we must celebrate the Jubilee, this is the time of grace that is offered to us so that peoples enslaved in all ways may be freed and able to hear the message that says, "God will speak peace to his people, to his saints, to those who turn to him in their hearts. Surely his salvation is at hand for those that fear him. Mercy and truth will meet, justice and peace will embrace, the Lord will give what is good to our land." (Psalm 85: 8-13)

Affirmation of ecumenical efforts for peace and justice
Letter to the Rev. Gaspar Domingos, Council of Christian Churches in Angola (SICA), 3 September 1999.

Prezado Rev. Domingos,

O Comité Central do Conselho Mundial de Igrejas, de 26 de agosto a 3 de setembro de 1999, recebeu com apreço a declaração do Comité Central do CICA sobre a paz em Angola. Reconhecemos a sua coragem e as ações que tomaram, as quais são um testemunho eloquente em favor da paz e justiça em seu país.

Nós estamos bem conscientes da enorme tarefa que têm diante de vocês. A necessidade de que os angolanos reunam-se e raciocinem em conjunto, nuca foi tão urgente. Esta necessidade é crítica para reverter a presente situação de assissinatos em massa. Como afirmam muito bem em sua declaração, a vida de cada angolano/a é um presente de Deus e ninguém tem o direito de destrui-la. Ao afirmarmos a santidade da vida, também apoiamos o seu objetivo mencionado de apêlo aos angolanos para que tomem decisões sábias. Decisões estas que poderão salvar a vida angolanos/as.

Agradecemos a sua presença e a do Rev. Caetano na reunião do Comité Central. Tal presença foi de grande beneficio. As discussões e decisões tomadas a respeito da Década cujo o objetivo é superar a violência (Decade to Overcome Violence) são de particular interesse e importáncia para os angolanos e para a situação de conflito está de acordo com a política geral do CMI e com o espírito da Década cujo o objetivo é superar a violência.

A luz do que foi mencionado acima, quero expressar que o CMI está pronto a acompanhar o Conselho de Igrejas Cristãs em Angola na busca da paz, jutiça e reconciliação. Esperamos receber em breve os seus planos de ação a serem implementados.

No aguardo do envio de seus planos, desejamos que seu ministério seja pleno de paz e reconciliação para o seu povo e país. Que a graça de nosso Senhor Jesus Cristo seja com bocês ao prosseguir este ministério tão importante.

Sinceramente,

Rev. Dr Konrad Raiser
Secretário Geral

[TRANSLATION]

Dear Rev. Domingos,

The Central Committee of the World Council of Churches, meeting in Geneva, 26 August – 3 September 1999, received with appreciation the statement of the Executive Committee of the SICA on peace in Angola. We appreciate your courage and the actions that you have taken that are an eloquent witness for peace and justice in your country.

We know well the enormous task that lies ahead of you. The need for Angolans to come together and to reason together has never been so urgent. This is critical to be able to reverse the present situation of mass assassinations. As your statement affirms so clearly, the life of every Angolan is a gift of God and no one has a right to destroy it. As we affirm the sanctity of life we also support the initiative mentioned in the appeal to Angolans to take wise decisions, decisions that could save Angolans lives.

We thank you for your presence and that of Rev. Caetano in the meeting of the Central Committee. That presence was of great benefit. The discussions and decisions taken with respect to the Decade to Overcome Violence are of particular interest and importance for Angolans and for the situation of your country. Your repudiation of all forms of violence in the resolution of conflict corresponds to the policies of the WCC and to the spirit of the Decade, whose objective is to overcome violence.

In the light of the above, I wish to express that the WCC is ready to accompany the Council of Christian Churches in Angola in the pursuit of peace, justice and reconciliation. We hope to receive soon news of the implementation of your plans of action.

In anticipation of receiving your plans, we express the wish that your ministry of peace and reconciliation be fulfilled for your people and your country. May the grace of our Lord Jesus Christ be with you as you pursue this important ministry.

Sincerely,

Rev. Dr Konrad Raiser
General Secretary

Expression of thanks and invitation from the Council of Christian Churches in Angola, Luanda, 29 September 1999.

Sua Excelência
Rev Dr. Konrad Raiser
Secretário Geral do CMI

Estimado no Senhor

Graça e Paz

Sirvo-me desta para expressar em meu nome e no do Conselho que represento, nossa sincera gratidão pela forma como pacientemente soube referir-se quer na vossa missiva como publicamente em relação a questão de Angola bem como os gestos de solidariedade demonstrado aos esforços das Igrejas neste conflito que já é o mais longo de África. Uma vez mais reiteramos nossa expressa vontade de "Não à guerra e sim a Paz". Que o decénio que se avizinha venha consolidar os esforços do fim da violência que a muito procuramos combater.

Desde já no espírito do Comité Executivo bem como de todas Igrejas em Angola, muito nos valeria se dentro do Calendário de Trabalho de S.Excia nos pudesse honrar com uma "Visita Pastoral" nos meses que testemunham o fim desse histórico milénio.

Com os votos de saúde e prosperidade

Somos com cordiais

Saudações Cristãs
Vosso Servo

Rev. Gaspar João Domingos
Secretário Geral do CICA

183

Luanda, 29 September 1999

Your Excellency
Rev. Dr Konrad Raiser
General Secretary of the WCC

Esteemed Sir,

Grace to you and peace

I take this opportunity in my own name and that of the Council which I represent to express our sincere gratitude for your kind open letter in which you refer to the question of Angola and speak of gestures of solidarity with the efforts of the churches caught up in this conflict which is now the longest in Africa. Once again we reiterate our express will to say "No to War and Yes to Peace." May the coming decade consolidate efforts to put an end to the violence which we try so much to combat.

Of course, in the spirit of the Executive Committee and according to the desire of the Angolan churches, we would greatly appreciate it if you were able to include in your schedule a "Pastoral Visit" in the months before the end of this historic millennium.

Wishing you health and prosperity,

We are cordially yours,

Christian greetings,
Your servant,

Rev. Gaspar Joao Domingos
General Secretary of the CICA

CONGO (REPUBLIC)

Appeals for international efforts for peace
Letter to UN Secretary-General Kofi Annan, 2 February 1999.

Dear Mr Secretary-General,

I would like to thank you again for your video-taped message to the World Council of Churches Eighth Assembly, held last December in Harare. It was presented in a plenary session of the Assembly, and viewed appreciatively by the some 5000 delegates, observers and visitors in attendance. We were grateful for the opportunity, on the occasion of the 50th anniversary of the adoption of the Universal Declaration of Human Rights, to be able to demonstrate through your presentation the close relationship we have with the United Nations. In a special declaration on the occasion, the Assembly reiterated the WCC's commitment to the principles of the Declaration, and to the central role of the United Nations in implementing them.

Meeting in Harare, Assembly delegates experienced in person the terrible human cost and pain inflicted on Africans by the many conflicts raging on the continent. This has raised the sense of urgency felt by churches around the world to support our African brothers and sisters in their efforts to achieve peace and embark on the human reconstruction of Africa.

One can and should not draw up a hierarchy of suffering among the many conflicts, all are terrible. But some are worsening because they tend to be ignored by the international press and institutions. One of these is the Republic of Congo (Brazzaville), where in the dark shadow of neighboring conflicts, there is a general breakdown of social structures and escalating fighting more and more openly along ethnic lines.

It is not the intention of this letter, Mr Secretary-General, to inform you of a situation you know well and which you have addressed in public statements. Rather it is to share with you our deep concern and to offer you our support in your efforts to bring this situation back into view in the international community in order that some relief for the suffering population might be sought.

To this end, I have today sent a letter to President Chirac of France, a copy of which is attached for your information, urging his government to give more visible and urgent attention to this situation. In that letter I detail the situation experienced by the Christian communities of the Republic of Congo. Many church leaders who were instrumental in recent efforts to promote national reconciliation have been killed, others have been forced into hiding.

Remarkably, most church leaders have chosen to remain in the country, as close as possible to their communities, in the hope that circumstances will soon allow for them to retake their ministry of peace, tolerance and national reconciliation. It is in their name, and giving expression to their urgent concerns that I write, in hope that their and other voices of the people of Congo-Brazzaville can be heard and responded to at the table of the Security Council and in other international forums.

Respectfully yours,

Konrad Raiser
General Secretary

Letter to H.E. Jacques Chirac, President of the French Republic, 2 February 1999.

Monsieur le Président,

Depuis quelques semaines des appels de plus en plus angoissés parviennent au Conseil œcuménique des Eglises de la part de ses églises membres du Congo-Brazzaville. Ces appels confirment des informations en provenance de différentes sources faisant état d'une détérioration dramatique de la situation et d'une tournure catastrophique des événements dans le sens de massacres basés de plus en plus ouvertement sur 1'appartenance ethnique des populations.

Comme vous le savez, les églises du Congo-Brazzaville ont joué un rôle très courageux pour contribuer à un processus de réconciliation nationale après la guerre de 1997; et cela, au prix de la vie de plusieurs de leurs membres et d'un engagement remarquable de nombreuses communautés chrétiennes agissant en tant qu'acteurs de paix sur le terrain. Tous ces efforts sont malheureusement stoppés, si ce n'est anéantis, avec la nouvelle vague de terreur qui s'est abattue sur le Congo depuis la fin de 1'annee 1998.

Plus encore qu'une assistance humanitaire, qui pourtant est d'une vitale importance, nos interlocuteurs en appellent avant tout a une mobilisation de la communauté internationale qui soit à la hauteur de la gravité de la situation afin de contribuer à mettre fin aux combats.

C'est dans ce contexte, Monsieur le Président, que je me permets d'intervenir auprès de vous aujourd'hui, en tant que dirigeant d'un pays qui dispose de très sérieux atouts pour jouer un rôle déterminant en faveur d'un engagement plus important de la communauté internationale au Congo-Brazzaville.

Nous savons que la France a déjà accompli des efforts dans ce sens. Mais devant 1'evolution tragique de la situation et les craintes d'une aggravation imminente du conflit, nous voulons croire que d'autres interventions sont possibles au plan diplomatique auprès du gouvernement du Congo pour qu'il négocie l'arret des hostilités et s'engage dans un processus de pacification et de réconciliation.

L'intervention des Nations Unies et de l'Organisation de l'Unite africaine nous paraît également indispensable, tant il est vrai que la détérioration actuelle est aussi le résultat d'un manque d'attention suffisante de la part de la communauté internationale. Un récent rapport de 1'ONU constatait avec amertume que « les efforts de réconciliation nationale entrepris après la guerre de 1997 ont été entravés par la très faible réponse de la communauté international aux appels consolidés d'urgence lancés à la fin des cinq mois de conflit. »

De notre coté nous nous engageons avec les églises membres du Conseil œcuménique, en particulier celles de France, d'Europe et d'Afrique, à accompagner les efforts des Eglises du Congo pour la paix et la réconciliation et à les soutenir dans les moments difficiles qu'elles connaissent actuellement.

La VIII Assemblée du Conseil œcuménique des Eglises qui vient de se tenir en terre africaine au Zimbabwe, en décembre 1998, a réaffirmé avec force l'engagement des églises à soutenir les processus de reconstruction et de réconciliation en Afrique. La crise qui déchire le Congo-Brazzaville en ce moment n'est pas la moindre des tragédies qui mobilisent notre soutien, et nous ne pouvons que regretter qu'elle n'ait pas reçu jusqu'à présent la visibilité médiatique qu'elle mériterait.

En souhaitant vivement que la France puisse accentuer son rôle d'acteur de paix dans ce pays et entraîner un engagement plus important de la communauté internationale dans ce sens, devant une situation qui risque de s'aggraver encore d'avantage, je vous prie de recevoir, Monsieur le Président, l'assurance de ma très haute considération.

Konrad Raiser
Secrétaire général

[TRANSLATION]

Mr President,

For several weeks the World Council of Churches has received ever more anguished appeals from its member churches in Congo-Brazzaville. These appeals confirm the reports we have received from different sources on the dramatic deterioration of the situation and on the catastrophic turn of events leading to massacres based more and more openly on the ethnic identities of the affected populations.

As you know, the churches of Congo-Brazzaville have played a very courageous role in contributing to a process of national reconciliation since the war of 1997 during which numerous Christian communities acted as exemplary peacemakers on the ground at the cost of the lives of a number of their members. All these efforts have been either stymied or annulled by the new wave of terror that has swept over the Congo since the end of 1998.

Even more than for humanitarian assistance, which is itself of vital importance, our partners appeal for a mobilization of the international community that would correspond to the gravity of the situation and help put an end to the fighting.

It is in this context, Mr President, that I place this situation before you as the leader of a country that is well equipped to play a significant role in engaging the international community in Congo-Brazzaville.

We know that France has already taken initiatives in this sense. However, in view of the tragic evolution of the situation and the fears of an imminent aggravation of the conflict, we believe that further diplomatic interventions with the government of the Congo, calling upon it to negotiate an end to the hostilities and to engage in a process of pacification and reconciliation, are urgently needed.

On our part, we are engaged with our member churches, especially those in France, Europe and Africa, in efforts to accompany the churches of the Congo in their efforts for peace and reconciliation and to support them in the present difficulties.

The Eighth Assembly of the WCC that met last December in Zimbabwe, on African soil, has strongly reaffirmed the churches' engagement to support the process of reconstruction and reconciliation in Africa. The crisis that now tears Congo-Brazzaville apart is one of those that demand the world's attention and we deeply regret that thus far it has not received the media attention that it deserves.

In the sincere hope that France might strengthen its role as an actor for peace in this country and vis-à-vis the international community, and in view of a situation that risks becoming still worse, I offer you, Mr President, the assurance of my highest esteem.

Konrad Raiser
General Secretary

Message to the Ecumenical Council of Christian Churches of Congo (COECC)
Sent in February 1999.

Chers frères et sœurs en Christ,

A l'occasion de la célébration de la Journée de l'œcuménisme au Congo, je vous adresse nos salutations chaleureuses et fraternelles au nom du Conseil œcuménique des Eglises.

Nous voulons vous dire que nous nous sentons très proches de vous en ces temps difficiles, en raison des conflits de pouvoir persistants et violents qui opposent plusieurs dirigeants politiques. Au moment de l'Assemblée du COE à Harare, en décembre 1998, nous avons entendu avec peine les témoignages de vos délégués, notamment sur le terrible incident qui avait coûté la vie à six membres d'une mission de réconciliation du COECC. Par la suite, nous avons suivi avec consternation les informations sur la reprise des combats, des tueries, des déplacements massifs et les souffrances de milliers de personnes. Nous savons que les églises n'ont pas été épargnées et nous exprimons toute notre sympathie à celles et ceux qui ont été victimes de ces tragiques événements.

Le COE s'est efforcé de maintenir le contact avec le Congo, malgré les difficultés de communication, et de briser le silence des médias internationaux sur la situation dans votre pays. Des approches ont été faites auprès du Président de la France et du Secrétaire général des Nations Unies. Ensemble avec plusieurs églises partenaires, notamment en France et en Suède, et avec la CETA, le COE s'est tenu prêt à envoyer une délégation œcuménique, pour témoigner de notre solidarité et contribuer, si possible, à la recherche d'une solution pacifique des problèmes dont souffrent votre pays et sa population.

Le document « Recherche de Paix au Congo » que vous nous avez fait parvenir indique clairement la mission que les églises entendent poursuivre à travers votre Conseil. Je voudrais vous assurer du soutien du COE dans vos démarches et de notre souhait que la visite prévue de la délégation puisse avoir lieu bientôt.

Sachez que nous vous portons dans la prière. Que le Seigneur vous garde et vous donne la force pour faire face aux difficultés et témoigner de l'espérance qui est en Lui.

Konrad Raiser
Secrétaire général

[TRANSLATION]

Dear brothers and sisters in Christ,

On the occasion of the celebration of the Day of Ecumenism in Congo, I send you warm and fraternal greetings from the World Council of Churches.

We assure you that we feel very close to you in these difficult times, due to the persistent and violent power struggles that oppose several political leaders. At the WCC Assembly in Harare in December 1998 we heard with sadness the reports of your delegates, especially on the terrible incident that had cost the lives of six members of a reconciliation mission of the COECC. Subsequently, we have followed with consternation the news of the new fighting, killings, massive displacements and the sufferings of thousands of persons. We know that the churches have not been spared and we express our deep sympathy to those who have been victims of these tragic events.

The WCC has made efforts to maintain contact with the Congo, despite the difficulties of communication, and to break the silence of the international media on the situation in your country. Approaches have been made to the President of France and to the Secretary-General of the United Nations. Together with several partner churches, notably those in France and Sweden, and with the AACC, the WCC has remained ready to send an ecumenical delegation to give witness to our solidarity and to contribute, if possible, to the pursuit of a peaceful resolution of the problems that bring suffering to your country and its population.

The document, "Pursuit of Peace in the Congo," that you have sent us indicates clearly the mission that the churches intend to pursue through your Council. I wish to assure you of the support of the WCC in your efforts and of our desire that the foreseen delegation visit can take place soon.

Know that we keep you in our prayers. May the Lord guard you and give you the strength to face the difficulties and witness the hope that is in Him.

Konrad Raiser
General Secretary

Appeal for Peace and Humanitarian Action in Congo-Brazzaville
Statement issued at the conclusion of a consultation of concerned church leaders, Paris, 29-30 November 1999.

On 29 and 30 November, the World Council of Churches, in collaboration with the French Protestant Federation, convened a consultation in Paris on the situation in the Republic of Congo (Brazzaville). It was attended by delegates from the Ecumenical Council of Christian Churches of Congo, the French Protestant Federation, Free Churches in Sweden, Norway and Finland, the All Africa Conference of Churches and the World Council of Churches.

The people of the Republic of Congo (Brazzaville) are experiencing an unimaginable tragedy as a result of a fratricidal war in which atrocities of the worst kind have been committed both by the militias and by the public forces of order (pillaging, humiliation, rape, murder). Vast sections of the population have fled into the forests, cut off from any form of help. The people are in a state of total disarray and destitution.

There are some voices calling for peace, and we are particularly touched by those of the women who, with the children, are the first victims of this war.

We want to let all these cries of suffering be heard, despite the blanket of silence that prevents international opinion from being informed of this human tragedy. This was the first objective of our meeting.

It is our duty as churches in France, in the Nordic countries, the Congo and in the worldwide ecumenical fellowship to echo this appeal for peace. We are ready to do all in our power to make it heard.

We welcome the peace initiatives that have been taken to date. But, once again, we fervently urge the principal warring parties to come to the negotiating table without further delay. We believe this negotiating table should be offered by a trusted international partner, acceptable to all and of guaranteed neutrality, who could undertake to accompany any peace agreements that might result from the negotiations. Under the leadership of the World Council of Churches, our churches are ready to accompany the implementation of this process and to follow it through to the end.

We draw attention to a desperate humanitarian emergency to which the response of international aid has so far been cruelly inadequate. We call upon the Congolese government and the international aid agencies to prepare a response in keeping with the scale of the people's distress.

190

We direct this appeal first to our own emergency aid instrument, ACT (Action of Churches Together), urging it to join in actions already started, notably by the Free Churches of the Nordic countries and other bodies present in Congo.

We appeal to all parties in the conflict to guarantee safe passage for the transport and distribution of humanitarian aid.

In the situation of distress confronting us in the Republic of Congo we draw inspiration from the biblical vision of Psalm 85:

"Steadfast love and faithfulness will meet;
righteousness and peace will kiss each other." (Psalm 85:10)

Nonetheless, we accept that we must begin by bringing an end to the suffering, addressing the immediate needs and restoring trust.

It is for the Congolese people to effect the work of truth and reconciliation.

CONGO (DEMOCRATIC REPUBLIC)

Message of solidarity
Letter to the member churches in the Democratic Republic of Congo, 5 February 2001.

Dear Sisters and Brothers in Christ,

As the Central Committee of the World Council of Churches meets these days in Potsdam, in the reunified and now peaceful land of Germany, we have again had you all in our prayers.

At this meeting we have also launched the Decade to Overcome Violence. Nowhere are our concerted Chrisitian efforts needed to overcome violence more than they are in the Democratic Republic of Congo. In the aftermath of the assassination of President Laurent Kabila and in the transition to another phase of the political life of your beloved land, we pray that God give you strength to witness for peace and the end to all violence in your land. We pray that all those in positions of civil and military responsibility, both in government and in the armed opposition, will hear your call for peace and non-violent resolution of the conflicts that have inflicted such suffering.

We recognize what a great burden for the restoration of peace and the establishment of justice in the DRC is upon you. During my recent visit I became even more deeply convinced that you are equal to that task. I want you to know that you are not alone in this difficult time. Churches in your neighboring nations, with whom you have decided to make common cause for peace and reconciliation through FECCLAHA, stand with you, as do the churches around the world gathered together in the WCC.

Receive, then, the prayers of the church leaders gathered in this Central Committee; and the blessings of Christ, the Prince of Peace, of the almighty God, who judges all with mercy, and of the Holy Spirit, who remains with you now and evermore.

Yours in the Risen Lord and Savior,

Konrad Raiser
General Secretary

ETHIOPIAN-ERITREAN CONFLICT

Communication to religious leaders in Ethiopia

Letter to the members of the Interfaith Committee in Ethiopia via the Rev. Yadessa Daba, General Secretary of the Mekane Jesu Church and member of the WCC Executive Committee, 13 May 1999.

Dear friends,

It has been several weeks now since our visit with you. Though we have been silent in our communication with your Committee, I want to assure you that we have been working continuously on our shared concern for peace between Eritrea and Ethiopia. Our time with you was enormously valuable, and we remain deeply grateful for your openness and willingness to take such extensive time to speak with us.

We are deeply troubled about the continuation and even intensification of the war, and its effects on the civilian populations, and are more convinced than ever that joint religious initiatives, both with respect to the present fighting and with regard to long-term peace and reconciliation initiatives are urgent.

The World Council of Churches has been in regular contact, since our visit, with Norwegian Church Aid in order to assure that ours is a common ecumenical engagement in support of your own efforts. We have agreed that, as soon as possible, another joint meeting should be held. The WCC is prepared to provide auspices for this in cooperation with NCA.

In order to move further in the direction of realizing this desire, Mr Stein Villumstad will be paying a follow-up visit to Addis Ababa next week. He comes also on behalf of the WCC, and as a new member of our Commission of the Churches on International Affairs.

We are prepared to convene a joint meeting as early as possible in the month of August. This could be held at a place near Nairobi where a protected meeting site could be arranged. It might also be held near Geneva. We believe that there are now sufficient grounds to believe that the two sides can reach agreement on joint initiatives, based on the positions you have represented to one another in Oslo and Frankfurt. Given the importance that all attach to this, there could be merits in holding the meeting here in Geneva with the possibility of announcing the agreement in a formal press conference with the UN international press corps. This we leave to you to decide.

We have reported the conversations we had with you to the officers of the World Council of Churches, who endorsed wholeheartedly this interfaith initiative for peace. We continue to pray for peace, and with you to work for it.

With warm fraternal greetings, and in the fervent hope that we may meet again soon, I remain

Yours respectfully,

Dwain C. Epps
Coordinator, International Relations

Minute on Peace and Reconciliation between Ethiopia and Eritrea
Adopted by the Central Committee, Geneva, 26 August - 3 September 1999.

The World Council of Churches and many of its member churches and related agencies around the world have been deeply concerned about the conflict between Ethiopia and Eritrea, which has been raging with ever greater intensity since May 1998. We have grieved at the terrible, mounting toll of human life this war is again inflicting on peoples who have suffered so terribly and for so long from war, repression and abject poverty. Immediately after the outbreak of hostilities, the General Secretary wrote to the leaders of the two countries, imploring them to stop the fighting and to resolve the border issue, which was the immediate source of contention, by peaceful means.

Earlier this year an ecumenical delegation led by the WCC, including a representative of the All Africa Conference of Churches (AACC) and the Fellowship of Councils and Churches in the Great Lakes and Horn of Africa (FECCLAHA), visited both Ethiopia and Eritrea, to express the concerns of the churches around the world and to offer whatever assistance the WCC and the wider ecumenical movement may be able to render. The delegations met with government leaders, and especially with Orthodox, Protestant, Roman Catholic and Muslim leaders, who on both sides have formed religious committees to promote a peaceful solution.

These two religious committees will be meeting for a third time soon at the invitation of Norwegian Church Aid. Fervently hoping that the conversations they resume now may lead to agreement on joint steps to be taken for peace, the Central Committee of the World Council of Churches, meeting in Geneva, 26 August - 3 September 1999, conveys to the religious leaders on both sides our encouragement and the assurance of our prayers.

We know from our own experience how difficult is the road to peace, but we know that God Almighty expects all those who believe in Him to travel that road. We know how demanding is the way to justice, but God is a God of Justice. We know how long is the way to reconciliation, but God wills that we live together as sisters and brothers who love and care for one another. Be assured that we stand ready to accompany and support you when you are ready and able to travel together for the sake of God and all God's people. May God inspire your deliberations, unite your spirits, and equip you to bring a word of hope, a word of peace to the leaders of your countries and to all those who look to you for spiritual guidance.

Message to the Participants in the Oslo Gathering of Religious Leaders
Letter conveying the minute of the Central Committee, 2 September 1999.

Your Holinesses, Your Eminences, Distinguished Friends,

It is with sincere pleasure that I transmit to you, through the courtesy of the Rev. Yadessa Daba, member of the Central Committee of the World Council of Churches, the message of encouragement and support which the Central Committee adopted today. The Central Committee is comprised of 158 members coming from all parts of the world, many of them from situations of severe internal or international conflicts. They represent the more than 340 Orthodox, Anglican and Protestant member churches of the Council in some 150 countries. With us have also been the leaders of the All Africa Conference of Churches (AACC) and of the Fellowship of Councils and Churches in the Great Lakes and Horn of Africa (FECCLAHA).

In these days we have prayed for you, and churches around the world shall continue to do so as you meet and as you labor for peace and reconciliation between your peoples.

I take this opportunity to send you my own warmest personal greetings, and those of the friends who accompanied me in the ecumenical delegations which visited you earlier this year. I have your faces in my eyes and your voices in my ears as I write to you this letter of peace.

May God truly bless you all and guide you in these days.

> Yours in the name of Him who offers us the promise of peace,
>
> Dwain C. Epps
> Director
> Commission of the Churches on
> International Affairs

Congratulations to H.H. Patriarch Abuna Paulos on the award of the Nansen Medal
Letter sent to the head of the Ethiopian Orthodox Tewahedo Church, 15 November 2000.

Your Holiness,

It was a pleasure to meet you, however briefly, when we were together in New York for the Millennium Summit of World Religious Leaders. I was encouraged to have through Norwegian Church Aid a report of the important meeting you had in that city between the Religious Committees of Ethiopia and Eritrea, and to see the further agreements for future actions you adopted there.

Now I have had the welcome news that you have been named as a co-recipient of the prestigious Nansen Medal for service to refugees this year. I want to congratulate you warmly for this merited recognition of your work, which includes the leadership you have given to the joint efforts of the Religious Committees. The granting of the Nansen Medal for 2000 to persons who themselves have suffered the rigors of exile and thus the fate of refugees is a significant step. We know well how you yourself were impacted in those difficult years of your own imprisonment and exile during which we accompanied you, and we can attest to the ways in which you have applied that personal experience in your years as spiritual leader of the Ethiopian Orthodox Tewahedo Church.

A mark of your commitment both to the plight of refugees and to the causes of uprootedness in your part of the world has been your effort to build bridges between the religious communities, the peoples and the leaders of Ethiopia and Eritrea at a time when they provided virtually the only contact across a growing divide. I am sure that this high distinction now given to you bodes well not only for your own ministry, but for the realization of the important goals the committees have set for themselves to build a lasting peace and harmonious relations between your two peoples.

Yours in Christ,

Konrad Raiser
General Secretary

Appeal for the release of Ethiopian human rights defender
Letter to H.E. Prime Minister Meles Zenawi, 10 May 2001.

Your Excellency,

The World Council of Churches has received with deep concern news of the arrests and detention on 8th May of Prof. Mesfin Wolde Mariam, Executive Committee Member of the Ethiopian Human Rights Council, and of Dr Berhanu Nega, lecturer at the Addis Ababa University. According to our information, a court hearing on the charges is scheduled to be held within 48 hours. We sincerely hope that this will be the case and that such a hearing will be held in a way that fully respects established international legal norms and the independence of the judiciary for which the Ethiopian Constitution provides.

195

We do not wish to interfere in the legal process, nevertheless it is appropriate for us to express considerable surprise at these actions taken against two distinguished defenders of human rights in your country. The two persons now in detention are well known to us and to other international organisations dedicated to human rights. Their non-partisan approach, commitments to non-violence, and their personal integrity have gained them high respect and esteem among international jurists and humanitarian organisations around the world.

We encourage you to take steps to secure the release of these two men from detention pending court hearings on charges brought against them.

It has also come to our attention that the offices of the Ethiopian Human Rights Council have been sealed by the authorities. According to our extensive knowledge of this Council, it has both in its actions and its statements been an impartial defender of human rights within the framework of the Constitution and the international norms to which your government has subscribed. It too has consistently advocated non-violence to achieve the goals of social justice through respect for human rights.

Respectfully yours

Konrad Raiser
General Secretary

IVORY COAST

Expressions of concern about internal conflict
Letter to WCC member churches in the Ivory Coast, 10 October 2002.

Chers sœurs et frères en Christ,

Le Conseil oecuménique des Eglises a suivi avec une inquiétude grandissante les événements qui secouent votre pays depuis plusieurs semaines. Nous voulons vous assurer de notre prière, notre solidarité et nos sentiments de profonde sympathie avec les familles et les proches des victimes de la violence.

Nous sommes très préoccupés par la nature du conflit qui oppose les Ivoiriens les uns aux autres. Votre pays a été pendant longtemps un exemple de stabilité politique et sociale en Afrique. Malgré les problèmes inhérents à chaque nation, une certaine conception de l'unité nationale et de la cohésion de la société avait permis à la Côte d'Ivoire d'éviter que des tensions internes ne dégénèrent en affrontements. Maintenant il est à craindre que votre pays à son tour soit menacé par le fléau de la fragmentation et des oppositions à caractère ethnique et religieux. Très probablement des facteurs de déséquilibre et d'inégalité économique entre différentes régions jouent également un rôle.

Le Conseil oecuménique des Eglises voudrait encourager les communautés religieuses en Côte d'Ivoire, et en particulier les églises chrétiennes, de faire tout leur possible pour éviter que le conflit ne dégénère en guerre civile qui plongera la population dans la misère et la souffrance. Avec vous, nous réprouvons les actes de ceux qui ont attaqué le pouvoir démocratiquement élu. Devant ce défi, la tentation est grande de chercher la solution par la force des armes. Pourtant nous croyons que la responsabilité première de tous ceux qui sont concernés est d'explorer les voies du dialogue et de persévérer autant que faire se peut dans la recherche d'un règlement pacifique. Refuser l'affrontement violent, même si celui qui s'est érigé en adversaire a saisi les armes, est dans l'esprit de la Décennie *Vaincre la violence* que les églises membres du Conseil oecuménique ont solennellement proclamé lors de la Huitième Assemblée à Harare, en décembre 1998.

Dans ce contexte, et malgré l'échec de leur première tentative que nous déplorons, nous souhaitons apporter notre soutien aux efforts des autorités de la CEDEAO en les appelant à continuer leur mission de médiation en vue de réunir les parties autour de la table de négociation. Par votre intermédiaire, nous demandons au gouvernement légitime de la Côte d'Ivoire de faciliter les efforts de la CEDEAO et éventuellement d'autres organismes africains et internationaux envers une solution négociée. Il y a urgence: des situations de conflit ailleurs en Afrique ont montré qu'une fois les affrontements déclenchés il devient très difficile d'arrêter la spirale de la violence avec toutes les souffrances qu'elle provoque pour les populations civiles.

Nous sommes heureux de trouver dans votre déclaration de responsables catholiques et protestants méthodistes de la Côte d'Ivoire l'esprit de tolérance et de réconciliation religieuse évoquant non seulement les temples et les églises mais aussi les mosquées. Le danger que le facteur religieux s'ajoute aux autres dimensions du conflit est réel. Nous espérons que les communautés chrétiennes et musulmanes de la Côte d'Ivoire trouveront la voie du dialogue et aideront leurs fidèles à se respecter et s'aimer mutuellement, pour faire échec à ceux qui voudraient fomenter des affrontements au nom de la religion.

Le Conseil oecuménique des Eglises se joint pleinement à votre appel à la prière et la mobilisation de toutes les forces spirituelles en faveur du rétablissement de la paix. Nous vous encourageons à analyser les causes profondes de la crise que traverse votre pays et d'y remédier dans la mesure de vos forces. Dans cet effort, nous voulons être avec vous et apporter le soutien de la grande famille oecuménique.

Sachez que vous êtes dans la prière de beaucoup qui de près ou de loin partagent vos peines et vos inquiétudes. Nous vous saluons dans la communion du Christ, le Prince de Paix.

Konrad Raiser
Secrétaire général

Dear Sisters and Brothers in Christ,

The World Council of Churches has followed with growing concern the events that have shaken your country during the past several weeks. We wish to assure you of our prayer, solidarity and deep sympathy with the families and those close to the victims of the violence.

We are very concerned about the nature of this conflict that brings Ivoirians into opposition with one another. Your country has been for a long time an example of political and social stability in Africa. Despite the problems inherent to each nation, a certain understanding of national unity and social cohesion have allowed the Ivory Coast to avoid the disintegration of internal tensions into confrontations. Now there is reason to fear that your country may also be threatened by the tide of fragmentation and conflict of an ethnic and religious character. Very likely, these factors of destabilization and economic inequality between the different regions also play a role.

The World Council of Churches wishes to encourage the religious communities of the Ivory Coast, and in particular the Christian churches, to do everything possible to avoid the degeneration of this conflict into a civil war that would plunge the population into misery and suffering. With you we condemn the acts and those who have attacked the democratically elected government. In the faces of such a challenge there is a great temptation to seek a solution by armed force. Nevertheless we believe that the primary responsibility of all concerned is to explore avenues of dialogue and to persevere as far as possible in the search for a peaceful resolution. To refuse violent confrontation, even when the adversary has taken up arms, is in the spirit of the Decade to Overcome Violence that the member churches of the WCC have solemnly proclaimed at the Eighth Assembly in Harare in December 1998.

In this context, and despite the failure of their first effort that we deplore, we wish to support the efforts of the ECOWAS authorities, calling upon them to continue their mediation mission in an effort to bring the parties to the negotiation table. Through you we ask the legitimate government of the Ivory Coast to facilitate ECOWAS efforts and eventually those of other African or international bodies in seeking a negotiated solution. This is urgent: as conflict situations elsewhere in Africa have shown, once confrontations have occurred it is very difficult to break the spiral of violence with all the suffering it inflicts on the civilian populations.

We are happy to find in the declaration issued by your Catholic and Methodist church leaders a spirit of religious tolerance and reconciliation that evokes not only churches but also the mosques. The danger that the religious factor be joined with other dimensions of the conflict is real. We hope that the Christian and Muslim communities of the Ivory Coast will find the path of dialogue and help their faithful to respect and love one another and to hold in check those who would foment confrontations in the name of religion.

The World Council of Churches joins you fully in your call to prayer and efforts to mobilize all the spiritual forces in favur of the reestablishment of the peace. We encourage you to analyze the underlying causes of the crisis through which your country is going and to seek remedies that are within your reach. In that effort we wish to stand alongside you and to offer you the support of the wider ecumenical family.

Be assured that you are in the prayers of many who from near or far share your pain and your worries. We salute you in the communion of Christ, the Prince of Peace.

Konrad Raiser
General Secretary

Letter to the Executive Secretary of ECOWAS (Economic Community of West African States), 10 October 2002.

Dear Sir,
The World Council of Churches has been following with growing concern the developments in Ivory Coast. As the international ecumenical organisation representing over 340 member churches in the world we add our voice to that of the All Africa Conference of Churches, our continental ecumenical partner, expressed in its letter to you of 1st October.

Ivory Coast, which has been for a long time an example of political and social stability in Africa, now seems to be in turn threatened by the curse of fragmentation and internal oppositions fueled by ethnic and religious divisions.

We reprove the acts of those who have resolved to attack the democratically elected authorities of Ivory Coast. Yet we believe that in the face of this challenge the primary responsibility of all concerned is to resist the temptation to respond by military action and to explore as much as possible the possibilities of resolving the conflict through negotiation.

We regret that the efforts of ECOWAS to avoid armed confrontation have not succeeded so far. I would like to express the support of the World Council of Churches for the ECOWAS mediation and encourage you and your organisation strongly to continue seeking ways of bringing the parties to the negotiation table.

The World Council of Churches is encouraging and assisting its member churches in Ivory Coast to promote dialogue and mutual understanding between the various ethnic and religious communities, and to contribute to a peaceful solution of the present conflict.

We assure you and the people, the churches and the authorities of Ivory Coast of our prayers.

Yours sincerely,

Konrad Raiser
General Secretary

LIBERIA

Appeal for the release of human rights defender

Letter to Mr Jeff Gongoer Dowana Sr, Head of Mission, Embassy of the Republic of Liberia in London, 22 November 2002.

Dear Sir,

We write to you in connection with the imprisonment of Mr Aloysius Toe who is being detained by the Liberian government on charges of high treason. Mr Toe is a human rights activist. He is a project officer at the National Human Rights Centre of Liberia, committed to the promotion and protection of human rights through peaceful means and has not indulged in any acts of violence or treason as alleged. It appears Mr Toe's only fault is he helped to organise a prayer service to draw attention to the plight of human rights defenders who have been in jail for over four months without proper charges being filed against them.

We call on the Liberian government through you for immediate release of Mr Aloysius Toe. In the alternative, it is requested that proper charges be filed against him and he be tried in accordance with the due process of law.

Yours sincerely,

Peter Weiderud
Director, Commission of Churches on
International Affairs

MADAGASCAR

Expression of concern about the post-election crisis

Open letter to the leaders of WCC member churches in Madagascar, 24 January 2002

Chers frères et sœurs en Christ,

Le Conseil oecuménique des Eglises suit avec une inquiétude grandissante la polémique et le mécontentement d'une large faction de la population malgache au sujet de l'élection présidentielle à Madagascar. Nous sommes conscients des efforts que vous, dirigeants de nos églises membres, avez faits et continuez de faire pour guider le processus électoral afin qu'il soit pacifique et que la volonté du peuple telle qu'elle a été exprimée par les bulletins de vote soit respectée. Peu d'églises en Afrique ont une expérience aussi riche que la vôtre dans le domaine de la médiation entre le peuple et les autorités politiques, et sont aussi bien placées que vous pour jouer ce rôle.

Nous avons appris que la Haute Cour a annoncé qu'elle rendra publique les résultats officiels du premier tour de l'élection présidentielle lundi 28 janvier prochain, qu'elle a refusé de prendre en compte les éléments recueillis par le Conseil national des élections, et que l'éventualité d'une décision qui rendrait caduque là tenue d'un deuxième tour suscite des manifestations populaires importantes, à Antananarivo et dans les Provinces. Nous comprenons que cette situation préoccupante peut déboucher sur une crise politique majeure qu'il serait difficile de contrôler et dont souffriraient le pays et la population.

Par l'intermédiaire de cette lettre ouverte nous en appelons aux responsables politiques qui détiennent le pouvoir à Madagascar de tout faire pour que le processus démocratique soit pleinement respecté. Nous demandons à ceux qui sont chargés du maintien de l'ordre publique d'éviter l'utilisation des moyens violents pour contenir ou empêcher les expressions des sentiments de la population.

Nous vous assurons de notre solidarité et de nos prières pour vous, pour le peuple malgache et pour ses dirigeants politiques en ces temps d'épreuve. Nous nous tenons prêt à vous aider dans vos efforts envers un avenir marqué par la paix sociale et politique et par l'harmonie dans votre pays bien-aimé.

Georges Lemopoulos
Secrétaire général adjoint

[TRANSLATION]

Dear sisters and brothers in Christ,

The World Council of Churches is following with growing concern the polemics and popular discontent of a large portion of the malagasy population surrounding the presidential election in Madagascar. We are aware of the efforts that you, the leaders of our member churches, have undertaken and continue to exert to guide the electoral process in a peaceful way and that the will of the people be respected as it was expressed by their ballots. Few churches in Africa have such a rich experience as you in the field of mediation between the people and the political authorities, or are so well placed to play such a role.

We have learned that the High Court has announced that it will make public the official results of the first round of the presidential election next Monday, 28 January, that it has refused to take into account elements gathered by the National Elections Council, and that the eventuality of a decision that would render useless the holding of a second round has given rise to large popular demonstration in Antananarivo and in the provinces. We understand that this worrying situation could lead to a major political crisis that would be difficult to control and that would bring suffering to the country and the population.

Through this open letter we appeal to the political leaders in power in Madagascar to ensure that the democratic process is fully respected. We appeal to those charged with the maintenance of public order to avoid the use of violent means to contain or block the expression of the population's feelings.

We assure you of our solidarity and our prayers for you, the malagasy people and for the political leaders in this time of trial. We remain ready to assist in your efforts toward a future marked by social and political peace and harmony in your beloved country.

Georges Lemopoulos
Deputy General Secretary

Letter to the churches of Madagascar, 22 February 2002

Sœurs et Frères en Christ,

En raison des récents développements suite aux élections présidentielles, les mobilisations de masse dans la capitale Antananarivo et les perturbations violentes ailleurs dans le pays;

En compassion avec tous ceux qui sont pris dans la passion de ces moments dans l'histoire de la nation;

Partageant votre désir de vérité et de justice; et

Nous rappelant que la démocratie dépend de la volonté de tous de vivre ensemble dans un esprit de tolérance et de respect les uns pour les autres;

Le Conseil oecuménique des Eglises renouvelle son appel au peuple malgache, ses parties politiques, et le gouvernement d'agir maintenant avec modération, évitant toute forme de violence qui pourrait vous diviser davantage et poser des obstacles à votre avenir commun.

Nous appelons aussi toutes les nations amies de Madagascar à faire usage d'une diplomatie de sagesse pour aider Madagascar à remettre en place une base solide de gouvernance démocratique qui puisse répondre à la volonté du peuple malgache dans son ensemble.

Nous vous assurons de nos prières en ces moments critiques.

Konrad Raiser
Secrétaire général

Sisters and Brothers in Christ,

In view of recent developments in the aftermath of the presidential elections, and of the mass mobilizations in the Capital and violent disturbances elsewhere in the country;

Out of compassion with all caught up in the passion of this hour in the nation's history;

Sharing your desire for truth and justice; and

Mindful of the fact that democracy depends on the will of all to live together in a spirit of tolerance and mutual respect:

The World Council of Churches renews its appeal to the people of Madagascar, their political parties and the government to act now with reason, avoiding any form of violence that would further divide and pose obstacles to your common future.

We appeal at the same time to all nations to use wise diplomacy to maintain calm and assist Madagascar to restore a firm basis for democratic rule responsive to the will of all its people.

Assuring you of our prayers in this critical time,

Yours in Christ,

Konrad Raiser
General Secretary

MOZAMBIQUE

Appeal for Debt Cancellation for Mozambique
Letter to WCC member churches in "Group of Eight" nations, 13 March 2000.

Dear Sisters and Brothers,

Images of the terrible devastation of Mozambique in recent weeks have brought forth an outpouring of compassion from neighboring countries in Southern Africa and around the world. There is a mounting will to assist this people and its churches in this time of great emergency and to support them as they begin the daunting work of reconstruction of homes and infrastructure. This, however, requires a form of international solidarity which goes beyond charity to offering justice to this beleaguered nation, to make "jubilee" a reality and to create conditions for them to "build houses and inhabit them, and to plant vineyards and harvest their fruits."

Mozambique's external debt has for decades frustrated or slowed its efforts to achieve development and a decent standard of living for its people. Under the present circumstances this debt is economically, ethically and morally intolerable. It must now be forgiven.

Mozambique has no hope of meeting the projected costs of emergency response, and much less those of recovery from the long-term damage to its economy unless its disabling debt burden is lifted. Its past and current obligations were already far beyond the country's capacity to pay current interest on the debt, and debt service costs are on the rise. We hope the churches and the wider international community will respond generously to the emergency needs of Mozambique, but this is not enough in the present grave circumstances.

We therefore urge you to appeal to your governments to forgive their bilateral debts with Mozambique and to advocate with multilateral creditors, especially the World Bank and the International Monetary Fund, for the immediate, total and unconditional cancellation of the money owed by Mozambique, and not simply postpone debt payment to a future date as they did for Honduras after the "Hurricane Mitch" disaster.

We also call on the churches and Government of Mozambique to take their own accountability seriously and to use the resources resulting from the debt cancellation for strengthening and building the social sector.

Mozambique is not the only country in Southern Africa that has suffered badly from the floods, nor is it alone in having to confront a debilitating debt. However, given the dramatic situation now in Mozambique action is most urgently needed here. We hope that this will lead soon to similar relief for its neighbors throughout the region.

Continuing our commitments. We address this appeal now in light of our long-standing commitments. You and other member churches have accompanied the churches and people of Mozambique during their costly struggles for independence before 1975. We have remained with them during the crippling sixteen years of civil war that followed, and through the years of subsequent drought and famine that claimed a million lives. We continued to support the churches' courageous peace and reconciliation efforts leading up to and since the 1992 peace agreement between the Government and RENAMO. Thus we know well the terrible waste of civil war and the economic instability that haunted the country even before the floods. More than 75,000 demobilized soldiers have yet to be reintegrated into society and the economy. Hundreds of thousands of land mines lie buried still and now hamper transport and relief work in remote areas of the country. Vast stocks of arms and ammunitions have yet to be recovered and pose a continuing threat to social stability and peace. Despite all this and the debilitating effects of the debt, a young democracy was emerging and the nation's economy was growing in strength in recent times. Last year for the first time

Mozambique was able to produce enough food to feed its population. These efforts of the people cannot now be sacrificed. They need to be strengthened.

Mozambique remains one of the world's poorest countries with a per capita annual income of some US$90. It is counted among the Heavily Indebted Poor Countries (HIPCs) with a debt burden of $8.3 billion. Even after initial debt relief was granted in June 1999, the annual debt service averages $73 million. Partly as a result of structural adjustment requirements, the health care budget is a mere $20 million and that for education only $32 million. Floods have destroyed a large part of Mozambique's infrastructure (roads, communication and buildings). Thousands of hectares of crops have been destroyed, and there is a looming health crisis. Well over a million people are affected. Early reconstruction cost estimates were $65 million, and the most recent torrents have done further damage. This, combined with the remaining debt burden, risks keeping the people of Mozambique in a state of permanent poverty and misery.

We therefore urge you to take action now. Please advocate with your governments for a collective decision by the "Group of Eight" leading industrial nations to take a lead in canceling all bilateral and multilateral debt for Mozambique, and that they spare no effort to help it and other affected Southern African nations to guarantee the economic, social and cultural rights of their peoples.

Please continue to keep the people and churches of Mozambique in your prayers during this time of crisis and reconstruction. Your prayers and expressions of solidarity, communicated to the Christian Council of Mozambique, will help to assure them of the spiritual and practical support of brothers and sisters around the world.

Yours in Christ,

Yorgo Lemopoulos
Acting General Secretary

NIGERIA

Minute on Nigeria
Adopted by the Central Committee, Geneva, 26 August - 3 September 1999.

Bishop Michael K. Stephen of the Methodist Church of Nigeria has informed the Central Committee about the actions taken by the churches in Nigeria in response to the Memorandum and Recommendations on Nigeria adopted by the Central Committee in 1997. Among those recommendations was an appeal to the churches to keep the human rights situation in that country under close review and to inform the WCC of their actions, and to encourage the churches of Nigeria in their witness for human rights, justice and peace in Nigeria. The political situation in Nigeria has changed significantly since then, and the leadership of the

Christian Association of Nigeria has taken a strong stand for justice, identifying itself with the suffering people of the country.

The Central Committee of the World Council of Churches, meeting in Geneva, 26 August - 3 September 1999,

• welcomes this report from the churches of Nigeria;
• commends them for their witness and their response to its earlier request; and
• requests the Officers to write to the Christian Association of Nigeria, conveying the gratitude of the Central Committee for the churches' efforts, encouraging them to continue to be a prophetic voice in the nation, and offering them support as they pursue reconciliation in Nigeria.

Expression of condolences on the death of Bola Ige
Letter to H.E. Olusegun Obasanjo, President of Nigeria, 10 January 2002.

Your Excellency,

It is with consternation and great sadness that we have received the news of the sudden passing away of Dr Bola Ige, Minister of Justice in the Federal Government of Nigeria, as a consequence of an attempt on his life shortly before Christmas.

On behalf of the World Council of Churches, I write to offer our sincere condolences to you and the people of Nigeria at the loss of a highly respected political leader and tireless advocate of the rights of people. Dr Ige has been recognized internationally as one of the outstanding sons of Nigeria, and his untimely and brutal death will leave a void that cannot be filled easily. I want to assure Your Excellency of our sympathy and prayerful accompaniment as you respond to this emergency situation.

The World Council of Churches has particular reason to keep a grateful memory of Dr Ige's involvement in the ecumenical movement, beginning with his active participation in the Student Christian Movement. At the time of the debates about development and liberation, and especially during the process leading up to the 1966 Geneva Conference on Church and Society, he was a prominent figure among a new generation of Christian political leaders from Africa. When, after the Uppsala Assembly of the WCC in 1968, the Programme to Combat Racism was launched, Dr Ige was the first Moderator of the Commission guiding this programme which became an ecumenical rallying point not only in Africa.

Dr Bola Ige will be remembered by many friends in the ecumenical family as a colleague with a sincere Christian commitment, a great and demanding vision and a profound dedication to the cause of justice, especially racial justice. We offer thanks to God for the life and witness of our brother Bola Ige. May he enjoy the light and peace in the eternal presence of our God.

With respectful regards,

Konrad Raiser
General Secretary

RWANDA

Unresolved questions related to the genocidal killings in Rwanda
Background information and suggestions for advocacy, issued in Geneva, June 1999.

An appeal addressed to the World Council of Churches Eighth Assembly in Harare last December has been given wide circulation by *African Rights*, a London-based non-governmental organization, and questions arising from this appeal have been addressed to the World Council of Churches. This note is to inform churches and related organizations of initiatives taken by the World Council of Churches in relation to the Rwandan tragedy.

Early warning and efforts to avoid the conflict

The WCC has followed the evolution of events in Rwanda and Burundi since at least the early 1970s, when a report on these conflicts was presented to the Commission of the Churches on International Affairs (CCIA). From 1991, the WCC sent signals to the governments directly involved, to the wider international community and to the churches, of the danger signs, and engaged together with the All-Africa Conference of Churches (AACC) in efforts to bring conflicting parties together to resolve their differences through negotiation.

- On 10 January 1991, the Director of CCIA addressed a letter to the President of Rwanda expressing alarm at the "persistent reports of arrests, torture and killings of civilians as a result of the actions" of Rwandan security forces, and calling for measures to be taken to correct "inhuman conditions" in Rwandan prisons and to guarantee respect for human rights as a means of restoration of peace and justice for all citizens of Rwanda.

- In response to an appeal by the churches of Rwanda, a joint WCC-AACC consultation on Rwanda was convened in Nairobi, 19-22 August 1991, bringing together church leaders and representatives of governments and refugees in the region. In his address to the Consultation, the WCC General Secretary drew attention once again to the crisis, and appealed to all parties to bring an end to violence and warfare.

- On 21 October 1993 the Acting General Secretary wrote to the Secretary-General of the United Nations, informing him of the peace accord in Rwanda recently concluded through the mediation of the churches with the support of the AACC, the WCC and the World Alliance of Reformed Churches. He

207

urged international action in response to the coup d'état which had taken place the previous night in Burundi in order to avoid a tragic destabilization of the situation in the region.

- These mediation efforts continued up to the time of the genocide, but were cut short by the deaths in Kigali of the presidents of Rwanda and Burundi when the plane in which they were travelling was apparently shot down.

- On 7 April 1994, the morning after this tragedy, the WCC General Secretary issued an "urgent appeal to the people of Burundi and Rwanda not to respond to the tragedy with renewed acts of terror and ethnic warfare", and appealed to the international community "not to abandon peoples long plagued by social and political chaos, ...misery and massive violence. He warned that the "ethnic conflicts in Rwanda and Burundi (threaten) to spill over into the wider region, exacerbating tensions in neighbouring countries... The peace and democratic future of the region, and to a great extent of the whole of Africa is at state." He called "on all nations and competent international organizations to redouble efforts to assure order in these countries in the wake of this tragedy."

- Two weeks later, on 18 April 1994, the WCC General Secretary condemned the widespread killings in Rwanda, recalling his own visit to Rwanda five months earlier. Noting that the "suffering of the Rwandan people has gone beyond the limits of understanding," he called on the international community to "be ready to assist in every possible way to bring about a cessation of hostilities, a peaceful solution to the conflict, and humanitarian assistance to the suffering."

- In May and June of 1994 other letters were sent to the Secretaries-General of the OAU and the UN, to the Chairman of the Rwandan Patriotic Front, to French Foreign Minister, Alain Juppé, and to the new Rwandan President Bizimungu.

Criminal responsibility for actions during the genocide

In the hope of establishing in Rwanda a process similar to that which had been followed earlier in El Salvador and in Guatemala, the WCC appealed to the UN to put in place an effective Human Rights delegation "to provide protection and to establish the facts with respect to responsibility for the massive violations of human rights which have occurred in that country."

Within months of the genocide, *African Rights* published a book with substantial information on individuals judged to be in complicity with or directly responsible for mass killings, listing among them many of the persons with churche leadership responsibilities, including most of those named in the document now in circulation. Following criticism that the facts on a number of cases cited were erroneous, *Africa Rights* published a corrected version of its charges.

At about the same time, the WCC published a book by Hugh McCullum, *The Angels Have Left Us*, which dealt with, among other things, the stories about both acts of heroism of Christians in the face of adversity and complicity of some church leaders. As an estimated ninety percent of the population of Rwanda is Christian, by sheer numbers the majority of the victims, and the perpetrators, of the 1994 genocide were Christians. A chapter on *The Church: Problems and Promises* goes into detail about the confusion and shortcomings of the Rwandan churches in this terrible period, but also points to hopeful signs for the resurgence of a faithful witnessing church.

In September 1994, the WCC Executive Committee considered a range of complex issues related to war in the context of reflections on the anniversary of the end of World War II. A paper provided to guide that discussion contained the following commentary:

> In Rwanda, there is growing evidence of the complicity of some church leaders with political groups and militia who appear to have organized the first massacres of Tutsis and politically suspect Hutus, and to have fanned the flames of ethnic hatred into the genocidal furore which ensued. According to reports gradually being gathered from refugees and people who stayed behind, pastors, priests and lay leaders may well have been among those who betrayed people of another ethnic group, or even participated directly in the killing.

> One must immediately add that some pastors, priests and lay leaders have accompanied their people to the refugee camps where they are seeking to minister to their pain. Stories are emerging of people, certainly many of them Christians, who sacrificed their own lives trying to shield members of another group.

> *More cases of both betrayal and martyrdom will certainly emerge in the days ahead. But the bitter memory of those who preached the love of God and served as leaders of churches who abandoned or betrayed members of their own flock will long remain in the land. Clearly, the ecumenical movement cannot ignore this reality. While insufficient evidence is in hand to name individuals related to the churches who may have been involved, the WCC and the AACC have taken the position that no one should be shielded from international inquiries aimed at establishing the truth about those responsible for this slaughter.* (Emphasis added)

It is not at all clear that one can apply the criteria to this situation that derive from the German church experience between 1933 and 1945, but the questions inevitably arise: Where are the prophets in these churches? Have there been the likes of a Dietrich Bonhoeffer here, whose message has been expressed in words and actions which have been ignored by or inaccessible to the churches outside? Has there been the equivalent of a "Confessing Church" in Rwanda which we have failed to recognize or to support? Had the churches abroad been more attentive to the attitudes of some church leaders in Rwanda, would their churches have been denied admission to the fellowship, or pressed harder to assume their responsibility as peacemakers and witnesses to the love of Christ for all people? Do we expect a confession from the new church emerging in Rwanda of Christians' complicity?

We must confess, as an ecumenical fellowship, along with our forebears in the First Assembly, that

> We have to accept God's judgment upon us for our share in the world's guilt. Often we have tried to serve God and mammon, put our loyalties before loyalty to Christ, confused the Gospel with our own economic or national or racial interests and feared war more than we have hated it. As we have talked with each other here, we have begun to understand how our separation has prevented us from receiving correction from one another in Christ. And because we lacked this correction, the world has often heard from us not the Word of God but the words of men.

The broad Church World Action - Rwanda programme being implemented now by the churches of Africa and beyond calls for intensive efforts to help rebuild multi-ethnic communities and a new, more tolerant Rwandan society. Central to those efforts will be to assist Rwandan Christians to reconstitute a faithful, servant church. How do we prepare ourselves for this? Of what corrections of our own behaviour are we in need in order to be regarded as bearers of the Word of God in a suffering Rwanda?

Post-conflict response

A massive ecumenical effort was engaged through the creation of a new international humanitarian response mechanism, Church World Action-Rwanda, on which full details are available now through ACT (Action by Churches Together). This response was a comprehensive one, seeking in a creative way to work with refugees who had fled Rwanda into neighbouring countries, and at the same time seeking to address the critical internal needs of the country through humanitarian assistance, trauma counselling teams, and capacity building in the local churches whose leadership had been decimated.

Consistent efforts were engaged to equip the churches in the Great Lakes Region to respond together to the ever-expanding crisis set in motion by the events in Rwanda.

In December 1994 the WCC convened a private meeting with leaders of nearly all the churches in the North which had historic links with Rwandan churches (including the Roman Catholic Church). The main purpose of the meeting was to share information and, in so far as possible, develop a common stance on issues related to alleged complicity of some Rwandan church leaders with the genocide and on the reconstruction of a witnessing church. The meeting started with a time of repentance and confession by the churches in order to establish a framework for participation in the process of forgiveness, reconciliation and healing.

210

In November 1996, the WCC brought together Rwandan church leaders to provide a platform for serious soul-searching on the part of the church leadership, and to begin in a small way the long process to repentance and confession. The meeting, held in Johannesburg, South Africa, was attended by church leaders from inside Rwanda (representing the remnant church) and church leaders in exile in neighbouring countries – Burundi, Democratic Republic of Congo, Uganda, Kenya, Tanzania and South Africa. The gathering brought out the tensions among the church leaders themselves. For 24 hours they would not sit in the same room even to pray. But eventually a way was found to bring the participants together for difficult, yet fruitful work.

From this meeting, a Core Group was formed to plan the next steps, including ecumenical visits, facilitated by the WCC, to the region and especially by church leaders from the region to stimulate a process of repentance, forgiveness and healing. In the following years ecumenical visits to Rwanda, Burundi, Uganda, Kenya and Tanzania took place. The Core Group called a second meeting in Entebbe, Uganda in March 1997, and another in Kigali, Rwanda in September 1997 which formulated the Kigali Principles for common Christian witness for peace and reconciliation.

In October 1997 the WCC convened the Global Ecumenical Forum on the Great Lakes region attended by church representatives from the Great Lakes region, Europe and North America. Among other things it endorsed the Kigali Principles and outlined a platform of action which eventually led to the formation in March 1999 of FECCLAHA (Fellowship of Councils and Churches in Great Lakes and Horn of Africa). The membership of FECCLAHA includes councils and churches of Rwanda, Burundi, Uganda, Democratic Republic of Congo, Kenya, Tanzania, Ethiopia, Eritrea and Southern Sudan. The main foci of FECCLAHA are peace, reconciliation, and the healing of memories.

Some conclusions

The WCC was energetic in seeking to provide early warning signs to the churches and the wider international community about the impending disaster in Rwanda. While no one could predict the dimensions of the conflict which ensued, its potential character and amplitude were foreseen, and every possible effort was made both directly and through wider advocacy to prevent it.

When the worst occurred, the WCC was equally energetic in seeking to limit the damage and to begin to help reconstruct the basis for peace among embattled ethnic groups, and to equip the churches to rebuild in a way which would help them learn from the past and become a faithful witness for peace and democracy to be reconstructed on the killing fields.

While the WCC was careful not to rush to judgment on individual cases, it was consistent with its long-standing positions in calling for effective international investigative missions to be sent to Rwanda to establish the truth about what had occurred, and to identify those responsible for crimes against humanity. It called for the creation of effective international tribunals to be created in order to bring those responsible for crimes to justice as a part of its broader efforts to counter the widespread trend of giving impunity to such persons. The WCC has excluded no one from accountability for such crimes rather, explicitly, has indicated that church leaders themselves must answer to charges made against them.

Neither the WCC nor its member churches are in a position to exercise such justice. Member churches whose members are among those against whom charges have been made are restricted to the application of ecclesial sanctions which vary from one confession to another. In fact, a private meeting was held early on with heads of mission boards of most churches who have historic ties with Rwandan churches to provide them an opportunity to consult together on this and related questions.

In the end, the administration of the law and legal sanctions rest with national and international systems and institutions empowered to apply the law. As the recent case of the charges placed against General Augusto Pinochet of Chile has shown, precedents are now clearly established that not only the government of the country where offenses were committed is responsible for pursuing crimes against humanity, but also that this is a shared international obligation. The WCC in general, and in the particular case of Rwanda, has repeatedly appealed for such precedents to be followed, for the International Tribunal on Rwanda to be adequately supported to pursue its appointed task, and for the creation of an International Criminal Court.

The WCC will continue to advocate for such means to guard against the injustice which is compounded by the granting by intent or default of impunity to authors of crimes against humanity. Churches, agencies, other civil society actors and individuals all have an advocacy role to play here with their national governments.

SIERRA LEONE

Support for UN peace efforts
  Letter to H.E. Kofi Annan, Secretary-General, 11 May 2000.

Dear Mr Secretary-General,

I write to express the energetic support of the World Council of Churches for your efforts to achieve the full implementation of Security Council Resolutions 1270 (1999) and 1289 (2000) establishing and expanding the mandate of UNAMSIL.

You are certainly right in emphasizing that "The UN can only be as strong as its Member States, and (their) political will and resources, and the willingness to commit resources." The members of the Security Council and indeed of the United Nations at large can have no excuse for not having foreseen the present
212

situation and taken appropriate measures to prevent it. In fulfillment of your responsibilities to provide early warning you have reported regularly and in detail to the Security Council on the dangerous developments in Sierra Leone. The Council itself has had the situation constantly under review and has taken firm actions several times in the past two years. Appealing to Chapter VII of the Charter, the major powers have been quick to respond to crises elsewhere in the world in recent times, often decisively, with massive force and at enormous expense. The peoples of the world, especially those of Africa, are well justified in judging harshly the failure of the same powers to act in an equally timely and decided way here in accordance with the mandate given under the same provision of the Charter.

I draw your attention especially to the statement issued by the Inter-Religious Council of Sierra Leone on 10 May (attached). The IRCSL, which has played a central and courageous role in achieving the peace accord in their country and in promoting its implementation, appeals to

- the United Nations to implement with vigour and strength its full mandate to protect peace in Sierra Leone, and
- the international community to fulfill its commitments to the government of Sierra Leone, the United Nations and relevant non-governmental organisations to enable them effectively to fulfill their respective mandates vis-à-vis the Lomé peace agreement.

The WCC knows first hand the suffering of the people of Sierra Leone in this terrible civil war. We are also aware that the death, maiming and other terrors of the war were controlled only as a result of the resolute actions of the ECOMOG forces. The churches and other religious communities of Sierra Leone have underscored for many weeks the concern you expressed in your own letter to the Security Council of 23 December 1999 "about the repercussions which a premature withdrawal of ECOMOG might have on the security situation in Sierra Leone." In the religious leaders' view, only immediate and equally decided action by UNAMSIL could prevent the country from descending again into chaos and destruction.

Thus the World Council of Churches joins and adds its voice to the urgent plea of the Inter-Religious Council of Sierra Leone, and to your own pleading that the nations act now before further lives are lost. Their failure to act after such long and detailed forewarning would certainly lead to the charge that their silence and inaction makes them complicit with the equally foreseeable consequences.

In saying this, we express through you our heartfelt gratitude to those nations that have responded to the call of the Security Council and sent soldiers willing to put their lives on the line to safeguard the peace and the safety of the people of this embattled land.

Our prayers are with you, and especially with the people of Sierra Leone in this most critical hour.

Respectfully yours,

Geneviève Jacques
Acting General Secretary

Peace in Sierra Leone

Statement of the Inter-Religious Council of Sierra Leone
Freetown, 10th May 2000

The deteriorating security situation and breach of the Lomé peace agreement resulting in the current spate of hostilities and renewed suffering of the people is of worrying concern to the inter-religious council of Sierra Leone.

The peoples of Sierra Leone want peace! Their long suffering has been borne with great courage, and this has only strengthened their commitment to reconciliation and the establishment of a society based upon respect for truth and justice.

The peoples of Sierra Leone want all the parties to the peace process to bear their full responsibilities for ending hostilities and building the peace. Genuine peace must benefit all. The people want the responsible, disciplined, and effective assistance of the UN mandated mission during this period of transition. And, in the final analysis, they want an honest process designed to ensure an effective representative government committed to the common good and the constructive engagement of all parties to the conflict.

Acts of commission or omission that threaten peace with justice are an attack on the peoples of Sierra Leone and a violation of their sovereign will. This has gone on for far too long and it must stop now! We acknowledge civil society for its great awareness and constructive approach in expressing the wish of the citizenry.

As leaders of the religious communities in Sierra Leone, we, the members of Inter-Religious Council of Sierra Leone (IRCSL), take as our sole standpoint a shared moral commitment to peace with justice, which is deeply held and widely shared by our religious communities.

The IRCSL hereby calls upon all concerned to immediately desist from any acts that violate the terms of the Lomé peace agreement or retard its progress. IRCSL also calls upon those with special designated responsibilities for peace-building to exercise their commitments with responsibility and vigour.

Specifically, the Inter-Religious Council of Sierra Leone calls upon:

4. Cpl Foday Sabanah Sankoh and his RUF Rebel Forces involved in recent hostilities to immediately and unconditionally release all captured UN personnel and other abductees, desist from all acts of violence, and re-enter in

full faith into the Disarmament and Demobilization Programme. The IRCSL further calls for effective leadership within the rebel movement designed to ensure full compliance with the peace process among all its members.

5. The Government of Sierra Leone and President Kabbah to exercise their due and legitimate responsibility of protecting and serving all the citizens of Sierra Leone in their desire for peace, right to protection, and demand for effective governance.

6. The United Nations to implement with vigour and strength its full mandate to protect peace in Sierra Leone, and

7. The International Community to fulfill its commitments to the government of Sierra Leone, the United Nations and relevant non-governmental organizations to enable them effectively to fulfill their respective mandates vis-à-vis the Lomé peace agreement.

As a religious body, the IRCSL offers its good offices to all concerned to re-engage the entire country in the process of comprehensive peace-building and reconciliation.

SUDAN

Appeal of the Sudan Ecumenical Forum* on Sudan peace negotiations
Issued in Geneva, 7 July 1999.

The Sudan Ecumenical Forum, convened in Geneva, 5-7 July 1999 by the World Council of Churches in cooperation with Caritas Internationalis, has reaffirmed the joint position of the Sudan Council of Churches and the New Sudan Council of Churches with regard to peace in the Sudan that:

• A just and lasting peace can only be achieved through meaningful and genuine dialogue; no party can maintain the illusion that a military victory is possible.

• The best hope for achieving a comprehensive cease-fire and a lasting peace is the negotiating framework provided by the Intergovernmental Authority for Development (IGAD).

The people of the Sudan are suffering immeasurably as a result of the civil war which has raged in the South for 16 years. This war must be stopped, and the IGAD *Declaration of Principles* for a lasting peace put in place without further delay.

A new round of negotiations will begin on 18 July in Nairobi, Kenya. We appeal to the Government of the Sudan, to the leadership of the SPLA/M, to the member states of IGAD, and to the IGAD Partners Forum to spare no effort to ensure their success. We appeal especially to the two parties to the conflict to engage in an open-ended process of negotiation, and continue until they have made measurable progress towards an agreement and committed themselves to a fixed schedule for further negotiations on the detailed terms of a full settlement.

The conditions for success are there. The Sudanese people in both North and South manifestly desire peace. The Government of Sudan and the Sudanese People's Liberation Army/Movement (SPLA/M) have both accepted the IGAD *Declaration of Principles* in 1998. The IGAD Partners Forum (IPF) has committed itself in Oslo in March 1999 to provide the necessary resources for an effective secretariat under the auspices of the Kenyan Ministry of Foreign Affairs to allow the IGAD process to move ahead in a sustained, determined and deliberate way.

The political stalemate which has lasted for nearly a full year must be broken now. These talks must mark a turning point for peace. Neither the people of the Sudan nor the wider international community can accept anything less. The fighting must stop on all fronts, and the rights of the communities of Sudan to a peaceful environment, to equity, to democracy, to justice, to the reconstruction of the physical and social infrastructure, and to development must be realized without further delay.

Statement on the situation in the Sudan
Adopted by the Central Committee, Potsdam, Germany, 28 January – 6 February 2001.

Background. The conflict in Sudan has been on the ecumenical agenda for over three decades. The roots of the conflict lie in its history of slavery and colonialism and date back to 1956 when the country gained independence from Great Britain. The situation today, however, has become increasingly more complex than when the almost thirty-year long conflict began. The main causes of the conflict are to be found in:

- The divide-and-rule policy of the colonial rulers, manifested in the "Closed District Act" of 1935 that barred freedom of movement between the Northern and Southern provinces of Sudan;
- Unequal development policies between the North and the South that gave rise to present disparities;
- Religious rivalry, enforcement of cultural hegemony, tribalism and racism;
- Failure of the Government of Sudan to implement the spirit of the 1972 Addis Ababa Peace Accord that gave rise to the present environment of total lack of faith and trust amongst the Southerners against the Government in the North;
- The reluctance on the part of the Government of Sudan to abide by the Declaration of Principles (DOP) agreed to between the parties in the framework of mediation by IGAD (the East African Intergovernmental Agency for Development); and
- The refusal by the Government of Sudan to accept separation of religion and state in the Constitution.

From 1971 the WCC, in cooperation with the AACC, engaged actively in a mediation effort with the South Sudan Liberation Movement and the Government of Sudan that led to the 1972 Addis Ababa peace agreement. Though this agreement brought a cessation of hostilities and a substantial reform of government of a united Sudan, it eventually collapsed, giving rise to a new civil war.

In view of the new intensification of the fighting, the WCC Central Committee adopted a Minute on the Sudan in August 1992, expressing concern about the situations in South, East and West Sudan that had displaced thousands of civilians, especially including children. It called on the United Nations to promote a cease-fire in Southern Sudan and a disengagement of troops, together with resumption of the stalemated Abuja negotiations. The Central Committee reaffirmed the need for the WCC to remain in contact with the parties to the conflict in efforts to promote a just and lasting peace.

Again in September 1997 the Central Committee adopted a Statement on Sudan, where it welcomed the common position taken by the church leaders in North and South Sudan in their paper: "Here We Stand United in Action for Peace." That paper called for a stop to the war and dialogue for peace among the armed factions in the South and between them and the Government of Sudan. The Central Committee urged all parties, their supporters abroad and those seeking to assist in the achievement of a negotiated peace to support the resumption of the IGAD Peace process, to cooperate with it, and to place their various initiatives within the framework of the IGAD principles.

The Sudanese churches have been unceasing in their own efforts to promote peace at all levels. The New Sudan Council of Churches has undertaken a significant, innovative new effort in this direction through a series of People-to-People Peace Conferences in Southern Sudan. These have resolved a series of ethnic and communal conflicts and brought hope and stability to some of the areas most affected by the hostilities. The Khartoum-based Sudan Council of Churches has also developed an active programme in advocacy and grassroots peacemaking, especially among women and youth.

At the regional level, the IGAD Peace Process -- that started with much promise and hope with the acceptance of the Declaration of Principles by the parties to the conflict -- now shows signs of stagnation despite zealous efforts of the IGAD Secretariat as well as of Northern States members of the IGAD Partners Forum to keep the negotiations on track. These have not been sufficient to remove the primary obstacle in the way of negotiations, namely the reluctance on the part of the Government of Sudan to accept the principles of separation of religion and state and to implement fully the IGAD Declaration of Principles. As a result, impatience with the slow progress of negotiations has led to insistent new calls by the people of the South, and of their churches, for self-determination and independence from the North.

The current situation. In the late 1990s the Government's oil exploration efforts in Southern Sudan, in cooperation with Western and Asian petroleum companies, succeeded in producing some 150.000 barrels a day in the Upper Nile. Oil production has contributed to an escalation of the conflict and hardened the

217

determination of the Government of Sudan to pursue a military solution to the conflict. The churches in Sudan, together with ecumenical partners abroad, have called for a just sharing of oil resources and have demanded that the oil revenue be spent on improving the situation of the people and not on promotion of the war effort through purchase with oil revenues of more sophisticated arms.

In its war effort the Government of Sudan has used air power ever since the war began in Southern Sudan. In recent times, however, aerial bombardment has targeted civilians and taken an increasingly heavy toll through high altitude bombing. Densely populated civilian areas like Kotobi and Lui have been bombed repeatedly, resulting in loss of life and destruction of property. One of these bombings that occurred in the hometown of Bishop Paride shortly after he addressed the Eighth WCC Assembly in Harare was vigorously protested immediately by the WCC Officers to the Government of Sudan through its embassy in Zimbabwe.

The continuing bombing has further increased the suffering of the people already caught in the midst of this seemingly endless conflict. Bombing missions have not spared NGOs involved in humanitarian relief operations, a number of whose aircraft have been destroyed. These air strikes eventually drew international attention. They were suspended for a period in the middle of last year after UN General Secretary Kofi Annan intervened, but were resumed with a vengeance later. On 29 December 2000 the Sudan air force bombed the Episcopal Church Cathedral in Lui, Equatoria Province, completely destroying it. The raids continue unabated taking a continuing heavy toll of casualties.

The Central Committee of the World Council of Churches meeting in Potsdam from 29 January to 6 February 2001, profoundly conscious of the unbearable suffering of the Sudanese peoples, especially those in the South, as a result of more than thirty years of civil war:

calls on the Government of Sudan to cease immediately the bombing of civilian targets of Southern Sudan, Nuba Mountains, Southern Blue Nile and other marginalized areas, and to abide by international law;

calls for the establishment of a no-fly zone in these areas, except for protected access of aircraft transporting humanitarian supplies;

urges the Government of Sudan, the SPLA and other warring parties to abide by the Geneva Convention and to allow independent observers to monitor the situation.

reminds the Government of Sudan of its responsibility to guarantee the safety and security of all its citizens both in the North and in the South;

notes with concern that the oil revenue earned by the Government of Sudan is diverted to its war effort and contributes to the escalation of fighting in Southern Sudan rather than being utilized to meet the urgent needs of the people affected by the hostilities;

requests member churches to undertake lobbying and advocacy efforts with governments and oil companies based in their countries for the cessation of further petroleum exploration and development in Southern Sudan until such time as a peace agreement is reached between the parties;

reiterates its conviction that any lasting peace in Sudan must be negotiated with the support of partner states in the region through the IGAD peace process and the Declaration of Principles enunciated thereunder;

reassures the churches of the Sudan of the continuing support and prayers of the World Council of Churches in their peace efforts;

appeals to WCC Member Churches to intensify their efforts to encourage and support the joint peace initiative of the Sudan Council of Churches and the New Sudan Council of Churches; and

urges churches and church-related agencies to continue to provide necessary humanitarian support to the Sudan for the needs of refugees and displaced persons, those in desperate situations of poverty, and the victims of war, including especially those disabled as a result of wounds inflicted through war, mines and bombing.

Minute on the peace process in Sudan
Adopted by the Central Committee, Geneva, 26 August - 3 September 2002.

At its last meeting (Potsdam, February 2001) the WCC Central Committee adopted an extensive statement on the situation in Sudan. That statement drew the attention to the urgency of efforts to resolve the conflict and called on the member churches, ecumenical partners and related agencies to engage in a series of advocacy actions to this end.

Through the Sudan Ecumenical Forum, the WCC and other ecumenical partners have intensified their monitoring of developments, and provided new support to the churches of Sudan and their advocacy for peace and reconciliation.

In late June 2002, the General Secretary visited the North and South Sudan at the invitation of the Sudanese churches. There he renewed the WCC's pledge to continue to accompany the churches in their struggle for a just and lasting peace in Sudan.

Simultaneously with this visit the Government and the Sudan Peoples Liberation Army / Movement (SPLA/M) met in Machakos, Kenya under the auspices of the Inter-Governmental Agency for Development (IGAD) for further negotiations on a peaceful resolution of the conflict. On 20th July 2002 they signed an agreement known as the "Machakos Protocol". The Sudanese churches, though still concerned with the increased incidents of violence in Upper Nile, have expressed unequivocal support for this commitment of the parties to enter into negotiations for a peaceful and comprehensive resolution of the conflict, based on the IGAD Declaration of Principles (DOP). They welcomed the Machakos Protocol as a valuable framework for the ongoing peace negotiations, and especially the specific

219

agreement of the Parties to incorporate provisions for the Right to Self-Determination for the people of South Sudan and on State and Religion in a Final Agreement.

The Central Committee welcomes the Machakos Protocol and reiterates its support for the IGAD Peace Process, and expresses appreciation for the persistent efforts of the Sudanese churches to pursue peace against heavy odds. At the same time, it is concerned about the reported escalation of fighting around Tam in Western Upper Nile and Yuai in Eastern Upper Nile, in serious breach of the provisions of the earlier Nuba Mountains Ceasefire Agreement brokered by the USA and Switzerland, resulting in further serious loss of life and displacement of civilian population.

In this new context, and in light of the Decade to Overcome Violence, the Central Committee urges member churches to:

- remain constant in prayer for the churches and people of Sudan;
- support and encourage the churches of Sudan in their continued witness and work for justice, peace and reconciliation;
- monitor and exchange information on developments related to the Machakos Protocol; and
- assist the Sudanese churches to gain access to future negotiations within the framework of the IGAD Peace Process.

Call for respect for the Machakos Protocol and revival of the peace process
Letter to H.E. President Omar Hassan al-Bashir, 7 October 2002.

Your Excellency,

The World Council of Churches has closely monitored the situation in Sudan since the early 1970s when together with the All Africa Conference of Churches it brokered the Addis Abba Peace Accord. In 1994 the WCC was instrumental in the creation of the Sudan Ecumenical Forum in which it has actively participated together with other ecumenical partners to support the Churches of Sudan in their advocacy for peace and reconciliation.

The WCC Central Committee that met in Potsdam, Germany, February 2001 adopted an extensive Statement on Sudan that called for urgent efforts by the Churches to resolve the conflict by engaging in a series of advocacy action to promote peace and reconciliation. In late June 2002 the General Secretary of the World Council of Churches, on an invitation of the Churches, visited the North and South Sudan. In Khartoum he met the officials of the government of Sudan. Around that time the government of Sudan and the Sudan Peoples Liberation Army / Movement signed a major Peace Agreement known as the *"Machakos Protocol"*.

220

The Central Committee of the World Council of Churches that met in Geneva from 26 August to 2 September 2002 took note of this significant and encouraging development and adopted a minute on Sudan, copy attached. It called on the member Churches to remember the Churches and the People of Sudan in their prayers and to support and encourage them in their continued witness and work for justice, peace and reconciliation.

We were disappointed to learn of the breakdown of the ceasefire agreement that has put in jeopardy the *"Machakos Protocol"*. We hope and pray that the peace process will be revived and the negotiations for a just and lasting peace will continue.

Respectfully yours,

Peter Weiderud
Director
Commission of Churches on International
Affairs

ZIMBABWE

Expression of concern about pre-election repression and violence
Letter sent to Mr Densen Mafinyani, General Secretary, Zimbabwe Council of Churches, 13 April 2000.

Dear Densen,

The World Council of Churches has been following with mounting concern the news from Zimbabwe in recent weeks. Reports we are receiving from various sources, and increasing requests to us from constituents and the press to comment on evolving events in the run-up to elections prompts us to write now to seek your assistance.

According to our information non-violent demonstrations are being severely repressed by security forces, and people are being jailed for what appears to be only their attempt to use the right of free expression of views. The encouragement of President Mugabe of the occupation of White farms is reported to have led to serious threats to Zimbabwean citizens and acts of physical violence. Given the fact that these invasions of property are being encouraged despite decisions of the Zimbabwean courts barring them is widely questioned around the world, and could have serious implications for Zimbabwe's international relations. All these together give the impression of a massive breakdown of the rule of law. Combined with the already tense economic situation they appear to threaten widespread chaos.

We have taken note with appreciation of the Communiqué issued by the "Workshop on the Role of the Church in Promoting Democracy and Good

Governance: The Role of the Church in the Forthcoming General Elections." The holding of the workshop does great credit to the ZCC and was a most encouraging sign of the witness the churches are providing. The analysis it has provided of the current obstacles in the electoral process is precise and enlightening. We have also been encouraged by the commitments taken by church representatives at the Kadoma Workshop, including a call for the elaboration of a "blueprint" on Land Reform before the Parliamentary election.

However, we are troubled by the stated intention of issuing press statements in support of "the current invasion of farms by war veterans." We share your concern that a just process of land reform is essential to complete the process of decolonization undertaken during the struggle for national liberation. Nonetheless, we are fundamentally convinced that this must be pursued in accordance with the law, and with respect for White farmers who have chosen to remain and to seek to contribute to the general welfare of the nation as loyal citizens of Zimbabwe.

We remain, as always, eager to accompany and assist you in whatever way the World Council of Churches can. To be able better to interpret your situation and the position of the churches to the wider ecumenical community we would be grateful for your interpretation of the current situation and guidance to us.

Awaiting eagerly your response, I reassure you of our fervent prayers for the ZCC and its churches, and for the Zimbabwean nation at this most critical juncture.

In Christ Jesus who reigns supreme,

Konrad Raiser
General Secretary

Pastoral letter to the churches

Joint letter to Mr Densen Mafinyani, General Secretary of the Zimbabwe Council of Churches, 25 April 2000.

Dear Densen,

Grace and peace to you in the name of the Risen Christ!

As we celebrate Easter together in separate places, we are again reminded of our bond of unity in Him who overcame death that we may be reconciled to God and to one another. Just as Christ called us into this fellowship, He continues always to strengthen us as disciples in his own ministry of justice, peace and reconciliation. This is our common calling, each in our own place and each on behalf of the whole Church, in order that the world might believe in Him.

We continue to be grateful for the Council's witness, and are especially pleased to hear that the Zimbabwe Council of Churches is holding tomorrow a consultative meeting with the leaders of the political parties to reflect with them on their responsibilities in this critical time of decision-making for the nation. No other body in Zimbabwe is better equipped than the Council to address the deep underlying causes of the current problems encountered by your people, and no one is better placed than the Council to lead them to lasting peace based on justice for all.

Thus we are confident that this gathering will call forth the best from the leaders of Zimbabwe, reminding them of the mutual obligations and responsibilities of government, political parties and the people to promote the common good. Narrow understandings of political power based on individual gain or group interests cannot achieve this. Now is the moment for those called to provide leadership to focus their thoughts and actions on the greater good and to act with honesty and integrity.

The churches of Zimbabwe share the responsibility for good governance of the nation, and the people look to you for clear ethical and moral guidance. To perform this role, we pray that you will prepare yourselves carefully and develop a common position that will enable you to offer a clear and decided witness to the people, its political parties and its government with respect to:

- the primacy of the rule of law;
- the need to eliminate official corruption and abuses of power;
- the need to establish a system of responsible stewardship of the nation's economy, including the equitable distribution of the land, other natural resources and wealth;
- the need to reverse the trend of deteriorating social services;
- the need to enhance human security through strengthening the basis for peace and social stability; and
- the need to re-consider the deployment of Zimbabwean troops in a neighbouring country.

We are aware that this will require courage and costly discipleship. As you pursue this task, we assure you of our prayers, solidarity and accompaniment. The global ecumenical fellowship that accompanied you through the daunting struggle for independence of Zimbabwe and in the process of building a new nation remains with you today. The difficult decision of the World Council of Churches to accept your invitation to hold its Eighth Assembly in Harare was a mighty sign of this resolve of the ecumenical movement to share the risks you take in standing for justice and peace. In this connection, we are prepared to send now a pastoral team to support you in this demanding hour.

In its letter to you of 14 April 2000, the World Council of Churches warmly welcomed and supported your Communiqué issued by the "Workshop on the Role of the Church in Promoting Democracy and Good Governance: The Role of the Church in the Forthcoming General Elections." We also would like to refer to the letter of the General Secretary, of the Lutheran World Federation, addressed to His Excellency Robert Mugabe dated 14 April 2000. We regret that in spite of national and international outcry the violence exercised with the tacit approval of the Government has not subsided, but rather has taken more lives and heightened tensions, further leading the country to the brink of collapse of order and the rule of law.

As we await your own reflections, we offer here our own convictions with respect to the especially critical issue of the land, in the hope that you will take them into account:

1. We reaffirm our support for fair distribution of land through a clearly defined, equitable and democratically-controlled land reform. Only thus can land ownership be democratized; without it no effort to redistribute and reallocate land can be either effective or just. The struggle for independence was fought and blood was shed over the ownership of land in Zimbabwe. The imbalance inherited from the colonial era remains and still needs to be redressed. But to leave this in the hands of individuals or groups cannot lead to the democracy for which Zimbabwe struggled. The churches have a moral and spiritual obligation to provide leadership and to advocate on behalf of and uphold the rights of all, especially the powerless, the voiceless and marginalised with respect to the redistribution of land.

2. An effective plan for land reform will require a wise and careful review of the commercial farming sector to ensure that the agro-based economy and the farm laborers are not unduly affected. Any action that will further disrupt the economy of the country at this time of grave financial crisis needs to be avoided. The rights of the 300,000 farm workers, some of them migrant workers from neighboring countries, need to be protected.

3. The rights of white farm owners who have chosen to remain in Zimbabwe and to contribute to its development must also be respected. The uncontrolled process of land occupation without a solid plan for land redistribution has led to racial violence and the deaths of black and white Zimbabweans alike. Violence is inadmissible as a means of resolving conflict, whether it is exercised by individuals, groups or government. Even one more act of violence or killing is a sin against God who created every person in his own image.

4. A fair land redistribution policy must compensate the landless for the deprivation of land by colonialists and the landowners for the labour and capital they have invested in developing the agricultural sector.

5. The international community, and in particular the former colonial power, must help finance the programme for fair and democratic distribution of land.

6. In order for land distribution to be carried out deliberately and without violence, the national and international media must report on the land debate and ensuing problems dispassionately and in an objective and balanced way.

We share these considerations with you in love and with great hope for your ministry on behalf of the whole Church of Christ in the place you have been called to witness and to serve. May God strengthen you in your convictions and in your witness in this troubled time.

Yours in Christ, the Lord of all,

Konrad Raiser
General Secretary
World Council of Churches

Ishmael Noko
General Secretary
Lutheran World Federation

Planned visit to Zimbabwe in view of forthcoming elections
Letter to Mr Densen Mafinyani, General Secretary of the ZCC, 9 May 2000.

Dear Densen,

Greetings in Christ Jesus.

Subsequent to the last letter Dr. Raiser sent you together with Dr Ishmael Noko, we have been in consultation with several of the agencies to which letters have gone from the ZCC with respect to monitoring of the elections. These conversations and the continuing difficulties in the situation in Zimbabwe have led us to the conclusion that we should seek an early opportunity to meet with you and others in the country to seek a deeper understanding of the situation. Dr Raiser has thus decided to send two staff colleagues, Ato Melaku Kifle and Dr Rogate Mshana, to Zimbabwe to consult about how we and other international partners can be most supportive of the churches' efforts. We have also asked Canon Clement Janda to designate one of his staff to join in the visit.

Situations like these are often difficult to deal with through correspondence, and we feel deeply the need to share with you in person our support. At the same time we need to be better informed in order to provide the guidance churches and partners around the world seek of us.

I sincerely hope that you will welcome this visit, which will have the following terms of reference:

- to express solidarity with the ZCC and its churches
- to gain a deeper understanding of the present economic and political situation;
- to discuss your plans for monitoring elections and what we might do to support them;
- to discuss the proposal we made to you to send an ecumenical pastoral team to Zimbabwe.

Melaku and Rogate plan to depart from Geneva on 13 May and to stay for about a week. Their plan is to meet with you and your staff, with other church leaders, with political and civil society actors, and with government representatives.

I sincerely hope you will welcome this visit as an expression of ecumenical solidarity and accompaniment. I would be most grateful to receive your agreement by prompt e-mail.

Yours ever,

Dwain C. Epps
Coordinator
International Relations

WCC team recommends deployment of ecumenical peace observers for Zimbabwe elections

Press Statement issued in Harare, 29 May 2000.

A World Council of Churches (WCC) delegation visiting Zimbabwe at the invitation of the Zimbabwe Council of Churches (ZCC) announced today its decision to send international ecumenical peace observers to Zimbabwe for a period leading up to and following the elections scheduled for 24-25 June 2000.

The five-member team sent by WCC General Secretary Dr Konrad Raiser with the support of the General Secretary of the Lutheran World Federation (LWF), Dr Ishmael Noko, has just concluded an eight-day visit to Zimbabwe. The team included senior members of the Geneva, Switzerland-based WCC International Relations staff, a representative of the General Secretary of the All Africa Conference of Churches (AACC), a South African member of the AACC International Affairs Commission and a representative of ICCO, a WCC-related agency in the Netherlands.

During its eight-day stay in the country, the team held extensive discussions with the General Secretary Mr Densen Mafinyani and the officers and staff of the Zimbabwe Council of Churches. It also visited groups of church leaders in the cities of Mutare, Bulawayo and Gweru. It heard the perspective of the "freedom generation" of youth represented through the Student Christian Movement. In addition, it met with a range of civil society organizations, including the ZCTU (Zimbabwe Congress of Trade Unions), and with political parties including the ruling party ZANU-PF, the major opposition party MDC (Movement for Democratic Change) and other minority parties.

Team leader Melaku Kifle, WCC International Relations staff member from Ethiopia, said that "the purpose of the visit was to offer support and encouragement to the churches of Zimbabwe at a critical moment in the nation's history. We have not come with fixed ideas, but rather to listen and learn from the churches and others in order better to understand the challenges now confronting the country, and to see how the world-wide ecumenical fellowship can accompany them now."

Reporting to the officers of the ZCC at the conclusion of their visit, the WCC team said that it had heard three primary concerns as it met church, government and political, and civil society leaders around the country: issues related to the land, the rising incidence of violence and matters related to the forthcoming general elections.

The Land

"Most of the church representatives we met regretted the recent land occupations led by war veterans and encouraged by government leaders," said Rev. Dwain Epps, WCC International Relations Coordinator. "All regretted the violence and the deaths of Black farm workers, White farmers and those involved in the invasions," he said, "and we join with them in denouncing these losses of precious, God-given life. The lasting injustice results from the dispossession of native Zimbabweans' lands by the colonizers, but the answer to this pressing problem must be found through respect for the law and the implementation of a considered land policy that has had the benefit of wide consultation among all concerned." The team reported that church representatives in different parts of the country had called for more intensive efforts by the churches to develop essential elements of such policy and recommend them to the nation, its government and political parties.

Violence

Recalling that at the Eighth WCC Assembly, held in Harare in December 1998, the churches had decided to declare an Ecumenical Decade to Overcome Violence, Kifle said "wherever we went now, people reported to us on the rising tide of violence in Zimbabwe. This alarms us and calls churches around the world to support those here who believe that there are more creative ways to deal with conflict than the resort to violence." The team heard concerns not only about the violence related to land invasions, but also that being used to intimidate citizens, especially the poor, in the period between the February referendum on a new constitution, and the forthcoming June elections.

Elections

The team heard almost universal complaints that the lead-up to the June elections had so skewed the democratic process that it would hardly be possible to anticipate an election that meets international standards. At the same time, it was impressed that ordinary citizens and opposition political parties insisted that everyone should come to the polls. Remarkable efforts were being made to make it possible for all citizens to vote without fear. The churches' campaign to educate voters and to convince them that their ballots would be confidential was encouraging. Based on the evidence presented to it, the delegation was deeply concerned that these elections could not be fully "free and fair" given the limitations on open expression of opinion through the media, in campaign rallies of various parties and through uninhibited voter education. "Nevertheless," Epps said "we respect and admire the determination of Zimbabweans to exercise their democratic rights to present candidates and to vote despite all the impediments. Given the fact that the greatest threat to citizens now is the fear of violence, we have decided to support the 'peace monitors' being put in the field by the churches here through the sending of ecumenical 'peace observers' from churches in Africa and other parts of the world to assist in protecting people's rights."

The role of the churches

The WCC delegation heard in several quarters sincere appreciation for the role the Zimbabwean churches were playing in providing a unified, non-partisan, principled approach to issues confronting society in this time. At the same time it noted Christians' confessions that they and their churches had not spoken out clearly or soon enough to prevent violence, and that their own divisions have weakened their witness for peace, justice and the dignity of all in the sight of God. It encouraged the churches in their will to speak out as faithful disciples of the Prince of Peace. It appealed to the political parties to respect the varieties of opinion which give strength and vitality to a democratic society and to do so without rancor or hatred. And it appealed to the government to fulfill its responsibility to protect the rule of law and the fundamental freedom of expression for all citizens without distinction. "Senior government officials and others have expressed appreciation to the WCC for its solidarity with the people of Zimbabwe during the liberation struggle and for having accompanied the independent nation ever since," Kifle said. "In holding the last WCC Assembly here churches around the world gave a strong sign to the nation that they intend to walk alongside the churches here and the society of which they are a part as they strive to fulfill the promises of the leaders of the freedom struggle. We pray that reason will now prevail over passion, and that the interests of the community will dominate over the individualism, narrow personal power interests and resort to violence that are so characteristic of this age of globalization. The eyes of this region and of the world are now on Zimbabwe. May God grant that what it does now may offer them a sign of hope and be pleasing in God's sight."

The members of the WCC delegation included Mr Melaku Kifle and the Rev. Dwain C. Epps from WCC headquarters in Geneva, Mr Noel Okoth from the AACC in Nairobi, Rev. Eddie Makue from the South Africa Council of Churches, and Mr. Aad van der Meer from ICCO in the Netherlands.

Pastoral letter to the church leaders gathered at Victoria Falls
Sent to Bishop Dr Ambrose Moyo, President of the ZCC, 19 July 2001.

Dear Brothers and Sisters in the Lord,

Peace and grace to you. We have followed and continue to monitor the situation in Zimbabwe with great concern. It is a situation that is part and parcel of our prayers and meditation.

We are aware of your efforts towards peace, reconciliation and justice. The church in Zimbabwe is facing a testing of its faith. It is indeed a critical moment when the church is called to be a peacemaker, called to advocate for truth and justice with love and humility. Your role as a church is more critical than ever because forces of evil reside and are perpetuated by those you consider brothers and sisters in Christ but also by descent. Indeed the words of Paul to the Ephesians are relevant to you as ambassadors of Christ (Eph. 6:19-20)

It is our prayer that the Lord almighty will grant you the courage he gave prophet Elijah to speak to Ahab and his team. That your ministry will not be compromised. Rather that you shall be the "salt" and the "light" at this critical moment of your history.

We continue to pray for you and seek God's guidance in the situation. Remember that you are not alone in this process. Your fellow sister churches in Africa are with you despite their own problems. Africa needs a church that will restore hope to the people – a church that has a dream for the people –. a church that will speak the truth in and out of season. And may God through the Holy Spirit grant you the power and commitment to be his vessel of honour.

God's blessings and peace,

WCC Africa President
Dr Agnes Abuom

Congratulations to church leaders on Victoria Falls communiqué
Letter to Bishop Dr Ambrose Moyo of the Evangelical Lutheran Church in Zimbabwe, President of Zimbabwe Council of Churches, 2 August 2001.

Dear Bishop Moyo,

We have read with deep appreciation the communiqué issued by the Heads of Denominations at your retreat in Victoria Falls in mid-July. It was a particular pleasure to see that three senior members of the Government and the ruling party accepted your invitation for extensive conversations.

According both to your communiqué and press reports in Zimbabwe, you have addressed straightforwardly the critical issues of the day facing your country and its people. You have done so based on your responsibility to proclaim the Gospel values of justice, peace and love for one's neighbour. This you have done in a non-partisan way, openly and transparently and with the most vulnerable of the citizenry much at heart. In this way, you have responded to the call of the Harare Assembly which reiterated the appeal of the early ecumenical movement:: "Let the Church be the Church".

We have been particularly impressed by the commitment the church leaders expressed to continue to give witness in their life and worship to stemming the tide of violence, to promote peace, to care for the victims of injustice without distinction, and to continue through dialogue with all those involved in the politics of the nation to promote the values of democratic governance.

I look forward eagerly to being with you again briefly in late August to renew our friendships and to do all that I can to bring the weight of the worldwide ecumenical movement to bear in support of the principled positions you have taken.

May God continue to guide you and to bless your efforts as followers of Jesus Christ, the Prince of Peace.

Yours ever in His name,

Konrad Raiser
General Secretary

Statement on Zimbabwe

Adopted by the Executive Committee, Geneva, 11-14 September 2001.

The Executive Committee of the World Council of Churches, meeting in Geneva, 11-14 September 2001, expresses its deep appreciation to the Zimbabwe Council of Churches and to the church leaders for the Pastoral Letter to the Nation made public in Harare in late August of this year.

The member churches of the WCC have become increasingly concerned about the deteriorating economic and social situation in Zimbabwe and the rising tide of violence there. Part of this violence has been instigated by the encouragement given by the government of Zimbabwe to the War Veterans to occupy white-owned commercial farms. These invasions have claimed many lives of both white and black citizens. Compounding this violence were widespread acts of political intimidation in the months before the 2000 parliamentary elections. These have continued almost unabated. Early this year, the War Veterans began to attack and occupy private businesses.

Pressures applied by international financial institutions for structural adjustments of Zimbabwe's economy have exacerbated the impact on the people of the nation by further undermining the social welfare system and public health services at a time when the HIV/AIDS pandemic had already stretched it to the limits.

Zimbabwe's African neighbours and others around the world have been deeply troubled by all these developments in this nation that they had regarded to be a model of how racial tolerance, economic development and political democracy can contribute to a successful transition from colonial rule.

The WCC has a deep and long-standing attachment to the people of this land and to their churches. This began during the period of colonial rule, continued through the struggle for independence, has been sustained in the years since, and was renewed with the holding of the Eighth WCC Assembly in Harare in December 1998.

The ZCC pastoral letter reflects our concerns and has been issued at a critical time. Its urgent call for an open national dialogue on the crucial issues facing the country was warmly welcomed by the people of Zimbabwe. It makes clear and constructive recommendations on ways to lead the society as a whole away from the brink of self-destruction. These are addressed to the government, all political parties, the private sector and civil society as a whole. We sincerely hope that no particular addressee, especially the government and the ruling party, will view it as an attack on them or their institutions; but rather that all will welcome the church leaders' offer to facilitate the national dialogue and cooperate with them in pursuit of non-violent approaches to conflict transformation.

It is noteworthy that the church leaders have chosen to assume responsibility for their own national situation, and have made little reference to those outside Zimbabwe's borders whose impact is continually felt in this land. It is crucial, however, that the international community also take the churches' words to heart. Threats of further economic sanctions or to suspend all foreign aid until after the 2002 presidential elections could well impair the national dialogue and push Zimbabwe over the edge.

We therefore commend the approach taken by the recent Commonwealth meeting in Abuja, Nigeria. It recognizes the fact that "Land is at the core of the crisis in Zimbabwe and cannot be separated from other issues of concern...such as the rule of law, respect for human rights, democracy and the economy. A programme of land reform is, therefore, crucial to the resolution of the problem."

Zimbabweans are capable of restoring responsible governance, the rule of law and the democratic process in their country, and can put in place a responsible process of land reform that will do justice to all involved. They cannot, however, do this alone. International financial institutions, and especially those governments that made financial commitments to facilitate a fair process of peaceful land redistribution during the Lancaster House independence negotiations, must fully assume their obligations as well. In Abuja, the United Kingdom renewed its commitment. We hope that the U.S.A. will follow suit. Without these nations' assistance and the understanding and help of the international community, the nation will remain in jeopardy.

We continue to pray fervently that the people of Zimbabwe, their government, political parties and civil society as a whole will heed the call of the churches now, before it is too late. May God continue to bless and guide Zimbabwe in this critical hour of need.

Statement of the international ecumenical peace observer mission on the Zimbabwe presidential election

Presented to the press in Harare, 13 March 2002.

We, international ecumenical peace observers from the World Council of Churches (WCC) and the All Africa Conference of Churches (AACC), have been invited by the president of Zimbabwe, under the auspices of the Zimbabwe Council of Churches, to observe the 9-12 March 2002 presidential election processes.

Because we believe in the universality of the Christian Church, we consider it both a privilege and an inherent part of our Christian calling to accompany the people of Zimbabwe in their search for peace and justice via the democratic election of a Zimbabwean president. We are committed to non-partisanship, seeking the will of God, and observing the election process in line with human rights. In fulfilling our observer mission, we have been guided by the principles of universality, transparency, secrecy, fairness and freedom.

Universality

Since the country's liberation from a racist regime, the principle of "one man, one vote" has guided elections in Zimbabwe. In a country struggling with economic hardships, reaching out to every voter in this country is not an easy task. We commend the efforts of polling officers and monitors who have concluded an enormous task, and we applaud the voters who turned out in millions, showing civic responsibility and endurance.

But huge numbers of people were denied the possibility of voting. In Harare Province, many people gave up queuing and thousands were turned away, even after waiting for days. Pregnant women and others were forced to endure this mismanagement, which became a violation of the dignity of the voters.

We were also concerned about the high denial rate at polling stations, commonly reaching more than 10%. This was due, among other things, to deficiencies in the voter education and registration procedures, and the rigid application of these procedures. The postal vote system only functioned for a limited and preferred group; polling agents like teachers, for instance, were sent outside their constituencies and could have been included in the postal vote.

Transparency

Technically, the voting and counting followed the prescribed procedures, and polling agents from the two leading parties were present at almost all the polling stations we visited.

We appreciate that the government invited international election observers from most countries, but regret that only 109 out of more than 3,650 local observers from the churches were accredited.

232

We think the fuller participation of the civil society in voter education and monitoring of the election process would have increased its transparency.

We are concerned about the lack of public awareness and insight into the registration process and the supplementary voters' roll.

We were reminded of a recommendation by the Zimbabwean Council of Churches in their 2001 pastoral letter to amend the electoral law to allow for an independent electoral commission.

Voting secrecy

Our impression is that people had their chance to vote in secret, with the possible exception of postal votes, which we did not observe. We observed that the majority of the people assisted to vote were women, due to illiteracy. This jeopardized their access to a secret ballot. Voter education would have helped them to practise their right in secret.

Fairness

We acknowledge the important role of media in informing and educating the public during an election. However, we observed that the print media in Zimbabwe were polarized, with government-owned media supporting the ruling party and most of the private-owned media supporting the opposition party. This polarization exacerbated an already hostile atmosphere, to which some Western media also contributed. In Zimbabwe, the radio, the sole medium in most of the rural areas, and TV are controlled by the governing party.

Some of the limitations on the universality of the votes also led to limitations in fairness, giving one party an advantage over the others. The disenfranchisement of voters in Harare is an example of this. Closer analysis of the registration process may also reveal some problems of fairness and justice, including the issues of postal votes, supplementary voters' roll, and dual citizenship.

The many cases of intimidation we observed or which were reported to us constitute a serious limitation to fairness during these elections.

Freedom

To participate actively in an election, freedom of expression, association and assembly, and from intimidation are essential. The most serious problem in Zimbabwe during this election was the political violence. We received detailed information from the churches and human rights organizations that about 150 people were killed in political violence since April 2001. Many incidents of harassment, rape, malicious damage to property and general breakdown in the rule of law were reported to us, some of which took place during the days of the election.

The violence comes from the rivalry between the two leading parties. Both parties were behind violent episodes, but documentation from human rights organizations as well as our own observations indicate that the clear majority of cases should be blamed on the ruling party.

The Zimbabwean churches have repeatedly and strongly appealed to all parties to stop the violence and the recruitment of young people for organized violent activities. A special responsibility rests with the police to be non-partisan in political antagonism and respond to all types of violence.

We appeal for an end to the many arrests of opposition parties' officials and of others voicing opposition. We are also concerned about the so-called "fast track laws" which have allowed freedom of assembly and press freedom to be obstructed.

These observations preclude us from confirming the elections to be universal, transparent, fair or free.

Peace

We hope there will be a road to peace from what the Zimbabwe Council of Churches calls "a very frightening culture of politically motivated violence". But there is no easy road to peace. The road to peace includes the values of truth, justice and reconciliation. As expressed in Psalm 85, "Mercy and Truth have met together, and Justice and Peace have kissed each other." There can be no sustainable peace without economic justice. Peace can only be initiated through honest and open dialogue between earlier antagonists.

The ecumenical movement, globally and in Africa and as it observes the Decade to Overcome Violence, is engaged in creative peace programmes. We call upon churches and all peace-loving persons around the world to pray for the people of Zimbabwe and not forsake them, but support them in these difficult times.

ECUMENICAL POLICY

Justice, Peace and People's Security in North East Asia

Report of the Ecumenical Consultation held in Kyoto, Japan, 26 February – 3 March 2001.

Historical background

Since the 5th WCC Assembly in Nairobi in 1975, the World Council of Churches (WCC) has worked substantially on the issues of militarism and disarmament in the context of giving guidance to the churches on their work for justice and peace. The following year, a major consultation on militarism and its impact on Asian societies was held in Kuala Lumpur, under the auspices of the Christian Conference of Asia (CCA).

Seventeen years ago, the WCC's Commission of the Churches on International Affairs (CCIA) organized a consultation in 1984 on Peace and Justice in North-East Asia in the Japanese town of Tozanso. This was during a period when the Cold War threatened to explode into nuclear conflagration. In light of various dangerous regional confrontations, church leaders decided to look at ways to defuse conflict and bring about the reconciliation of people in the region.

Of particular concern was the division of Korea, which prevented Christians of North and South to work together to explore possible ways of reducing tensions and building peace on the peninsula. In the wider framework of regional concerns and within a caring ecumenical community, it was possible to reflect theologically on the calling of Christians to seek reconciliation on the basis of repentance and the hope which comes through faith in Christ. Affirming that a loving God would not leave any people without witnesses, church leaders from South Korea took the courageous step of trusting in the authenticity of Christians in the North who sent greetings to the consultation. They asked the WCC to initiate direct contact with the Korean Christians Federation (KCF) and to invite them into dialogue with South Korean Christians within the ecumenical family.

In its report to this consultation, the National Council of Churches in Korea expressed appreciation for the continued concern of the WCC and the churches around the world in raising awareness about the imperatives of Korean reunification. The stimulus that this gave to the Korean churches in their own effort to seek dialogue across political barriers has contributed significantly to the new political, economic, and human relationships, including the emotional reunions of separated families.

The collapse of the Soviet Union and the end of the Cold War have had their impact also on North East Asia. Major political and economic changes have affected all the countries in the region. This is a time of hope, but it is also a time of danger. While creative thought and committed action have helped to improve

235

the lives of the poor and the weak, these gains are overshadowed by the ascendance and impact of global economic interests, backed by the aggressive military projections of the powerful.

Purpose and participation

This consultation meets at a time when the yearnings for justice, peace and people's security have been heightened by recent political and strategic developments.

From 26 February to 3 March 2001, some 45 participants from churches in the region, ecumenical partners from Europe, North America and the Pacific, as well as staff members of the WCC, the CCA and the Council for World Mission (CWM) met at Kansai Seminar House in Kyoto, Japan. They set about discussing the capacity and tasks of churches and the ecumenical movement in meeting the significant new challenges to peace, justice and people's security in the North East Asian region.

Opening worship was held using traditional Japanese elements. Professor Masao Takenaka gave a message using the image of bamboo to convey Jesus' emptying himself to the point of death on the cross.

Keynote addresses were presented by Victor Hsu ("From Black Ships to Star Wars to a New Heaven and a New Earth") and Muto Ichiyo ("People's Security in Post-Cold War Situation"). Presentations by representatives of the National Christian Council in Japan (NCCJ), the National Council of Churches in Korea (NCCK), the China Christian Council (CCC), and the Presbyterian Church in Taiwan (PCT), outlined different perspectives on people's security in North-East Asia.

Stories were also shared about the struggle of Okinawan people against the destruction of the environment and the disruption of the life of the people by the presence and expansion of American military bases on their land, as well as the struggle of indigenous people of Taiwan for their land, heritage and dignity.

The consultation was disappointed that the Korean Christians Federation of the Democratic People's Republic of Korea could not be present. A message was received from the KCF during the consultation commending the WCC for this timely initiative, and expressing regret at being unable to attend. Nevertheless they sent warm Christian greetings and prayers for a successful consultation. They underlined the hope that the consultation would proceed in the spirit of the June 15 Joint Declaration of the Korean summit of 2000, and encouraged participants to support the process of peaceful reunification of Korea.

Theological understandings

Peace, justice and people's security are rooted in God's call for life abundant for all (I came that they may have life, and have it abundantly." John 10:10). A WCC "Consultation on Militarism" in 1977 affirmed that:

"Security for humanity has as its basis the loving will of God who desires that none shall perish and that all his creation should enjoy this fullness of life. False notions of security blind the nations and they should be challenged. The peace we seek is a 'warm peace': not merely the absence of war, but a peace best defined in the biblical word "shalom", which expresses a positive state of justice, mutual respect for differences, welfare, health, security; a community embracing all humanity which is a loving concern for all."

The biblical vision of security is not based on the security of the state, nation or king. Rather, it calls the state or "king" to do justice and seek God's *shalom* (Isaiah 10:1-2). In both Isaiah and Micah, the vision of *shalom* weaves abundant life inseparably into people's security that includes gender justice, social, ecological, economic and political conditions for peace with justice, both internally and internationally.

"The wolf shall live with the lamb, the leopard shall lie down with the kid... the lion shall eat straw like the ox... the weaned child shall put its hand on the adder's den... they will not hurt or destroy..." (Isaiah 11:6-9)

"...they shall beat their swords into ploughshares, and their spears into pruning hooks; nation shall not lift up sword against nation, neither shall they learn war any more; but they shall sit under their own fig trees, and no one shall make them afraid." (Micah 4:3-4)

All nations, economic systems and rulers stand under the judgment of the shalom vision wherein justice and peace are both the conditions for and the fruit of abundant life for all. This vision is for all persons and generations for fullness of life. It is historical and concrete. The sins of the past must be remembered and repented. Women, children, the old and the excluded must be full and equal participants. Impunity must be replaced by truth, justice and a reconciled community.

Reconciliation restores broken and unjust relations between persons, communities and nations. It is this *ministry of reconciliation* to which churches are called today, but reconciliation is a difficult and costly process which requires courage and prophetic witness.

The emphasis of the writer of the Psalms is always on the needs and dignity of the poor, the widow, the orphan and the sojourner. Jesus takes Isaiah's vision and puts the oppressed, the captives, the blind and poor at the centre of his mission. (Luke 4:16ff) For Jesus, a sure sign of the reign of God was that the blind be enabled to see, the lame to walk, and the poor to receive good news. (Matt. 11:5) This is the biblical test for human and people's security. There can be no just measure of society based on GDP, capital growth, size of the army, or average wealth. People's security requires addressing the structural realities of the global and local situations.

From the perspective of faith, the security of all is judged by the "shalom security" of the poorest, the weakest, the excluded, the subjugated, the people, the *minjung*. Christians are called into the struggle for security of women, for children, for tribal and aboriginal peoples, for all those undervalued and marginalized by corporate-led, market-driven globalization.

The measure of people's security is abundant life for "the least of these" in a globalized world economy afflicted by extreme poverty, disease, injustice, environmental degradation and militarized hegemony.

In the eyes of faith, peace, justice and people's security in North-East Asia today require that we seek to realize Isaiah's vision:

"For I am about to create new heavens and a new earth... No more shall there be an infant that lives but a few days, or an old person who does not live out a lifetime... They shall build houses and inhabit them; they shall plant vineyards and eat their fruit... They shall not labour in vain, or bear children for calamity; for they shall be offspring blessed by the Lord – and their descendants as well... They shall not hurt or destroy on all my holy mountain, says the Lord." (Isaiah 65:17-25)

The new context

The consultation celebrated the significant improvements in this region over the past two decades. However, new threats to the security of people have emerged. Important points of contention continue to divide societies and even churches in this region.

In 1984, many of the churches of the region suffered under repressive military dictatorships and their national security ideologies. Most of these regimes have now been replaced by democratically elected governments. In some cases, churches have gained a very considerable political influence with their governments. In other cases, relations have improved but the relationship is still uncertain and churches proceed with caution. In still others, churches are a minority with little means of direct influence.

Participants noted both positive and negative aspects of globalization. For example, the means of communication have increased dramatically, making it easier for civil society groups, non-governmental organizations and people's movements to communicate rapidly, to share information and to engage in common advocacy.

In its report, the PCT drew attention to the rapid growth in numbers of transnational non-governmental organizations and to their positive influence for justice, peace, human rights, development and protection of the environment. To achieve these goals, we cannot rely on governments alone.

The consultation encouraged churches to form new alliances with other partners in civil society, other faith groups and academic research institutes and coalitions.

238

There is a noticeable "globalization from below" by which citizens effectively organize themselves for common action across national boundaries.

Globalization has made us aware of our interdependence across national and geographical boundaries. As the CCC noted in its report, among the negative effects of globalization are the marginalization and exclusion of workers, job and income insecurity. There is a need for common commitment to better standards of living for all, a better quality of life for those who suffer most, so that economic benefits can accrue to all, and the environmental heritage can be protected for future generations.

Reliance on military solutions to human problems and divisions persists and in some ways has grown. The consultation questioned the justice and value of human security based on military security. Solutions to conflicts too often rely on military power. But this cannot be the ultimate basis for people's security. There is a need to decrease the potential for major conflicts through confidence-building measures and increase peace-building through peace education and conscientization. This necessitates dialogue between parties in conflict, so that legitimate grievances can be addressed.

After the collapse of East European socialist states in 1991, there was an expectation that the nuclear threat would recede into the background. Recent developments show a new reliance on military strategies and technology. Recent strategic directives coming from the US Pentagon have served to create new fears and insecurities in the region. New developments in missile defense – National Missile Defense (NMD) and Theatre Missile Defense (TMD), if implemented, will almost certainly lead to a new arms race. The projection of military power as a method to confirm and protect economic hegemony was disparaged by the consultation as was the continuing arms sales and the purchase of new generations of weapons by countries in the region.

The consultation heard in a report by NCCJ that Japan is being pushed by the USA to assume a greater military role with support from significant sectors of Japanese society. Major financial resources are being transferred for US forces in Japan. There is pressure for Japan to amend its peace constitution and strengthen more directly its military role. Japan is gradually being strengthened in the new strategic scheme, causing alarm from neighbours who have not forgotten Japan's aggressive historical role in the entire region. In this regard the churches have been particularly courageous and prophetic in emphasizing non-violence as a means of securing peace and security for all.

Based on the conviction that conflict flash points can be more effectively addressed regionally, there is recognition that sub-regional and regional mechanisms and common security systems should be explored and encouraged.

The consultation nevertheless believed that in their ecumenical witness, churches have continued responsibility for peace, justice and security for the people. In group discussions, participants therefore sought to identify some common understandings about the threats which exist in their societies and in the region. They affirmed the desire to be instrumental in building bridges of caring humanity across the divides of ideology, politics and nation. They sought to find the parameters of a process by which to continue to consult together about alternative approaches to security in this region—alternatives that would replace reliance on nuclear weapons and military forces, with new people-based systems of security, in the framework of the Decade to Overcome Violence.

Many of the threats to peace, justice and peoples security addressed at this consultation were experienced equally by all churches represented. However one source of conflict in the North-East Asia region – the tension across the Taiwan straits – gave rise to continuing disagreement.

Representatives from CCC and PCT expressed different understandings and agreed that the best way to resolve all the issues should be sought by peaceful means. Any attempt to resort to military violence can only endanger people's security in the region.

Recognizing the complexity and sensitivity of this issue, the consultation was unable to reach a consensus on how to resolve these differences. Participants agreed to continue ecumenical efforts to provide forums for this question to be discussed in a way which maintains the unity of the fellowship of the churches joined together in the World Council of Churches. It urged the wider ecumenical movement to keep these two churches in its prayers, and to seek every opportunity to promote exchanges and face-to-face encounters between them.

Participants hoped that through worship and prayer, and the sharing of their stories with one another, Christians from both sides of the Taiwan straits might enhance their fellowship as a first step towards discussing common concerns.

Statement on South Asia
Adopted by the Central Committee, Geneva, 26 August – 3 September 2002.

The situation in the South Asia region poses a major threat to world peace. Two nuclear powers, India and Pakistan, remain in a state of perpetual and growing military confrontation. The region has been the scene of inter-state and intra-state violence and conflict for the last five decades. It is home to over a billion people and provides a contrast of two different worlds – that of the rich elite minority and a poor, disadvantaged and socially marginalized majority. Its societies are being torn asunder as a result of nationalism, ethnocentrism and religious extremism.

Three smaller countries, Nepal, Sri Lanka and Bangladesh, are also in crisis. Nepal, the only Hindu kingdom in the world, is faced with a growing "Maoist" insurgency that has resulted in immense loss of life, prosperity and security for its people. The ethnic conflict in Sri Lanka has taken a heavy toll of human lives and has brought the country's economy to a virtual standstill. The signing of the agreement in February 2002 to cease hostilities between the Sri Lankan government and the Liberation Tigers of Tamil Eelam (LTTE) provides a sign of hope. However, since it gained independence from Pakistan through a liberation war in 1971, Bangladesh remains unable to overcome the confrontational nature of its politics. Opportunist politicians and repeated military interventions have brought the country to virtual ruin. Its economy remains stagnant and wholly dependent on massive external assistance.

South Asian societies are plagued by endemic corruption and confrontational politics that often result in grave and serious human rights violations of opposition political parties. In an ever-growing environment of intolerance, religious minorities and religious freedom are under attack not only at the hands of the authorities but also in several cases from the majority communities.

The churches and Christians in the region are overall a small minority faith. The growing climate of religious intolerance and nationalism seriously threatens their and other religious minorities' rights to manifest their faith in public worship and practice. Christians are often pressured to be silent, suffering witnesses to hope in turbulent times. In such critical times the participation of Christians in the life and action of the community comes out of their understanding and exercise in faithfulness to the power of the gospel. In the midst of brokenness, violence and conflicts, Christians and churches are challenged to be messengers of peace and provide space for healing and reconciliation.

Against this background, and in the context of the Decade to Overcome Violence, the Central Committee takes the following actions:

1. *Religion, Politics and Intolerance*

1.1 The South Asian Region has been the dwelling for major religions of the world, Islam, Hinduism, Buddhism, and Christianity. For centuries people practising these religions have lived in peace and harmony. That situation now seems to be changing. In the last decade religion has emerged as a significant and sometimes a dominant factor in intra-state conflicts. It has been manipulated to promote narrow political or nationalist interests and objectives. Religious intolerance has grown almost universally and South Asian societies are no exception to it.

1.2 In India the emergence of Bhartiya Janata Party (BJP) as a major force on the political scene has seriously undermined the secular base of the country. During recent years, Christians and Muslims have come under attack and their places of worship have been burnt. Attacks against the Dalit community too have increased. Despite all the constitutional guarantees Dalits continue to suffer indignities and discriminations not only at the hands of the authorities but also at the hands of the majority. In Pakistan the environment of religious intolerance, which was nurtured during the 11 years period of General Zia's military rule, has made the lives and properties of Christian minorities insecure. Many families have suffered because of indiscriminate use of the blasphemy laws that have targeted innocent Christians. Christian villages and churches have come under attack at the instigation of Islamic extremist groups. The situation has worsened as a result of the US-led war in Afghanistan. In Sri Lanka and Bangladesh, Buddhist and Islamic groups have often used religion for political purposes to incite hatred and violence against religious minorities.

1.3 The increasing religious intolerance in the whole of South Asia has claimed many victims. It has undercut the multi-cultural, multi-religious and pluralistic base of societies in the region. Intolerance has encouraged a new wave of ideologies, which distort and seek to rewrite history and which incite communal violence, building walls of separation and hatred between communities and peoples.

The Central Committee *calls on the churches* including those in the region to:

* *raise awareness* of the spread of religious extremism that is affecting most religions - Islam, Hinduism, Christianity and Buddhism - negatively. This negative influence of religion often originates with groups acting out of ignorance and obscurantism in order to impose their particular religious views on society;

* *encourage and support* civic educational projects that promote understanding, tolerance, peace and inter-communal harmony at local, national and regional levels;

* *engage in dialogue on human rights* with people of other faiths and convictions in order to build a culture of peace and address such issues as rights of minorities and intolerance;

* *draw attention to the plight of the Dalits* suffering from the discriminatory practices and policies of the Indian government and to help secure the implementation of constitutional guarantees through legal recourse, awareness building and advocacy at the national and international levels;

* *mobilise* national and international support for the repeal of the Blasphemy Laws in Pakistan.

2. India – Pakistan Confrontation and the Kashmir Dispute

The post September 11th developments have again brought Pakistan and India to the brink of a major war. The war in Afghanistan and the US presence in the region have added a new dimension to an already tense situation in the sub-continent. The military establishment in Pakistan is again being rewarded for its support to the US-led international coalition against terrorism. Yet while the military regime actively participates in the war against Taliban and Al-Qaida networks in Afghanistan, it remains lukewarm in its political will to disband the militant Islamic groups at home that are engaged in violent actions in Kashmir.

2.1 The Kashmir dispute remains a thorn in the side of India and Pakistan. Since the partition of the sub-continent in 1947, the two neighbours have fought three
242

major wars. The present deployment of millions of troops across the borders could lead to open hostilities with prospects of a nuclear war that neither side can afford.

2.2 Despite the UN Security Council Resolutions of the 1940s and 1950s and the Simla Agreement of 1972, there is presently an impasse with little prospect of the parties returning to the negotiating table to seek an amicable settlement of the dispute through dialogue. The situation in Kashmir took a turn for the worse in the late 1980s, when India, instead of listening and responding to the grievances of the people of Kashmir, sent in the military forces to the valley to quell a popular uprising. The situation since has continued to deteriorate with no signs of return to normalcy. The Pakistan-sponsored incursions by Islamic militants to support the struggle of the Kashmiri people have further aggravated an already grave situation.

2.3 The people of India and Pakistan have paid a high price because of this perpetual state of military confrontation between the two countries. It has led to a steady increase in defence expenditure. Such increase has come at the cost of health care, food, education, adequate housing and other projects in the human development sectors further adding to the sufferings of the common people.

The Central Committee

affirms that the Kashmir dispute be resolved in accordance with the wishes of the people of Jammu and Kashmir. The basis for such resolution should be the principles enunciated in the UN Security Council Resolutions of the 1940s and 1950s and it should be pursued in the spirit of the Simla Agreement of 1972;

reiterates that there is no military solution to the Kashmir dispute and the two parties should return to the negotiating table without delay;

appeals to the governments of India and Pakistan to take immediate steps to restore and normalise relations by undertaking confidence-building measures that could pave the way for a political dialogue;

calls on the government of India to allow increased access to the Kashmir Valley by non-governmental organisations concerned with human rights; and *on the government of Pakistan* to refrain from providing support to Islamic militant groups involved in cross border terrorism;

encourages WCC member churches to be in solidarity with churches in India and Pakistan and assist them in their ministry of healing and reconciliation in the region;

urges the churches in India and Pakistan to undertake the following actions to facilitate the process of an amicable settlement of the Kashmir dispute:

- to build awareness amongst the churches in the two countries about the urgency of resolving the Kashmir dispute;

- to encourage and support people-to-people relations between India and Pakistan for better understanding and for promotion of peace and reconciliation in the region;

- to organise prayer vigils, where possible on an inter-faith basis, to promote peace and reconciliation between the two countries.

3. The Nuclear Threat

The May 1998 nuclear tests by India and Pakistan caught the international community unawares. Tensions between the two countries increased, giving rise to the prospects of an accelerated arms race in the region. The tests were condemned worldwide and on 6th June 1998 United Nations Security Council adopted Resolution 1172 calling on the two countries to refrain from further nuclear tests. The Resolution laid down a set of guidelines to bring the two countries into the mainstream of non-proliferation regime. The ecumenical community is of the considered view that it is dangerous to rely on the assumption that nuclear weapons will not be used in South Asia. The Kargil episode in 1999 and the December 13th, 2001 attack on the Indian Parliament have shown that there is little appreciation of the changed situation in the sub-continent since the May 1998 nuclear test.

The Central Committee *calls on the governments of India and Pakistan* to:

- *dismantle* their nuclear weapons and become parties to the Nuclear Non-Proliferation Treaty and the Comprehensive Test Ban Treaty;

- *place* all their civilian nuclear programmes under internationally recognised safeguard arrangements; and

- *cooperate* with other states in the region in working towards a nuclear-weapon free zone in South Asia.

calls on both governments in the meantime to immediately implement measures to reduce the risk of deliberate or inadvertent nuclear attacks by:

- *jointly committing* to a policy of no first use and formalising that commitment through a bilateral agreement;

- *refraining* from arming delivery systems;

- *ensuring* effective central civilian political control over nuclear policies and facilities; and

- *expanding* **and enhancing** the existing agreement prohibiting attacks on each other's nuclear installations.

further calls on the governments of India and Pakistan to:

- *halt* all further research, development and production of nuclear weapons or weapons components; and

- *cease* production of fissile materials and to support international negotiations towards a global ban on the production of fissile materials.

244

calls on other governments to:

- *end immediately* all material and political support to India and Pakistan for the development and production of nuclear weapons and/or their delivery systems.

calls on its member churches in South Asia to:

- *urge* their respective governments to work towards a South Asia nuclear-weapon-free zone; and to
- *undertake* public awareness programmes in support of the abolition of nuclear weapons in South Asia and globally.

calls on churches in other parts of the world **to:**

- *support* the churches and ecumenical bodies in South Asia in their efforts to promote a nuclear-weapons-free zone in that region; and to
- *call upon their own governments* to withhold all support related to nuclear weapons research, production and deployment by India and Pakistan and encourage achievement of the goal of a nuclear-weapons-free zone in South Asia.

4. *Sri Lanka's Ethnic Conflict*

The conflict in Sri Lanka, since it escalated in 1983, has claimed over sixty thousand lives on both sides of the ethnic divide. The war has left the country's economy in tatters. For over two decades people – mostly Tamils – have been subjected to draconian laws. Torture, detention without trial, extra-judicial killings and curtailment of freedom of the press are common practices of the state. The LTTE has imposed strict conditions in areas under its control where extortion, summary executions and forced recruitment, particularly of children, for war purposes are common practices.

The escalation of the war in 1980s and 1990s resulted in the mass exodus of Tamil refugees to India, Western Europe, North America and Australia; in addition a large number of people in the North and East were uprooted as internally displaced persons. Several attempts were made to mediate a peace agreement between the Sri Lankan government and the LTTE without much success. The situation unexpectedly changed in February 2002, however, when the Norwegian Government facilitated a Memorandum of Understanding between the Sri Lankan government and LTTE to cease hostilities, pending the peace talks that are scheduled to take place in Bangkok, Thailand.

The Central Committee:

- *welcomes* the Memorandum of Understanding arrived at between the government of Sri Lanka and the Liberation Tigers of Tamil Eelam;
- *urges* the ecumenical community to
  - *accompany* the sister churches in Sri Lanka in their journey to peace;

- *pray for, encourage and provide solidarity support* to the National Council of Churches in Sri Lanka and the Church of Norway in their joint efforts to build awareness and mobilise support for the peace process;
- *mobilise support* nationally and internationally in favour of the Peace Process in Sri Lanka;
- *provide human and material resources* for reconciliation and reconstruction of Sri Lanka.

5. *Bangladesh and Religious Minorities*

After three decades of Independence, Bangladesh has failed to evolve a viable constitutional framework of democratic governance. The country has suffered frequent changes of government and bloody military coups. Its founding principle of "Secular Bengali Nationalism" has collapsed and the country is presently caught between the throes of abrasive right-wing Islamic political parties and opportunist politicians. Lack of development of parliamentary political culture has paved the way for destructive politics of the street. There is an urgent need for building a culture of tolerance and peace in the country.

The Central Committee *calls on the churches* to:

• *monitor* the situation of the religious minorities in the country, and provide pastoral and solidarity support to the churches and Christians in the country;

• *provide* human and material resources to the churches of Bangladesh to enable them to initiate inter-religious cooperation and dialogue to promote tolerance and build a culture of peace.

AFGHANISTAN

Statement on the initiation of bombing in Afghanistan
Issued by Mr Georges Lemopoulos, Acting General Secretary, Geneva, 8 October 2001.

The initiation of bombings and missile attacks against Afghanistan last night, while not unexpected, is nevertheless of profound concern to the World Council of Churches. As the churches joined in the ecumenical movement have done so often over the past century, they have again in recent weeks sought to avoid this renewed use of overwhelming military power. The WCC has reflected this consistent and widely held stance of the churches in a letter sent last week to UN secretary-general Kofi Annan by Dr Konrad Raiser, the general secretary of the WCC.

We abhor war. The first WCC assembly in 1948 called it a sin against God and humanity. We do not believe that war, particularly in today's highly technologized world, can ever be regarded as an effective response to the equally abhorrent sin of terrorism. Our experience of ministry to the victims of war convinces us that acts of war can never spare civilian populations despite all the precautions of military planners. Nor do we believe that war can be described as an act of humanitarianism or that the practice of war can be legitimately linked to the promise of humanitarian assistance.

We therefore pray that the United States of America and the United Kingdom will bring a prompt end to the present action, and that no other state join with them in it. We pray for those who live under the bombs and missiles, hoping against hope that they will be spared. We pray for the minority Christian churches and communities who are placed in danger as a result of such action: especially now for those in Pakistan who, despite their own poverty and small minority status, began planning last week to assist the present wave of Afghans fleeing from terror. We pray for the Muslim and other religious communities who despite President Bush's and Prime Minister Blair's affirmations to the contrary, are likely to consider themselves the targets of this and the other military actions foreseen to follow. We pray for the leaders of these and all nations that God will invest them with wisdom and compassion in this terrible time; that they turn away from the temptation of the sword and toward actions for global justice that provide the chief hope to overcome terrorism in all its forms and to provide true peace and security for the nations and peoples of our world.

BANGLADESH

Expression of condolences after church bombing
Letter to H.E. Mr Iftekhar Ahmed Chowdhury, Ambassador of Bangladesh to the United Nations Office in Geneva, 12 June 2001.

Your Excellency,

It was with great sadness that we received the sad news of the bombing of the Roman Catholic Church in Baniarchar, Muksedpur, Dist. Gopalgonj, on 3rd June, conveyed to us by Mr Subodh Adhikary, General Secretary of the National Council of Churches in Bangladesh.

I write to express through you to the Government and people of Bangladesh, and especially to the friends and loved ones of the deceased and injured our most sincere condolences.

The outpouring of public condemnations of this atrocity, the prompt visit of the Home Minister to the site of the tragedy, and the assurances of the Prime Minister that a full enquiry will be undertaken as to the responsibility for this violent act all attest to the will of your nation to hold firmly to the principles and practice of tolerance.

We are confident that every possible effort will be made to bring those responsible to justice as a means of assuring all that strict respect for the rule of law will reign in your nation. In a global climate that too often witnesses today the resort to violence as a result of religious bigotry and intolerance, these timely and

247

decisive measures are clearly essential to the public welfare of believers of all faiths and that of the public as a whole.

Sincerely and respectfully yours,

(Rev.) Dwain C. Epps
Coordinator
International Relations

CHINA, PEOPLES REPUBLIC

Message to the seventh national conference of the China Christian Council
Conveyed from Geneva, 16 May 2002.

Sisters and brothers in Christ,

Grace to you and peace from God our Father and the Lord Jesus Christ!

I send you warm greetings and congratulations of the World Council of Churches on the occasion of the convening of the Seventh National Conference of the China Christian Council. We are profoundly aware of the significance of this event in the life of the CCC. Aware of the important matters before you during this session, I assure you of our fervent prayers as you address matters related to the management of the church and the choice of new leaders. At this first National Conference in the new century, you face great challenges of providing spiritual nurture to your congregations as the number of Christians continues to grow at an impressive rate. You will be addressing the continuing need to train thousands of new lay leaders and pastors and to equip them to guide the congregations into a vital witness to the wider society that is itself experiencing an era of unprecedented economic expansion and rising expectations. In fulfilling these tasks you may count on the full support of the World Council of Churches for the life and ministry of the China Christian Council.

We give thanks to God for the blessings he has spread upon you and for the vitality of the faith amongst you. May you feel anew the power of the Holy Spirit that descended upon the first church in Jerusalem in this season. Be assured that you will be accompanied by the prayers of the worldwide ecumenical fellowship as you worship, pray and deliberate day by day.

Yours ever in Christ,

Konrad Raiser
General Secretary

Message on the extension of the mandate of UNAMET
Letter to UN Secretary-General Kofi Annan, 3 September 1999.

Dear Mr Secretary-General,

The Central Committee of the World Council of Churches, which has met here in Geneva for the past ten days, has again carefully considered the situation in East Timor. During these discussions, the role of the United Nations in negotiations which have led to the referendum just held has been held up as a sign of the effectiveness of the UN in promoting the peaceful resolution of disputes. On behalf of the Central Committee, I congratulate you and the staff of UNAMET for the successful culmination of the electoral process. Member churches of the WCC have participated in this process by sending observers and monitors who, together with the WCC member church in the territory - Gereja Kristen di Timor Timur - have worked in close coordination with UNAMET and kept us informed of developments on a daily basis.

We have been gratified by the high turnout of voters despite threats and intimidation. The United Nations deserves credit for organizing this historical exercise of self-determination that allowed the East Timorese people an opportunity to express their hopes and aspirations for the future.

While we commend the work undertaken by the UNAMET to determine the will of the East Timorese people, we remain concerned about the security of the population in the post-referendum period between the interim and the implementation phase. We therefore welcome the decision of the United Nations Security Council to extend the mandate of the UNAMET until the 30th November, and to add to the civilian police and military liaison components.

Given the present conditions in East Timor, the WCC is of the view that the United Nations should maintain a strong presence in the territory to defuse conflict and tension between the pro-integration and pro-independence groups in order to establish peace and promote stability and reconciliation. In order for this process to be brought to a successful conclusion, it is important that steps be taken in consultation with the parties to ensure that all factions in East Timor are disarmed. All sectors of the population, irrespective of the result of the ballot, must be integrated into the political life of the country in a free and democratic environment.

As you will see from the attached decision of the Central Committee (cf. p. 257), we are of the view that the mandate and term of UN presence in East Timor need to be reviewed and adjusted as appropriate in order to respond to the continuing need. I therefore urge you to propose such measures to the Security Council.

Assuring you of our deep appreciation for your efforts in the field of peace-making which respects the Charter mandate that every effort should be made to avoid the use of force to settle disputes, and assuring you of our prayers, I remain

Respectfully yours,

Konrad Raiser
General Secretary

INDIA

Expression of solidarity with Christian leaders
Letter to the Rev. Dr Ipe Joseph, General Secretary of the National Council of Churches in India, 1 February 1999.

Dear Brother in Christ,

Your letter of 29 January and the information you sent on the initiatives taken by NCCI and its member churches on the tragic events in South Gujarat and elsewhere in India were very welcome. We have been following the unfolding situation with growing anxiety, and many of the member churches have sought our advice about how they could helpfully respond to reports of the violence on Christmas against churches and Christians, and to the tragic murders of Dr Graham Stewart Staines and his sons, Timothy and Philip.

We are grateful for the witness the churches of India are giving on behalf of the worldwide ecumenical fellowship in this time of trial. Our hearts go out to all those who have suffered, to their families, to their churches, and to all those in your beloved land who are bereaved as a result of these senseless and brutal acts of violence.

We understand, and shall respect your wish that the World Council of Churches issue no public statement on the matter for the moment, and will share the information you have sent with concerned churches and ecumenical councils around the world.

We are grateful to know of the meeting scheduled tomorrow at CNI Bhavan between leaders of the several Christian traditions to consult together on the situation and on next steps to be taken. We await eagerly the results of your deliberations and your further guidance. We assure all those present of our prayers that this night of darkness will soon be dispelled by the light of the love, tolerance and interreligious harmony to which the people of India have been so committed.

We are especially dismayed that some of the media in your country have so falsely and maliciously mis-stated the positions and intentions of the churches joined in the World Council of Churches. From its very beginnings, the ecumenical movement has stood for the principle of religious freedom and tolerance in a way which is in consonance with Art. 25 of the Constitution of
250

India. From the first time this concern was mooted, at the 1910 International Missionary Conference, the churches advocated that religious freedom is a basic right shared by all citizens, irrespective of their faith, and warned Christians and churches against claiming this right as their exclusive privilege. Throughout this century, the WCC has actively defended the equal claim of all religious communities to the full rights of religious freedom articulated in Art. 14 of the Universal Declaration of Human Rights.

As your appeals make clear, it is the responsibility of the Central and State Governments to maintain the present Constitution of India, to guarantee respect for its provisions related to the rights of religious and other minorities, and to uphold the obligations India has assumed by ratifying the International Covenants on Human Rights. Only when the rule of law prevails, when the rights of all, of every community and individual, are respected, can there be hope for justice, peace and well-being of both the majority and the minorities. As a result of their bitter experiences with religious intolerance at the time of the birth of their nation Indians know this better than most. The founders of the Indian nation thus provided constitutional guarantees to protect against a recurrence of such tragedies. The present-day leadership must assume its responsibilities to the Constitution, to fairness and equity, and to maintain order in the face of extremist acts.

We pray constantly that God may give you the strength to persevere in your commitment to serve the whole Nation and the people of India. We remain with you in spirit as you consider what you are called to do now as Christians together with people of other faiths throughout the land who share your devotion to peace, progress and mutual respect.

In the name of Christ, to whom be the glory for ever and ever,

Konrad Raiser
General Secretary

Condemnation of inter-communal violence in Gujarat
Letter to member churches and the National Council of Churches in India, 5 March 2002.

Dear Sisters and Brothers in Christ,

The World Council of Churches has received with shock and profound sorrow the news of the tragic outbreak of indiscriminate communal violence in the cities and towns of Gujarat that has already resulted in over hundred deaths and threatens to engulf the entire country. Together with you, we condemn and deplore such wanton acts of violence that have resulted in immense sufferings of people of both Muslim and Hindu communities. Through you, we convey our heartfelt condolences to the bereaved families of the victims.

In recent times there has been an almost universal increase in incidents of religious intolerance and violence. This trend must be stopped before our societies are further torn asunder by hatred and senseless killings at the hands of extremists. It is the responsibility of each and every person to prevent such ruthless acts of destruction and disruption that are certainly contrary to all religious beliefs. It is imperative for people of all faiths to rise to the challenge to defuse violence and conflict and promote inter-communal peace and harmony amongst the people.

India has been a model of secular democracy founded on principles of plurality and diversity. These must be preserved in the interest of all. The spiritual teachings of Mahatma Gandhi, who belonged to Gujarat, are based on *"Ahimsa – non violence"*. During his lifetime the great Mahatma worked for communal harmony and mutual tolerance as a necessity for all times and for all races and called for the sharing of each other's sorrow to strengthen the bonds of common humanity. The tragic events in Gujarat today discredit the spirit and teachings of this great leader who held both Hindus and Muslims dear to his heart.

We share the pain and sorrow of the Indian people. Our prayers are with you ever as you seek to uphold non-violence and act as bridge builders and agents of peace and reconciliation in your beloved nation.

Yours in Christ,

Georges Lemopoulos
Acting General Secretary

INDIA-PAKISTAN DISPUTE

Expression of hope for the success of India-Pakistan summit
Letter to member churches and councils of churches in India and Pakistan, 11 July 2001.

The World Council of Churches welcomes the Summit Meeting in Agra from the 14–16 July 2001 between the prime minister of India, Atal Behari Vajpayee, and the president of Pakistan, General Pervez Musharraf.

At the Agra Summit the two leaders face an urgent challenge to resolve all outstanding issues to ensure an environment of peace and security. The two neighbours have fought three major wars since they gained independence from the British colonialists in 1947. Caught in a vicious cycle of enmity and hatred, the two have diverted scarce resources towards defence spending in a suicidal arms race that has driven millions of their people into despair and destitution. The nuclear tests carried out in 1998 contributed to further aggravation of tensions between the two countries and caused de-stability in the already troubled South Asian region. High on the agenda of the summit is the resolution of the long-standing festering Kashmir dispute and the dangers posed by nuclear weapons of both the countries, the latter underlining the importance of avoiding a conflict which could spiral into a war, possibly a nuclear war.

Given the history of dismal relationships of animosity and broken promises, the World Council of Churches shares the hope of the churches and the people of goodwill in the two countries that the Agra Summit can help to restore much-needed mutual trust and confidence to overcome the obstacles on the path to peace in the subcontinent. For far too long, the two countries have suffered as a result of the continuous orchestration of mutual hate by a section of the people on both sides. As a result, not enough has been done to create a culture of peace. The summit provides an opportunity for the leadership to pave the way for normal and cooperative relations that can open doors for new opportunities in this period of globalization, to concentrate on accelerating economic growth, social development and justice for their people.

The churches in India and Pakistan together with civil society organizations and people of goodwill have been engaged in efforts to promote peace and reconciliation in the sub-continent. At a time when the World Council of Churches has proclaimed the years 2001–2010 as the Decade to Overcome Violence and has called on Christians and churches to be bridge-builders and to address issues of violence in their own context, it is important that the churches uphold the Agra Summit in their intercessions.

In the name of Jesus Christ the Lord of Peace who has called us to His service,

Geneviève Jacques
Acting General Secretary

Appeal to the Governments of India and Pakistan for normalization of relations with Pakistan

Identical letters to H.E. Mr Atal Bihari Vajpayee, Prime Minister of India, and H.E. General Pervez Musharraf, President of Pakistan, 7 October 2002.

Your Excellency,

The World Council of Churches is a fellowship of three hundred and forty Churches all around the world. It was founded in August 1948 in Amsterdam and has its offices in Geneva, Switzerland. The aims of the World Council of Churches amongst others include expressing the common concern of the Churches in the service of human need, the breaking down of barriers between people, the promotion of one human family in justice and peace.

Over the years the Council has closely monitored developments in South Asia. Of particular concern has been the growing incidents of religious intolerance and violence in India and Pakistan. Also, the continuing military build-up and confrontation between the two countries has raised the spectre of a nuclear war that has serious implications for the lives of the people in the region.

Taking note of these developments, the Central Committee of the World Council of Churches adopted the accompanying Statement (copy enclosed) on South Asia including India and Pakistan. The Statement amongst others calls on the member Churches of the Council to be in solidarity with Churches in India and Pakistan and assist them in their ministry of healing and reconciliation in the region.

The World Council of Churches appeals to Your Excellency to restore and normalise relations between India and Pakistan by undertaking comprehensive confidence building measures that could pave the way for a political dialogue. Such a dialogue in turn would create an environment where other important and complex issues like Kashmir and nuclear proliferation could be addressed.

We assure Your Excellency of our continuing prayers and support in the efforts to seek a peaceful resolution of the conflict between the two countries.

Respectfully yours,

Peter Weiderud
Director
Commission of Churches on International Affairs

INDONESIA

Ecumenical delegation visit on request of the WCC eighth assembly
Press release issued at the conclusion of the visit to Indonesia, 27 January – 3 February 1999.

Following a visit to Indonesia, a joint World Council of Churches (WCC)/Christian Conference of Asia (CCA) team has called on the Indonesian government urgently to identify and bring to justice those responsible for the burning and destruction of places of worship, as well as communal violence involving Christians and Muslims, and members of the ethnic Chinese minority.

During the visit, which took place 27 January - 3 February 1999, the nine-member team held talks with President B. J. Habibie and told him they found it difficult to understand why the Indonesian government had so far failed to identify those who in the May 1998 riots and subsequently had organised or carried out acts of violence against people and property.

Indonesians are proud of their tradition of religious pluralism. However, despite this, 544 churches have been destroyed since the country's independence in 1945 and this phenomenon continues today. In mid-January 1999, a few days before the delegation arrived in Jakarta, the port city of Ambon, where Muslims and Christians have long lived side by side in peace, witnessed a wave of communal violence and destruction that left over forty people dead and many mosques and churches destroyed.

In discussions with the WCC/CCA team, President Habibie and other senior government officials spoke strongly against those responsible for the violence, and condemned the attacks on churches and mosques, as well as the fostering of religious hostility. The president pledged to bring the perpetrators to justice. However, in the context of recent developments in Indonesia, the President told the team, " I am involved in Mission Impossible".

The ecumenical team is convinced the violence in Indonesia is not primarily an expression of religious hatred but rather the result of economic and political factors. Also, Indonesia is a place where freedom of expression was repressed for many years but now the country is experiencing a new kind of liberty. No one is sure what will happen in the future, particularly after the parliamentary elections in June for which over 200 parties have registered. The team says the situation in Indonesia is one of absolute confusion in which religion and ethnicity have been exploited by members of power elites. The delegation was encouraged to hear of Muslim neighbours who had provided shelter to Christian families under attack, and of Muslim young people who had protected a church from being destroyed.

As well as a smooth election process and the bringing to justice of the perpetrators of violence, the team also concluded that conflict resolution in Indonesia requires the enactment of legislation to ensure greater autonomy for the provinces, a just resolution of the demands for self-determination in East Timor and Irian Jaya, the establishment of social organisations to build harmony among the country's diverse religious and ethnic groups, increased capacity to mobilise domestic and foreign human and financial resources in order to eradicate persistent poverty and improve the overall economic outlook of the country, and a change in the conditions imposed by Indonesia's international creditors, particularly the International Monetary Fund and the World Bank.

The WCC/CCA team visit included time in Irian Jaya. Here, the team found a clear wish for independence among all sectors of society, including the churches. However, in Jakarta, government officials, including Foreign Minister Ali Alatas, made it clear to the team that Irian Jaya is an integral part of Indonesia and there is no parallel with East Timor. Nevertheless, the team found that the hopes of Irianese people were understandably raised by the government's recent announcement on the independence of East Timor.

The team discovered the delay in convening the National Dialogue, proposed in September 1998 and agreed to by President Habibie, has caused frustration and confusion in Irian Jaya. The delegation was concerned that church leaders, both Protestants and Catholics, as well as tribal chiefs, NGOs and student representatives had spent little time in discussion with each other, in preparation for the National Dialogue.

The WCC/CCA delegation now calls on the Indonesian Government to initiate the National Dialogue without delay and to ensure the people of Irian Jaya are properly represented in that dialogue without conditions.

The team also calls on the UN Commission on Human Rights to look into human rights violations in IRIan Jaya which include arbitrary arrests, extra-judicial killings, and the violation of the right to freedom of expression and of the socio-economic and cultural rights of the Irianese people as a result of the Indonesian government's programme of transmigration.

Appeal for decided action to stop inter-communal violence
Letter to H.E. President Bacharuddin Jusuf Habibie, 1 March 1999.

Your Excellency,

The World Council of Churches has closely followed the developments in Indonesia since the May 1998 riots. The Council and its member churches have watched with growing concern the unfolding ethnic violence and communal conflicts that have left thousands of families in pain and despair. These events are all the more appalling because they are against the very spirit and proud traditions of the Indonesian people for religious pluralism.

Concerned by these developments, the Eighth WCC Assembly, held in Harare last December, decided to send an ecumenical delegation on a pastoral visit to Indonesia from the 26th of January to 4th of February. I take this opportunity to thank you and your other senior cabinet colleagues for taking the time to meet with the delegation on the 2nd of February. The meeting not only provided the delegation with the opportunity to express the concern of the churches around the world on the situation in Indonesia, but it also helped the delegation to understand and appreciate the difficulties encountered by your government as it endeavours to defuse the present climate of violence and conflict that has affected large parts of Indonesia. At the meeting Your Excellency deplored these acts of violence and condemned those responsible for the attacks on churches and mosques, as well as the fostering of religious hostilities. The delegation was assured that the government was doing everything in its power to bring the perpetrators responsible for these reprehensible acts to justice. The delegation returned hopeful with the assurance given by you.

It is now a month since that visit, yet the violence and communal conflicts continue unabated. New areas have been engulfed in a frenzy of fresh communal violence. Those responsible for the killings and arson have yet to be brought to justice.

We are distressed by these developments, more particularly with the situation in Ambon where the trouble began in mid-January last and continued while the delegation was in Indonesia. At that time the General Secretary of the Indonesian Council of Churches together with the leaders of other religious communities accompanied government officials to Ambon to help authorities in their efforts to restore peace and harmony in the region. This is a region where Muslims and Christians have long lived side by side in peace.

We have now received reports from our member churches that Ambon remains in the grip of communal frenzy, never witnessed before. There are daily reports of casualties and of attacks against Christian homes and places of worship, particularly in Batu Merah Dalam in the northern part of the city. It is a matter of deep concern for us that the special army units whose duty it is to protect the lives and properties of all Indonesians are accused of a partisan approach. This has spread insecurity and unrest amongst the members of the Christian community.

We urge Your Excellency to ensure that military personnel act as custodians of law and order and carry out their duties in accordance with the guiding principles of 'Pancasila'. Also that immediate steps are taken to apprehend those responsible for violence, arson and killings and that they are brought before the courts of law to stand trial. Failure to do so will encourage the perpetrators to continue to indulge in these heinous crimes with impunity, thus further damaging Indonesia's image in the comity of nations.

We trust that, in accordance with the assurances given to the Ecumenical Delegation, Your Excellency will give this matter urgent and serious consideration.

Sincerely yours,

Konrad Raiser
General Secretary

Minute on Indonesia
Adopted by the Central Committee, Geneva, 26 August - 3 September 1999.

The WCC, in pursuance of the minute adopted by the Eighth Assembly at Harare, Zimbabwe, in December 1998, and in cooperation with the Christian Conference of Asia, sent an ecumenical delegation to Indonesia in late January 1999. This was followed up with a staff visit to East Timor in late June and early July 1999 related to the planned United Nations supervised referendum. Since the fall of Suharto in May 1998, the Council has monitored developments in the country and has kept close contact with the churches, particularly those in East Timor and Irian Jaya. The WCC sent a message to the government of Indonesia expressing concern about the growing incidence of communal violence and attacks on places of worship in Ambon and other parts of Indonesia, and about continuing human rights violations by the security forces, particularly in East Timor and Aceh, where women and children have suffered most. The WCC and many of its member churches and partner agencies have provided support to the Indonesian churches' efforts to assist the people and provide witness in these difficult circumstances.

The Central Committee of the WCC, meeting in Geneva, 26 August - 3 September 1999, expresses particular concern now about the dangers confronting East Timor in the post-referendum period, as a consequence of the division of the community between the pro-autonomy factions, some of whom have been armed by the Indonesian military, and pro-independence sectors. In light of the present climate of hostility and conflict, the Central Committee requests the General Secretary to address an appeal to the Secretary-General of the United Nations, urging him to consider an alteration and a further extension of the mandate of the UN presence in East Timor beyond the referendum period until peace and security there is restored.

The continuing communal violence in Ambon and the increase in repressive measures by the security forces in Aceh and Irian Jaya remains a matter of grave concern for the WCC. The Central Committee assures the churches in Indonesia of the WCC's ongoing support for them as they struggle through this difficult period.

The Central Committee calls upon WCC member churches to:
- *pray* for the churches and people of Indonesia;
- *continue to monitor* developments and exchange information; and
- *offer support and encouragement* to the churches of Indonesia as they work for peace and reconciliation, for human rights and for justice for all.

Protest of travel ban imposed on Central Committee member

Letter to H.E. M. N. Hassan Wirajuda, Ambassador of Indonesia to the United Nations in Geneva, 3 September 1999.

Your Excellency,

The World Council of Churches has learned with deep concern that a six-month travel ban, effective 23 June 1999, has been imposed on Mr Welly Mandowen, a member of the WCC Central Committee from the Evangelical Christian Church in Irian Jaya. Mr Mandowen was elected by the WCC Assembly in Harare, Zimbabwe, last December. This ban has prevented him from attending the first meeting of the Central Committee held here in Geneva over the past ten days. He was not made aware of the ban, apparently issued two months earlier, until he arrived in Jakarta in late August when he was scheduled to depart for Geneva.

According to our information, the notification of the ban issued to Mr Mandowen does not specify any clear reason for this action by the Indonesian authorities. We believe that such an action is wholly unwarranted, and constitutes an infringement of the fundamental right of all Indonesian citizens to the right to leave and return to their home country.

The news of this ban troubled the 158-member Central Committee, made up of persons from churches in every region of the world, and reflected badly on your Government. We would be grateful if you would convey our concern to the appropriate government ministry, along with the expression of our hope that corrective action will be taken forthwith to remedy this injustice.

Respectfully yours,

Dwain C. Epps
Director
Commission of the Churches on
International Affairs

Appeal to Indonesian Government to end impunity

Letter sent to H.E. President Abdurrahman Wahid, 12 January 2000.

Your Excellency,

The World Council of Churches has closely monitored the developments in Indonesia over the past year. Last January, an international ecumenical delegation sponsored by the World Council of Churches and the Christian Conference of Asia made a pastoral visit to Indonesia. The delegation in its meeting with former President B. J. Habibie and his senior cabinet colleagues expressed concern, amongst others, at the communal violence and destruction taking place in the port city of Ambon. The delegation was assured by the former President that perpetrators responsible for acts of violence and for fostering religious hostilities would be brought to trial before courts of law.

In the aftermath of the violence between Muslims and Christians, the churches and the National Council in Indonesia have unfailingly cooperated with the authorities in their efforts to restore peace and harmony in the Malukus region. It is one year since the trouble began, yet there is no sign of the situation being brought under control. Several attempts were made to restore peace and to defuse tension; the most recent one was the signing of the Declaration to End the Conflict by the leaders of the two communities. This was followed by Your Excellency's own visit to the region in mid-December 1999. All these efforts seem to have gone in vain as the spate of killings and destruction continues unabated. The burning of the Silo Church in Ambon a day after Christmas came as a rude shock not only to the Christians in Indonesia but also to the people at large.

In recent days the situation in the Moluccas has rapidly deteriorated despite heavy deployment of the additional units of the Indonesian security forces. It is the primary task of the security forces to maintain law and order and to protect the lives and property of the people; in this however they have not succeeded. In fact the perceived partisan approach of the personnel of the security forces has further aggravated an already difficult situation. The inability of the security forces to restore law and order and to bring the killings to an end is a sad reflection on the Indonesian Government.

We are convinced that Your Excellency personally and the leaders of your Government sincerely seek a solution to this matter which will reduce the violence, stop the killings and contribute to communal harmony and the well-being of the people. Nevertheless, as your National Human Rights Commission has documented, some leaders of the security forces are either responsible for or have directly committed grave abuses of human rights in the past, adversely affecting the credibility of these forces. Part of the process of containing violence and restoring harmony in the Moluccas must certainly be to place such officials under charges and to try them for crimes they are alleged to have committed. To allow impunity for official actors to continue will tarnish the image of the Indonesian Government in the eyes of the international community. This will postpone the restoration of the process to encourage interfaith dialogue between the Islamic and Christian communities which is badly needed to restore normalcy and peace in the region.

We are deeply concerned at the loss of lives of both Muslims and Christians and express our profound sympathy for all who have suffered as a result of the continuing violence in the region. We want to assure the Indonesian people that the ecumenical community upholds them in prayer and is ready to render all possible assistance and to work with them for reconciliation with a view to restoring peace and harmony in the Moluccas region.

Respectfully,

Georges Lemopoulos
Acting General Secretary

Minute on Indonesia
Adopted by the Executive Committee, Geneva, 29 February – 3 March 2000.

In light of the report it has received on the situation in Indonesia, and in particular on the terrible suffering inflicted on Christians and Muslims alike as a result of the inter-communal strife in recent months, the Executive Committee of the World Council of Churches:

• *extended* to the Communion of Churches in Indonesia (PGI), and especially to the churches and Christians in the Malukus its deep compassion with them in this terrible, trying time, and mourns with them the deaths of so many of their fellow Christians;

• *shared* with to the Muslim community of Indonesia its sorrow at the suffering it has undergone, including the loss of many lives;

- *recalled* that Indonesia has provided in the past a model of tolerance which respects the cultural diversity and religious pluralism of its people;

- *acknowledged* the efforts of the present government of Indonesia to introduce much needed political reforms; to revitalize the economy in a way which would share out the wealth of the nation equitably among its citizens, irrespective of race, culture or religion; to promote full respect for human rights and to bring offenders to justice; and to re-establish law and order through security forces under strict civilian control;

- *called* upon Muslim and Christian leaders in Indonesia to redouble their efforts to mediate in this dispute and to restore harmonious inter-communal relations;

- *called* upon the member churches of the World Council of Churches to pray for the people of Indonesia and to offer generous assistance to the victims of violence and for the rebuilding of their communities and places of worship.

Appeal for the restoration of law and order in the Malukus

Letter to H.E. Dr N. Hassan Wirajuda, Ambassador of Indonesia to the United Nations in Geneva, 27 June 2000.

Your Excellency,

Earlier this year, in a letter addressed on 11th January to the President of Indonesia, Dr Abdurrahman Wahid, the World Council of Churches expressed its concern at the increased incidence of communal violence in the Malukus region. The Council emphasized the need for the government of Indonesia to contain violence and take steps to restore inter-communal harmony. In February you were kind enough to receive me and my colleague, Mr Clement John, to discuss the planned visit to Indonesia of the General Secretary of the World Council of Churches, Dr Konrad Raiser. At the time we discussed the Council's concerns about the attacks on Christian minorities and the insecurity they had created.

In March Dr Raiser visited Indonesia in connection with the inauguration of the Assembly of the Communion of Churches of Indonesia (PGI). During that visit Dr. Raiser met and discussed the situation in Indonesia with President Abdurrahman Wahid. Particular reference was made to the inter-communal violence in Ambon and Halmahera. President Wahid explained the complexities of the situation in the Malukus and assured Dr Raiser that the government was taking all possible steps to restore law and order and to bring an end to the violence in the region. He requested understanding and patience to allow his government to address this complex problem.

It is now three months since these assurances were given but the situation has not improved. On the contrary it has become worse. The violence in the region continues unabated with no signs of respite, despite the fact that the government has deployed additional forces. In recent days we have received reports of the bombing of Churches in North Sumatra, a region which has hitherto remained peaceful and with good inter-communal relations. Church leaders in the region have called on their followers to exercise restraint and not to be provoked into retaliation. In Central Sulawesi, another region known for inter-communal harmony, communal tensions and violence have increased in recent days.

The World Council of Churches is deeply disturbed by these developments, and particularly those in the Malukus region where in recent days over a hundred people have been killed, and churches and houses belonging to members of the Christian community burned. Late last week, the day after we received warnings of imminent danger, the Indonesian Christian University and the Roman Catholic hospital in Ambon were burned. This has come as a shock not only to the people of Indonesia but also to people all over the world.

The continuing influx of intruders in the Malukus region from Java and other parts of the country troubles us deeply. Outsiders entering the region are armed and are held largely responsible by citizens in the region for the present state of lawlessness. The heavy deployment of security forces by the government has failed to deter the miscreants from carrying out their nefarious activities. Needless to say, this state of affairs tarnishes the good name of the Indonesian government both at home and abroad. Christian minorities that have been the target of these attacks are increasingly vulnerable and insecure. There is a growing feeling that the government has not taken adequate steps to enforce law and order and to provide for the safety and well-being of its people.

The World Council of Churches has repeatedly reiterated that it is concerned about the impact of continuing violence and loss of lives of Muslims and Christians alike. We are particularly dismayed that local efforts on the part of both communities to restore community harmony and peace are being destroyed by armed zealots from outside.

We therefore ask that you convey our sentiments to President Wahid, with the request that his Government take the strongest possible measures to restore law and order in the Malukus region, ensure the impartiality of security forces deployed there and in other affected regions, and apprehend and bring to justice those suspected of responsibility for killings and destruction.

With the assurance of our deepest respect, and looking forward to an early response, I am

Respectfully yours,

Dwain C. Epps
Director
Commission of the Churches on
International Affairs

Appeal on the situation in the Malukus

Letter to H.E. Mrs Mary Robinson, UN High Commissioner for Human Rights, 13 July 2000.

Dear Madame,

The World Council of Churches is concerned at the increase in violence in the Malukus region that has resulted in scores of people being killed and properties belonging to Christians, including church buildings and schools, destroyed. The state of Civil Emergency declared on 27 June by the Government of Indonesia has failed to stop the death and destruction taking place. The situation is particularly precarious in Ambon, Halmahera and Poso. We have received regular information from our member churches and from the Communion of Churches in Indonesia about these attacks on Christians and their establishments by armed religious zealots from Java. In the face of this onslaught, many Christian villages have been forced to evacuate for security reasons. There is a complete breakdown of law and order.

The Indonesian military personnel who have the responsibility to ensure the safety and security of the citizens and their properties have miserably failed in discharge of their duties. In fact, some members of the security forces are alleged to have joined hands with the intruders in attacks against Christians.

The World Council of Churches has, on several occasions in the past, brought to the attention of the Indonesian Government the rapidly deteriorating situation in the Malukus. Despite assurances of the Government of Indonesia that measures were being taken to restore law and order, the situation has failed to improve. The Council has just received reports that Waai and Batugandung in Ambon have been subjected to mortar attacks by the intruders supported and backed by the personnel of the Indonesian military. In Batugandung seven people have lost their lives. There are reliable reports of an imminent attack on Tobelo in the coming days.

It is now two weeks since the Indonesian Government declared a state of Civil Emergency, an action of extreme measure, to control the violence in the Malukus, but it continues unabated resulting in grave and serious human rights violations and crimes against humanity. The recent attacks of the intruders indicate a design to annihilate Christians or force them out of the Malukus. To save the Christian community from this ordeal church leaders in the region have been constrained to call on their followers to evacuate their homes and move to secure areas.

Given the gravity of the situation, the World Council of Churches appeals to you to undertake an immediate visit to Indonesia and urge the Government to stop the human rights violations and atrocities being committed in the Malukus by intruders backed and supported by the Indonesian army. The Indonesian Government should be asked to take steps to effectively stop the entry of intruders into the Malukus region. The Government should also immediately bring to trial those guilty of committing human rights violations.

Sincerely,

Konrad Raiser
General Secretary

Appeal on sectarian violence in Central Sulawesi

Letter to H.E. Mrs. Mary Robinson, UN High Commissioner for Human Rights, 10 December 2001.

Dear Mrs. Robinson,

The World Council of Churches has received with concern reports from its member churches in Indonesia as well as from other parts of the world about the increase in the level of sectarian violence in Central Sulawesi and Indonesia. This has resulted in grave and serious human rights violations. The violence is likely to further increase if immediate steps are not taken to bring the situation under control.

In Poso during the last week of November 2001, 600 houses and 6 churches were burned; 1500 Christians were forced to flee the city in search of security. Since the beginning of December, another 21 Christian villages and 5 churches have been destroyed in Poso. The Christians living in the area have fled Poso and sought shelter in Tentena – the headquarters of the Christian Church in Central Sulawesi (GKST).

The attacks resulting in destruction of property and displacement of people were carried out by the forces of the Laskar Jihad that came largely from East Java. The groups were armed with rocket launchers and automatic weapons. They have presently surrounded Tentena, cutting off essential supplies to the region.

The church leaders in Sulawesi have repeatedly appealed to the central government in Jakarta to save them from these attacks that are being organized and carried out by the Laskar Jihad. To this date the government has not responded to their appeals, nor has it taken adequate measures to ensure their security and prevent further violations of human rights.

We therefore urge you to call upon the Indonesian government: to pay serious attention to the sectarian violence taking place in Sulawesi before it degenerates into another situation such as that of the Malukus; to ensure the safety of the people of Sulawesi; to ensure that perpetrators responsible for the acts of violence are brought to justice; and further to take necessary steps to disarm private armed groups such as the Laskar Jihad.

Sincerely,

Konrad Raiser
General Secretary

Minute on Indonesia

Adopted by the Central Committee, Potsdam, Germany, 29 January – 6 February 2001.

The Central Committee of the World Council of Churches notes with great pain and sorrow that the inter-communal violence in the Malukus region which began in January 1999 has left over 5,000 people dead, some 500,000 displaced, and property worth billions of rupiah destroyed. Trust between the Muslim and Christian communities has seriously eroded. Though cease-fires and moratoriums on killings have periodically been agreed between the two communities, these have all been of short duration and fighting has been renewed with a vengeance. The Indonesian security forces have often been irresponsible and inept in the carrying out of their responsibilities, and have repeatedly failed to stop or control the violence and bring the perpetrators to justice. In fact there is clear evidence that members of the Indonesian army and police forces have participated directly in some of these attacks. National authorities have to date failed to take any disciplinary action against such offenders.

The situation has been further compounded by the organized entry of the Java-based radical Islamic group called "Lashkar Jihad," thousands of whose members have indulged in systematic "religious cleansing" of Christians and acts of forced religious conversions. This group has been provided arms and training by a section of the Indonesian armed forces and has also received support and encouragement from Jakarta-based politicians.

The Central Committee:

reiterates the WCC's expressions of solidarity and continuing prayers for the people and churches in Indonesia in this trying time;

reiterates the WCC's call upon religious, political and military leaders in Indonesia to spare no effort in pursuing a peaceful resolution of the conflict, the disarming of militias on all sides, and the restoration of law and order;

calls upon the WCC to continue to monitor developments here and to support and encourage the efforts of the Communion of Churches in Indonesia to engage the Islamic Community in dialogue to promote a just and lasting peace;

asks the WCC, as a matter of priority, to explore further avenues of cooperation amongst the world faith communities to address together the underlying causes of inter-religious violence in the Malukus and Poso, and the situation in Aceh, particularly the victimization of women;

calls to the attention of the member churches and related agencies the large-scale displacement of people; the rehabilitation needs of large numbers of persons injured or maimed in the fighting, and other humanitarian needs and urges them to respond generously through Action by Churches Together (ACT).

Note on Indonesia
Minuted by the Central Committee, Geneva, Geneva, 26 August – 3 September 2002.

The Public Issues Committee also considered the request made related to continuing religious and communal tensions in Indonesia and informs the Central Committee that it has responded to this, according to the procedures for public issues, as part of the ongoing work of the WCC. As indicated in the Preliminary Report on Public Issues prepared by the International Relations staff, the Council has given high priority to the continuing tension and conflict between Muslims and Christian in Indonesia, especially in Aceh and in the Malukus. Of particular concern now are the developments in South and Central Sulawesi where, despite the Malino Agreements I & II between the Muslim and Christian communities and the Government of Indonesia, violence and killings continue almost unabated. In response to the above-mentioned request, a letter will be prepared to reiterate ecumenical concerns to the President of Indonesia. International Relations staff of the Council will continue to monitor developments closely, in regular contact with the churches in Indonesia and the Christian Conference of Asia, and plans are being made for a pastoral visit by staff and key partners to give a further expression of ecumenical solidarity with the churches in the hope of helping them to restore harmonious inter-communal relations.

Expression of concern and condolences to the families of victims of the bombing in Bali
Letter to member churches and national councils in Indonesia and Australia, 16 October 2002.

Dear sisters and brothers in Christ,

We are shocked and grieved by the car bomb explosion near the Kuta Beach in Bali that killed nearly two hundred innocent Indonesians and foreigners, mostly Australians. The World Council of Churches has been deeply disturbed by the increase and spread in incidents of violence in the archipelago which have claimed hundreds of innocent lives in the last couple of years. In letters addressed to successive Indonesian governments, the Council has expressed our deep concern about these developments and the failure of the law enforcement agencies in the country to guarantee the safety and security of the people.

The tragic event in Bali last week should reinforce our resolve not to allow forces of evil and darkness to use violence as a tool to spread fear, division and despondency. On the contrary, it should stimulate us to revive our commitment to the Decade to Overcome Violence in order to build just, sustainable and reconciled communities. In a country like Indonesia churches and other religious communities are also under obligation to work together for the creation of a culture of peace with justice.

We welcome the unequivocal condemnation of the perpetrators of this horrendous act by the Indonesian officials and appreciate particularly the statement of President Megawati that "the bombing is a warning to all that terrorism is a real danger and potential threat to national security". We sincerely hope that every effort will be made to identify the culprits and to bring them to trial before courts of law and ensure that justice is done.

Please express our profound sympathy to the families of the victims and our fervent prayers for the injured. Assuring you of our prayers and support for your communities at this difficult time.

Yours sincerely,

Konrad Raiser
General Secretary

Appeal for protection of human rights in West Papua
Letter to H.E. Mme Megawati Soekarnoputri, President of the Republic, 20 September 2002.

Your Excellency,

The World Council of Churches is deeply concerned at the deteriorating human rights situation in West Papua. Since the death of Theys Hiyo Eluay, the Chairperson of the Papuan Presidium Council and the Paramount Chief of Sentani tribe in mysterious circumstances, there has been an increase in incidents of torture, kidnappings, rape, illegal detentions and arbitrary executions. Despite assurances by the government, those responsible for his death have not been brought to trial before a court of law. The Commissions of Enquiry set up by the government have failed to arrive at any conclusive findings. The demand of the people for an independent Commission of Enquiry, without members of the military, have not been met.

The unchecked influx of Lashkar Jihad to Sorong, Fak Fak, Biak and Jayapura has further compounded an already complex situation. Among the new arrivals are young men from Java, who are sponsored by the military for nefarious activities. They have been recruited for the militia 'Satgas Merah Putih' that operates hand in glove with the military and the Lashkar Jihad to intimidate the Papuan people engaged in a struggle for socio-economic, cultural and political rights. According to the reports received by us the developments in West Papua seem to follow, the same pattern as those in East Timor in the early 1990s. The military by encouraging and inducting the Lashkar Jihad in the region is using religion to create a 'horizontal conflict' to deflect attention from the demands of the people for justice and human rights. The security forces are unable to effectively control this developing conflict.

We are also concerned by the reports of surveillance of Church leaders and human rights defenders by the military intelligence. Some Church leaders have received threats and are fearful of their safety and security.

To defuse the present state of tension and conflict in the region it is necessary that the government put an end to the influx of outsiders, restrain the military from destabilising the situation by committing acts of harassment and repression of the Papuan people. The government must take immediate steps to revive the national dialogue initiated by Your Excellency's predecessor. The grievances of the Papuan people for equitable sharing of economic resources and political power should be addressed through the implementation of the autonomy law. The people of Papua remain committed to peace through a process of consultation and multilateral decision-making.

The member churches of the World Council of Churches in Indonesia, including West Papua, are of the considered opinion that national dialogue is the only way forward to peace and reconciliation in the region.

Yours sincerely

Dr Konrad Raiser
General Secretary

KOREA

Congratulations to President Kim Dae-jung on the award of the Nobel Peace Prize
Letter from the General Secretary, 13 October 2000.

Your Excellency,

May I take this opportunity to express my deep satisfaction and joy at the decision of the Norwegian Nobel Committee to award you with this year's Nobel Peace Prize.

This decision honors you as a statesman who has committed his entire life to the struggle against authoritarian rule and to work for democratization and for the unification of the Korean peninsula. In this long and arduous journey, Your Excellency has undergone much pain and suffering. I recall the tragic events of Kwang-ju when you had to suffer incarceration followed by a period of trials and tribulation in exile. Those were difficult days. Along with you many Christians and church leaders underwent imprisonment and torture for raising their voice against injustice. It was at the height of this repression in January 1981, when I had the opportunity to visit South Korea with a WCC-sponsored ecumenical team. The purpose of the visit was to express pastoral concern and solidarity of the ecumenical community with the life and witness of the local churches. The Council at the time was deeply concerned by the developments that were taking place and the repression that was being unleashed on the people. The WCC made an impassioned appeal to the Korean government to ensure that Your Excellency and other defendants received a fair trial with due process.

I recall the several meetings I had with you over the years when I visited Korea, the last one being in April 1999, when I was on my way back from North Korea. We discussed, among others, the response of the North Korean government to your "sunshine policy". I was impressed by your readiness to set aside serious ideological and political concerns in the pursuit of peace. The international community placed much hope in your single-mindedness to pursue peace despite temporary setbacks and difficulties. Your visit to North Korea early this year was a major breakthrough and a well-deserved reward for your untiring efforts. The "sunshine policy" is very much in line with the ecumenical framework for peaceful reunification of Korea. The World Council of Churches, as you know, has been working towards the reunification of Korea since the Church Leaders' Consultation at Tozanso in 1984. This consultation paved the way for a series of meetings between Christians of North and South Korea. I am hopeful that the award of the Nobel Peace Prize will go a long way to accelerate the unification process.

As you continue to implement your "sunshine policy" we offer you congratulations on receiving the Nobel Peace Prize and assure you of our continuing prayers and support.

With respectful greetings,

Yours,

Konrad Raiser
General Secretary

PAKISTAN

Appeal for the release of blasphemy law protestors
Letter to H.E. General Pervaiz Musharraf, Chief Executive of Pakistan, 15 January 2001.

Your Excellency,

The World Council of Churches has learnt with deep concern of the arrests of Fr Arnold Heredia, former Executive Secretary of the Committee for Justice and Peace, and presently the priest of St Francis Parish in Karachi, and a Council member of the Human Rights Commission of Pakistan; Mr Aslam Martin, project co-coordinator for the Committee for Justice and Peace; Mr Riaz Nawab of

Caritas, Karachi; and fourteen others on 10th January, while they were engaged in a peaceful demonstration near the Rainbow Center, Saddar, Karachi. The protestors were taking part in the procession to the Governor's House, organised by the newly formed All Faith Spiritual Movement, to submit a memorandum demanding the repeal of the Blasphemy Law.

According to reports we have received, the peaceful demonstrators were not only restrained from proceeding to the Governor's House but they were also tear-gassed and beaten by the security forces. As a result Fr Heredia and some of the other protestors were injured. The seventeen protestors are presently under detention on remand by the authorities at the Preedy Police Station

The World Council of Churches has previously drawn the attention of the Government of Pakistan to the serious situation that has arisen as a result of discriminatory practices and of persecution of religious minorities in Pakistan including Christians, Ahmadiyas and Hindus. Extremist forces and groups have in particular used the blasphemy law to incite religious hatred and animosity against these religious minorities. These incidences have been well documented by both national and international organisations, including the Human Rights Commission of Pakistan. They have greatly contributed to the growing environment of religious intolerance often resulting in serious disturbances of law and order and serious abuses of human rights.

These developments are in violation of Article 36 of the Constitution of Pakistan that guarantees the legitimate rights and interests of the minorities. Despite the assurances given to the religious minorities by Quaid-e-Azam, Mohammed Ali Jinnah that "minorities are a sacred trust of Pakistan," their security is not protected and they continue to be victimised at the hands of unscrupulous sections of the society. We have thus appealed to the Government of Pakistan to take immediate steps to repeal Section 295 C of the Pakistan Penal Code.

It was not in defiance, but in defence of the Constitution of Pakistan that the above-mentioned persons presently under police detention peacefully protested, demanding repeal of the blasphemy law. We therefore urge you to assure their immediate release, their protection from unlawful abuse from any quarter, and at the same time to guarantee the security and physical integrity of others under your jurisdiction presently charged under the blasphemy law.

Respectfully yours,

Georges Lemopoulos
Acting General Secretary

Expression of deep concern about the safety and security of the Christian minority in Pakistan

Letter to H.E. General Pervaiz Musharraf, President of the Republic, 29 October 2001.

Your Excellency,

The World Council of Churches is deeply concerned by the act of terror committed in Bahawalpur on 28 October, when masked gunmen attacked the St Dominic's Roman Catholic Church where Sunday's services were being conducted by Pastor Emmanuel Allah Ditta of the Church of Pakistan. As a result of indiscriminate firing by the gunmen, 17 worshippers were killed and around 30 others were injured including women and children.

The World Council of Churches has followed with concern the recent developments in the region. In a letter sent to United Nations Secretary General Kofi Annan on 2 October by Dr Konrad Raiser, the WCC General Secretary, the Council expressed its apprehension of the military action initiated by the International Coalition in Afghanistan. The Council appealed to the United States and the United Kingdom to bring a prompt end to this action.

We are aware of the difficulties faced by the people of Pakistan and your government as a result of the continuous bombings in Afghanistan that have resulted in an increasing number of civilian casualties. This has caused resentment and division within Pakistan society. While appreciating the manner in which Your Excellency's government has handled the present crisis, we nevertheless are deeply concerned about the safety and security of the Christian minority in the present highly charged environment of religious intolerance.

The National Council of Churches in Pakistan has supported the government's decision to join the International Coalition to fight terrorism. In view of Sunday's killings in the church at Bahawalpur, it has asked that a judicial inquiry be held into the incident so that those found guilty of this heinous act can be brought to justice.

The World Council of Churches supports the demand of the National Council of Churches in Pakistan. While we remain supportive of Your Excellency's government in these difficult times, we urge that all necessary measures be undertaken to provide safety and security to the Christian minority in Pakistan.

Respectfully yours,

Georges Lemopoulos
Acting General Secretary

Condemnation of the assassination of human rights defenders

Letter to H.E. General Pervaiz Musharraf, President of the Republic, 1 October 2002.

Your Excellency,

The World Council of Churches deplores the September 25th terrorist attack on the office of Idara-e-Amn-o-Insaf, Karachi in which seven of its Christian staff were ruthlessly gunned down at close quarters, after being blindfolded. This is the fourth in the series of such terrorist attacks that have targeted Christian churches, hospitals, schools and other institutions in Pakistan. In all these attacks precious innocent lives have been lost.

On October 29th 2001 in a letter addressed to Your Excellency, in the aftermath of the terrorist attack on St Dominic's Roman Catholic Church, the World Council of Churches while appreciating the manner in which the government had handled the crisis, asked that a judicial enquiry be held into the incident so that those found guilty could be brought to justice. Much to our dismay neither the culprits of the attack on St Dominic's church nor those involved in subsequent attacks at the hospital and school in Taxela and Murree have been arrested and brought to trial before a court of law.

The violent killings of the staff of Idara-e-Amn-o-Insaf are all the more deplorable because the organisation works for the poor and socially marginalised in Pakistan society, irrespective of their religious beliefs. It provides a platform for interreligious cooperation in the area of social justice and for promotion of human rights.

These recurring incidents of terrorist violence, you will no doubt agree, if allowed to go unchecked and unpunished will not only encourage those who indulge in such wanton acts of violence but will also tarnish the image of Pakistan. It is therefore necessary that law enforcement agencies in the country undertake all necessary steps to apprehend the perpetrators of these heinous crimes and bring their cases before courts of law for prosecution and judicious conclusion.

The World Council of Churches calls on Your Excellency's government to provide safety and security to the Christian minority in Pakistan.

Respectfully yours,

Dr Konrad Raiser
General Secretary

Open letter to member churches and the National Council of Churches in Pakistan, 1 October 2002.

Dear sisters and brothers in Christ,

The World Council of Churches has received with shock and profound distress the news of the terrorist attack on the office of Idara-e-Amn-o-Insaf, in Karachi in which seven of its staff were killed. This is the fourth in the series of terrorist attacks that have targeted Christian churches, hospital, school, and other institution in Pakistan. In all these attacks precious innocent lives have been lost. The Council is deeply disturbed by the present environment of religious rage and intolerance in the country that has given rise to such attacks. On October 29, 2001 in a letter addressed to President Pervez Musharraf, in the aftermath of the terrorist attack on St Dominic's Roman Catholic Church, the World Council of Churches expressed its concern about the safety and security of the Christian minority in the highly charged environment of religious intolerance. It called on the government to undertake all necessary measures to provide safety and security for the Christian minority in the country.

The violent killings of the staff of Idara-e-Amn-o-Insaf is all the more deplorable, because the organisation works for the poor and socially marginalised in Pakistan society, irrespective of their religious beliefs. The Idara-e-Amn-o-Insaf is an instrumentality of the church that not only manifests concern for involvement in social justice and human rights but also, provides a vision of a new and just society for all.

We take this opportunity to convey through you our condolences and sympathy for the families of the victims of the September 25th massacre. May our Lord's blessings be with the kith and kin and give them courage to bear this tragic loss. We vehemently condemn such senseless and wanton blood-letting of innocent people. These acts of violence that result in taking away of innocent human lives deserve to be denounced by all peace-loving people.

Be assured of our continuous prayers and solidarity with the Christians in Pakistan at this difficult time.

Yours sincerely

Dr Konrad Raiser
General Secretary

Expression of concern about developments in the Philippines

Letter to the National Council of Churches and WCC member churches in the Philippines, January 2001.

Dear Sisters and Brothers in Christ,

The World Council of Churches has followed with deep concern the developments in the Philippines particularly since I visited you last March. At that time I witnessed and heard testimonies of general discontent because of the ineptitude and corruption that characterized the rule of President Estrada and his unfortunate response to events unfolding in the Southern Philippines at that time.

Our concern is consistent with our long history of involvement in the struggle of the Filipino people for justice, peace and democracy. A WCC-CCA delegation was there after the *'Velvet Revolution'* that overthrew the dictatorship of Ferdinand Marcos to accompany the Churches in the Philippines and to commend them on the role they played in the struggle against the injustices and human rights violations of that military dictatorship. The delegation paid a courtesy call on former president Corazon Aquino on her assumption of office.

There was much promise of political and economic reforms and a period of relative calm under the democratically-elected governments of Presidents Aquino and Fidel Ramos. However, conflict and corruption continued to afflict Philippines society. Despite its promises the government consistently failed to address the underlying causes of discontent and conflict. President Fidel Ramos entered into peace negotiations with the Moro Islamic Liberation Front and the National Democratic Front, but these initiatives were never sincerely followed through. As a result, the situation in the Southern Philippines and the rural areas deteriorated dramatically as fighting once again broke out early last year between the armed forces of the Philippines and the fighters of MILF. Unfortunately the Estrada government's response was to embark on military operations, remilitarising the rural areas by sending a large number of armed forces personnel there. This led to massive displacement and human rights violations.

It is ironic that while large numbers of Filipino people toil abroad in distant lands to sustain their families and provide the much needed foreign exchange to the country, the ruling elites have been oblivious of their sacrifices and continue with impunity to indulge in waste, corruption and abuse of power. It is time that measures be taken to bring an end to this system that has perpetuated disparities, social contradictions and injustice in Philippines society. The impeachment proceedings against President Estrada that ended without a verdict revealed again the inadequacies of the present political system. Despite evidence of corruption and public outrage the President defiantly held onto office at great cost to the country's economy.

We commend the churches in the Philippines for standing once again by the people in that critical hour. Let us hope that this time around, the response to the massively expressed will of the people will lead to thoroughgoing reforms in the political system to make it democratic not only in form but truly participatory and dedicated to the principles of justice, transparency and accountability.

In this Kairos we thank God for the unfailing witness of Christians in the Philippines and of their churches to justice and basic human rights for all. You can be assured of our continuing solidarity, prayers and support in your struggle for justice and righteousness. May God almighty strengthen you and the people of the Philippines as you embark anew on the road to building and revitalising society.

Yours in Christ,

Konrad Raiser
General Secretary

SRI LANKA

Message to Member Churches and the National Christian Council
Sent by the General Secretary, August 1999.

The World Council of Churches has followed with deep concern the recent political developments in Sri Lanka. Faced with a political crisis because of the decision of the Sri Lanka Muslim Congress to withdraw from the ruling coalition and the move by the major opposition party, the United National Party, to introduce a "No Confidence Motion" against her Government, President Chandrika Kumaratunga decided to prorogue the Parliament. She also decided to issue a call for a Referendum in August, on the adoption of a new constitution. The decision of the President has caused widespread unrest and has been condemned by the leadership of political parties, religious groups and civil society organisations. There have been protests and demonstrations all over the country, resulting in street battles between the people and the security forces that have caused deaths and injuries to civilians.

To add to this political problems of the government, the attack on the morning of 24th July, by a group of suicide bombers of the Liberation Tigers of Tamil Eelam (LTTE) on the Bandaranaika International Airport and the adjacent Air Force Base, caused heavy damage to military and civilian aircraft raising concerns about the overall security situation in the country. Since the present government took over the government, the country has suffered much with fluctuating military fortunes in the North negating Government's claims of "War for Peace". In the South there has been one political crisis after another.

The political instability and the on-going war have taken a heavy toll of the country's economy. With prices soaring and the general security situation at its lowest ebb, common citizens have been the major victims of this never-ending spiral of violence and uncertainty.

As the 24 July statement of the National Christian Council of Sri Lanka points out: "A National priority must be the establishment of a new political culture through which a political space will emerge for the strengthening of democratic institutions ushering in peace and the development of the country". "There should be an end to confrontational politics in the larger interest of the country and its people".

The Norwegian Peace initiative that was welcomed by both parties to the conflict and has the backing of the international community provided a ray of hope for the people of Sri Lanka before the current political crisis began. It is imperative that the Government not only initiates a dialogue with the opposition political parties in the South to overcome the present Constitutional crisis, but also, takes steps to revive the Norwegian Peace initiative for talks with LTTE.

Statement on the situation in Sri Lanka
Issued by the CCIA and communicated to the parties to the conflict on 9 May 2000.

The Commission of the Churches on International Affairs of the World Council of Churches is deeply troubled by developments in Sri Lanka during the last few days. The military gains made by the Liberation Tigers of Tamil Eelam (LTTE) in Northern Jaffna peninsula have once again drawn the attention of the international community to the fratricidal ethnic conflict that has resulted in decades of misery and suffering of the Sri Lanka people. The capture of Elephant Pass by the LTTE and the withdrawal of the Sri Lankan armed forces to highly populated areas have dramatically intensified the climate of fear, tension and uncertainty in the whole island.

The ethnic conflict that escalated in 1983 has continued for nearly three decades with large sectors of both the Tamil and Sinhalese population caught in the middle as the warring parties achieved fluctuating military gains. It has long been clear that any pursuit of a final military solution of the conflict is an illusion. The parties concerned need to seek alternative means to resolve it.

During this period the country has suffered economically and politically. Its development programmes have been impeded as precious human and material resources have been squandered on war efforts. The announced decision of the government to buy still more arms to counter this offensive and the addition by the LTTE of new heavy weapons to its arsenal can only bring further suffering. The warring sides must now make an honest assessment of the situation and the human costs that continued armed confrontation will inflict on all the people. It is time also for the propaganda war to cease. Censorship should be removed.

Independent news media should be allowed to expose the facts as they see them. Internationally recognised international humanitarian organisations should be given free access to protect civilians in zones of conflict and allowed to provide much needed relief to the people in affected areas.

The Commission of the Churches on International Affairs warmly welcomes the statement recently issued by the National Council of Churches in Sri Lanka saying that the conflict in Sri Lanka cannot be solved by military means and appealing to the parties to engage in serious negotiation for peace. The international community has repeatedly offered good offices to this end. Such offers should be accepted in the legitimate interests of the people.

We appeal to the Government of Sri Lanka and to the leadership of LTTE to lay down their arms now and to assume fully their shared responsibility to prevent further loss of precious human lives.

Dwain C. Epps

Director
Commission of the Churches on
International Affairs

Message of congratulation on the signing of the Memorandum of Agreement between the government of Sri Lanka and the Liberation Tigers of Tamil Eelam (LTTE)

Letter to H.E. President Chandrika Bandaranaike Kumaratunga, 7 October 2002.

Your Excellency,

The World Council of Churches has closely followed developments in Sri Lanka since the escalation of the ethnic conflict in 1983. The Council has been deeply concerned not only with the loss of life and property but also with the massive displacement of people as a result of the war in the North. Over the years the Council and its member churches have provided much needed humanitarian relief and assistance to those affected by the conflict.

The World Council of Churches is delighted and welcomes the signing of the Memorandum of Agreement between the government of Sri Lanka and the Liberation Tigers of Tamil Eelam (LTTE). This positive development provides a sign of hope and promises to usher in a period of peace and national reconciliation in Sri Lanka.

The Central Committee of the World Council of Churches meeting in Geneva from 26th August to 2nd September took note of this development and was encouraged by it. In a statement adopted on the situation in South Asia including Sri Lanka (copy enclosed), the Central Committee of the World Council of Churches called on its members around the world to accompany the churches

277

in Sri Lanka in their journey to peace and to mobilise support nationally and internationally in favour of the peace process. The Council was particularly encouraged by the joint efforts of the National Council of Churches in Sri Lanka and the Church in Norway to bring awareness amongst the people in support of the peace process.

The World Council of Churches would like to avail itself of this opportunity to assure Your Excellency of its continuing support for peace and national reconciliation in Sri Lanka.

Respectfully yours,

Peter Weiderud
Director
Commission of the Churches on International Affairs

AUSTRALASIA

AUSTRALIA

Expression of concern about treatment of asylum seekers
Letter to WCC Member Churches in Australia and the National Council of Churches in Australia, 29 August 2001.

Dear Brothers and Sisters in Christ,

Over the last few days, we have been watching the unfolding story of the *Tampa*, the ship filled with asylum-seekers which has been standing off Christmas Island that has been prevented from landing in Australia and is apparently unable to travel elsewhere. Like many around the world, we have been dismayed by the initial reaction of the Australian government and hope that the government will allow the asylum-seekers to land, to receive the assistance they need, to be allowed to tell their stories and to present asylum claims. The right to seek and enjoy asylum is a basic human right (Universal Declaration of Human Rights, Art.14) which must be upheld throughout the world – and on Christmas Island.

We know, through our participation in the NCCA Forum and a staff visit on these issues to Australia last month, that the situation of refugees and asylum-seekers has become a burning political issue in your country. While Australia is certainly not alone in the world in implementing measures to deter asylum-seekers, such policies stand in stark contrast to Australia's history as a country of immigration and of refuge. Over the years, Australia has played a leading role in creating and supporting an international regime to protect those forced to flee their countries because of persecution, human rights violations and wars. It is truly sad to see the public debate in Australia now characterized by stereotyping, xenophobia and lack of compassion. Moreover, it is deeply troubling to see Australia's role in the international community changing from one of support and leadership for a collective response by the international community to one of questioning international obligations.

The *Tampa* case is not an isolated example. Together with the churches joined in the NCCA, the World Council of Churches is particularly concerned about the wider pattern of policies toward asylum-seekers currently being followed by the Australian government:

mandatory, unlimited detention of asylum-seekers in detention centres located in isolated parts of the country where community support is minimal;

asylum-seekers who are recognized as refugees are given temporary protected visas which delay them from being reunited with family members and beginning new lives;

the government's agreement with Indonesia under which asylum-seekers en route to Australia are detained by Indonesian security forces;

recent reports that the government is calling for fundamental changes in the 1951 Refugee Convention precisely at a time when other governments and churches around the world are commemorating the 50th anniversary of the Convention.

All of these developments have repercussions far beyond Australia's shores. When the government of such a democratic and prosperous country refuses landing privileges to a ship loaded with asylum-seekers rescued from peril at sea, other governments take notice. When the Australian government calls for changes in the 1951 Refugee Convention to prevent people from seeking asylum in other countries, the whole international regime of refugee protection is weakened.

We share the concern expressed by the government that the practice of trafficking in human lives must be stopped. However, we reject the notion that the victims of such practices be further punished rather than the traffickers themselves. We understand that it is difficult to speak out on such divisive political issues in the current climate in Australia poisoned by government spokespersons and media that label asylum-seekers as "illegals" and "queue-jumpers." Yet the Gospel tells us that Jesus made the love for strangers and enemies a hallmark of the inclusive community of the children of God. In this, he followed the Old Testament tradition of receiving the stranger (Exodus 23:9; Leviticus 19: 33-34; Deuteronomy 24:14-19; Jeremiah 5-7). We are therefore greatly encouraged by several recent statements by Australian churches that offer both an alternative vision of a culturally diverse society and which outline concrete steps the churches are taking. We commend you for these actions and express our solidarity with you as you struggle to live out your faith in difficult times.

As the WCC Central Committee said in 1995: "Christians are called to be with the oppressed, the persecuted, the marginalized and the excluded in their suffering, their struggles and their hopes. A ministry of accompaniment and advocacy with uprooted people upholds the principles of prophetic witness and service – diakonia. We cannot desert the 'needy', nor set boundaries to compassion (Hebrews 13:2; Luke 10: 25-37; Romans 12:13)."

May God bless and sustain you in your witness now to a government and a society in need of such words of wisdom, mercy, peace and justice.

Yours in Christ,

Konrad Raiser
General Secretary

Expression of concern and condolences to the families of victims of the bombing in Bali
Letter to member churches and national councils in Indonesia and Australia. 16 October 2002 (cf p. 266).

CARIBBEAN

HAITI

Appeal to the government and leaders of the ruling Lavalas political party to put an end to violence and injustice
Open letter addressed to the Haitian Protestant Federation, 19 December 2001.

Chers frères et Sœurs en Christ,

Le Conseil œcuménique des Eglises suit avec une inquiétude grandissante la détérioration de la situation politique et sociale en Haïti de ces derniers temps. La recrudescence de la violence, les lynchages comme celui du journaliste Brignol Lindor le 3 décembre dernier à Petit-Goâve, les assassinats et les exécutions sommaires font régner un climat d'insécurité insupportable pour la population, et risquent de rendre impossible l'accord politique pour lequel ont œuvré le parti au pouvoir et les forces de l'opposition.

Tout porte à croire que ces violences ne sont pas gratuites et ne s'expliquent pas seulement par la pauvreté extrême à laquelle est condamnée la majorité du peuple haïtien. Des groupes agissent pour provoquer la terreur et visent l'élimination physique de certaines personnes ciblées. Il semble bien que les autorités publiques ne fassent pas tout ce qui serait nécessaire pour réprimer ces actes. Des témoignages fiables indiquent même qu'elles puissent y être impliquées ou tout au moins les tolèrent.

Les récentes informations parues dans la presse internationale sur les exécutions sommaires perpétrées par des agents de la police, basées sur un témoignage authentique, font craindre le pire pour l'intégrité et l'autorité de l'Etat. Le principe de « zero tolérance » fixé par le gouvernement est compréhensible et répond à l'exaspération d'une population qui n'en peut plus. Mais cela ne saurait en aucun cas justifier que des personnes soupçonnées d'actes criminels ou même prises en flagrant délit soient exécutées sans aucune forme de procès.

Face à cette situation préoccupante, le Conseil œcuménique des Eglises se joint aux appels lancés par le Centre œcuménique des Droits de l'Homme, le Comité des Avocats pour le Respect des Libertés Individuelles, et d'autres organisations en Haïti pour que les droits humains soient réellement respectés. Nous demandons instamment au gouvernement d'assurer le comportement correct de la Police nationale haïtienne et d'améliorer le fonctionnement des instances judiciaires, dans le respect de la loi.

Le Conseil oecuménique des Eglises appelle les partis politiques, notamment la Famille Lavalas et la Convergence démocratique, de tout faire pour poursuivre et conclure l'accord politique en négociation. Dans ce contexte, nous demandons au gouvernement et aux responsables du parti politique au pouvoir d'empêcher les réactions violentes à la récente tentative de coup d'état, comme la mise à feu des locaux de la Convergence démocratique, qui réduisent les chances de faire aboutir les pourparlers. Nous voulons croire que la conclusion et la mise en œuvre d'un accord politique entre les principaux partis peut redonner espoir au peuple haïtien et ouvrir une voie d'avenir. Sans la volonté de mettre fin à l'engrenage de la violence et des injustices le pays va au-devant du chaos total.

Le Conseil oecuménique des Eglises encourage la Fédération protestante d'Haïti et toutes les églises et communautés chrétiennes de persévérer dans la recherche du bien pour le peuple haïtien, à travers la prière, la proclamation de la volonté de Dieu et les actions, en s'associant à tous ceux que s'engagent pour sortir le pays du cercle vicieux de l'injustice et de la violence. Nous vous assurons de notre solidarité et de notre soutien.

En ce temps d l'Avent, où les chrétiens du monde entier se préparent pour accueillir Celui qui est le Prince de paix, nous nous souvenons que l'amour manifesté en Jésus Christ est plus fort que le mal et nous rend capable d'être des ambassadeurs de la réconciliation. Que Noël soit pour vous un temps de paix et de renouveau spirituel, qui vous permette à continuer le bon combat. (2 Tim. 4 :7) Que Dieu vous bénisse et bénisse le peuple d'Haïti.

Konrad Raiser
Secrétaire général

[TRANSLATION]

Dear Brothers and Sisters in Christ,

The World Council of Churches is following with increasing concern the recent deterioration of the political and social situation in Haiti. The fresh upsurge of violence, lynchings such as that of the journalist Brignol Lindor on 3 December at Petit-Goâve, assassinations and summary executions have created a climate of insecurity that is unbearable for the population, and could make it impossible to achieve the political agreement that the government and the opposition are seeking.

Everything points to the fact that the violence is not gratuitous and cannot be explained only by the extreme poverty to which the majority of the Haitian people are condemned. Groups of people are aiming to provoke terror and to physically eliminate certain targeted individuals. It would seem that the authorities are not doing everything necessary to stop these actions. Reliable witnesses say that they may even be implicated in them or at least tolerate them.

Information supplied by reliable witnesses and recently published in the international press about the summary executions perpetrated by police officers leads us to fear the worst for the integrity and authority of the state. The principle of "zero tolerance" adopted by the government is understandable and responds to the exasperation of a population that cannot stand the situation any longer.

However, there is no justification for executing individuals suspected of criminal acts or even caught red-handed, without any form of trial.

In the light of this worrying situation, the World Council of Churches adds its voice to the appeals that human rights be properly respected made by the Ecumenical Centre for Human Rights, the Committee of Lawyers for the Respect of Individual Freedom, and other organizations in Haiti. We demand that the government act to improve procedures in the courts and to ensure that the national police behave with due respect for the law.

The World Council of Churches appeals to the political parties, especially the Lavalas Family and the Democratic Convergence, to do everything possible to bring the political agreement currently being negotiated to a successful conclusion. In this context, we ask the government and the leaders of the political party in power to prevent violent reactions to the recently attempted coup d'état, such as the setting on fire of Democratic Convergence offices, as such reactions reduce the chances of successful talks. We would like to believe that the conclusion and implementation of a political agreement between the main parties could bring hope to the Haitian people and open a way forward for them. But, without the will to put an end to the spiral of violence and the injustices in the country, the country will descend into total chaos.

The World Council of Churches encourages the Protestant Federation of Haiti and all Christian churches and congregations to persevere in the search for a better life for the Haitian people, through prayer, the proclamation of the will of God and practical action, in association with all those involved in trying to break the vicious circle of injustice and violence in the country. We assure you of our solidarity and support.

During Advent, when Christians throughout the world prepare to welcome the Prince of Peace, we remember that the love manifested in Jesus Christ is stronger than evil and makes us able to be the ambassadors of reconciliation. Let Christmas be, for you, a time of peace and spiritual renewal, that will allow you to continue to fight the good fight (2 Tim.4 :7). God bless you and the people of Haiti.

Konrad Raiser
General Secretary

Support for the joint appeal by the Roman Catholic Church and the Protestant Federation of Haiti for prayer for peace, justice and integrity
Letter to the churches and Christian communities in Haiti, 6 May 2002.

Chers sœurs et frères en Christ,

C'est avec beaucoup de joie que j'ai pris connaissance de l'appel conjoint de l'Eglise catholique romaine et la Fédération protestante d'Haïti pour un temps de prière et d'adoration en faveur de la paix, la justice et la probité, les 11 et 12 mai prochains.

Cette action commune à laquelle le peuple haïtien tout entier est invité à se joindre est un signe fort qui traduit la détermination des églises de promouvoir une prise de conscience et un changement radical dans la société haïtienne. Le recueillement devant Dieu, dans un mouvement qui rassemble et engage le plus grand nombre de fidèles est une manière profondément chrétienne de dire non à la violence, l'injustice, le mensonge et la corruption. C'est en se tournant vers Dieu que le peuple chrétien peut se mettre en route, puisant sa confiance et sa force auprès de Celui qui a dit : *« Voici, je fais toutes choses nouvelles »*.

Au nom du Conseil œcuménique des Eglises et de ses Eglises membres dans le monde entier, je vous apporte notre soutien et notre solidarité. Je vous assure de notre communion fraternelle. J'encourage toutes les églises, toutes les communautés chrétiennes et tous les fidèles d'Haïti à participer à ce temps de prière et de recueillement. Je salue votre initiative d'appeler les chrétiens à porter un vêtement blanc, en signe d'engagement commun et pour que votre action dans l'union de tous soit visible.

En vous mettant ainsi en marche, vous allez entamer un long chemin. Il vous faudra persévérer. Sachez que vous n'êtes pas seuls. Le peuple haïtien a beaucoup d'amis. Les églises d'Haïti font partie d'un réseau d'amour, de charité et de solidarité. Nous voulons cheminer avec vous.

Que Dieu vous bénisse et bénisse le peuple d'Haïti.

Konrad Raiser
Secrétaire général

[TRANSLATION]

Dear Sisters and Brothers in Christ,

It was a great joy for me to receive the joint appeal of the Roman Catholic Church and the Protestant Federation of Haiti, calling for a time of worship and prayer for peace, justice and integrity this coming 11 and 12 May.

This common action, in which all the people of Haiti are invited to take part, is a strong sign of the determination of the churches to promote a new awareness and a radical change in Haitian society. An act of reverence before God, which gathers together and involves as many church members as possible, is a deeply Christian way of saying No to violence, injustice, falsehood and corruption. By turning to God, the Christian community can make a new start, drawing confidence and strength from the One who said, "See, I am making all things new."

In the name of the World Council of Churches and its member churches throughout the world, I offer you our support and our solidarity. I assure you that we are in communion with you as sisters and brothers. I would encourage all the churches, all Christian communities and all faithful Christians in Haiti to participate in this time of worship and prayer. I applaud your initiative in calling on Christians to dress in white, as a sign of their common commitment and so that your action may be visible, in the unity of all.

In making this new start, you will be setting out on a long road together. You will need perseverance. Know that you are not alone. The people of Haiti have many friends. The churches of Haiti are part of a network of love, kindness and solidarity. We want to walk this road with you.

God bless you, and God bless the people of Haiti.

Konrad Raiser
General Secretary

Report of ecumenical election observers
Issued in Port-au-Prince, 27 May 2001.

Un groupe de 13 observateurs électoraux est venu de Suisse, de France, d'Allemagne et des Etats-Unis. La présence de ces observateurs exprime l'intérêt et la solidarité de la communauté mondiale des églises chrétiennes pour le peuple haïtien dans cette étape importante de la construction démocratique que représente ce scrutin.

Nous avons admiré la volonté manifeste des citoyens haïtiens de participer au scrutin, et ceci en dépit de sa complexité et des difficultés matérielles et techniques de son organisation que rendaient presque impossible la stricte application de la loi électorale. Nous avons pu constate, également, la présence, dans les bureaux de vote, de nombreux observateurs nationaux et de mandataires des différents partis. Nous soulignons le sérieux et le sens civique des membres de la majorité des bureaux de vote observés, malgré une formation souvent insuffisante. Cet engagement a permis un déroulement satisfaisant du vote dans ces bureaux. Par contre, dans plusieurs bureaux de vote, nos avons été témoins de certaines irrégularités : pressions, intimidations, secret du vote non assuré. Les opérations de dépouillement se sont déroulées dans des conditions particulièrement difficiles (durée, manque d'éclairage, exiguïté des locaux, fatigue de membres des bureaux de vote, départ ou exclusion des mandataires) et des irrégularités ont été observées, notamment en ce qui concerne les procès verbaux (incomplets, non signés ou non rédigés sur place). Nous n'avons pas observé l'acheminement des résultats vers les bureaux électoraux communaux (BEC) ni, la plupart du temps, leur compilation qui n'a pas, généralement, été achevé dans les délais légaux de 48 heures. A partir de cette étape de compilation des résultats nos observations ont été rendues très difficiles par le désordre qui régnait dans la plupart des BEC que nous avons visités. Dès le lendemain du vote, nous avons observé, en plusieurs lieux, une dégradation du climat, caractérisée par une montée des tensions (arrestations de candidats, manifestations de rues, actes de violence, interventions des forces de police).

Dans ces conditions, toute appréciation sur l'ampleur et les conséquences des irrégularités observées nous paraît prématurée : une vérification rigoureuse par département et pour tous les postes électifs est nécessaire.

Il est du devoir de Conseil Electoral Provisoire, des autorités nationales, des partis politiques, de la société civile, de tous les acteurs de ce processus électoral et des représentants de la communauté internationale, d'agir, en fonction de leurs compétences respectives, afin que l'ensemble des règles de fonctionnement de la démocratie soit garanti. Il importe que la volonté de tous les électeurs soit respectée.

Pour le groupe des observateurs œcuméniques,

Philippe Verseils   Aves Mignot   Christian Delord

[TRANSLATION]

A group of 13 election observers has come from Switzerland, France, Germany and the United States. The presence of these observers expresses the interest and the solidarity of the world community of Christian churches for the Haitian people in the important stage of democratic construction this vote represents.

We have admired the manifest will of Haitian citizens to participate in the vote despite the complexity and material and technical difficulties in its organization that rendered almost impossible the strict application of the electoral law. We have also been able to confirm the presence of numerous national observers and representatives of different parties. This engagement has permitted a satisfactory development of the vote in the election bureaus. However, in several voting places we have been witnesses to certain irregularities: pressures, intimidations, secrecy of the vote not guaranteed. The counting of ballots has taken place under particularly difficult conditions (time elapsed, lack of lighting, small quarters, fatigue of the members of the voting offices, departure or exclusion of official observers) and irregularities have been observed, notably in the minutes (incomplete, unsigned or not written on the spot). We did not observe the transfer of results to the communal voting offices (CVO) nor, most of the time, their compilation that has not, generally, been completed within the legal limit of 48 hours. From this point of the compilation of results, our observations were made very difficult by the disorder that reigned in most of the CVOs that we visited. From the day after the vote we have observed, in several places, a degradation of the climate, characterized by rising tensions (arrests of candidates, street demonstrations, acts of violence, interventions by police forces).

Under these conditions, any estimate of the breadth of the consequences of the irregularities observed seems to us premature: a rigorous verification by department and of all the voting places is necessary.

It is the duty of the Provisional Electoral Council, the national authorities, the political parties, civil society, all actors in the electoral process and the representatives of the international community to act, in terms of their respective competences, in order that all the rules of the functioning of democracy be respected.

For the group of ecumenical observers,

Philippe Verseils   Aves Mignot   Christian Delord

PUERTO RICO

Appeal for the cessation of US military exercises on the Island of Vieques
Letter to U.S. President Bill Clinton, 30 November 1999.

Mr President,

The people of Vieques, Puerto Rico, widely supported by the churches there and in the United States, have for some months been engaged in non-violent actions seeking the cessation of US military use of this island for weapons testing and bombing practice.

The World Council of Churches fully supports this initiative. We join with Puerto Ricans and the residents of Vieques in appealing to you, in your role as Commander in Chief of the Armed Forces, to declare a halt to these practices, and to remove the U.S. Navy from the island and the surrounding maritime areas.

U.S. military exercises in and around Vieques over many years have inflicted serious environmental damage. Worse still, they have repeatedly resulted in accidental deaths of civilian residents.

We urge you to take leadership in this matter, and in this period of Advent to exercise your authority in a way that would show respect for the human rights of the people of Puerto Rico and give them a sign of peace.

Yours sincerely,

Dwain C. Epps
Director
Commission of the Churches
on International Affairs

Excmo. Sr. Presidente

El pueblo de Vieques, Puerto Rico, apoyado por las iglesias locales y las iglesias de los Estados Unidos, se ha comprometido desde hace varios meses a realizar acciones no violentas para obtener el cese del uso de la isla como zona de pruebas por los militares estadounidenses.

El Consejo Mundial de Iglesias apoya completamente esta iniciativa. Nos unimos al pueblo puertorriqueño y a los habitantes de Vieques para apelar ante Ud., en su rol de Comandante en Jefe de las Fuerzas Armadas, para que declare el alto a estas prácticas y que ordene la salida de la Marina de Guerra de los Estados Unidos de la isla y de las zonas marítimas circundantes.

Los entrenamientos militares que realizan en Vieques y en sus alrededores desde hace muchos años han deteriorado seriamente el medio ambiente. Peor aún, han causado muertes accidentales de civiles.

Por lo tanto, le instamos a tomar las medidas que se imponen y que, en este período de Adviento, ejerza su autoridad de manera que muestre el respeto de los derechos humanos del pueblo puertorriqueño y les haga llegar un mensaje de paz.

Respetuosamente,

Dwain C. Epps,
Director,
Comisión de las Iglesias en
Asuntos Internacionales

Appeal for protection of non-violent protesters on the Island of Vieques
Letter to H.E. President Bill Clinton of the U.S.A., 2 May 2000.

Mr. President,

On 29 November 1999 we conveyed to you the support of the World Council of Churches for the non-violent actions undertaken on the Island of Vieques in Puerto Rico by the Ecumenical Coalition on Vieques. At that time we urged you then to exercise your authority as Commander in Chief of the Armed Forces to call a halt to the use of this island for weapons testing and bombing practice. We also appealed to you to respect the human rights of the people of Puerto Rico and to give them a sign of peace.

We are now informed that a decision has been taken to send US Marshals and FBI personnel to remove protestors from the Island, and that such action is imminent. News reports yesterday indicated that this action is being supported with a massive show of naval force off the coast of Puerto Rico.

We are grateful that you sent your representative, Mr. Jeffrey Farrow, to meet with the Ecumenical Coalition recently. Through that meeting, you should be informed that the non-violent presence in Vieques has the wide support of the churches in Puerto Rico, both Protestant and Roman Catholic, and that among those engaged in this vigil in the restricted area on Vieques are representatives of the churches, including bishops.

We have also been grateful for your leadership in seeking to restore the confidence of the people of Puerto Rico by taking action on humanitarian grounds to release most of the long-term prisoners held in US prisons for political actions they had taken many years ago.

The present action apparently to be taken today runs directly counter to such efforts, and will hardly be understood by the churches or the wider international community. They do not bring credit to your Administration.

The spectacle of police action backed up by the presence of warships and which is likely to involve arrests of church leaders will contribute little to the pursuit of a lasting solution to this problem. We therefore urge you to call a halt to this intervention immediately and to heed the request of the churches of Puerto Rico that the people of Vieques be consulted with respect to their own will on the future of their land.

We pray for you and that a spirit of dialogue can soon replace confrontation with the people of Puerto Rico.

Respectfully,

Dwain C. Epps
Director
Commission of the Churches on
International Affairs

EUROPE

CYPRUS

Minute on Cyprus
Adopted by the Executive Committee, Geneva, 29 February – 3 March 2000.

The Executive Committee of the World Council of Churches, meeting in Geneva, Switzerland, 29 February – 3 March 2000, received with appreciation information on the WCC delegation visit to Cyprus in October 1999, which included a first WCC visit to the Turkish-occupied territory of Cyprus since the "Turkish Republic of Northern Cyprus" was unilaterally declared in 1983.

Recalling its Statement on Cyprus (1997), the Executive Committee

Warmly welcomed the resumption of UN-led proximity talks on Cyprus and prays that they will pave the way as soon as possible for substantive negotiations leading to a just and peaceful resolution of the conflict;

Expressed its support for the UN Secretary-General's efforts to bring about a comprehensive settlement of the Cyprus problem;

Requested staff and member churches to continue to monitor closely developments in Cyprus and to encourage the Church of Cyprus and all members of the Greek and Turkish Cypriot civil society in efforts for justice, peace and reconciliation.

Minute on Cyprus
Adopted by the Central Committee, Potsdam, Germany,. 29 January – 6 February 2001.

Meeting in the reunified Germany, the Central Committee recalls that it was during its meeting in Berlin, in August of 1974, that Turkish armed forces invaded Cyprus causing the exodus of more than 250,000 people from their lands, and occupied thirty-seven per cent of its territory. We renew the World Council of Churches' appeals for justice, peace, reconciliation and the reunification of Cyprus, and reassure the people and the Church of Cyprus of our continuing prayers that this long-standing conflict will soon be settled through negotiation and this last wall of separation in Europe finally be brought down.

ROMANIA

Appeal for continued dialogue on church-state legislation
Letter to President Emile Constaninescu, 4 February 2000.

Your Excellency,

As a worldwide fellowship of churches, the World Council of Churches has always been concerned with issues of church-state relations. In this regard, it has come to our attention that the government of Romania is continuing its consideration of legislation on religions. Some of our member churches in Romania have expressed to us their concerns about this legislation, particularly the requirements for registration of religious communities.

We strongly encourage further dialogue and negotiation involving the representatives of churches and religious communities themselves before the legislation is finalized.

As you are aware, we have signaled this concern previously to your Government. In a spirit of constructive dialogue I sent our Coordinator for International Relations, the Rev. Dwain Epps, to Romania to share our experiences. In his extensive conversations with Dr Gheorghe F. Anghelescu on the broader issues of church-state relations in 1998, Rev. Epps offered our continuing support in the resolution of some of these issues.

It is in this same spirit that I reiterate our sincere hope that you and your Government will respond positively to this new request.

Respectfully yours,

Konrad Raiser
General Secretary

RUSSIAN FEDERATION

Expression of condolences to victims of the bombings in Moscow
Letter to H.H. Alexei II, Patriarch of Moscow and All Russia, 15 September 1999.

Your esteemed Holiness,

We have received with shock and great dismay news of the bombings of apartment buildings in Moscow in which scores of innocent victims have been killed. On behalf of the World Council, I wish to convey through Your Holiness our most profound sympathy and condolences to the families and loved ones of all those whose lives have been taken through these acts of terrorism. Christians in our member churches around the world share a deep sense of revulsion, and hold you, the families, and the Russian nation in their prayers in these difficult and frightening times.

It is one of the characteristics of our time that acts of isolated extremists are used by some to create suspicion, intolerance and even hatred against the religious groups of which they are assumed to be a part. Few churches have been as diligent as the Russian Orthodox Church in building relationships of mutual respect between believers of different faiths in and beyond your own society. You yourself have sustained this long tradition of spiritual leadership, and have spoken out clearly against all efforts to divide Russian society along religious or other lines, or to demonize any group because of the faith they hold. We are sure that you will not fail now, in this time of dramatic need, to renew your call for tolerance and national unity in the face of such adversity.

I assure you of our readiness to assist you in any way you may find helpful in your ministry to the victims and their families, and in the witness you give to your people.

With deep respect,

Yorgo Lemopoulos
Acting General Secretary

Expression of profound concern about the continuing intervention in Chechnya by Russian armed forces.

Joint letter to His Holiness Alexei II, Patriarch of Moscow and All Russia, 15 November 1999.

Your Holiness,

We greet you in the name of our Lord and Saviour Jesus Christ 'for He Himself is our peace' (Eph. 2:14).

On behalf of the Conference of European Churches and the World Council of Churches we express our profound concern at the continued escalation of the conflict in Chechnya and the human tragedy in the North Caucasus region, and we acknowledge with gratitude the recent statement of Your Holiness on this very matter.

The CEC and WCC recognize the context of lawlessness and terrorism which has preceded the current armed intervention by the Russian armed forces. We remember the many victims of terrorist acts, kidnapping and executions in Chechnya, including a number of Christian pastors and workers. However, we raise our voices that even legitimate political or military objectives cannot justify the innocent victims and suffering of peoples in the region.

We deplore the disproportionate and irresponsible use of force employed by the Russian military forces, which is contributing to a humanitarian crisis of the utmost seriousness. We appeal to the Russian and Chechen political authorities, and to the combatants on all sides, to manifest mercy to all people, especially the civilian population, the prisoners and the wounded.

The CEC and WCC appeal to Your Holiness and to the leadership of the Russian Orthodox Church to do everything in your authority to enable unimpeded and secure international humanitarian assistance to be brought to those uprooted by this conflict, and to promote a peaceful resolution of the crisis. The ecumenical organizations will continue to work closely with the Russian Orthodox Church and with other partners to provide relief to those most in need, through its emergency office ACT - Action by Churches Together.

We share with the Russian Orthodox Church the rejection of any attempts to manipulate religion for political ends, which Your Holiness has drawn attention to in previous statements. We oppose any radicalisation on religious grounds, and we encourage all efforts by Islamic and Christian leaders which actively promote peace, tolerance and a real solution to the conflict.

The CEC and WCC pray with the Russian Orthodox Church and other churches, and with all people of good will, that a political solution, which expresses the genuine will of the Chechen people, may be found, and which will lead to the restoration of the rule of law, a lasting and just peace for all the peoples of this region.

Konrad Raiser	Keith Clements
General Secretary	General Secretary
World Council of Churches	Conference of European Churches

Reiterated appeal to stop indiscriminate Russian military actions in Chechnya
Joint letter to His Holiness Alexei II, Patriarch of Moscow and All Russia, 10 December 1999.

Your Holiness,

At this season of Advent, we greet you in the name of our Lord Jesus Christ the Prince of Peace, the Saviour of the world who came in humility as a homeless child in Bethlehem and who will come in glory as the judge of all the world.

We wish to make known to you again the concerns which we expressed in our letter to you of 15 November 1999 on the conflict in Chechnya, concerns which are widely felt in the member churches of CEC and the WCC. It is above all the plight of the many innocent civilians which is on our hearts, both those trapped inside Chechnya and those who have become refugees.

First, in this context we greatly welcome the forthcoming visit by the President of the Organisation for Security and Cooperation in Europe (OSCE), Mr Knud Vollabaek, to Chechnya. Our ecumenical organisations have, as you know, been strongly supportive of the OSCE since its inception, believing it to be

293

a crucial instrument for promoting peace, stability and human rights throughout Europe. We deplore the way in which its role was marginalised during the Kosovo crisis. It is our hope that Mr Vollabaek's visit will receive every facility needed for making an objective assessment of the situation inside Chechnya. To this end, we would welcome any opportunity you could take to meet with Mr Vollabaek if and when he passes through Moscow in order to encourage him in his task, and to help ensure that he receives from the Russian authorities every means required to make his visit to Chechnya as wide-ranging and thorough as possible.

We further greatly appreciate the appeal which you made in your statement of 12 November, that the Russian military authorities should not inflict suffering on innocent civilians, and that 'the army should show an attitude of high responsibility in choosing the means and ways of conducting their military operations and that all the authorities should pay exceptional attention to the needs of the civilians . . .' The many reports which we are receiving on the military actions, however, indicate that this call for discrimination in the use of force is not being heeded. We are particularly concerned at the reports that the Russian military authorities have given notice that total destruction of the city of Grozny will soon be implemented, and that all remaining people in the city will be regarded as military targets. Such an order fails to take into account that, due to the present conditions in the city, many civilians will not have been able to receive this information, and many, especially the weak, the elderly, the sick, the very young and their parents, will not be in a position to leave. This ultimatum, we therefore believe, is contrary to all accepted international conventions and codes of conduct in warfare and is unacceptable to the Christian conscience. We therefore appeal that with all the spiritual authority at your disposal as the head of the Russian Orthodox Church, you speak to the Russian government in the name of just conduct and humanity and in reiteration of your earlier appeal.

We are aware that, as stated in our letter of 15 November, the Russian authorities have been faced with a highly complex and difficult situation in Chechnya, which for so long has been in the grip of terrorist and criminal activity. Experience of dealing with endemic violence in other contexts, however, does not suggest that military action of this kind leads to any genuine solution and in fact, in the longer term, exacerbates it and creates further problems. We are also sensitive to the feelings among the Russian people at large, that external criticism of the military action is invalid, especially in view, for example, of the NATO action on Kosovo. At the same time, we would point out that our two ecumenical organisations first strongly opposed then repeatedly called for a halt to the NATO aerial attacks, and that our reports based on visits to Serbia during the conflict called attention to the sufferings being inflicted on its civilian population by that action. Our appeal to you, and to the Russian government, is motivated by the same fundamental concern.

Mindful of the high and holy responsibilities laid upon you as leader of the great Russian Orthodox Church during these tense and difficult days, and remembering the promise of our Lord, 'Lo, I am with you always', we assure you of our cordial regard and our heartfelt prayers that you may experience all needed grace, strength and joy in the Lord, and that peace and hope may be brought to the people of Chechnya and the surrounding region.

With our sincere good wishes,

Yours in Christ,.

Konrad Raiser
General Secretary
World Council of Churches

Keith Clements
General Secretary
Conference of European Churches

Statement on Chechnya
Adopted by the Executive Committee, Geneva, 29 February - 3 March 2000.

The roots of the present-day conflict in Chechnya lie deep in the histories of the peoples of the region. Since 1991, however, ethnic and national tensions have been aggravated by the breakdown of authority in Chechenya. Human rights violations and breaches of personal security there have been of concern to the international community. One manifestation of this has been the rampant practice of taking individuals and groups hostage for political or financial gain. Hundreds of people, including Orthodox Christian clergy and Muslim religious leaders, UN personnel, humanitarian workers, journalists, citizens of neighboring territories and numerous Chechens – including children – have been kidnapped, brutalized, and sometimes killed. This lawlessness also led, it is strongly suspected, to acts of terrorism by Chechen militants in the Russian Federation. In late summer 1999 Chechen fighters undertook a violent assault on Daghestan, Chechnya's neighbor in the Russian Federation.

In response to this deteriorating situation, and with considerable popular support, the government of the Russian Federation has once again intervened militarily in Chechnya. While the stated aim of that intervention was to restore law and order, it was undertaken with massive, often indiscriminate force, which has resulted in the deaths and maiming of many non-combatants and forced hundreds of thousands to flee. An undetermined number of young Russian and Chechen soldiers have also been killed. Russian forces have restricted the movement of affected people in Chechnya and the surrounding region, including those voluntarily seeking to return to their homes. International organizations report wide-scale human rights abuses in Russian-controlled areas, including detention camps, and there are serious allegations of involvement of Russian military personnel in criminal acts, including arbitrary killings of civilians.

While the Russian authorities have denied these charges, the fact that they have barred access by the International Committee of the Red Cross to Chechen detainees, and severely restricted access of journalists and other independent observers, puts into question the credibility of their affirmations. Military actions continue on both sides, trapping civilians behind Russian lines and incurring continued loss of human life. Tens of thousands of civilians have extremely limited access to water, food, medical care, and electricity or gas.

This continued suffering must be brought to an end. The pursuit of this war is unlikely to provide the basis for a stable peace. Instead, hatred and desire for revenge as a result of these actions raise the specter of unending war, further acts of terrorism and still more suffering for the population. This war also risks isolating Russia from other European nations and important partners, as shown by the recent action of the Council of Europe's Parliamentary Assembly that found Russia to be in violation of international humanitarian law in its conduct of military operations.

The Executive Committee of the World Council of Churches, meeting in Geneva, Switzerland, 29 February - 3 March 2000 therefore:

noted with appreciation the appeal by His Holiness Patriarch Alexei II on 12 November 1999 for "common efforts (to) help heal the physical and spiritual wounds of those who suffer" from this situation, and for all concerned to "work together for reconciliation and pray for peace so that the Lord may return it to the divided and embittered people" of Chechnya;

assured the Russian Orthodox Church of its prayers as it seeks to guide the leaders and people of its nation, to ensure merciful treatment of the victims of the war, to offer constructive alternatives to the use of armed violence, and to seek a just, peaceful solution;

called for an immediate end to hostilities and dialogue with Chechen representatives who have the respect of their people in pursuit of a lasting resolution which respects the will of the people, and is set within a democratic framework respecting the rule of law and human rights norms;

urged all parties to avail themselves of the resources available through the Organization for Security and Cooperation in Europe (OSCE) to achieve these ends;

welcomed efforts by Russian authorities to investigate reports of human rights abuses in Russian-controlled areas of Chechnya and urges the authorities to allow access to these regions by the competent United Nations bodies and the OSCE;

urged the Government of the Russian Federation to establish firm guarantees for the human rights and humanitarian needs of people affected by the war, including provision of adequate assistance, the establishment of humanitarian corridors so that civilians in conflict zones can leave, and to allow access to the region by responsible international humanitarian agencies; and

called upon the international community to assist the Government of the Russian Federation in the reconstruction of homes and infrastructure in the region, in the provision of adequate assistance for displaced persons who choose to return voluntarily in order that people can begin re-building their lives and communities, and in efforts to seek reconciliation.

TURKEY

Statement on the situation of the Kurdish People and the arrest of Abdullah Ocalan

Statement by Ms Kristine Greenaway, Director of Communication at a press conference held jointly with representatives of the Kurdish community in Switzerland at WCC headquarters in Geneva, 19 February 1999.

At around 14:00 this afternoon, Friday, 19 February, members of the Kurdish community in Switzerland came to the World Council of Churches at the Ecumenical Centre in Geneva.

Leaders of the group met the WCC General Secretary, Rev. Dr Konrad Raiser, and presented him with an appeal concerning Abdullah Ocalan.

The group expressed its concern over the arrest and detention of their leader Abdullah Ocalan by the Turkish authorities and called on the WCC to intervene in this matter.

The WCC has followed the issue of the Kurdish people over the years. Given the WCC's stated commitment to human rights and self-determination, the WCC calls on its member churches in Europe to seize this opportunity and urge their respective governments to seek a peaceful political solution to the plight of the Kurdish people.

The Kurdish community has expressed concerns about the physical safety and security of Abdullah Ocalan. The WCC appeals to the Turkish government to ensure Mr Ocalan's safety and that he can receive visits from his lawyers. The WCC further appeals to the Turkish authorities to ensure Mr Ocalan receives a fair trial in accordance with international norms and procedures of the Rule of Law.

Expression of concern about the abduction, detention and trial in Turkey of Mr Abdullah Ocalan

Letter to Mr Daniel Tarschys, Secretary-General of the Council of Europe, 11 March 1999.

Mr Secretary-General,

On behalf of the World Council of Churches and the Conference of European Churches, bodies in consultative relationship with the Council of

Europe, we wish to convey our concern about the abduction, detention and trial in Turkey of Mr Abdullah Ocalan.

As ecumenical organizations with a long-standing dedication to the strengthening of and respect for the international rule of law, we are deeply concerned about the broad implications of this case with respect to jurisdiction, international standards on the treatment of prisoners, and the right of every person to an open and fair trial.

The abduction of Mr Ocalan in Kenya, and his forcible transfer to Turkey cannot, we believe, be allowed to establish a precedent, and it renders the jurisdiction of the courts of Turkey in this case questionable under international law with respect to extradition.

We are grateful that the European Committee for the Prevention of Torture and Inhuman or Degrading Treatment or Punishment has visited Mr Ocalan in pursuit of their mandate. We now look forward to the publication of its report in accordance with Article 11 of the European Convention for the Prevention of Torture and Inhuman or Degrading Treatment or Punishment. We sincerely hope that this timely visit and the Committee's continuing oversight in this case will ensure full respect for the rights and physical integrity of Mr Ocalan so long as he remains in detention.

We wish to support and encourage you and the Council of Europe in your efforts to assure Mr Ocalan's right to be presumed innocent until proved guilty in a fair, public trial in a civil court in accordance with Article 6 of the European Convention on Human Rights. This should include his right to a defense attorney of his own choice, and sufficient time and facilities for the preparation of his defense, and access to the proceedings by international observers.

We trust that the Government of Turkey will be held to the axiom that the administration of justice must be carried out in such a way that it be publicly acknowledged as just and fair. For this to be so in this case, the question of legitimate jurisdiction must be allowed should Mr Ocalan's defense choose to put it.

We urge the Council of Europe to assume its full responsibilities in this case vis-à-vis its member state which has freely accepted the terms of the Charter and the relevant Conventions. In so doing you bear responsibility on behalf of the wider international community for respect of the rule of law and of human rights.

Respectfully yours,

Konrad Raiser
General Secretary
World Council of Churches

Keith Clements
General Secretary
Conference of European Churches

Appeal to commute the death sentence of Abdullah Ocalan

Letter to H.E. Süleyman Demirel, President of the Republic, 2 July 1999.

Your Excellency,

On behalf of the World Council of Churches I appeal to you not to carry out the death sentence pronounced by the Security Court against Abdullah Ocalan.

The World Council of Churches adopted a decade and a half ago a position which opposes the use of capital punishment. The WCC has taken this position on theological grounds, and on the basis of our conviction that the death penalty is a form of cruel and inhuman punishment which denies compassion and leaves no room for the possibility of rehabilitation of the offender. At the same time, we are concerned that steps be taken now to break the vicious cycle of violence in your country. Both Turks and Kurds must now know that the use of retributive violence contributes not to healing, but only to further suffering on both sides.

On these grounds, and trusting in your own wisdom and the value you place on the sanctity of life, we appeal to you to grant clemency and commute the death sentence given Abdullah Ocalan.

Respectfully yours,

Dwain C. Epps
Director
Commission of the Churches
on International Affairs

Expression of condolences to earthquake victims

Letter to H.E. Süleyman Demirel, President of the Republic, 20 August 1999.

Your Excellency,

As the dimensions of the terrible tragedy in your country resulting from the recent earthquake grow, the hearts of Christians around the world go out to the people of Turkey. As an expression of this concern, I offer you, and through you, to all those in your country who mourn losses of loved ones and remain stunned by the destruction of homes and communities, the deepest condolences and sympathy of the World Council of Churches.

I have sent similar messages to the churches in Turkey related to the World Council of Churches, asking them to share these with their friends and neighbors. From the first hours after news of this disaster came, churches and church-related agencies which cooperate with Action by Churches Together (ACT), a joint humanitarian response program of the WCC and the Lutheran World Federation, began to mobilize emergency assistance and to contribute to the enormous task of rebuilding. This aid, which will be channeled through our churches in Turkey and through other international response channels, is a tangible expression of the pain

Christians feel, and the solidarity they are compelled by faith and common human feeling to offer to all the victims without distinction.

We mourn with you and the people of your land your losses, and hold you always in our prayers to the one loving and merciful God, that He may bring you consolation and invest you with the hope and courage to face up to the daunting task of healing and reconstruction.

Very sincerely yours,

Konrad Raiser
General Secretary.

YUGOSLAVIA (FORMER)

Message to the Conference on Peace and Tolerance in Kosovo
Conveyed to the conference held in Vienna, 16-18 March 1999.

To the distinguished participants in the First Summit of Kosovo Religious Leaders,

The World Council of Churches (WCC) has closely monitored the civil conflict in Kosovo over recent months, and welcomes all attempts to seek a just and peaceful settlement to the crisis in the region. The WCC supports the statements and actions of the churches and religious communities that seek to promote a lasting peace, including the present summit of Kosovo religious leaders of the Serbian Orthodox, Catholic and Islamic communities.

As churches and religious leaders in the Federal Republic of Yugoslavia and elsewhere have said from the beginning of this conflict, violence cannot bring peace. The use of force and intimidation cannot secure a lasting and just solution to this complex and painful conflict. The only viable future for the region lies in a negotiated settlement based on the establishment of full democracy and respect for the human rights of all communities, majority and minority, and the due recognition of the need for tolerance and peaceful co-existence. The WCC affirms the principle that the representatives of all national communities in Kosovo should be involved in any political settlement, if this is to be just and durable.

The Council condemns in the strongest terms the use of violence in any form by the conflicting parties. The efforts by the international and regional organizations and mechanisms to actively promote a settlement to the conflict, in particular the Rambouillet peace process, and all supportive measures short of military force to achieve this end, are commendable and need to be encouraged. The WCC welcomes the active involvement of the Organization for Security and Cooperation in Europe (OSCE), which is in accordance with the resolutions of the UN Security Council. The WCC emphasizes the necessity for the international institutions to ensure that any future political settlement enhances stability in the region and builds confidence among all its peoples.

The Council remains greatly concerned about the humanitarian disaster created by the armed conflict which has resulted in the displacement of tens of thousands of civilians. The WCC therefore urges all parties, and especially the authorities in the Federal Republic of Yugoslavia, to honour their commitments to maintain and uphold the right to access by international humanitarian organizations to the affected region, and to facilitate the safe return of all those displaced by the fighting. The WCC, through its emergency office ACT-Action by Churches Together, will continue to provide assistance to the victims of the humanitarian crisis, regardless of their origin.

The WCC expresses its profound solidarity with all the peoples of Kosovo, and joins the common prayer of the faithful of all religious communities that justice and peace may be restored in this land.

Konrad Raiser
General Secretary

Pastoral letter to WCC member churches in the Federal Republic of Yugoslavia

Letter to leaders of the three WCC member churches in Yugoslavia, 25 March 1999.

H.H. Patriarch Pavle
Serbian Orthodox Church

Bishop Istvàn Csete-Szemesi
Reformed Christian Church in Yugoslavia

Bishop Ján Valent
Slovak Evangelical Church
of the Augsburg Confession in Yugoslavia

Your Holiness, Brothers in Christ,

I am writing to you on behalf of the World Council of Churches to express our profound emotion following the NATO-led bombing of Yugoslavia, and to express our solidarity with you at this critical time.

The attack signals a failure to reach a negotiated agreement, and a breakdown in human relations. War can only bring further destruction and human suffering to a region which has already experienced so much pain, and will open new wounds and enmities.

I have stated on previous occasions the position of the WCC on the crisis, and have condemned violence and intimidation in any form, as only a negotiated solution can bring a durable and just peace. This conviction was most recently reiterated in a message to the Summit of Kosovo Religious Leaders in Vienna, 16-18 March 1999, in which the Serbian Orthodox Church was represented, a copy of which is attached.

301

During this Lenten season Christians remember Christ's passion and crucifixion. But we also together proclaim that in the midst of human suffering and weakness comes our greatest hope, that of His Resurrection, and the invitation to eternal life.

I would like to assure you of the thoughts and prayers of the member churches of our fellowship, and of the staff here in Geneva, during this critical time. The WCC remains available to respond to the requests and needs of its members, and will maintain its humanitarian assistance to all victims of the situation, regardless of their origin.

Konrad Raiser

General Secretary

Appeal for an immediate moratorium on the NATO military intervention

Letter to H.E. Kofi Annan, Secretary-General of the United Nations, from the general secretaries of the WCC, CEC, and LWF and endorsed by the general secretary of WARC, 29 March 1999.

Dear Mr Secretary-General,

We write to express our profound concern at the current military intervention of NATO in the Federal Republic of Yugoslavia, and appeal to you to immediately initiate efforts of the United Nations to seek a just and lasting peace to the conflict in Kosovo.

The NATO-led intervention in the Federal Republic of Yugoslavia manifests the failure of the international community to achieve a credible, negotiated solution. Each day of bombing makes the solution more distant, and increases the risk of regionalisation of the conflict. It also enhances the danger of a renewed divide within Europe.

We therefore appeal for an immediate moratorium on the NATO military intervention, in order to allow for a renewal of the political process under your leadership and under the auspices of the United Nations.

We agree with the appeal of His Holiness Patriarch Pavle, head of the Serbian Orthodox Church on March 25, 1999 urging 'the governments of all countries of the world for their action in order that the bombardment should be stopped and that a just solution to the current crisis may be found through negotiations. The Serbian Orthodox Church appeals to the military and civilian authorities of Serbia and Yugoslavia to do everything possible so that peace may be established'.

We affirm the declaration of Kosovo religious leaders for a non-violent resolution of the conflict based on guaranteed rights of all communities.

We reiterate our conviction that decisive progress was made in the Rambouillet process towards a durable political settlement, and this should not be lost. In the present situation, however, we believe that the United Nations alone can offer a framework for a new initiative which can break the present deadlock.

On behalf of our member churches we confirm our willingness to back and support any initiative taken by Your Excellency to stop the present acts of military violence and seek a non-violent resolution of this conflict in the Federal Republic of Yugoslavia.

Konrad Raiser
General Secretary
World Council of Churches

Keith Clements
General Secretary
Conference of European Churches

Ishmael Noko
General Secretary
Lutheran World Federation

Milan Opocensky
General Secretary
World Alliance of Reformed Churches

Easter appeal for a cessation of armed conflicts
Issued from Geneva, 31 March 1999.

In this season of Easter, Christians around the world share the profound pain of all those caught up in tragedies such as Kosovo. Our hearts go out to all those who are suffering the terrible consequences of the violence being inflicted on God's children in this region and in many other parts of the world. We lament the failure of imagination, collective will and human spirit made manifest in the incapacity to address the causes of conflict through peaceful means. As we remember again the sacrifice of Jesus Christ, the one proclaimed by the prophets as the Messiah, the Prince of Peace, our hearts are heavy for we recognize that we have not yet been able to overcome our inclination to turn to the sword in moments of doubt and fear.

Kosovo is but one of the many conflicts around the world today where people take up arms against one another out of fear, hate, greed or hopelessness. Many of these wars are largely hidden from the view of the wider world, and some of them have claimed an even more terrible toll than is now being inflicted in the Balkans. So we pray this Easter for all of those in Yugoslavia and elsewhere whose lives are shattered by war.

Leaders of christian churches in both East and West, and leaders of other religious faiths have appealed in recent days for a cessation of such acts of violence and for the settlement of conflict by negotiation. Regrettably, such voices have not yet been heard over the clamor of charges and countercharges, and the roar of bombs, landmines and guns.

One of these leaders, His All Holiness The Ecumenical Patriarch Bartholomew, has summarized many of these sentiments in his appeal of 29 March 1999, saying,

in the name of God who loves humankind, in the name of the human race, in the name of civilization, at this season of the religious feast of the

303

Muslims, the Easter of Roman Catholics and Protestants, the Passover of the Jews and the Pascha of the Orthodox, on bended knees (I) fervently appeal from the tormented depths of my heart to all world government leaders, to military commanders and to those who bear arms throughout the world, that they cease fire immediately and permanently. We beseech them to use mutual understanding and mutual concession to resolve peacefully their regional, international and worldwide disputes, in order that the God of peace and mercy might bless them and all people.

In this same spirit, we appeal to Christians around the world in these high holy days to join their hearts and spirits in this prayer that the bombings may cease and that the guns may fall silent. May the Spirit descend among us and inspire in us the courage to sacrifice our individual wills in order that the peace of the Risen Christ may prevail.

Konrad Raiser
General Secretary
World Council of Churches

Keith Clements
General Secretary
Conference of European Churches

Joe Hale
General Secretary
World Methodist Council

Denton Lotz
General Secretary
World Baptist Alliance

Ishmael Noko
General Secretary
Lutheran World Federation

Milan Opocensky
General Secretary
World Alliance of Reformed Churches

John L. Peterson
Secretary General
Anglican Communion

Statement on Protection of Humanitarian Principles in Kosovo Refugee Response

Issued jointly by the WCC, CEC, LWF and WARC, Geneva, 15 April 1999.

The war in Yugoslavia and especially acts of ethnic cleansing committed by Serbian forces against the Albanian population in Kosovo have created a humanitarian crisis of dramatic proportions which presents immense challenges to international humanitarian organizations as well as to political and military actors.

Within this context the Lutheran World Federation (LWF), the World Council of Churches (WCC), the Conference of European Churches (CEC) and the World Alliance of Reformed Churches (WARC) are deeply concerned that basic principles of humanitarian assistance which are fundamental to humanitarian refugee response be recognized and protected. These principles include the right to asylum under the same terms and conditions to which any other group of refugees is entitled, including evacuation on a voluntary basis only, respect for the unity of the family and priority for the elderly and vulnerable.

Established international humanitarian organizations and institutions have responsibility to ensure that such basic humanitarian principles are protected. In the present context the military has a necessary role in providing logistical support, in the establishment of infrastructure and in the safeguarding of both refugees and humanitarian personnel, but such support must be provided within the framework of humanitarian principles and under the coordination of these humanitarian organizations

Therefore the LWF, WCC, CEC and WARC call on all member churches and their related humanitarian agencies to press their respective governments:

- to support the presence and coordination role of established international humanitarian agencies and institutions to ensure that established humanitarian principles are protected in all aspects of refugee response, including provision of sufficient support and resources to allow for assistance which meets the standards set out in the *Code of Conduct for the International Red Cross and Red Crescent Movement and Non-Governmental Organizations in Disaster Relief* and the *SPHERE Humanitarian Charter and Minimum Standards in Disaster Responses*;
- to ensure that lead humanitarian organizations such as UNHCR and ICRC be given sufficient support and prominence to equip them to coordinate humanitarian response;
- to ensure that the actual management of refugee services be handled by humanitarian organizations and their personnel and that the role of military actors be limited to logistics, infrastructure and security.

Yorgo Lemopoulos
Acting General Secretary
World Council of Churches

Keith Clements
General Secretary
Conference of European Churches

Agneta Ucko
Acting General Secretary
Lutheran World Federation

Milan Opocensky
General Secretary
World Alliance of Reformed Churches

Yugoslavia's double tragedy
Ecumenical delegation Report, Novi Sad, Belgrade, 16-18 April 1999.

Introduction

A joint delegation of the Conference of European Churches (CEC), the World Council of Churches (WCC) and the Lutheran World Federation (LWF) visited the Federal Republic of Yugoslavia (FRY), 16-18 April 1999.

The aim of the visit was to meet with the leaders of member churches in the Federal Republic of Yugoslavia, and to discuss with them the causes and consequences of the current crisis in Kosovo, and of the NATO bombardment of

305

Yugoslavia. The delegation visited member churches in the Yugoslav cities of Novi Sad and Belgrade, but was unable to enter the province of Kosovo itself due to restrictions on movement resulting from the intensive conflict situation there. Visits to member churches in Albania and other countries in the region are also being planned.

The visit was held soon after the start of the bombing campaign against targets throughout the Federal Republic of Yugoslavia. The ecumenical delegation was organized in the context of widespread international concern provoked by the massive and tragic exodus of over half a million Kosovar Albanians into neighbouring Albania and Macedonia, and the accounts and allegations of serious human rights violations, forced deportation, and arbitrary executions perpetrated in the province of Kosovo, detailed by the United Nations High Commissioner for Refugees, the UN High Commissioner for Human Rights, and others.

The World Council of Churches, the Conference of European Churches and the Lutheran World Federation have repeatedly appealed for a negotiated and peaceful resolution to the conflict situation in the region of Kosovo, and have consistently opposed any violence or use of military force by the involved parties. The relevant statements and press releases have been made public.

The purpose of this report is to communicate the results of the visit and the discussions with the Yugoslav church leaders, and to summarize the preliminary findings of the delegation.

The objectives of the visit were:

- to be present and manifest solidarity with member churches in Yugoslavia at a critical time;
- to listen to the churches and receive information about their situation.
- to discuss the conflict in Kosovo, and the massive exodus of the Albanian Kosovars and its causes;
- to discuss possible ecumenical initiatives in the country and region, including further humanitarian assistance, with the churches.

Delegation members were:

Rev. Dr Keith Clements, General Secretary, CEC
Mr Alexander Belopopsky, Europe Secretary, WCC
Rev. Dr Olli-Pekka Lassila, Europe Secretary, LWF

Meeting with Protestant Church Leaders (Novi Sad)

The delegation met with the leaders of the minority Protestant churches (Reformed, Lutheran and Methodist) in Novi Sad (Vojvodina) in northern Serbia. The region is home to important ethnic Hungarian and Slovak minorities. The group's arrival coincided with the first night that Novi Sad had not been targeted since the start of the NATO bombing. The church leaders welcomed the solidarity and understanding of the broader Christian family manifested by the visit, and

306

especially valued the letters and Easter peace appeal of the international church bodies.

There are a number of responses of the church communities in Yugoslavia to the crisis in Kosovo, and especially to the NATO intervention and its consequences, including statements and joint prayers. The church leadership is generally well-informed about the refugee crisis and deportation in Kosovo, and its dramatic consequences on the civilian population and the neighbouring countries. All church leaders forcefully condemn any violence, intimidation, ethnic cleansing and forced displacement of the civilian population in Kosovo, and support calls for a negotiated and peaceful resolution to the conflict. However, there are different perceptions about the immediate causes of the violence and refugee crisis in Kosovo. For most of the churches, the role of the Kosovar Albanian armed separatist forces is an important factor in the radicalization of the situation in the region, together with the violent response of Yugoslav and Serbian military and paramilitary forces, and the intensive NATO bombardment is perceived as having aggravated the exodus of people from the region.

The conflict situation and the NATO intervention were the main areas of discussion. Novi Sad has been hit by aerial strikes every night for three weeks, and several sites in the suburbs and the central bridges in the city have been destroyed. The local churches unanimously condemn the NATO attack which is perceived as an unjust and inhuman response to a complex sequence of events which have led to the crisis around Kosovo, and which is understood by them as an illegal and immoral attack on a sovereign State. The church leaders emphasize that the bombing campaign has undermined democracy, has strengthened the regime's control of the country, and has radicalized the extremist forces in Yugoslavia and among ethnic Albanians.

Bishop Istvan, head of the Reformed Church in Yugoslavia, is certain that war in Kosovo could have been avoided if the Western powers had not interfered and created "impossible expectations". According to the Lutheran church leader Bishop Valent "the humanitarian tragedy facing the Albanians has been exacerbated by NATO and KLA (Kosovo Liberation Army) actions". The crisis in Kosovo is the result of the dismantling of the delicate Yugoslav balance of nationalities constructed by Tito, and of extremist Kosovar Albanians who were encouraged by Western powers to seek secession from Yugoslavia, it was stated by the church representatives. Methodist Superintendent Hovan adds that now "the whole country is in crisis" and he expresses his gratitude for the assistance and support of the ecumenical family for all victims of the conflict.

The ethnic minorities in the province of Vojvodina (mainly Hungarians and Slovaks) "are not responsible for the crisis in Kosovo", explained Bishop Valent, "but the consequences on the local situation here are direct and important". Young men are facing mobilization, the economic impact is serious, and there are isolated examples of a xenophobic attitude towards minority groups, which had

307

not existed prior to the NATO raids. The introduction of a state of war in Yugoslavia also means that churches must seek permission to organize any non-worship gathering.

The profound sense of injustice and outrage engendered in the traditionally multi-ethnic and multi-cultural region is articulated by a local university professor, Dr Svenka Savic, whose text is being circulated abroad by the churches. "Bridges are constructions (...) of the spirit, which join people and objects (...) The bombardment of the bridge in Novi Sad symbolizes division between nations, parts of the world, the division within ourselves. The bombardments of the bridge in Novi Sad is only one of a series of bombardments in our (former) country (...) and today we stand in front of our destroyed bridge, each of us recalls how we lived with it, and we all cry. We cry because we hate those who took it away from us. Destroying the bridge in Novi Sad as a strategic point, they have moved the emotional point of our balance, and now we are limping in search of support."

Meeting with the Roman Catholic Church (Belgrade)

The delegation was received by Archbishop Perko, head of the Roman Catholic Archdiocese of Belgrade. The Archbishop received the delegation in the same dining room where Serbia was presented with an ultimatum by the Western Powers which led to the First World War. The Roman Catholic Church and the Holy See through the Papal Nuncio in Yugoslavia have vigorously intervened to seek to end the international bombardment of Serbia as a response to the Kosovo crisis, and are actively promoting diplomatic solutions. According to Archbishop Perko, the churches are all united against the Nato bombing, and must never cease struggling for dialogue and negotiation between the warring parties in Kosovo. The inevitable result of the Nato bombing of Yugoslavia is a strong and popular Serbian reaction to the West, he says. "We are for dialogue, but the tragedy is that dialogue is now impossible (..) there seems to be no mutually acceptable understanding of what is possible as a solution to the conflict". The Archbishop remains pessimistic about the immediate future. He thinks the culmination of events around Kosovo is a "tragedy and disaster" for the Serbian people, which he compares to the plight of the Jews during the time of the Prophet Jeremiah. He is supportive of the "moral duty" of European churches to stop the Nato bombing, which can only worsen the situation, and to contribute to dialogue and peaceful solutions, but he fears that this is a "cry in the wilderness".

Meeting with the Serbian Orthodox Church (Belgrade)

The delegation was received by the head of the Serbian Orthodox Church Patriarch Pavle, and separately, by two diocesan Bishops, Irinej of Backa and Bishop Ignatije of Branicevo. The visit was warmly welcomed as a "visible manifestation of concern and solidarity for the churches in Yugoslavia and the cause of peace" said Patriarch Pavle. The Patriarch emphasized that the visit came at a time of great difficulty and misfortune for both Serbs and Albanians. The Patriarch repeated his condemnation of war and violence and he repeated his

308

public appeals for the ending of all military actions by all forces, to allow for the guaranteed return of all civilians to their homes, and a solution which allows for peaceful coexistence. "From the very beginning of this situation I have appealed to our State authorities, military forces and civilian leaders to do everything in their power to prevent an escalation of the conflict", he stated. "All war is evil" he says, "but civil war is doubly evil as it provokes neighbour to fight neighbour".

The Patriarch reminded the delegation that he lived for 34 years in Kosovo, and knows at first hand the situation there. He expressed his profound concern at the human suffering and tragic destruction taking place in the province. He thinks it is important to understand the causes and reasons for the current situation. In his view, the Yugoslav State is faced with an impossible position, as armed separatists seek independence from the rest of Yugoslavia. The Nato intervention is perceived as an attack by Western powers on the sovereignty and freedom of the country, and does nothing to promote a negotiated solution. What does the Gospel tell us when our integrity and freedom is attacked? he asks. The Church is against war, but a State has the right to defend its integrity. But the Gospel also says that we must answer before God for our actions and lives, and "all our work in this crisis must be to serve justice, truth and love", he emphasized.

The Serbian Church leader welcomes the actions and statements of the international church organizations, and especially of the Roman Catholic Church, to promote a peaceful solution to the conflict. The Serbian Orthodox Church is working directly to promote alternative solutions, and has been consistently critical of the actions of the Yugoslav political leadership in Kosovo, and sent a delegation to present its views at the Rambouillet peace conferences, without success. Specific annexes were drafted by the church as additions to the Rambouillet draft proposals, which propose broad autonomy and secure rights of all minorities within Kosovo. A memorandum proposing urgent alternative solutions to the policy of the Yugoslav government was presented to Madeleine Albright in person by Bishop Artemije of Raska-Prizren. The Patriarch and Holy Synod support the statements and actions of the Orthodox Bishop in Kosovo, Bishop Artemije, for a cantonisation of the province within a democratic and federal Yugoslavia, with guarantees for all ethnic and national groups. These positions have been articulated for over two years, and have provoked strong criticism of the Orthodox Church from the Yugoslav political leadership. The Patriarch expressed his interest in the proposals that European churches together take a new initiative to call for a cessation of hostilities, an end to Nato bombing and the establishment of a humanitarian corridor into Kosovo in favour of those displaced and suffering from the fighting.

In conversation with Bishop Irinej, the Serbian Orthodox Bishop in Novi Sad, it was emphasized that the NATO bombing has aggravated the situation and cannot contribute to a solution of the crisis. The psychological approach of NATO has been disastrous, as it has dramatically reduced any possibility of a political solution. The delegation raised the issue of the reported atrocities, forced deportation and ethnic cleansing by Yugoslav forces in Kosovo. The church leaders expressed grief at the human suffering in the province, but accused the separatist forces and the Nato intensive bombing as having encouraged and even directly provoked the massive exodus of people. "We weep for the plight of the refugees from Kosovo" he says, and the church will not look at who is Albanian and who is Serb. However, he remains sceptical about the humanitarian motives of the NATO operation. "Almost no help was given to Yugoslavia from outside or even by our State authorities to assist the 700,000 refugees who were forced to leave homes in Croatia and Bosnia", he said. Yugoslavia had many problems and was a far from perfect democracy, but it was still the most open country in the communist system, he emphasized. "The difficulties are a thousand times greater after the NATO intervention. Western policy towards Yugoslavia has now produced the greatest anti-Western factor in Europe".

According to the Bishop, the Serbian Orthodox Church has struggled to propose alternatives solutions for the Kosovo crisis, but the NATO intervention has now actually created new conflicts, with tensions emerging even in his region of Vojvodina. He thinks that Yugoslavia should give full autonomy to the Kosovar Albanians within the existing international borders, with the rights of the other minorities in Kosovo being guaranteed by an international peace-keeping force "without NATO countries", who cannot offer a neutral role after the intervention. The Bishop cannot believe that the disastrous reactions to the Nato bombing were not analyzed and predicted by Western policy makers, and he therefore raises the question about the broader geopolitical interests of the intervention in the region. The Bishop emphasized that the church "does not speak in the spirit of government but rather in the spirit of the Gospel". "We too are Europeans," he said, and he appealed for European churches to raise awareness about the Yugoslav churches' situation and positions, and about the human impact of the bombing and the displacement in the Federal Republic of Yugoslavia.

The Humanitarian Situation in Yugoslavia

During conversations with church representatives, the critical social, humanitarian and political situation provoked by the bombing, and the continued violence and military action in Kosovo, were discussed. The full scale of the humanitarian impact remains difficult to measure, and is evolving daily. The massive displacement of people in Kosovo, and the arrival of over half a million Kosovar Albanian refugees in neighbouring Albania and in FYR Macedonia, has created a massive humanitarian disaster and suffering. At the time of the visit, the precise situation within Kosovo, and the full extent of the human and material catastrophe, were not known. The international humanitarian organizations and the United Nations agencies estimate that some hundreds of thousands of people remain displaced within the province itself, with limited access to food and shelter.

Many major cities in Yugoslavia have been heavily affected by the Nato bombing of bridges, energy supplies and military targets. The most intensive bombing has

310

been in Kosovo itself, and in the Southern cities of Yugoslavia. There have been civilian deaths directly from bombing, although the authorities are reluctant to release any figures. Some people displaced by the fighting in Kosovo, including Albanians, Serbs and others, are making their way as far North as Vojvodina and Novi Sad, although many prefer to avoid the big agglomerations. Over 100,000 displaced people are present in Montenegro, according to the Yugoslav Red Cross. The existing refugee populations from the fighting and forced movements of population in Bosnia and Croatia are also seriously affected. According to UNHCR figures there are over 760,000, mainly Serb, refugees still in the Federal Republic of Yugoslavia, many of whom are dependent on international aid. Pharmaceuticals and imported necessities (e.g. baby food and milk) are already in limited supply. The heating, water supply and sanitation systems have been seriously damaged in many cities. The Red Cross is increasing stocks of blood, and is developing first aid training. Hospitals are being emptied of non-emergency cases, and in some areas water and heating supplies are disrupted. The psychological and trauma impact on the civilian population is becoming apparent, and it appears that the suicide rate is rising especially among vulnerable groups such as the elderly.

Another direct impact of the conflict has been the potential mobilization of men for the army. Men of conscript age are not allowed to leave the country. Some examples of desertion and draft-dodging are reported especially among the non-Serb minority communities, which are reluctant to serve in Kosovo. Conscientious objectors, especially among Jehovah's witnesses and Nazarenes, are subject to punishment.

However, it is the long-term impact which is most feared according to Karoly Beres, the leader of the Ecumenical Humanitarian Organization based in Novi Sad. "The bombing of factories, fuel depots, and civilian transport routes, following ten years of international sanctions, is rapidly creating an economic disaster" he says. Of deeper concern is the slow breakdown of normal life that is being engendered, as schooling and medical services are halted. "It seems immoral for us to ask for aid when the Kosovars are suffering so much" he stresses, "but the rising waves of hatred [caused by Nato bombing] are taking effect and the consequences frighten us". The EHS leader expressed his recognition and gratitude for the support given by Western church agencies for the work of the organization. According to Beres, the churches can have an important role in overcoming conflict, if they can avoid the mistakes of politicians and look to the future and not only refer to the past. "our great task as churches is to find ways for all nations to live together as part of a broader European life". But he admits that the continued crisis in Yugoslavia is making this expectation a distant dream.

The joint ecumenical visit was welcomed by the churches as a manifestation of real concern and solidarity, and was organized at a critical and tense time in the Federal Republic of Yugoslavia.

The delegation recognized the double tragedy experienced by people in Yugoslavia: the devastating civil war and forced movement of populations in the region of Kosovo, and the subsequent massive impact of the Nato bombardment throughout Yugoslavia.

The Yugoslav church leaders condemn any violence, intimidation, ethnic cleansing and forced displacement of the civilian population in the province of Kosovo.

The Serbian Orthodox Church explicitly appeals for the guaranteed right of return of all people displaced from their homes by the fighting.

There are differences of perception about the immediate causes of the massive exodus of refugees, as some churches see the NATO bombing and the armed confrontation within Kosovo as important causes.

All churches emphasize the need for any solution to the conflict to respect the territorial integrity of the Federal Republic of Yugoslavia and the multi-ethnic character of the province, with protected rights for all ethnic and religious groups.

There is unanimity of all the churches, Orthodox, Protestant and Catholic, in opposing the NATO bombing. According to the churches, the NATO intervention, far from changing Yugoslav policy, has led to an escalation of the crisis. The intervention is perceived as an unjust attack on a sovereign country and on a civilian population, despite the insistence of NATO that it is directed against the Yugoslav leadership and military capability in Kosovo.

The Nato intervention is seen as having effectively silenced any political and democratic opposition in the country, and has largely paralyzed the emerging civil society, as the country rallies itself against perceived foreign aggression. The Yugoslav authorities have closed down or restricted the previously thriving independent media, especially in Serbia. According to Democratic Party leader Zoran Djindjic, quoted at the time of the visit in the Western media, the NATO intervention has actually strengthened Milosevic, and will lead to social unrest in Yugoslavia. In Belgrade, 17 leading peace organizations and independent NGOs have appealed for an end to the bombing, and reports speak of increased intimidation and fear among civil society activists since the start of the bombing. Paradoxically, some of the areas most affected by bombing were also centres of support for opposition political parties, while Kosovo was a strong centre of support for Milosevic due to the abstention of the Kosovar Albanians in elections. The churches themselves do not articulate any support for the leadership or policy of the current Yugoslav regime.

The Nato military intervention risks further destabilising the fragile ethnic and political balance within Yugoslavia, and threatens to reopen differences and conflicts among countries in the region.

The overall humanitarian impact of the bombing in the Federal Republic of Yugoslavia is much wider and deeper than reported internationally. "Collateral damage" includes the frequent, usually indirect, damage of hospitals, schools and residential areas, and the economic, psychological and trauma impacts are very significant. In many regions, the disruption of transport routes is isolating vulnerable communities. For example, an important bridge linking Serbia and Croatia has been destroyed, effectively isolating the last remaining Serbs in the area around Vukovar. The economic impact is devastating, and weakens the distribution of water, energy and food supplies in some parts of the country. The Yugoslav Red Cross has released detailed information on the situation, and is actively developing its disaster preparedness measures. Some groups in Yugoslavia have protested the environmental impact of the NATO bombing of oil and chemical installations, especially in the Danube, and the alleged use by NATO of depleted uranium ammunition and indiscriminate anti-personnel bombs in Kosovo itself.

The role of media and the transmission of information has a dominant role in shaping perceptions. The Yugoslav State media concentrate on the impact of the Nato bombing on civilians in other parts of Yugoslavia. Yugoslavs who have access to satellite television, foreign radio and the internet are aware of the mass deportation, ethnic cleansing and tragic plight of refugees forced to leave Kosovo. The Western media, with limited access to regions in Kosovo, gives little account of the armed conflict in the province, and of the complexity of its causes. Very little account is given anywhere of the alternative and moderate positions of the Yugoslav democratic movement and of the churches. The deliberate influencing of media by all parties, and the new power of direct information through the internet, have created a "live" war, in which the image and perception at times seem to override the content and direction of actions on all sides.

8. RECOMMENDATIONS TO INTERNATIONAL CHURCH ORGANIZATIONS

The international ecumenical organizations should further assist the churches in Yugoslavia to articulate and communicate their experience and understanding of the current crisis.

The ecumenical community should encourage an international prayer for peace, for example each Wednesday afternoon, in solidarity with churches in Novi Sad. An international prayer for peace in Yugoslavia is also being proposed by Yugoslav churches for 16 May.

The international church organizations should encourage the more systematic sharing of information with member churches in FRY, especially about the conflict and refugee crisis in Kosovo, and the international church reactions.

313

The ecumenical response to the humanitarian needs of all victims, displaced people and refugees must be continued and strengthened through ACT-Action by Churches Together. Disaster preparedness is a priority, and a coordination meeting could be arranged with Serbian partners. Particular emphasis must be given to strengthening the capacity of local churches and organizations in FRY to assist those in need.

Assistance for the revival of the Yugoslav ecumenical council of churches is important and necessary, and was requested by the Protestant church leaders.

The further networking and mobilization of churches worldwide to discuss the crisis and their respective positions, and to promote a just and negotiated settlement to the crisis, could be encouraged. The special concern of European churches could be focused in a united appeal for a cease fire, cessation of bombing and establishment of a humanitarian corridor into Kosovo.

Similar visits to other churches and partners in the Balkans region should be organized as early as possible, with a view to promoting possible sub-regional inter-church collaboration.

To overcome the isolation and to enhance ecumenical exposure, an increased involvement of FRY churches in the activities and life of the international church organizations should be encouraged.

Church leaders consultation on the churches and the crisis in the Balkans
Report of the consultation convened by the WCC and CEC in collaboration with the LWF, WARC and the Ecumenical Council of Hungary, Budapest, Hungary, 26-27 May 1999.

Over 40 church leaders and representatives from Eastern and Western Europe as well as from North America met in Budapest, Hungary, from 26 to 27 May to discuss the churches' response to the crisis in the Balkans region. Representatives of the churches in the Federal Republic of Yugoslavia (Lutheran, Methodist, Reformed and Serbian Orthodox churches) participated in the meeting.

The consultation was jointly organized by the World Council of Churches (WCC) and the Conference of European Churches (CEC) in cooperation with the Lutheran World Federation (LWF) and the World Alliance of Reformed Churches (WARC), and was hosted by the Ecumenical Council of Churches in Hungary. The consultation benefited from the presence of a representative of the Council of European Bishops' Conferences (CCEE). The international ecumenical organizations have taken several initiatives in response to the crisis, including the sending of delegations to the Federal Republic of Yugoslavia, to Albania and to the Former Yugoslav Republic of Macedonia.

The main purposes of the consultation were:

- To exchange information on the churches' actions and statements in response to the crisis in the Balkans;
- To engage in a dialogue aimed at a better understanding of the different perceptions and positions of the churches;
- To discuss the churches' role and witness in response to the crisis and in promoting peace.

The consultation shared in the widespread international concern about the escalation of the conflict and the reports of massive human rights violations in Kosovo, the devastating impact of the NATO air strikes and the tragic effects on the civilian population, and the plight of almost a million refugees from Kosovo.

The consultation recognized the complex historical roots of the crisis, and the different perceptions of the nature of the conflict and of the immediate causes of the massive exodus of Kosovar Albanians.

In a context of renewed division and hostilities in Europe, the church representatives expressed their commitment to staying together in prayer and in solidarity. In this situation the churches should seek common Christian witness and action by affirming the following principles:

- To recognize the fundamental and urgent priority of negotiations as the only basis for a durable solution to the crisis, and to urge the parties to use all possible opportunities to end hostilities.
- To support initiatives which foster a peaceful and lasting resolution of the conflict, and which recognize the equal rights of all nationalities and ethnic groups to co-exist within the same territory.
- To promote the guaranteed right of return and security of all those displaced by the conflict.
- To recognize and promote the central role of the United Nations and the OSCE in any negotiated solution to the crisis.
- To contribute to the process of reconciliation and rehabilitation of communities.
- To support efforts to render justice to all victims of the conflict.
- To continue the response to the humanitarian needs of all those affected by the crisis, through WCC/LWF ACT-Action By Churches Together and local churches and partners.

The consultation recognized the need for further dialogue and discussion of the following issues:

- The concept of just war and the means of peaceful resolution of conflict.
- The competing claims of national sovereignty and of humanitarian intervention.
- The relationship between religion, identity, territory and nation.
- The role which national contexts, minority/majority status and history play in the formation of perceptions.

- The identification and nature of reliable sources of information and its accurate dissemination.

Follow-up and possible future actions:

The consultation recognized that the crisis affects the entire region of South-Eastern Europe. A lasting solution will be furthered decisively if the national, ethnic, cultural and historical features can be brought into the process of European integration. In particular, the Orthodox tradition must be acknowledged as an integral part of the European heritage.

A special expectation for follow-up focuses on the Conference of European Churches. In particular, cooperation with the CCEE and other appropriate Roman Catholic partners can be strengthened in response to the regional challenges. The framework of cooperation with the churches and ecumenical organizations in North America should also be reinforced, drawing on the experience of the churches' human rights programme.

The creation of new instruments for a Christian response at the South-Eastern Europe level should be seriously considered in order to generate and nurture a future-oriented approach, emphasizing preventive action, education, interreligious dialogue and building on existing and new networks within civil society.

Ecumenical delegation visit to the FYR Macedonia and Albania

Conclusions from the report of the joint delegation sent by the WCC, CEC and the LWF, 18-25 May 1999.

In April 1999, the World Council of Churches, the Conference of European Churches and the Lutheran World Federation sent a delegation to Yugoslavia to meet with the churches to discuss the causes and the consequences of the present conflict in the Balkans. As part of their continuing response to the war, WCC and CEC in cooperation with LWF, organized a second delegation to the Former Yugoslav Republic of Macedonia and Albania from 18-25 May. This delegation was asked:

- to express solidarity with the churches and related organizations that are ministering to the needs of the Kosovar Albanian refugees;
- to learn about the actual situation facing refugees in the Former Yugoslav Republic of Macedonia and Albania, including church ministry to uprooted people, the actions of non-governmental and inter-governmental organizations, and the response of refugees to their present situation;
- in consultation with local partners and ACT members, to recommend specific actions to be taken by the churches to support humanitarian principles in the region.

Members of the Delegation

Wilhelm Nausner, United Methodist Church, Geneva area
Antonios Papantoniou, Church of Greece
Sylvia Raulo, Evangelical Church of Finland
Elizabeth Ferris, World Council of Churches
Alessandro Spanu, Federation of Italian Protestant Churches (Albania only)

Observations and general conclusions

1. The present conflict in the Balkans is *not a religious war*. While ethnic identities are deeply held, people of different ethnic and religious groups have lived together with respect and tolerance for centuries. Efforts to portray the war as a religious conflict are very dangerous. In this highly politicized context, neither the churches nor other religious communities should allow themselves to be used by governments or political groups for political purposes.

2. The present crisis in the Balkans is a *long-term one*. The effects of this war will last for many years - while the attention of the international community will most likely be short-lived. The refugees from Kosovo have many needs which demand both immediate and long-term attention. At the same time, we are deeply concerned about the impact of the conflict and the presence of refugees on the countries which host them. If a new global crisis develops or if humanitarian agencies are able to work inside Kosovo, it may be that attention will shift from the on-going needs of refugees in Albania and Macedonia to other areas. Given the volatile situation in both of these countries, this could have devastating consequences for those countries and for the region as a whole.

3. The war is creating a very dangerous situation for the neighboring countries and deserves more *sustained attention* from the international community. It is impossible for the countries of Macedonia and Albania to continue to host large numbers of refugees without the sustained support of the international community. We must also remember that in both countries the transition from communist rule to democratic institutions is a very difficult one.

4. People throughout the region are afraid of the *de-stabilizing effects* of the arrival of large numbers of people of different ethnicities and express concern that the conflict will "spill over" into their countries. Thus, the *problems of the region are inter-related* and a comprehensive plan needs to be developed in response to the region as a whole. A peace agreement, for example, would need to take into account not only the return of refugees to Kosovo from Macedonia and Albania, but also the impact of the war on Greece, Italy, Hungary, Bulgaria and other countries in the region.

5. *Yugoslavia is the center of the Balkans.* What happens in Yugoslavia has repercussions throughout the region in terms of trade and economic transactions, infrastructure, transportation, and political developments. Until there is democracy in Yugoslavia, the whole region will be at risk.

6. The challenge for the churches in the region is to *build and sustain pluralistic societies* where people of different ethnic and religious backgrounds can live together in peace and mutual respect. Although recent years have witnessed conflicts on a large scale, we must also remember that there have been periods of peace in which multi-cultural societies have functioned well. In this context, proposals to re-define national borders are very dangerous.

Ecumenical statement on the peace agreement for Kosovo
Issued jointly by the WCC, CEC, LWF and WARC, Geneva, 11 June 1999.

Churches, Christians and people of other faiths around the world have worked and prayed for an end to the terror of ethnic cleansing, and to the destruction inflicted on Kosovo and Serbia by eleven weeks of NATO bombing. They have contributed aid and stood in solidarity with the hundreds of thousands of ethnic Albanians, Serbs and others who have been forced to flee Kosovo and other parts of Yugoslavia. We thank God that the parties have finally reached an agreement to bring an end to the conflict, and for the efforts of the Secretary-General of the United Nations and all others who have worked so tirelessly to achieve this result.

We welcome especially the agreement of the parties to return to the framework of the Charter of the United Nations in pursuit of a lasting settlement of this dispute, believing that it is only in this context that peace and harmonious relations among the peoples of Yugoslavia and in the wider Balkans region can be appropriately and effectively pursued. We welcome and affirm the reiteration by the Security Council that a lasting solution must be sought which respects the sovereignty and territorial integrity of the Federal Republic of Yugoslavia. We also strongly support the affirmation of the United Nations High Commissioner for Human Rights that any durable solution to this crisis must be built on the solid foundation of respect for human rights.

Reconstruction in Kosovo is a central task and a prerequisite for the return of refugees, but the repair of damage done in Serbia and the removal of punitive economic constraints are also essential to the establishment of peace, to alleviating the suffering of the people, and to reconciliation in the region. The delegation sent two weeks ago to Albania and Macedonia by the World Council of Churches and the Conference of European Churches underscored the fact that the impact of the war extends far beyond Yugoslavia's borders. The international community must give priority to rebuilding infrastructure, homes and economies throughout Yugoslavia, and take a comprehensive, regional approach to reconstruction and reconciliation in order to create conditions for economic and political stability, and peace throughout South-East Europe.

All those who have been internally displaced or expelled from Kosovo must be allowed to return to their homes in safety. At the same time, the international principles with respect to the protection of refugees hold that no one should be forced to return against their will so long as there is a well-founded fear of persecution or violation of their human rights. The principle of reuniting separated families must also be fully respected both in Kosovo and in the diaspora. As refugees return, the local ethnic Serb communities in Kosovo must be protected from reprisals and violations of their human rights.

The Security Council has clearly indicated that the task of establishing and building the peace on the ground and of restoring an effective civilian administration has both military and civilian components. These roles should not be confused. Those who will assume military responsibilities for security must exercise the greatest possible restraint with respect to the use of armed force. Responsibility for the reestablishment of civil administration and an effective civilian police force should be the exclusive responsibility of the civilian component in which the OSCE should have a leading role. The UN High Commissioner for Human Rights should be given clear responsibility and support for monitoring during the implementation phase of the peace accord and for the establishment of effective local and national human rights mechanisms.

The churches will have a key role to play in the enormous task of reconstruction, refugee repatriation and reconciliation which must begin immediately. We call upon the churches, especially those of Europe and North America, to respond actively and generously to this challenge, in Kosovo and the other Yugoslav Republics, in Albania and Macedonia, and among refugees who have sought asylum in their own countries.

The agreement reached will, we pray, stop the war; but a just and lasting peace will require a long-term, intensive commitment by the international community, the national government, and the churches to the promotion of reconciliation.

May God bless and guide the way to such a peace for all those who have suffered so much before and during this war.

Konrad Raiser	Keith Clements
General Secretary	General Secretary
World Council of Churches	Conference of European Churches
Ishmael Noko	Milan Opocensky
General Secretary	General Secretary
Lutheran World Federation	World Alliance of Reformed Churches

Pastoral letter to the Holy Synod of the Serbian Orthodox Church
Letter to H.H. Patriarch Pavle, 24 June 1999.

Your Holiness,

We greet you in the name of our Lord and Saviour Jesus Christ.

On behalf of the World Council of Churches and the Conference of European Churches we would like to express our sincere appreciation for the statement of the Holy Synod of the Serbian Orthodox Church on 15th June, which includes a call for the resignation of the president and the government of the Federal Republic of Yugoslavia. In taking this clear and courageous position the voice of the Church has been heard, not only in your country, but also by the international community and in the churches in Europe and beyond. Those of us in the WCC and CEC, and in the churches who have been in close relationship with you over the past years, knew that the Serbian Orthodox Church had been critical of the regime of Mr Milosevic for a long time. The statement has helped many better to understand the position of the Church.

We know that you have been concerned with the plight of the Kosovar Albanians. As more facts are being revealed about the atrocities of which they have been victims, we are aware of the crucial role the Church will be called to fulfill in assisting the Serbian nation and the faithful to come to terms with what has happened under the responsibility of the federal president and government.

We are moved and encouraged by the decision of your Holiness to move your patriarchal residence temporarily to the historic site of Pec. This will certainly be an encouragement for many members of the Serbian community in Kosovo, persuading them to stay. We are concerned about the lack of security for the Serbian community and support your call to the authorities of KFOR to provide swift and effective protection for everybody. We were particularly sad to learn about attacks directed at some of the monasteries, obliging Bishop Artemij and some of the monks to leave Prizren.

It is our sincere hope that with time, the Serbian people and the Kosovar Albanians will again be able to live together in peace. Reconciliation may take many years, but it must be the long-term objective of the churches and the international community. In this spirit, Your Holiness and the Church have consistently affirmed the right of all the refugees and displaced persons to return to their homes, and called on the Serbian people in Kosovo not to leave theirs. As WCC and CEC, we would like to assure you of our prayers and our willingness to assist the Serbian Orthodox Church, and the other churches, in the present difficult situation as well as in the long term.

With regard to humanitarian relief to all in need, Action by Churches Together (ACT), which is acting on behalf of the WCC and the Lutheran World Federation, is already in Kosovo. In the coming days and weeks ACT will establish cooperation with the Serbian Orthodox Church.

320

In order to discuss with Your Holiness, and with the bishops and clergy, other ways in which our organisations can be of assistance, and to gain a better insight into the situation, we are planning to send a WCC/CEC delegation to Kosovo next week, from 29th June to 1st July. We hope that Your Holiness will bless this initiative and will receive the delegation in Peç.

Yours ever in Christ,

Konrad Raiser
General Secretary
World Council of Churches

Keith Clements
General Secretary
Conference of European Churches

Ecumenical delegation visit to Kosovo
Findings of the delegation sent by the WCC and CEC, 29 June – 2 July 1999.

Following the visits of delegations from organisations based at the ecumenical centre in Geneva to Novi Sad and Belgrade 16-18 April, and Macedonia and Albania 18-25 May, during the time of the NATO bombing, the World Council of Churches (WCC) and the Conference of European Churches (CEC) decided to send a delegation to Kosovo as soon as possible after the war. This visit took place 29 June to 2 July 1999.

The aims and objectives of the visit were:
- to strengthen first-hand contacts with the religious communities, in particular with the Serbian Orthodox Church, in Kosovo
- to gather information about the present situation, especially with regard to security and the implementation of human rights for all peoples in the region
- to assess the future role of churches and ecumenical bodies in establishing a civil society to discuss humanitarian aid
- to suggest mid-and long-term ecumenical action. …

Findings and Conclusions

Humanitarian Aid. Wherever the ecumenical delegation went, the signs of war were highly visible. We met convoys of Albanian refugees returning home. According to UNHCR officials, 500,600 had returned so far and these were the ones who had some resources and a home to return to. In fear of revenge, Serbs are forced to leave the country, to live in ghettos or to seek refuge in monasteries under the protection of KFOR troops. It is feared that large parts of Kosovo are covered with land mines and unexploded devices that may take years or even decades to trace and remove. Accidents and new victims are reported daily, but the full scale of the problem is not yet clear. In all parts of the region we saw destroyed and burnt houses, including churches and mosques; the further north, the higher the degree of devastation. People of all ethnic and cultural backgrounds are suffering and lack food and medical supplies. According to the Muslim leader, Mr Naim Ternava, humanitarian aid for the region around Drenica is a high priority. Bishop Artemije referred to those Serbs that live in fortresses and are unable to move freely.

Humanitarian aid needs to continue and even be increased, especially in the light of the forthcoming winter, which starts in some parts of Kosovo as early as October. A sustained commitment to Kosovo by all aid organisations should be encouraged. ACT should continue to follow its principle of helping all those in need beyond religious or ethnic border-lines. Coordination among the many relief organisations present in Kosovo should be strengthened.

The ecumenical organisations should support the establishment of a UN Kosovo Mine Action Centre as well as the NGO mine clearance efforts

Towards a multi-ethnic and multi-religious Kosovo. All of our contacts expressed their vision for a multi-ethnic and multi-religious Kosovo. The present situation, however, forces the ethnic Serbian population as well as the Gypsies/Roma to leave Kosovo. Though the KFOR troops do their utmost to bring about stability and security, they are unable to protect every civilian of the minority population. Serbs have either left (Prizren), live in fortresses, seek refuge in monasteries or are separated from the ethnic Albanian majority by the KFOR troops (Mitrovica). We have seen little evidence that Kosovo can remain multi-ethnic under the present circumstances.

We recommend that the KFOR and UN civil administration mandates which guarantee the security of ethnic minorities and all citizens be made explicit and that personnel and resources be provided to complete the task. Advocacy for the rights of Serbs and other ethnic minorities as well as maintaining a multi-ethnic and diverse Kosovo is critical. The number of KFOR troops originally planned (50,000) should be fully deployed in Kosovo and the civilian police force must immediately be oriented, trained and put to work in communities across Kosovo. We urge the demobilisation of small arms. All of our contacts based their hopes on a strong KFOR presence. The presence of international protection forces, however, cannot guarantee the peaceful coexistence of the different parts of the population.

Therefore we strongly recommend the establishment of a civil administration and the re-building of a civil society as soon as possible. The fact that the KFOR troops and the UN moved in too slowly allowed the UCK to take over the civil administration in many parts of Kosovo. We regard it as indispensable that the religious communities be invited and heard at the EU meeting on reconstruction scheduled for 31 July.

Even these efforts will not prove to be sufficient in the long-run to guarantee the peaceful co-existence of ethnic Albanians, Serbs and Gypsies in Kosovo. Therefore the ecumenical delegation tested with all contacts the possibilities for mediation and civil conflict transformation. The response was, however, that it would be much too early to think about initiatives to this effect. Nevertheless we want to encourage those organisations which have experience in this field to jointly explore possibilities in the mid-term future. It may be that some local communities can be identified, which are already working towards reconciliation, or that representatives from different communities can be invited for training courses in civil conflict management in the near future. It would be advisable for mediation efforts to link with intergovernmental bodies, such as the OSCE or SIMIC. In addition, we recommend that a collection of resource materials on peace, tolerance and reconcilation etc. should be collected in Serbo-Croatian and Albanian in order to duplicate and spread it in Kosovo as widely as possible. The Patriarch himself spoke about the need for public repentance and forgiveness. The Patriarch also reacted positively towards the idea of a pastoral meeting of the ecumenical community and the Serbian Orthodox Church. We therefore recommend that plans for a pastoral meeting be developed and an invitation be issued.

We heard from all religious communities about their commitment to a multi-ethnic Kosovo which respects human rights, justice and the rule of law. We therefore call on all nations to share intelligence data gathered during the conflict that might lead to indictments by the ICTY. We urge nations to provide additional professional staff (e.g. forensicists, criminal investigators) to support the efforts of the ICTY.

Reacting to a quickly changing reality. The visit of this delegation was too short to prepare a full assessment of the situation in Kosovo. Moreover, the situation is changing by the day, if not by the hour. At the same time the media seem to be losing interest. We saw several media representatives leaving Kosovo. We recommend that the ecumenical organisations strengthen their efforts to keep in close contact with the Serbian Orthodox Church and all visited contact persons. Additional contacts within the religious communities as well with other NGOs and the intergovernmental organisations will have to be made. The director of the Muslim Academy explicitly invited us to continue the dialogue and to also meet with all leaders of the Muslim community. We also suggest that another small delegation be sent to the region in August in order to re-assess the situation, to express solidarity with the peoples in Kosovo and to recommend appropriate actions to be initiated by the meetings of the Central Committees of WCC and CEC in September.

Members of the delegation
- Ms Penny Panayiota Deligiannis (Diaconia Agapes, Orthodox Autocephalous Church of Albania)
- Ms Linda J. Hartke (Church World Service and Witness, National Council of Churches of Christ in the USA)
- Mr Saso Klekovski (Macedonian Centre for International Cooperation)
- Mr Artan Kosti (Orthodox Autocephalous Church of Albania)
- Ms Miriam Lutz (Action by Churches Together)
- Rev. Rüdiger Noll (Conference of European Churches)

- Mr Huibert van Beek (World Council of Churches)
- OKR Klaus Wilkens (Evangelical Church in Germany)
- Mr Vladimir Shmaly (Russian Orthodox Church) could not join the team due to technical problems.

The crisis is not over ! Europe, the Kosovo Crisis and the Churches

Report of the consultation convened by CEC in cooperation with the WCC and the Serbian Orthodox Church, Oslo, 14-16 November 1999.

Church leaders and representatives from the Balkan region and other parts of Europe and North America met in Oslo, Norway, from 14 to 16 November 1999 to assess the Kosovo crisis and its impact on the Balkan region and the rest of Europe.

The Conference was organised by the Conference of European Churches in cooperation with the Serbian Orthodox Church, the World Council of Churches and the informal Vienna group of church leaders. We express our thanks and gratitude to the Church of Norway and the Norwegian government for hosting and generously supporting the conference.

We offer the following conclusions to the churches in Europe and North America and through the churches to governments and a wider public. Meeting just prior to the OSCE Summit, which is meant to adopt a European Security Charter, we also address ourselves to the heads of state and government gathered in Istanbul on 18 and 19 November.

1. The Kosovo crisis is not over. It is a European tragedy and also has consequences for global, international relations. Large parts of Kosovo and also other parts of Yugoslavia have been devastated. Hundreds of thousands of people have become refugees or internally displaced people. Neighbouring countries have had to share their scarce resources with an overwhelming number of refugees. Some refugees return, finding their houses bombed, burnt or looted. Others are fleeing just now or do not see any possibilities for return.

National and international political and religious leaders support the idea of a multi-ethnic and a multi-religious Kosovo. The reality is that Kosovo day by day is becoming more and more mono-ethnic. We are far from lasting peace and reconciliation among the different communities. The crisis has revealed a complex situation which requires careful analysis anda multifaceted approach before stable solutions can be found.

2. The crisis in Kosovo has again reminded us about the need to understand Europe as one organic entity. We have seen that the recent crisis and other recent conflicts have exploited the old differences in Europe between the part which adheres to the Eastern Christian legacy and the part which emerges from the Latin-Roman legacy - the dividing line from the year 1054. In this situation, it is important to underline that the Orthodox and Western Christian traditions are as

two lungs in one European organism. Any attempt to deny the contribution of either of these traditions for European identity is a denial of our common heritage. There is no place for paternalism either between churches or between church agencies. All churches must be respected for the insights they have in their own societies and for the ability they have for contributing to the welfare and well-being of the peoples they serve.

> We recommend that CEC organise a study of theological and historical reasons for present divisions in Europe and encourage the churches in Western and Eastern Europe to engage in renewed efforts to understand one another better and come closer to one another.

3. This crisis has again shown us how easily we accept stereotypical images of each other, and how easy it is for mass-media to contribute to the demonisation of individuals or groups of people. There is a need to counter this with balanced information and by seeking human and ecumenical fellowship with each other.

> We recommend: The churches need to devise mechanisms whereby they together can share and evaluate information about potential conflicts with religious and ethnic components and also act to help prevent the escalation of conflicts.

4. Religion is an element in many conflicts, and it is also being exploited by many politicians. In the light of recent crises, there is an urgent need for dialogue among churches, and more especially for dialogue between churches and Muslim communities. There needs to be contact and cooperation between religious leaders, but first and foremost these dialogues have to take place primarily at the local level. In this way religious communities can play a role in conflict prevention and mediation. The future of Europe is also dependent upon its ability to let people and peoples with different religious convictions live side by side - all with equal rights and duties.

> We recommend: The participating states of OSCE should also recognise the important role religious communities can play in conflict prevention and mediation.

5. The NATO bombing did not bring an end to human suffering in the area. It contributed to the humanitarian disaster and had devastating effects on the environment. One group of victims was replaced by another. The results of the military intervention show that this kind of action is not what is required to solve complex conflicts such as this one. As churches, we are committed to peace and reconciliation. If more resources and energy had been used as part of a long-term strategy in conflict prevention, military action could have been avoided. Such a strategy is less costly, saves human lives and helps build a culture of peace and friendly coexistence.

> We recommend: As a contribution to the stability of the area, CEC should initiate the establishment of a centre for the support and coordination of

peace and reconciliation work of religious communities across conflict lines in the Balkan region.

6. We are watching with great concern the developments in the Northern Caucasus, where civilians are becoming victims of military intervention. While fully understanding the necessity to overcome terrorism, we urge all parties involved in the conflict to ensure that the civilian population is not victimized and that the OSCE code of conduct of 1994 is fully respected, and to do everything possible to bring the conflict to a peaceful solution.

7. There is an urgent need to start the reconstruction of Yugoslavia. Nobody is served by a Yugoslavia in the midst of Europe which is physically devastated and isolated. It is a joint European and North American responsibility to secure funds and other resources for this effort. We do not believe that the present sanctions regime serves the reintegration of Yugoslavia into Europe. In fact the victims of the sanctions are primarily innocent people, including children and elderly persons.

We recommend that the Security Council of the UN review the effects of the present sanctions against Yugoslavia.

We recommend: There is a need for a cooperative mechanism to facilitate interchurch aid, information sharing and a continuous discussion of current problems in Yugoslavia with political leaders and other important sectors of the society. We invite ecumenical organisations and churches in the region to consider how this might best be given effect.

We recommend: The Churches should devise proposals and projects for immediate reconstruction. One such project could be an ecumenical effort to rebuild a bridge across the Danube, Europe's river of life. This bridge would be a symbol of the bridges we need to build between different parts and religious traditions of Europe.

8. The immediate need in the Balkan area is to help people through the winter with proper housing, food and energy supply. Churches and humanitarian organisations have already raised and distributed sizable funds to aid afflicted people and regions. This must be continued. Care should be taken to secure good cooperation with local church leaders as the most effective way of aiding people.

9. Young people are an integral part of the present reality in the Balkan region. It is important to see that they can be a yeast of peace and reconciliation. It is crucial to involve young people in dealing with the complex implications of the Kosovo crisis. Support offered to youth networks and organisations is necessary in order to create a secure and non-violent society in the future.

10. As churches, we are painfully aware of the inadequacy of our own response to the tragedy in Kosovo. We have learned once more that peace-building is costly, in terms of spiritual stamina, political courage and physical resources. But peace-

making is our calling and we can fulfill it in many ways. Strengthening links between churches in different countries will give us early warning of situations which can lead to conflict. When we support each other and our communities, we can speak with credibility to political decision-makers. By doing this we also fulfill our biblical calling: *Carry one another's burdens, and in this way you will fulfill the law of Christ.* (Gal.6,2)

Condemnation of the destruction of churches
Joint letter to H.H. Patriarch Pavle of the Serbian Orthodox Church, 3 December 1999.

The continuing tragedy facing the communities in Kosovo and Metohija remains a cause of serious preoccupation for the World Council of Churches and the Conference of European Churches. In your recent letter, Your Holiness highlights a particularly disturbing aspect of the current situation.

The systematic violation of churches and holy places of the Serbian Orthodox Church is a painful manifestation of the division and hatreds which dominate this region even today. The desecration of these often ancient churches represents a loss not only for the Christian community, but for the cultural and spiritual heritage of the world, and is vigorously denounced by WCC and CEC.

Places of worship are often both the visible face and the living memory of the community. The recent history of former Yugoslavia, and most recently in Kosovo and Metohija, has been marked by a frenzy of destruction of communities and of cultures, including both Christian churches and Muslim mosques. The WCC and CEC, and the families of churches which they represent, remember with sadness all those who have fallen victims to the violence and evil in this region, and those who have been left homeless and orphaned as a result. The continuous persecution of the minority Serb, Roma and other communities in the region must come to an end if peace and security are to be established.

We appeal to the interim civilian and military structures responsible for public order in Kosovo and Metohija to ensure that every possible measure is taken to ensure the safety and tranquillity of all religious and civilian communities and monuments, and in particular the churches and monasteries of the Serbian Orthodox Church which are specifically targeted at this time. The cause of human rights which motivated the international intervention in this region will be weakened indeed if those which now have authority are unable to ensure the survival of minority communities and the protection of their religious and material patrimony.

The revival of hope in this region can only be founded on a renewal of stable human communities. As we approach the Feast of the Nativity of Christ our Lord, the 'Prince of Peace', we pray that healing and reconciliation can be brought to all peoples in this region, and that societies may once again be built on mutual tolerance and trust. May the churches and religious communities do all that is possible to contribute to the softening of hearts and opening of minds at this time.

Sincerely yours in Christ,

Konrad Raiser	Keith Clements
General Secretary	General Secretary
World Council of Churches	Conference of European Churches

Expression of solidarity with the churches in Yugoslavia
Joint letter sent 6 October 2000.

To: H.H. Pavle, Patriarch of the Serbian Orthodox Church
Bishop Ján Valent of the Slovak Evangelical Church of the Augsburg Confession in Yugoslavia
Bishop István Csete-Szemesi of the Christian Church in FRY
Superintendent D. Martin Hovan of the Evangelical Methodist Church in Yugoslavia

Brothers in Christ,

The World Council of Churches and the Conference of European Churches express their sense of solidarity and fraternal encouragement for the churches and people of the Federal Republic of Yugoslavia at this critical time.

Churches around the world have been following with concern and emotion the unfolding events in Yugoslavia in the last days and weeks. It is with a sense of great respect that all have watched the efforts of the newly elected democratic leadership in the country to assume responsibilities and seek to ensure a political and negotiated transition, which respects the will of the people and democratic principles.

We assure you of our thoughts and prayers at this time when the people of Yugoslavia are confronted with such important choices for the future. May our Risen Lord bless and guide all those who seek to contribute wisdom, discernment and truth to the solution of the political crisis in your country. We pray that the leadership of the churches in Yugoslavia will be given the strength and courage to guide and accompany the process of change, and thus contribute to the building of a lasting order of peace and justice in this long-suffering region.

For many years, the WCC and CEC have worked alongside the member churches in Serbia and Montenegro to manifest Christian solidarity in times of need, to communicate the voice of churches there to the broader world, and to assist them in responding to the most important social and humanitarian needs in the communities.

We stand prepared to work ever more closely with your churches, and seek ways together with you for a more effective response to the situation and needs of people.

To this end we hope to have an early opportunity of meeting with you and other leaders of the Yugoslav churches in order to determine how the wider ecumenical community might be of assistance.

With fraternal greetings,

Sincerely yours in Christ,

Konrad Raiser   Keith Clements
General Secretary   General Secretary
World Council of Churches   Conference of European Churches

Appeal for religious tolerance
Letter to His Holiness Pavle, Patriarch of the Serbian Orthodox Church, 16 August 2002

Your Holiness,

We greet you in the name of Our Lord Jesus Christ.

On behalf of the leadership of the World Council of Churches and of the Conference of European Churches, we are writing to express our profound concern at the continued violence facing members of the Serbian Orthodox Church and its cultural and spiritual property in Kosovo and Metohija in the recent period. The WCC and CEC have been closely following developments, and note with dismay an increase in the level of these attacks during the last months.

The deliberate attacks on the churches and holy places of the Serbian Orthodox Church occurring in Kosovo and Metohija at this time are a painful and scandalous manifestation of the extremism and instability still affecting parts of this region. We condemn these and all acts of violence and destruction, and remember with sadness all of those, from all communities, who have fallen victim to extremism and intolerance in recent years. As the WCC and CEC have stated on several occasions, it is our firm belief that a lasting solution for peace in this region can only be based on a situation of mutual tolerance and respect for all ethnic and religious communities. The WCC and CEC will therefore continue to work with the Serbian Orthodox Church and with other churches to promote all efforts of dialogue and peace-building in this region.

This situation also reflects the inadequacy of the international protection provided by the interim authorities in Kosovo to the minority communities, and particularly to the Serbian community. It is our intention, therefore, as WCC and CEC have done in the past, to intervene with the appropriate international authorities to raise awareness about this situation, and to appeal for effective international guarantees for all the peoples and their spiritual and cultural inheritance in South-East Europe.

We pray that a spirit of peace and healing may be brought to all peoples in the troubled region of South-East Europe. May the churches and religious communities do all that is within their possibilities to contribute to an opening of minds and a calming of hearts at this time.

Sincerely yours in Christ,

Rev. Dr Konrad Raiser   Rev. Dr Keith Clements,
General Secretary   General Secretary
World Council of Churches   Conference of European Churches

Letter to H.E. Mr Michael Steiner, Special Representative of the Secretary General, United Nations Interim Administration in Kosovo, 16 August 2002.

Dear Mr Steiner,

On behalf of the leadership of the World Council of Churches and of the Conference of European Churches, we are writing to express our profound concern at the continued violence facing members of the Serbian Orthodox Church and its cultural and spiritual property in Kosovo in the recent period. The WCC and CEC have been closely following developments in the region, and note with dismay an increase in the level of these attacks during recent months.

The deliberate attacks on the churches and holy places of the Serbian Orthodox Church occurring in Kosovo and Metohija at this time are a painful and scandalous manifestation of the extremism and instability still affecting parts of this region. We condemn these and all acts of violence and destruction, and remember with sadness all of those, from all communities, who have fallen victim to extremism and intolerance in recent years. These attacks are a major obstacle to the hope of a normalisation of inter-communal relations in the province.

This situation also reflects the inadequacy of the international protection provided by the interim authorities, including UNMIK, in Kosovo to the minority communities, and particularly to the Serbian community. We appeal to you and to the responsible authorities in Kosovo to ensure effective security and justice for all the peoples and the protection of their spiritual and cultural inheritance in Kosovo.

It is the firm belief of our organizations that a lasting solution for peace in this region can only be based on a situation of tolerance and respect for all ethnic and religious communities. The WCC and CEC will continue to work with the Serbian Orthodox Church and with other churches to promote all efforts of dialogue and peace-building in this region. May the churches and religious communities do all that is within their possibilities to contribute to an opening of minds and a calming of hearts at this time.

Sincerely yours,

Rev. Dr Konrad Raiser   Rev. Dr Keith Clements,
General Secretary   General Secretary
World Council of Churches   Conference of European Churches

LATIN AMERICA

ARGENTINA

Congratulations on the granting of the World Methodist Council's Peace Prize to the Grandmothers of the Plaza de Mayo
Conveyed by letter to Bishop Aldo M. Etchegoyen of the Evangelical Methodist Church of Argentina, 13 August 1999.

Estimado Obispo Etchegoyen,

Por intermedio de esta carta, el Consejo Mundial de Iglesias desea estar presente en el evento histórico de entrega del Premio Metodista por La Paz a las Abuelas de Plaza de Mayo.

Congratulamos al Concilio Mundial de Iglesias Metodistas por destacar el papel ejemplar de las Abuelas a través de su Premio por La Paz, que da reconocimiento internacional a organizaciones y personas que han tenido una postura ejemplar en la defensa de los derechos humanos y de la paz.

Felicitamos a las Abuelas, a quienes queremos reiterar nuestra profunda admiración y nuestra indefectible solidaridad por su incansable lucha para encontrar a sus nietos.

Es sumamente simbólico que el ultimo Premio por La Paz de este siglo sea otorgado a mujeres de coraje que han sido capaces de superar su propio dolor para dedicar su energía y la fuerza de su amor a buscar la verdad y la justicia por los desaparecidos en la Argentina.

Al final de un siglo marcado por tantas violaciones a los derechos humanos que han quedado impunes, las Abuelas formarán parte de la historia como un ejemplo para el mundo entero: un ejemplo de tenacidad y de creatividad; un ejemplo de la efectividad de una lucha comprometida con los valores esenciales de la dignidad humana.

Su mensaje ha llegado al mundo entero, como un signo de esperanza que transmite inspiración y coraje a otras mujeres y hombres que están enfrentados a los mismos desafíos.

Oramos para que tantos esfuerzos logren su objetivo: el reencuentro de los nietos con sus familias, la verdad sobre los desaparecidos y la justicia para las víctimas.

El Consejo Mundial de Iglesias reitera su compromiso de seguir acompañándolas en esta lucha. ¡Que el Señor de la Vida ilumine su camino!

Konrad Raiser
Secretario General

Esteemed Bishop Etchegoyen,

By this letter the World Council of Churches wishes to be present in the historic event of the granting of the Methodist Peace Prize to Grandmothers of the Plazy de Mayo.

We congratulate the World Methodist Council for having underscored the exemplary role of the Grandmothers through the granting of its Peace Prize and thus giving international recognition to organizations and persons who have distinguished themselves in their defense of human rights and peace.

We congratulate the Grandmothers, to whom we wish to reiterate our deep admiration and our unconditional solidarity for their untiring struggle to locate their grandchildren.

It is highly symbolic that the last Peace Prize of this century be granted to women of courage who have been able to overcome their own pain in order to dedicate their energy and the strength of their love to seek truth and justice for the disappeared in Argentina.

At the end of a century marked by so many violations of human rights that have gone unpunished the Grandmothers take a rightful place in history as an example to the world of the effectiveness of a committed struggle for the essential values of human dignity.

Their message has reached the whole world as a sign of hope that transmits inspiration and courage to other women and men who are confronted with the same challenges.

We pray that all these efforts may achieve their aim of reunion of the grandchildren with their families, the truth about the disappearances and justice for the victims.

The World Council of Churches reiterates its commitment to continue to accompany them in this struggle. May the Lord of Life light their way!

Konrad Raiser
General Secretary

Appeal on behalf of the "Prisoners of La Tablada"
Letter to H.E. President Fernando De La Rua, 7 July 2000.

Excelentísimo Sr Presidente,

Le escribo para expresar la profunda preocupación del Consejo Mundial de Iglesias frente a la actitud tomada por su Gobierno frente la situación impérente de las llamadas "Presos de la Tablada."

Durante de los sombríos anos de sucesivos dictaduras, de violaciones masivas de los derechos humanos, y de la lucha del pueblo argentino por la democracia, el CMI era una de las primeras organizaciones internacionales en denunciar los abusos a la Comisión de los Derechos Humanos de las Naciones Unidas y a la opinión publica mundial. Hemos seguido de cerca los acontecimientos a través de nuestras iglesias miembros, y las organizaciones ecuménicas y de la sociedad civil defensores de los derechos humanos, quienes acompañamos con fondos y acciones de solidaridad durante más de una década. Con ellos anhelábamos por la democracia en su país querido y por su pueblo valiente y también querido.

Llegada la democracia, hemos seguido preocupados por las consecuencias de las violaciones anteriores, continuando nuestro apoyo a los que buscaban desesperadamente sus parientes y amigos queridos desaparecidos. En todo esto hemos querido ser fieles al Señor que predicaba la justicia y el amor al prójimo.

Reconocemos que la búsqueda de la justicia ha sido una de las metas de los gobiernos democráticos argentinos. Y reconocemos también lo difícil que es aplicar los principios de la justicia en una sociedad que tanto a sufrido y que sigue siendo divido por los acontecimientos del pasado reciente. Pero la democracia precisa no solamente un estado capaz de mostrar su firmeza, sino que también sepa aplicar su sabiduría, la tolerancia y la gracia.

Los "Presos de la Tablada" han declarado por su parte una "voluntad y actitud...de tolerancia y su compromiso...con la democracia." Pero ellos, apoyados por muchos de sus compatriotas y por la Comisión Interamericana de Derechos Humanos – entre otros en el mundo – reivindican la justicia frente a las arbitrariedades y errores cometidas por el tribunal que les juzgó y condenó.

Sus abogados y la Comisión Interamericana han hecho los argumentos del derecho, y no entramos en ello. Queremos más bien subrayar que la justicia tiene caras diferentes. Una forma es retributiva, lo que trae en ella las semillas de un ciclo de violencia continua. Para que la sociedad disfrute los beneficios de la democracia sin violencia, es necesario aplicar una forma de justicia restorativa, que lleve en sí la promesa de paz y de reconciliación.

Por todo ello, y a la luz de los 37 días que llevan los prisioneros en huelga de hambre, le pedimos con urgencia, y en el nombre del Dios de amor y de justicia, de darles a ellos y a la nación argentina un signo publico de tolerancia y de gracia antes de que sea tarde.

Su Excelencia, Usted tiene en su poder la posibilidad de responder no tan solo a la letra, sino también, lo que es mas importante, al espíritu de las conclusiones de la Comisión Interamericana. Sumándonos a lideres de nuestras iglesias y a otros defensores argentinos de los derechos humanos le suplicamos en esta hora dar evidencia de una forma de liderazgo iluminado y generoso que le honraría a Usted y a su Nación.

Respetuosamente,

Rvdo Dwain C. Epps
Director
Comisión de las Iglesias en Asuntos Internacionales

[TRANSLATION]

Your Excellency,

I write to express the deep concern of the World Council of Churches with respect to the attitude your government has taken concerning the dramatic situation of the so-called "Tablada Prisoners".

During the dark years of successive dictatorships, of massive violations of human rights, and of the struggle of the Argentine people for democracy, the WCC was among the first international organizations to denounce the abuses to the United Nations Commission on Human Rights and to world public opinion. We have followed closely events through our member churches, ecumenical organizations and civil society associations of defenders of human rights, many of whom we accompanied with funds and solidarity actions for more than a decade. With them we longed for democracy in your dear country and for its valiant and equally dear people.

When democracy arrived, we remained concern about the consequences of earlier violations, continuing our support to those who searched desperately for their disappeared relatives and friends. In all of this we wished to be faithful to the Lord who preached justice and love for one's neighbour.

The "Tablada Prisoners" have declared their "will and attitude...of tolerance and their commitment...to democracy." But they, supported by many of their compatriots and by the Inter-American Commission of Human Rights – among others in the world – continue to call for justice in the face of the arbitrary decisions and errors committed by the tribunal that judged and condemned them.

For all of these reasons, and in view of the 37 days that these prisoners have spent on hunger strike, we ask you urgently, and in the name of the God of love and justice, to give them and the Argentine nation a public sign of tolerance and grace before it is too late.

Your Excellency, you have it in your power to respond not only to the letter, but also more importantly to the spirit of the conclusions of the Inter-American Commission. Joining with leaders of our churches and with other human rights

335

defenders in Argentina we plead with you in this hour to give evidence of an illuminated and generous act of leadership that would honor you and your nation.

Respectfully,

(Rev.) Dwain C. Epps
Director
Commission of the Churches on
International Affairs

Follow-up to the appeal on behalf of the "Prisoners of La Tablada"
Letter to H.E. President Fernando De La Rua, 13 November 2000.

Excelentísimo Sr. Presidente,

Con fecha del 5 de julio pasado, le hice llegar una comunicación para expresar la profunda preocupación del Consejo Mundial de Iglesias frente a la actitud tomada por su gobierno frente la situación imperante de los llamados "Presos de la Tablada."

En esa carta, sumándonos a líderes de nuestras iglesias y a otros defensores argentinos de los derechos humanos, le suplicamos buscar una solución honorable para cumplir con las recomendaciones de la Comisión Interamericana de Derechos Humanos sobre este caso.

Después de haber terminado su huelga de hambre, motivados por promesas hechas para ir al encuentro de sus reivindicaciones, los presos reanudaron esta acción. Según nuestra información, los presos se encuentran en un crítico estado de salud después de dos meses de huelga de hambre.

Entendemos que en el Congreso no ha habido una voluntad de cambiar las leyes de la Nación para resolver el caso. Dios quiere que la vida humana sea considerada sagrada, y el Señor Jesucristo nos enseña el amor al prójimo y que actos de gracia, aún al enemigo, es un deber a sus discípulos. En consecuencia, y dada la situación actual, le pedimos una vez más, y con un sentido de gran urgencia, que tomé Ud., Sr. Presidente, una acción humanitaria para salvar las vidas de estas personas.

Respetuosamente,

Rvdo Dwain C. Epps,
Director,
Comisión de las Iglesias en Asuntos
Internacionales

Your Excellency,

On 5 July I sent you a letter expressing the deep concern of the World Council of Churches with respect to the attitude taken by your government in the urgent case of the so-called "Tablada Prisoners".

With this letter, joining with leaders of our churches and with other human rights defenders in Argentina, we plead with you anew to seek an honorable solution to comply with the recommendations of the Inter-American Commission of Human Rights on this case.

Since they terminated their hunger strike, motivated by promises made to move in the direction of their demands, the prisoners have renewed their action. According to our information, the prisoners are in a critical state of health after two months of hunger strike.

We understand that there has been no will in Congress to change the laws of the nation in order to resolve this case. God wills that human life be considered sacred, and the Lord Jesus Christ teaches love for one's neighbor and that acts of grace, even towards one's enemy, is a duty for his disciples. This being so, and given the present situation, we ask you once again, and with a great sense of urgency, Mr President, to take a humanitarian action to save the lives of these persons.

Respectfully,

(Rev.) Dwain C. Epps
Director
Commission of the Churches on
International Affairs

Expression of appreciation for action to overcome impunity
Letter to the Hon Dr Gabriel Cavallo, 29 March 2001.

De nuestra mayor consideración:

Con profunda satisfacción nos enteramos de su sentencia del 6 de marzo de 2001, en relación a la causa Nro. 8686/2000 carátulada "Simón, Julio, Del Cerro, Juan Antonio s/sustracción de menores de 10 años".

La misma realiza un profundo análisis histórico en relación a los crímenes de lesa humanidad, la competencia del Derecho Internacional y la jurisprudencia relativa al tema.

En nuestra perspectiva la sentencia, en el ámbito jurídico, contribuye, de manera señera, a posibilitar la justicia en relación a crímenes que en diferentes países de América Latina, han escapado a la órbita judicial por decretos o leyes del mismo tenor que las de Punto Final y de Obediencia debida que, según su sentencia "llevan consigo una nulidad insanable".

Indudablemente, su sentencia no es sólo un avance significativo en el campo de lo jurídico. Es, asimismo, una contribución a la consciencia ética de la sociedad argentina y de la latinoamericana en su conjunto. En reiteradas oportunidades, el Consejo Mundial de Iglesias ha señalado la estrecha vinculación existente entre el ámbito de lo jurídico y el ámbito de lo ético, en lo que atañe a violaciones de los derechos humanos, su juicio y la impunidad.

Con pertinencia, la sentencia recoge algunos párrafos de documentos eclesiásticos (Cf. e.g. la alusión a la Constitución Gaudium et spes en V. d. *La valoración jurídica que hace la ley. La obediencia jerárquica y sus límites*) que manifiestan la preocupación compartida que las iglesias han tenido sobre esta problemática.

Sabemos lo difícil que significa en el marco actual de las sociedades latinoamericanas una sentencia de esa naturaleza. Por eso lo felicitamos por su coraje, por el amor a la justicia que revela la sentencia y, si bien aún queda mucho trecho por andar, consideramos que su contribución ha sido significativa en el proceso de justicia y reconciliación de la nación argentina.

Cuente con nuestro apoyo y nuestra oración para su gestión en estos momentos tan apremiantes en su país, que tiene resonancia que sobrepasa fronteras nacionales.

Atentamente,

(Rvdo) Dwain C. Epps
Director
Comisión de las Iglesias en Asuntos Internacionales

[TRANSLATION]

With our great respect:

We have received with great satisfaction the news of the sentence you have handed down on 6 March 2001 in case no. 8686/2000 "Simon, Julio, Del Cerro, Juan Antonio for separation of minors of 10 years of age".

This judgment contains a deep historical analysis of crimes against humanity and the application of international law and jurisprudence relative to this matter.

From our perspective the sentence contributes objectively in the juridical realm to the possibility of justice related to crimes that have evaded the judicial sphere in different countries of Latin America as a result of decrees or laws similar to those of "Punto Final" (Ed. "the end of the matter") and of due obedience that according to your finding "carry in them an unhealthy nullity".

Undoubtedly, your sentence is not only a significant advance in the field of jurisprudence. It is also a contribution to the ethical conscience of Argentine society and that of Latin America as a whole. The World Council of Churches has repeatedly called attention to the close relation between the juridical and ethical realms in that which pertains to violations of human rights, their judgment and impunity.

Pertinently, the sentence contains some paragraphs of ecclesiastical documents (e.g. the allusion to the Constitution Gaudium et Spes in *The juridical valuation that makes law. Heierarchical obedience and its limits*) that manifest the shared concern that the churches have expressed on this problematic.

We know the difficulty that a sentence of this sort poses in the contemporary context of Latin American societies. For this reason, we congratulate you for your courage, for the love of justice that this sentence reveals and, even though there remains a long road to travel, we consider that your contribution has been significant in the process of justice and reconciliation in the Argentine nation.

We assure you of our support and our prayer for your initiative in these critical times in your country that has a resonance that spans national borders.

Sincerely,

(Rev.) Dwain C. Epps
Director
Commission of the Churches on
International Affairs

Expression of solidarity with the churches and people of Argentina
Letter to member churches in Argentina, 10 January 2002.

Queridos hermanas y hermanos:

¡Cuánto sentido tiene en estas horas el saludo que el Apóstol Pablo dirigía a las iglesias: "Permanezcan con ustedes la gracia y la paz"! (1 Ts 1: 1)

En las últimas semanas, diversas informaciones han mostrado el doloroso proceso que ha vivido y continúa viviendo vuestro país, Argentina. Los medios masivos de comunicación han mostrado una y otra vez los violentos enfrentamientos entre ciudadanos y fuerzas policiales, los saqueos a comercios, las manifestaciones frente al Congreso y la Casa Rosada. Nos consterna el saldo de decenas de hombres y mujeres muertos, principalmente jóvenes, y varios miles de personas detenidas. Asimismo hemos recibido noticias del trabajo y la oración que cristianos e iglesias en Argentina han llevado adelante en este tiempo.

Junto a las iglesias y al movimiento ecuménico en todo el mundo, hemos sufrido con ustedes, y junto a ustedes hemos intentado oír el clamor del pueblo y discernir la presencia del Espíritu en medio de la situación que están viviendo. Situación marcada por mucha confusión, ira y violencia, pero también por signos de solidaridad, y de preocupación genuina de parte del pueblo argentino por su futuro. Desde un primer momento, hemos estado orando para que se restituya y fortalezca la institucionalidad democrática en ese querido país. Damos gracias a Dios por el testimonio que cristianos e iglesias en Argentina han dado en momentos tan difíciles y le rogamos que los confirme en la fe, la esperanza y el amor solidario.

Indudablemente, como lo han señalado numerosos analistas y las mismas iglesias y organismos ecuménicos, la magnitud de la crisis que atraviesa Argentina es muy preocupante. Tal vez lo más llamativo ha sido la renuncia consecutiva de dos presidentes de la nación en unos pocos días. Pero lo más preocupante es la situación de pobreza e inseguridad en que viven millones de personas en Argentina, debido en gran medida a la política económica de los últimos años. No nos toca a nosotros analizar ahora las causas de esta crisis, que ustedes conocen con detalle. Sólo quisiéramos decir que esta situación nos desafía a continuar profundizando nuestra reflexión ética y espiritual sobre el rol y el comportamiento de los dirigentes políticos locales, de los organismos financieros internacionales y de los diversos sectores de la sociedad. Es también un momento para continuar profundizando sobre nuestra acción comprometida con la vida, la justicia y la solidaridad.

Conmueven el clamor del pueblo argentino y las respuestas que las iglesias, organismos ecuménicos y otros actores de la sociedad civil están dando a lo que es también una crisis ética y espiritual. En el marco del Decenio para Superar la Violencia, que se inauguró a comienzos del 2001, alentamos a los cristianos, a las iglesias, a otras confesiones religiosas, a todos los hombres y todas las mujeres comprometidos con la paz, a aunar esfuerzos para superar esta crisis y construir una Argentina más justa y fraterna, fortaleciendo los lazos con la región. Será imprescindible, como han señalado iglesias y otros actores sociales, apelar a la responsabilidad de la clase política, superar la corrupción, la impunidad, el abuso de poder y dar pasos concretos e inmediatos hacia una verdadera reconciliación nacional basada en la justicia. En la presente situación, esto sólo se consigue con un afianzamiento de la democracia, y el respeto y la defensa de los Derechos Humanos, expresión del cuidado de la vida que el Dios Creador ha puesto en nuestras manos.

Recientemente escribía en el Mensaje de Navidad de 2001 que "nuestro mundo no podrá ser redimido sino por gracia y misericordia. Dios da y perdona con generosidad y ofrece vida en abundancia (Juan 10: 10) sobre todo para quienes son perdedores en nuestro mundo sin misericordia". Esta lógica de la misericordia es extraña para la lógica del poder, de la violencia, del mercado, que rige muchas veces nuestro mundo. Y sin embargo, desde la perspectiva cristiana, entrar en la misericordia de Dios es condición sine qua non para obtener la justificación.

Junto a cristianos de todo el mundo, me uno a ustedes para que se sientan reconfortados en la fe y hago mías las palabras del salmista, conocedor de la angustia, la miseria y la violencia: "Desde el abismo clamo a ti, Señor, escucha mi clamor... mi alma aguarda al Señor, mucho más que el centinela a la aurora... porque el Señor tiene misericordia y hay en él abundante redención" (Salmo 130).

En Cristo,

Rvdo Dr. Konrad Raiser
Secretario General

[TRANSLATION]

Dear Sisters and Brothers,

"Grace to you and peace" (1 Thess.1:1) - the apostle Paul's words of greeting to the churches seem specially significant at this time.

Many reports in recent weeks have drawn attention to the distressing situation afflicting your country, Argentina. Time and again the mass media have shown pictures of violent clashes between the population and the police, looting of shops, demonstrations outside Congress and the *Casa Rosada*. We deeply deplore the deaths of dozens of men and women, many of them young, and the thousands of arrests that have been made. At the same time, we have also heard about the work being done by the churches and Christians of Argentina and their prayers for the situation.

Together with churches and the world-wide ecumenical movement we have shared in your suffering and we have been with you as you try to hear the cry of the people and discern the presence of the Spirit in the midst of this crisis. It is a situation marked by great confusion, anger and violence but also by signs of solidarity and genuine concern for the future on the part of the Argentinian people. From the very beginning we have been praying that the democratic institutions of your beloved country may be restored and strengthened. We give thanks to God for the witness borne by Christians and churches in Argentina at this difficult time and we ask God to strengthen them in faith, hope and love.

As many analysts, and indeed churches and ecumenical organizations themselves, have pointed out, the scale of the crisis in Argentina is alarming. Perhaps the most striking thing has been the resignation of two presidents within the space of a few days. But most worrying of all is the state of poverty and insecurity in which millions of people in Argentina find themselves living today, largely as a result of the economic policy of recent years. It is not for us to analyse the causes of this crisis, which you know only too well. Let us simply say that the situation challenges us to continue our ethical and spiritual reflection on the role and behaviour of political leaders, international financial institutions and the different sectors of society. It also gives us cause to reflect further on our own commitment to action for life, justice and solidarity.

We are moved by the cry of the Argentinian people and the way in which the churches, ecumenical organizations and other members of civil society are responding to this crisis, which is to some extent also ethical and spiritual. In the context of the Decade to Overcome Violence, launched at the beginning of 2001, we urge Christians, churches, people of other faiths and all men and women committed to peace to join forces to overcome this crisis and build a society of greater justice and solidarity in Argentina, strengthening ties with other countries in the region. As churches and other social groups have said, politicians must be called upon to act responsibly, to put an end to corruption, impunity and abuse of power and to take immediate steps that will lead to genuine national reconciliation based on justice. In the present situation this can only be done by strengthening democracy and ensuring respect and protection of human rights, as a mark of our concern for the life which God the Creator has entrusted to our care.

In the WCC's Christmas message for 2001, I recently wrote that our world will only be saved by grace and mercy. "God gives and forgives generously and offers life in fullness (John 10:10) especially to those who are losers in our merciless world". The logic of mercy is foreign to the logic of power, violence, market forces which often governs our world. Yet, from the Christian point of view, participating in God's mercy is the condition *sine qua non* for obtaining justification.

With Christians all over the world I pray that you may be comforted in the faith and recall the words of the Psalmist, who was acquainted with grief, suffering and violence: "Out of the depths I cry to you, oh Lord. Lord, hear my voice! ... my soul waits for the Lord more than those who watch for the morning... for with the Lord there is steadfast love" (Psalm 130).

Yours in Christ,

Konrad Raiser
General Secretary

Expression of indignation at court decision to absolve officials charged with responsibility for the massacres of landless peasants

Letter to H.E. Dr Fernando Henrique Cardoso, President of the Republic, with copies to the president of the court of the State of Para, José Alberto Soares Maia, and to the minister of justice, 25 August 1999.

Dear Mr President,

On behalf of the World Council of Churches I must convey to you our consternation and sense of indignation at the decision reached by the Court in Belem on August 18th, by which it absolves three of the officials charged with responsibility for the massacre of 19 landless rural workers in El Dorado do Carajas in April 1996.

Soon after that massacre, at the invitation of ecumenical bodies in Brazil, the WCC sent an international ecumenical delegation there to ascertain the facts on the ground. Our delegation heard eye-witness accounts in which the perpetrators were clearly identified. It also heard directly the long-suffering landless people, and shared abroad their poignant cry for justice. Subsequently we have followed closely developments in this case and the peoples' demands both from a distance and through further visits to your country.

On the basis of the massive evidence which has been gathered by the prosecutor in this case, much of which we could also confirm, we and many others around the world assumed that justice would be done. To our astonishment, what has happened in Belem has rather mocked justice, and the victims of this heinous crime.

As you are aware, the WCC played an important supportive role during the brutal years of the military dictatorship to document and denounce the massive violations of human rights in that dark period. Since then, we have supported the growing movement in Brazil, elsewhere in Latin America and in other parts of the world to bring an end to impunity for such crimes. We sincerely believed, along with many Brazilians, that this case would mark a substantial turning point in the justice system of your country when it comes to the practice of impunity. We held out this hope, knowing full well that the granting of impunity for those responsible for massive violations of human rights is an incentive for the repetition of such crimes. This response to those who witnessed and who suffered the consequences of the massacre in El Dorado do Carajas can only feed the rising incidence of violence in Brazil, in much of which, it has been amply shown, police and other officials of the Government have been directly involved.

This, Mr President, cannot be the last word in this case. We therefore appeal to you and to the responsible ministers of your Government to override this judgement in the name of the principles of human rights and the international instruments to which Brazil is a party, and in fulfillment of the provisions of your own Constitution.

In anticipation of your favorable response, and of your positive corrective action, I remain

Respectfully yours,

(Rev.) Dwain C. Epps
Director
Commission of the Churches on International Affairs

CHILE

Expression of concern about police intervention in FASIC headquarters
Letter to Amb. Javier Illanes Fernández, Permanent Representative of Chile to the UN in Geneva, 26 May 1999.

Excnmo Sr Embajador,

El Consejo Mundial de Iglesias quiere expresar su profunda preocupación por los hechos acontecidos recientemente en la sede de la Fundación de Ayuda Social de las Iglesias Cristianas (FASIC), en Santiago de Chile.

Según informaciones recibidas de FASIC, el 19 de mayo, carabineros pertenecientes a la dotación de Fuerzas Especiales ingresaron violentamente a FACIC con el objeto de deterner a trest estudiantes universitarios que minutos antes havian ingresado a la sede. Al interponerse para proteger la integridad físic de estos jóvenes, el Secretario Ejecutivo, Sr. Claudio González, recibió golpes, puntapiés y empujones.

FASIC ha presentado ante la 2nda Fiscalia de la Justicia Militar una denuncia respecto a la violación de domicilio de que ha sido objeto, y el duro castigo y aprehensión de las personas que se encontraban en forma pacífica en sus oficinas. El Consejo Mundial de Iglesias quiere destacar que FASIC es un organismo vinculado a las iglesias que durante décadas ha trabajado en la defensa y promoción de los derechos humanos.

La Asamblea de las Naciones Unidas adoptoó en diciembre de 1998 la Declaración sobre el derecho y el deber de los indivíduos, los grupos y las instituciones, de promover y proteger los derechos humanos y las libertades fundamentales universalmente reconocidos. En dicho documento se destaca la responsabilidad primordial del estado en prover y proteger los derchos humanos y las libertades fundamentales.

Aprovechamos la ocasión para reiterar la responsabilidad del gobierno chileno en garantizar la seguridad de organismos de derechos humanos, incluso de organismos vinculados a las iglesias.

Esperamos que el anhelo profundo del pueblo chileno por el respecto de los derechos humanos y de la justicia sea respondido con acciones concretas de parte de su gobierno.

Muy atentamente,

Salpy Eskidjian
Asuntos Internacionales

[TRANSLATION]

Your Excellency,

The World Council of Churches wishes to express its deep concern about recent events in the headquarters of the Foundation for Social Action of the Christian Churches (FASIC) in Santiago de Chile.

According to information received from FASIC, on 19 May members of the armed forces attached to the Special Forces violently entered FASIC with the intention of detaining three university students who had just entered the headquarters. When he sought to protect the physical integrity of these young people, Executive Secretary Mr Claudio González was hit, kicked and pushed.

FASIC has denounced before the 2nd Military Court this violation of domicile to which is was subject, and the heavy-handed punishment and detention of the persons who had entered the headquarters offices minutes before. The World Council of Churches wishes to emphasize that FASIC is a body related to the churches that has worked for the defense and promotion of human rights for decades.

The General Assembly of the United Nations adopted in December 1998 the Declaration on the Right and Duty of Individuals, Groups and Institutions to Promote and Protect Human Rights and Universally Recognized Fundamental Freedoms. That document underscores the primordial responsibility of the state in promoting and protecting human rights and fundamental freedoms.

We take this occasion to reiterate the responsibility of the Chilean government to guarantee the security of human rights bodies, including those related to the churches.

We hope that the profound longing of the Chilean people for respect of human rights and justice will be met with concrete actions on the part of your government.

Respectfully,

Salpy Eskidjian
International Affairs

COLOMBIA

Ecumenical Cooperation Forum with Colombia
Report of meeting held in Geneva, 25-26 September 2001.

On 25 and 26 September 2001, we met as a delegation of Colombian Churches and civil society, and representatives from international ecumenical organizations and European cooperation agencies. The meeting was convened by the World Council of Churches (WCC) and the Lutheran World Federation (LWF) and was held in the Ecumenical Center in Geneva. Continuing the long-standing process of support, the objectives of the "Ecumenical Cooperation Forum with Colombia" were to exchange information about the current situation in Colombia and the role of the churches in the prevailing circumstances. Another objective was to strengthen international support for the peace process in Colombia, a process in which the churches are involved. The Forum also considered meetings with diplomatic missions to the United Nations and international Human Rights NGOs. We began our meeting with a service in which we pondered the words of Isaiah (Isa. 62: 6-7) where the prophet invites us to stand sentinel, to pray, raise our voice and work for reconciliation.

Throughout the meeting, we participants from other countries were challenged by the delegation's profound testimony of hope and its conviction that the violent conflict in Colombian society can be overcome through talks and political negotiations. This is based on the belief that the root of the conflict lies not, as has so often been said, in drug-trafficking but in the historical social injustice that has seen economic and political power concentrated in too few hands. From our standpoint of faith, we also recognize that sin has taken hold in Colombian institutions, in the country's laws and in many social and individual practices. We believe that Colombian society is built on pillars of exclusion, impunity and deep-rooted inequalities that must be remedied if there is to be lasting peace. (Mic 2: 1-2).

We value the efforts made in civil society to reinforce and give voice to the aspirations and experience of peace and to have a greater say in decision-making. We particularly stress the fact that the churches, too, have been part of those efforts, putting forward their identity and mission as communities of faith to help build peace processes, providing training themselves and promoting the training of their leaders in various theological and pastoral areas including dignity and human rights.

The churches' commitment has found especial expression in caring for displaced men and women, whose situation is one of the worst after-effects of the conflict. This commitment has shown the enormous potential of the Christian communities and of local congregations as places of healing and hope.

We share the clear rejection of the Plan Colombia because it serves to heighten armed conflict in the country. Indeed, the prophetic denunciation made by several actors in civil society of the escalating armed conflict, increasing numbers of displaced persons, the deteriorating human rights situation, the extension of the conflict to the region through the Andean initiative, and its environmental impact through crop-dusting, today adds up to a picture that bears out the previous statement. We therefore welcome the European Parliament's rejection of the Plan Colombia and its recommendations for European aid to obey different criteria.

After agreeing with this diagnosis, the Forum went on to draw up some proposals and strategies for future work and cooperation.

From the standpoint of our faith and pastoral practice, we affirmed that peace is built with:

- social justice and by ensuring the dignity of all individuals as God's creatures;
- the participation of all segments of society in seeking reconciliation based on truth;
- a legal system that combats impunity and ensures necessary reparation;
- the non-violent settlement of disputes; and
- the responsible stewardship of creation.

On this foundation, the following strategic areas and priorities were identified as starting points for strengthening valuable action already being taken at various levels.

1. Locally

Support for displaced persons. This includes attending to the material and spiritual needs of displaced people and also to organization, education and the development of community projects for them.

Skills and other training. Such training includes human rights, social leadership, mediation and dispute settlement, Bible and theological training and so on.

Exploring and expressing experience. It is hoped that through strengthening local experience, a culture of peace can be created. Special attention will be paid to work with indigenous people, women and Afro-Colombians, women and children affected by violence.

Strengthening spirituality. Through prayer and the celebrating of faith, an attempt will be made to give symbolic and practical expression to the churches' call for peace.

2. Nationally

Coordinating efforts. Support for the Commission on Human Rights and Peace (CEDECOL) in seeking common platforms and for wider ecumenical initiatives that include other sectors of civil society.

Arranging action to support displaced persons. Seeking machinery that could influence Government policies relating to the displaced population. Strengthening the pastoral ministry of the churches in their work with displaced people.

Strengthening processes of communication. Developing effective tools for communication to facilitate exchanges among the various parts of the nation and between society as a whole and the international community.

3. Regionally

Setting up an Andean forum. Supporting efforts to build an ecumenical meeting place in the Andean region where the challenges raised by the Plan Colombia and the Andean Initiative could be addressed. Link this process to existing regional networks in civil society.

4. Internationally

International ecumenical presence in Colombia. Such a presence would seek to protect and reinforce the initiatives of the churches and civil society. It would make itself felt through delegations that express brotherly love among local congregations and also convey the facts of the Colombian situation in their various churches.

Defense. Here the emphasis would be on strengthening existing international instruments for the protection of human rights (Office of the High Commissioner for Human Rights, observers, recommendations of the Commission on Human Rights, and so on); joint action by leaders of agencies, international ecumenical organizations and NGOs in approaching intergovernmental organizations and foreign governments.

Strengthening international ecumenical action. It is proposed that the work of the churches for peace in Colombia fall within the Ecumenical Decade to Overcome Violence (DOV). Within that framework, it is recommended that there be closer coordination between the WCC, the LWF and the Latin American Council of Churches (CLAI), other councils of churches, sister churches and ecumenical agencies.

Follow-up. A group of four people is being set up, comprising the WCC, the LWF, the agencies and the Colombian delegation, to provide follow-up to this meeting and draft practical proposals for implementing the recommendations in close cooperation with other ecumenical efforts. Within six months, there will be an assessment made of how implementation is progressing and possibly a similar meeting will be convened a year from now to continue the process.

We consider that this Forum has made a significant contribution to peace-building in Colombia. As a result of this Forum, the conciliating role of the churches has been given a higher profile and the efforts of the churches and society as a whole in Colombia have been given greater expression in working with the European churches, agencies and international ecumenical organizations. It has also helped to reinforce the commitment of the international ecumenical community in seeking peace with justice in Colombia. We pray for God's guidance and wisdom in working for peace in Colombia and the world. May He grant us the gift of love, forgiveness and reconciliation.

Rev. Milton Mejia	Lic. Marta Palma	Peter Prove	Rev. Karl Appl
For the Colombian	WCC	LWF	European ecumenical
delegation			agencies/churches

Minute on Colombia
Adopted by the Central Committee, Potsdam, Germany, 9 January – 6 February 2001.

The United States of America has approved and is implementing its "Plan Colombia." This plan, that includes the provision of additional military equipment and action in Colombian territory was denounced by the Latin American Council of Churches (CLAI) at its Assembly in Barranquilla, Colombia (14-19 January 2001). This plan has also been denounced in the "Letter of the Excluded" prepared by non-governmental organizations in Latin America and sent to the United Nations last year.

The Latin American churches consider that this plan is adding more violence to the already critical situation in Colombia and there is a serious danger of expansion of the conflict into other Latin American countries. In fact, the neighboring countries are already deploying military forces on their borders with Colombia. As a consequence of this, the number of refugees and displaced people has grown dramatically. In the year 2000, 38,000 people were killed. Thousands more have disappeared, been maimed or displaced from their homes. The Afro-Colombian communities and Indigenous Peoples have been particularly affected.

The churches in Colombia are in dialogue with sister churches in other parts of the world, including the churches in the USA, in order to inform them about the situation and develop joint actions of advocacy and solidarity. The General Secretary of the National Council of the Churches of Christ in the USA recently led a delegation to Colombia to assess the expansion of violence and seek ways to be supportive of the churches in Colombia and the region.

Convinced that military aid does not help the cause of peace, the Central Committee joins with the CLAI Assembly in opposing this Plan. It expresses its solidarity with the Colombian people, especially the families of those killed, maimed, disappeared or displaced, and with the Colombian churches in their work to support peace. It urges the staff of the Council to intensify its efforts in support of a negotiated peace to end the decades-long violence in Colombia.

Message on the massacre in the church of Bellavista
Letter to the churches of Colombia, 10 May 2002.

Hermanas y hermanas en Cristo,

De diversas fuentes nos ha llegado la noticia de la muerte de más de cien civiles refugiados (entre ellos unos cuarenta niños), en una iglesia de Bellavista, Municipio de Bojayá-Chocó, en medio de enfrentamientos entre los paramilitares y las FARC, ocurrida el pasado 2 de mayo. Una vez más, vuelve a nuestra memoria el claro precepto bíblico "No matarás" (Exodo 20, 13), cuyo incumplimiento se ha convertido, lamentablemente, en habitual en diferentes lugares en Colombia.

La magnitud de la tragedia no hace sino mostrar, una vez más, las consecuencias que el conflicto armado tiene en la población civil. Nuestro corazón se acongoja ante un espectáculo de violencia que trasciende los límites de lo imaginable. Pensamos en los familiares de los niños, jóvenes, mujeres y hombres muertos o gravemente heridos y nos solidarizamos con su dolor.

En reiteradas ocasiones hemos expresado nuestra preocupación por la agudización de la confrontación armada, que también ha tomado como objetivo las iglesias, las cuales históricamente han cumplido un rol de santuarios en diferentes conflictos en todo el mundo y cuya función ha sido preservada en el derecho internacional humanitario.

Una vez más apelamos a la paz, conocedores que es un anhelo profundo del pueblo colombiano. Rechazamos enérgicamente aquellas posiciones que reclaman una salida armada al conflicto. Los últimos años han mostrado, en la práctica que la implementación del Plan Colombia ha recrudecido la violencia en varias regiones. Reconocemos y apoyamos en este contexto el esfuerzo que las iglesias cristianas hacen en aras de la paz y reconciliación y a través de Uds. hacemos llegar a los familiares de las víctimas nuestro sentido pésame.

Rogamos a las iglesias compartan nuestro mensaje con los actores involucrados, FARC y paramilitares, así como al gobierno, que había sido alertado previamente por varias ONGs, la Oficina del Alto Comisionado de las Naciones Unidas para los DDHH y la Defensoría del Pueblo respecto del peligro que acechaba a las poblaciones de Bojayá y Vigía del Fuerte.

A la vez que oramos por la paz para el pueblo colombiano seguiremos acompañando las diferentes iniciativas ecuménicas que trabajan por la superación de la situación actual. Comprometidos en el "Decenio para superar la violencia. Las iglesias en busca de reconciliación y de paz", pondremos todas nuestras energías en seguir empecinada y creativamente el precepto del salmista "busca la paz y sigue tras ella" (Salmo 34,14).

Rvdo Dwain C. Epps
Director

Comisión de la Iglesias para Asuntos Internacionales

Sisters and brothers in Christ.

News has reached us from several sources of the deaths during a confrontation between paramilitary forces and those of the FARC on May 2nd of more than a hundred civilian refugees (including forty children) in a church in Bellavista in the Municipality of Bojayá-Chocó. Yet again we are reminded of the clear biblical commandment, "You shall not kill" (Exodus 20:13), and of the fact that lack of obedience to this commandment has regrettably become habitual in different places in Colombia.

The magnitude of this tragedy shows yet again the consequences of armed conflict for the civilian population. Our hearts grieve at the spectacle of violence that exceeds the limits of the imaginable. We think particularly of the families of the children, youth, women and men who have died or been gravely injured, and we share their pain.

We have repeatedly expressed our concern about the intensification of the armed confrontation that has also targeted the churches, which historically have been regarded as sanctuaries in different conflicts around the world, a role recognized in international humanitarian law.

Once again we appeal for peace, knowing that the Colombian people deeply longs for it. We energetically reject all notions that an armed solution is possible. Recent years have shown that the implementation of "Plan Colombia" has in fact increased violence in various regions. We recognize and support the efforts for peace and reconciliation made in this context by the Christian churches, and through you we extend to the families of the victims our sincere sympathy.

We ask the churches to share our message with the actors immediately involved – the FARC and the paramilitary – and with the Government, which had been alerted ahead of time by several NGOs, the Office of the United Nations High Commissioner for Human Rights and the People's Defense organization that the populations of Bojayá and Vigía del Fuerte were in danger.

As we pray for peace for the Colombian people, we shall continue to accompany the different ecumenical initiatives that work to overcome the present situation. Committed to the "Decade to Overcome Violence: Churches Seeking Reconciliation and Peace," we shall spare no effort to pursue diligently and creatively the injunction of the Psalmist, "seek peace, and pursue it." (Psalm 34:14).

(Rev.) Dwain C. Epps
Director
Commission of the Churches on
International Affairs

Statement on violence in Colombia
Adopted by the Central Committee, Geneva, 2 September 2002.

The "Violence in Colombia" has besieged this nation for decades. After a period of comparative calm, the violence has intensified dramatically in the past few years, with an average of twenty persons per day – three children among them – being killed or "disappeared" in the midst of the continuing social and political turmoil. A relatively new feature is the targeting of Christian leaders and laypersons. A tragic example was the murder of more than a hundred persons (including at least 40 children) who had sought shelter in a church in Bellavista during a military confrontation in May 2002.

Once again, the violence in Colombia knows no limits; the plight of its people is reminiscent of the words of the Psalmist,

> *My mouth is dry as a potsherd and my tongue sticks to my jaw; I am laid low in the dust of death. The huntsmen are all about me, a band of ruffians rings me round and they have hacked off my hands and my feet... Lord, do not abandon me! Come quickly to my aid! Deliver my soul from the sword, my life from the power of the evil ones! (Psalm 22)*

Churches and the broader civil society in Colombia have for many years opposed the military escalation, engaged in massive non-violent protests and in actions for a peaceful, negotiated solution. Many have paid with their lives and many others have been driven into exile by threats on their and their families' lives. The number of people forcibly displaced from their communities is now over two million – five percent of the total population – nearly one-fourth of these displaced in 2001 alone. Most of those displaced by the violence and the consequences of the implementation of Plan Colombia are indigenous people and Afro-Colombians; and as is so often the case in civil conflicts, women and children are the most seriously affected.

For the Colombian churches and other civil society organizations, the root of the conflict does not lie in drug-trafficking or in the violence of the armed guerrilla movements (though these too are held to account), but in the long history of social injustice, the concentration of economic and political power in a few hands, competition for control of potentially rich oil fields, and a social structure built on the pillars of exclusion, inequality and impunity.

After years of efforts to achieve a negotiated solution to the violence, early this year the government discontinued its peace negotiations with the Fuerzas Armadas Revolucionarias de Colombia (FARC) and ceased to respect the demilitarized zones. New elections brought Alvaro Uribe Veles to power, and shortly after his inauguration in August 2002, the new government declared a state of emergency, and said that it would double the size of the country's armed forces, and begin negotiations with the paramilitary forces.

These developments come in the context of "Plan Colombia" that is backed financially, militarily and politically by the USA. The Central Committee sharply condemned this military-based strategy when it met in Potsdam (February 2001), calling on the churches and the WCC to intensify their ecumenical efforts in support of a negotiated peace. "Plan Colombia" has subsequently been transformed into the "Andean Initiative" with military actions in different countries in the region.

In response, the WCC, in cooperation with the Lutheran World Federation, hosted an Ecumenical Forum on Colombia at the Ecumenical Center in Geneva, in which representatives from Colombian churches and civil society, the Latin American Council of Churches (CLAI), and European churches and partner agencies met to develop a strategy for responding to the war in Colombia. It too called for a strengthening of international ecumenical action and an emphasis on working for peace in the framework of the Decade to Overcome Violence (DOV).

In the light of this tragic situation and the threat it poses to the entire Latin American continent, and in the context of the Decade to Overcome Violence, the Central Committee of the World Council of Churches, meeting in Geneva, 26 August – September 3, 2002,

Reiterates its expressions of solidarity and prayers for the Colombian people, especially the families and friends of those killed, maimed, disappeared or displaced, and with the Colombian churches in their courageous and sacrificial witness and work for peace;

Calls upon all political, military and religious leaders in Colombia to spare no effort in pursuing a peaceful resolution of the conflict, the disarming of the paramilitary and the restoration of the rule of law;

Calls upon all the armed opposition movements to respect the rules of engagement applicable in situations of armed conflict, to desist from all actions that endanger the civilian population, and to seek a return to good-faith negotiations for peace;

Denounces once again "Plan Colombia" and all strategies based on the preemptive use of military force;

Urges the Government of Colombia to rescind all emergency measures, to guarantee full respect of the human rights of its citizens, and to respect fully those provisions of international rule of law applicable in times of civil conflict, especially including the protection of civilian populations in areas of armed conflict;

Calls insistently upon the Government of the United States of America to withdraw all its military forces, including military and other related advisors, from Colombia and from its other installations in the Latin American region without delay;

Urges all governments in the region to take all possible actions to encourage a peaceful resolution of the civil conflict in Colombia and to respect the rights of those forced to flee the violence in Colombia and to attend to their humanitarian needs;

Expresses appreciation to the UN High Commissioner for Human Rights for the work done through her Office in Colombia, and to Human Rights NGOs and church-related organizations for their efforts to protect and assist victims and to develop peacebuilding programs;

Draws once again to the attention of the member churches and related agencies the urgent situation in Colombia, expressing deep appreciation to those who have already made it a priority, and calling for prayers and actions of concrete solidarity with the churches, victims, and the endangered population in areas of armed conflict;

Calls especially upon the churches in the United States to press their government for an immediate cessation of their role in "Plan Colombia," and for foreign assistance to Colombia to be redirected from military to humanitarian purposes and for a renewed emphasis on strengthening respect for human rights in that country; and

Calls upon the staff of the Council to continue and strengthen its efforts to support peace and reconciliation initiatives in cooperation with the Colombian churches, CLAI, and other church and ecumenical partners around the world.

GUATEMALA

Oral interventions at the UN Commission on Human Rights
See p. 163.

MIDDLE EAST

IRAQ

Appeal to the UN Security Council to lift sanctions with direct and indiscriminate effect on the civilian population

Letter to H.E. Kofi Annan, Secretary-General of the UN, 18 February 2000.

Mr Secretary General:

The resignations of Mr Hans von Sponeck, United Nations Aid Coordinator and of Ms Jutta Burghardt, World Food Program Chief in Iraq have again drawn attention to the disastrous effects of the Security Council's sanctions on the people of this nation. Explaining his decision, Mr von Sponick said that the "Oil for Food" régime failed to meet even the "minimum requirements" of the civilian population, and that "as a UN Official I should not be expected to be silent to that which I recognize as a true human tragedy that needs to be ended".

The World Council of Churches has issued statements along similar lines and shared them with you. It is therefore heartening to see that persons of the quality of these two senior UN staff have acted according to their conscience at potential personal sacrifice. They bring credit to the United Nations and to the role of the international civil servant.

These international civil servants have now rightly suggested that such sanctions are tantamount to violation by the United Nations itself of the fundamental rights inscribed in international law through the Universal Declaration of Human Rights and the Covenants established to implement its provisions. We believe they are right.

We sincerely hope that the international community and especially the Security Council will pay heed to the gruesome situation they have again described. For over a decade the people of Iraq have suffered under a sanctions regime that is unrelentingly punitive of the people of Iraq who are hardly to blame for the actions of their government. The comprehensive application of an economic embargo in a manner that ignores the fundamental humanitarian needs and rights of 22 million people to basic health care, food and shelter is unacceptable. This is not new information. It has been amply documented by competent UN Agencies, the International Committee of the Red Cross and other international non-governmental organizations that the majority of the Iraqi people are denied the bare level of sustenance necessary to live a life of human dignity. The WCC has consistently received reports over the past decade on the deteriorating conditions of the population, especially of children, from its member churches and the Middle East Council of Churches Ecumenical Relief Service in Iraq. We also sent an expert delegation to Iraq in early 1998 to review the position.

The World Council of Churches holds that sanctions can be a legitimate and valuable tool available to the international community to enforce compliance with international law when applied prudently by a responsible international authority. Precisely in order to address situations like that prevailing in the case of Iraq, the WCC Central Committee adopted in 1995 a set of criteria for the just and effective application of sanctions. These were shared with you and the relevant Security Council committee at that time. In the preambular section of the resolution containing these criteria, the Central Committee cautioned that:

Even when appropriately applied under the authority of the UN Charter, sanctions have not always been consistent, impartial or effective. ... The absence of a clear, consistent, and effective system of enforcement by the UN further complicates the picture. This, and the ambiguity of international law, has allowed individual governments to use the term sanctions to provide a cloak of moral and legal justification for some of their own foreign policy initiatives. Especially since 1990, powerful states have sought UN endorsement of their intention to apply what they have termed sanctions. This practice requires careful scrutiny by the churches and by the international community.

The WCC "Criteria for Determining the Applicability and Effectiveness of Sanctions" include, *inter alia*:

Clear and limited purpose. Sanctions should have a *clearly defined* purpose and explicit criteria should be given for determining the conditions under which that purpose will be seen to be achieved, and the sanctions lifted.

Sanctions *may not have a punitive purpose beyond compliance,* nor may they be used for self-aggrandizement, or applied to further the economic, ideological political, military or other narrow national self-interest of a state or a group of states.

Having received the report of the WCC delegation which visited Iraq, the WCC Central Committee in 1998 appealed through you to the UN Security Council to undertake a thorough review of the sanctions regime on Iraq, taking into account its impact on the civilian population, and with a view to defining clear and agreed goals with a specific timeframe and benchmarks for the full lifting of sanctions.

We believe that economic sanctions can provide a non-violent alternative to war when applied under strict conditions and carefully monitored. Though in its Res. 1284 (1999) the Security Council returned to the question of delivery of humanitarian goods, it has still not appropriately or clearly defined sanctions against Iraq, nor has increasing monitoring diminished the suffering of the Iraqi people. The World Council of Churches therefore believes that the time is overdue for the Security Council to lift with immediate effect all sanctions that have direct and indiscriminate effect on the civilian population of Iraq.

356

I would be grateful if you would bring this concern to the attention of the Security Council.

Respectfully yours,

Konrad Raiser
General Secretary

Statement on the threats of military action against Iraq
Adopted by the Central Committee, Geneva, 26 August - 3 September, 2002.

The Central Committee of the World Council of Churches, meeting in Geneva 26 August to 3 September, 2002:

Profoundly concerned and alarmed about the persistent efforts of the Government of the United States of America to gather international support for a new military action against Iraq with the stated objective of overthrowing the present government of Iraq;

Recalling and reaffirming the words of the WCC First General Assembly (1948): *War as a method of settling disputes is incompatible with the teaching and example of our Lord Jesus Christ. The part which war plays in our present international life is a sin against God and a degradation of man.*

Recalling and reaffirming the 1991 Seventh Assembly Statement on the Gulf War, the Middle East, the Threat to World Peace and its statement on the Situation in Iraq of February 1998, where it warned against renewed military action which would result in large scale casualties and increased suffering by the Iraqi people;

Recalling and reaffirming subsequent WCC actions and public statements calling upon the United Nations Security Council to lift immediately all sanctions that have direct and indiscriminate effect on the civilian population of Iraq;

Reiterating its conviction that "under the sovereignty of God, no nation or group of nations is entitled to prosecute vengeance against another. Nor is any nation entitled to make unilateral judgements and take unilateral actions that lead to the devastation of another nation and the massive suffering of its people." (*Central Committee, Potsdam, 2001*);

Shares the fears and concerns of the churches in the Middle East and as expressed by the Middle East Council of Churches in its statement of August 5, 2002, and supports its call for "a sustained and determined diplomatic and political effort that engages the Iraqi government directly, and a sustained campaign to re-empower the Iraqi people and restore their dignity";

Welcomes The Christian Declaration launched in mid-July by Pax Christi UK which considers the pronouncements of war plans against Iraq by the USA, with a possible British support as immoral and illegal, deploring the fact that the world's

357

most powerful nations continue to regard war as an acceptable instrument of foreign policy, in violation of both the United Nations and Christian teachings;

Further welcomes the positions taken by churches in the USA, the UK, Canada, Australia and other nations expressing grave concerns about the threat of war against Iraq;

Calls upon the Government of Iraq to respect the resolutions of the UN Security Council, including demands that it destroy all weapons of mass destruction and related research and production facilities, to cooperate fully with UN inspectors deployed to oversee compliance, and to guarantee full respect of the civil and political, economic, social and cultural human rights for all its citizens;

Calls insistently upon the Government of the United States of America to desist from any military threats against Iraq and any further development of plans for military actions against that country;

Urges the international community to uphold the international rule of law, to resist pressures to join in preemptive military strikes against a sovereign state under the pretext of the "war on terrorism," and to strengthen their commitment to obtain respect for United Nations Security Council resolutions on Iraq by non-military means;

Calls upon all member churches and ecumenical partners to prevail upon their governments to address the root causes of the conflict itself and to put an end to the dire humanitarian crisis in Iraq; and

Reiterates its expression of solidarity with and prayers for the churches and people of Iraq.

Appeal to Iraq to respect the resolutions of the UN Security Council
Letter to H.E. Saddam Hussein, President of Iraq, 19 September 2002.

Your Excellency,

The Central Committee of the World Council of Churches, meeting in Geneva in early September 2002, adopted a statement on *the threats of military action against Iraq* which expresses "concern and alarm about the efforts of the US government to gather international support for a new military action against Iraq." I am attaching a copy of the statement for your consideration.

I draw your attention especially to the statements calling upon the Iraqi government "to respect the resolutions of the UN Security Council, including demands that it destroy all weapons of mass destruction and related research and production facilities, to cooperate fully with UN inspectors deployed to oversee compliance, and to guarantee full respect of the civil and political, economic, social and cultural human rights for all its citizens."

Please be assured of our on-going concern for the people of Iraq and for our prayers for peace.

Respectfully yours,

Peter Weiderud
Director
Commission of the Churches on
International Affairs

Appeal to the US Government

Letter to Amb. Kevin Edward Moley, Permanent Mission of the USA to the UN in Geneva, 19 September 2002.

Your Excellency,

I write to you in my new capacity as Director of the Commission of the Churches on International Affairs (CCIA) following Rev. Dwain Epps's leaving this same position after some three decades of ecumenical ministry in the field of international affairs – twenty years of which on the staff of the CCIA. I am very much looking forward to our future cooperation in addressing the challenges that confront the world at the international level. I am a layman – a trained journalist – from theChurch of Sweden and have up to now been Director for the international work of my church.

The Central Committee of the World Council of Churches, meeting in Geneva in early September 2002, adopted a statement on "the threats of military action against IraqI which expresses "concern and alarm about the efforts of the US government to gather international support for a new military action against Iraq."

The Central Committee also adopted a minute on *the tragedy of September 11th 2001 and the implications of the US government's response.* I am attaching copies of both of these statements and ask that you forward them to the appropriate officials in your government.

We earnestly hope that the dangers of military action in an already-troubled region can be averted. We assure you of our highest consideration and our support and prayers for efforts for peace.

Respectfully yours,

Peter Weiderud
Director
Commission of the Churches on
International Affairs

Appeal to the governments of China, France, Russia and the UK

Letters to the Permanent Representatives to the UN in Geneva, 19 September 2002.

Dear Sirs,

The Central Committee of the World Council of Churches, meeting in Geneva in early September, adopted a statement on *the threats of military action against Iraq* which expresses "concern and alarm about the efforts of the US government to gather international support for a new military action against Iraq." I am attaching a copy of that statement.

I draw your attention especially to the statement's call to the "international community to uphold the international rule of law, to resist pressures to join in preemptive military strikes against a sovereign state under the pretext of the 'war on terrorism,' and to strengthen their commitment to obtain respect for United Nations Security Council resolutions on Iraq by non-military means."

Our prayers are with you as you seek to maintain the international rule of law and to avert the dangers of military action in an already-troubled region. As you intensify those efforts to promote all necessary diplomatic initiatives, we assure you of our highest consideration and our support and prayers for efforts for peace.

Respectfully yours,

Peter Weiderud
Director
Commission of the Churches on
International Affairs

Appeal against military action in Iraq

Individual letters to Members States of the Security Council and to the Secretary General of the UN, 15ᵗʰ October, 2002.

Your Excellency,

The World Council of Churches (WCC) remains extremely concerned with the continued calls for military action against Iraq both by the US and UK governments despite Iraq's compliance with United Nations Resolution for UN weapons inspection, agreeing for the "immediate, unconditional and unrestricted access to sites in Iraq".

We were greatly alarmed and saddened by the US Congressional Joint Resolution to authorize use of force against Iraq passed by the US House of Representatives and Senate on 10ᵗʰ October, 2002, authorizing, *inter alia,* the President of the USA to use its armed forces in order to enforce all relevant UN Security Council resolutions regarding Iraq.

As you prepare for further deliberations of the United Nations Security Council this week, I would like to draw your attention to the numerous voices of Christians around the world, who, committed to the teachings of Jesus Christ and the prophetic vision of peace, strongly believe that preemptive war against Iraq is illegal, immoral and unwise.

The World Council of Churches' governing body meeting in September this year, urged *the international community to uphold the international rule of law, to resist pressures to join in preemptive military strikes against a sovereign state under the pretext of the "war on terrorism", and to strengthen their commitment to obtain respect for United Nations Security Council resolutions on Iraq by non-military means.*

They deplored *the fact that the most powerful nations of this world continue to regard war as an acceptable instrument of foreign policy, in violation of both the United Nations Charter and Christian teachings.*

The WCC has always advocated for every member state to comply with binding UN resolutions and to resolve conflicts by peaceful means. Iraq can be no exception. Since the end of the Gulf War we have repeatedly called the Government of Iraq to destroy its weapons of mass destruction and related research and production facilities, to cooperate fully with UN inspectors deployed to oversee compliance, and to guarantee full respect of the civil and political, economic, social and cultural human rights for all its citizens.

We are deeply concerned by the potential human costs of a new war and the prospects of large-scale displacement of people. The people of Iraq have suffered enough under a sanctions regime since 1991. Inflicting further punishment on innocent civilians is not morally acceptable to anyone. Churches around the world also caution against the potential social, cultural, and religious as well as diplomatic long term consequences of such a war, especially a unilateral one. Further fueling the fires of violence that are already consuming the region will only sow more seeds of intense hatred strengthening extremist ideologies and breeding further global instability and insecurity.

The WCC joins its voice with church leaders and Christian communities around the world, especially from the USA and UK, praying that you focus your attention on addressing the root causes of this conflict and to put an end to the dire humanitarian crisis in Iraq and the Middle East region as a whole. I call upon you as members of the United Nations Security Council to act wisely, responsibly and courageously.

We pray that God will guide you to take decisions based on moral principles and legal standards.

"No nation shall lift up sword against nation, neither shall they learn war any more." Isaiah 2:4.

Yours sincerely,

Rev. Dr. Konrad Raiser
General Secretary

Appeal to church leaders in member states of the UN Security Council

Letter to WCC member churches and Central Committee members, specialized ecumenical agencies, national and regional councils of churches, 24 October 2002.

Dear Brothers and Sisters in Christ,

As the United Nations Security Council continues its deliberations this week on Iraq and the threat of war in that country persists, the World Council of Churches (WCC) looks to you, the churches, national and regional councils and specialized ecumenical agencies from the United Nations Security Council member states, for guidance and cooperation in averting this war. It is in this context that I share with you the contents of the WCC General Secretary's letter to members of the United Nations Security Council sent October 15, 2002 (attached).

The General Secretary's letter conveys three main policy elements of the WCC, based on the WCC Central Committee Statement of September 2, 2002:

The need to uphold the international rule of law, resist pressures to join in preemptive military strikes against a sovereign state and to search for solutions by non-military means. The WCC opposes unilateral military action by any state and deplores the view held by many of the most powerful nations in the world that war is an acceptable foreign policy instrument, in violation of both the United Nations Charter and Christian teachings.

Deep concern for the potential human costs of a new war and the large-scale displacement of Iraqi citizens. Action by Churches Together (ACT), on behalf of the WCC, is currently preparing for a potential crisis in Iraq in co-operation with the Middle East Council of Churches. Together they are working on a regional emergency preparedness plan in consideration of the potential magnitude of the conflict and the humanitarian consequences both in Iraq and throughout the region.

Caution against the potential social, cultural, and religious as well as diplomatic long term consequences of such a war, especially a unilateral one. The WCC, through its Inter-Religious Relations team, recently hosted an international consultation on "Christians and Muslims in Dialogue and Beyond" which addressed how the already considerable division between East and West would be exacerbated by a conflict with Iraq. The conference delegates subsequently called on political leaders to resist the temptation to resort to simplistic and populist assignation of blame and demonisation of whole communities, and to resist the identification of violence and terrorism on any one particular religion or community; and for leaders of all religions at all levels to draw attention to the social, economic and other injustices which influence their environment and to resist the exploitation of these injustices to rouse religious hatred.

The WCC has been encouraged by the many actions and statements made by ecumenical councils and member churches, as well as various Christian peace movements, expressing consternation with recent political developments relating to the threat of war against Iraq (ref.: compilation attached). The next issue of *Behind the News*, due this week, will also include these actions for your information and further use.

In order for the WCC to ensure a coherent and collective ecumenical response, we urgently request information on any actions or advocacy plans you may have to help avert a military strike against Iraq. We would also welcome any suggestions you would like the WCC to further consider.

I pray that God will guide your actions in these troubled times.

Sincerely,

Peter Weiderud
Director
Commission of the Churches on
International Affairs

ISRAEL

Expression of condolences to victims of suicide bombing
Letter to H.E. Mr Yaakov Levy, Ambassador of Israel to the United Nations in Geneva, 6 June 2001.

Your Excellency, Mr Ambassador,

On behalf of the World Council of Churches General Secretary, Rev. Dr Konrad Raiser, I would like to extend our sincere condolences to the families of the victims of the suicide bomb attack on June 1st. May God grant them consolation where human words and efforts fail.

We are saddened and appalled to see and read the daily accounts of violence that continues in Israel and the Palestinian Occupied Territories. I want to assure you, Mr Ambassador, that we continue to mourn with every Israeli and Palestinian family that loses yet another loved one and keep both peoples deep in our prayers.

The World Council of Churches has consistently advocated a non-violent, peaceful resolution of this tragic conflict. We can never justify indiscriminate attacks on civilians, especially when directed to children and youth, nor can we justify disproportionate use of armed force, military occupation and impunity. As Rev. Raiser stated in his letter dated 10.10.00 to UN Secretary General Mr. Kofi Annan, "History bears witness to the truth that so long as this underlying injustice persists there can be neither peace nor security for either Israel or Palestine".

We are alarmed at the level of instability and insecurity in the region and strongly believe that any further escalation of the conflict must be avoided for the sake of the Israeli and the Palestinian people alike. Neither side can afford more pain and suffering. In memory of the innocent youth who lost their lives, we pray that the government of Israel will be able to embrace a real truce and address the root causes of this conflict for the sake of its children and future.

Cordially yours,

Salpy Eskidjian
International Relations

ISRAELI-PALESTINIAN CONFLICT

Letter of encouragement to the UN Secretary-General for his initiative for a resumption of negotiations

Letter to H.E. Kofi Annan, Secretary-General of the UN, 10 October 2000.

Mr Secretary-General,

I write to commend you for your decision to intervene personally in the Israeli-Palestinian conflict, and to assure you of the prayers of the churches joined in the World Council of Churches as you meet with the respective leaders.

We welcome Security Council resolution 1322 (2000) and its call for the immediate cessation of violence and all further acts of provocation. In adopting this resolution the Security Council speaks for the overwhelming majority of the peoples of the world. We share the call for the immediate resumption of negotiations and the need expressed for a 'speedy and objective inquiry into the tragic events of the last few days with the aim of preventing their repetition' to which reference is made in the resolution.

The roots of the present violence lie deep in the history of the conflictive relationship between Israelis and the Palestinians, in particular since the creation of the State of Israel, in the injustice done to the Palestinian people, and in the persistent refusal of Israel to abide by the terms of repeated demands of redress issued by the Security Council and the UN General Assembly over the past half century. History bears witness to the truth that so long as this underlying injustice persists there can be neither peace nor security for either Israel or Palestine.

Both sides have suffered from this renewed violent confrontation. But once again it is the Palestinian people, especially Palestinian youth, who pay by far the greater price in God-given life as a result of the disproportionate use of armed force by Israel.

We pray that Prime Minister Barak and President Arafat and all those caught up in the terrible, rising spiral of violence will respond to your initiative and to the appeals of governments and peoples around the world by stepping back from the brink before they and the region as a whole are cast again into the abyss of full-scale war.

This is not a time for ultimatums or threats of more violent acts of retribution, but the hour to join together in declaring a truce and days of public mourning for the victims of the violence on all sides.

As the Security Council has noted, this last wave of violent confrontation was set off by a provocative act in Jerusalem. This defies the shared belief of Christians, Jews and Muslims alike that Jerusalem is a Holy City that God intended to be a haven of peace, the symbol of harmony among the nations. As the heads of the churches in Jerusalem reminded us all on the eve of this outbreak, the Psalmist wrote, 'The Lord will write a list of the peoples and include them all as citizens of Jerusalem.' (Ps 87.6)

Ten days ago the Executive Committee of the World Council of Churches adopted a Resolution on Jerusalem Final Status Negotiations which reiterated our firm belief 'that Jerusalem can be a source of peace, stability and coexistence rather than of division and conflict that destroy human dignity and hope'.

The paper prepared as background for that action said that, if approached the right way, Jerusalem could be the reservoir of spiritual as well as the political refreshment that would nurture peace instead of being a poisoned well that threatens it. Jerusalem should be the engine for peace, a source of stability and coexistence, rather than a casual inheritor of the peace process, or worse: a continuing source of division and conflict.

We pray that all concerned will now draw on this source of peace and harmony, recalling the words of Christ, "Blessed are the peacemakers, for theirs shall be called people of God." (Mt. 5:9)

Respectfully yours,

Konrad Raiser
General Secretary

Sharing the land, the truth and the peace

Written submission by the CCIA to the Fifth Special Session of the United Nations Commission on Human Rights devoted to grave and massive violations of the human rights of the Palestinian people by Israel, Geneva, 17 October 2000.

Justice delayed, justice denied. The resolutions and reports relating to the rights and duties of Israelis and Palestinians adopted by or submitted to the General Assembly, the Security Council and this body since the Partition of Palestine and the creation of the State of Israel in 1948 fill volumes. Israel has most often either ignored or openly violated those related to its practices, thus delaying and often denying justice to the Palestinian people, both in the Occupied Territories and within Israel.

In the post-Oslo period Israel has continued and even accelerated its unilateral practices of changing "facts on the ground." These have included:

- the confiscation over the past three years of an estimated 2,200 Palestinian identity cards, some 900 in 1999 alone, affecting in all nearly 2,500 citizens;

- the continuing issuance and execution of demolition orders against Palestinian houses in the occupied territories – the Israeli Municipality of Jerusalem issued 141 demolition orders in East Jerusalem alone and carried out 19 in 1999 and demolished another three by the end of August 2000;

- continuing harassment and interference with the work of Palestinian institutions providing essential human services in East Jerusalem despite promises to desist; continuing expansion by Israel of illegal settlements in territories occupied since 1967 and denial of Palestinian's exercise of their right to return;

- repeated closures restricting movement of Palestinians and their access, *inter alia*, to the Holy Places in Jerusalem.

The Special Rapporteur on the Question of the violation of human rights in the occupied Arab Territories, including Palestine inferred in his last report, and events following the provocative visit on 28 September to Al-Haram Al-Sharif have again shown that the consequence of this repeated defiance of international law, of continuing systematic violations of human rights, including the application of collective punishments, has been to incite to violence and to deny peace and security to both peoples. Israel's particularly harsh response through the use of excessive force against its own Palestinian minority in recent days has contributed to their further vulnerability and alienation and to a deeper polarization of Israeli society.

In a letter of 10 October to Secretary-General Kofi Annan, Dr Konrad Raiser, General Secretary of the World Council of Churches (WCC) offered support and prayers for the success of the mission he has undertaken to the region. Dr Raiser said there:

Both sides have suffered from this renewed violent confrontation. But once again it is the Palestinian people, especially Palestinian youth, who pay by far the greater price in God-given life as a result of the disproportionate use of armed force by Israel.

We pray that Prime Minister Barak and President Arafat and all those caught up in the terrible, rising spiral of violence will respond to your initiative and to the appeals of governments and peoples around the world by stepping back from the brink before they and the region as a whole are cast again into the abyss of full-scale war.

This is not a time for ultimatums or threats of more violent acts of retribution, but the hour to join together in declaring a truce and days of public mourning for the victims of the violence on all sides.

Sharing the land. Most Israelis and Palestinians fervently desire peace, but many also despair at the lack of progress towards it. Jerusalem – home to Arabs and Jews, and considered holy by Christians, Jews and Muslims alike – has been regarded as the most complicated and difficult issue and has repeatedly been left to the end of the negotiation process. Believing that a resolution of this question could open the way to agreements on equitable sharing of the land and resources in Palestine, the last WCC Assembly (Harare, 1998) called upon the parties not to postpone further but to include final status negotiations on Jerusalem as an integral part of negotiations on a general settlement of the wider Middle East conflict. In fact an approach along these lines was taken during the most recent talks in Camp David. For the first time, both sides tabled constructive proposals for shared sovereignty in Jerusalem. Recent events have cut short this hopeful process. Once again the exercise of peoples' rights to peace and sovereign development has fallen victim to the enemies of peace.

Sharing the peace. It was not surprising that these confrontations began in Jerusalem, the nerve center of the conflict. In a resolution adopted on 29 September the WCC Executive Committee nevertheless shared the conviction expressed by Their Beatitudes the Patriarchs and Heads of Churches and Christian Communities in Jerusalem in their statement of 26 September 2000 that a successful conclusion of final status negotiations on Jerusalem would contribute greatly to "true peace with true justice and security for the 'two peoples and three religions' of this land - Palestinians and Israelis, Jews, Christians and Muslims alike." The WCC is firmly convinced that God intended the Holy City to be a source of peace, stability and coexistence rather than of the division and conflict that destroy human dignity and hope. We hope that the present special session of the Commission on Human Rights will draw on the spiritual resources God offers through Jerusalem and contribute constructively to this end.

Sharing the truth. Few international conflicts have been so marked by the dominant power's defiance of its obligations under the Charter to abide by decisions of the Security Council and its treaty obligations such as those of the Fourth Geneva

Convention. Here as elsewhere self-asserted claims to impunity pose barriers to peace and reconciliation between nations and peoples. Thus the WCC welcomed the important decision of the Security Council in res. 1322 (2000) that stressed "the importance of establishing a mechanism for a speedy and objective inquiry into the tragic events of the last few days with the aim of preventing their repetition". Such an investigation could provide an essential beginning to revealing, sharing and mutual acceptance of the truth about past systematic violations of peoples' rights. Without such a process there can be little hope for justice, peace or reconciliation between Israeli Jews and Palestinian Christians and Muslims within and beyond Israel's legitimate borders.

Recommendations

The Commission of the Churches on International Affairs of the World Council of Churches therefore recommends that this Fifth Special Session of the Commission on Human Rights:

- Respond to Security Council res. 1322 (2000) by contributing within its mandate to a "speedy and objective inquiry into the tragic events of the last few days with the aim of achieving an early final settlement between the Israeli and Palestinian sides;"

- Continue to support the work of the Special Rapporteur on the Question of the violation of human rights in the occupied Arab Territories in the pursuance of his mandate to investigate Israel's violations of the principles and bases of international law, and the 1949 Geneva Conventions relative to the Protection of Civilian Persons in Time of War in the Palestinian territories occupied by Israel since 1967, and to propose means of compliance with relevant resolutions through regular reports to the Commission;

- Encourage the Special Committee to Investigate Israeli Practices affecting the Human Rights of the Palestinian People and Other Arabs of the Occupied Territories to continue and intensify its work;

- Reiterate its demand that Israel cooperate fully with these investigations, including the granting of full access to the occupied Arab Territories, and respond to the content and recommendations contained in the reports;

- Encourage the Working Group on Minorities of the Sub-Commission on the Promotion and Protection of Human Rights, in response to the appeals of Israeli Palestinian leaders, to investigate systematic violations of the human rights of the Palestinian minority in Israel particularly in light of recent official abuses and failure to provide protection;

- Reiterate its demand that Israel comply fully with its obligations under the Fourth Geneva Convention;

- Follow up the work on impunity of the Sub-Commission on the Promotion and Protection on Human rights with respect to holding states and individuals suspected of having committed mass violations of the right to life accountable for their acts.

A three-member Palestinian ecumenical delegation is attending the Special Session of the United Nations Commission on Human Rights. The delegation is hosted by the Commission of Churches on International Affairs (CCIA) of the World Council of Churches (WCC).

Delegation members include:

Archimandrite Theodosios Hanna, representing His Beatitude Patriarch Diodoros, Greek Orthodox Patriarchate, Greek Orthodox Patriarchate of Jerusalem

The Rt. Rev. Riah Abu El-Assal, Bishop of the Episcopal Church in Jerusalem and the Middle East

Dr Marwan Bishara, author, journalist from Nazareth, research fellow, Ecole des Hautes Etudes en Sciences Sociales

Father George Tsetsis, member of the WCC Central and Executive Committees, will accompany the delegation along with WCC International Relations staff.

Three other people are unable to join the delegation in Geneva due to the military closure of Palestinian territories:

Ms Jean Zaru, Ramallah, Quaker, vice-chair of the board of Sabeel Ecumenical Liberation Theology Center, Jerusalem

Mr Constantine El'Dabbagh, Gaza Strip, Department for Services for Palestinian Refugees/Middle East Council of Churches

Ms Nahed Awwad, Beit Sahour, The Palestinian Center for Rapprochement between People

In Pursuit of Lasting Peace with Justice
Oral intervention by the CCIA to the Fifth Special Session of the United Nations Commission on Human Rights, Geneva, 17 October 2000.

Thank you, Mr Chairman, for the opportunity to bring to this Special Session a message of peace and hope from the churches and Christians of Jerusalem and the Holy Land.

I am Father Georges Tsetsis from the Ecumenical Patriarchate of Constantinople, and a member of the Central and Executive Committees of the World Council of Churches.

I speak on behalf of the Commission of the Churches on International Affairs of the World Council of Churches whose practice it is to bring to meetings of the Commission on Human Rights representatives of our member churches and individual Christians who can bear first-hand witness to the systematic violation of human rights in their lands. Members of our delegation include Archimandrite Theodosios Hanna, the personal representative of His Beatitude Patriarch

369

Diodoros of the Greek Orthodox Patriarchate of Jerusalem, the Right Reverend, Riah Abu El-Assal, Bishop of the Episcopal Church in Jerusalem and the Middle East, and Dr Marwan Bishara, a young Arab Israeli journalist and scholar. It is with deep regret that three other members of our delegation were prevented from attending this Special Session due to the military closure of the Palestinian Territories. They included Ms Jean Zaru, a pacifist Christian from Ramallah and former member of the WCC Central Committee, Mr Constantine El'Dabbagh, from Gaza engaged with the Department for Services for Palestinian Refugees of the Middle East Council of Churches, and Ms Nahed Awwad from Beit Sahour, a young woman actively engaged in dialogue between Palestinians and Israelis through the Palestinian Center for Rapprochement between People.

We have submitted a written statement for inclusion in the record of this meeting. It and information detailing our decades-long engagement for peace in Jerusalem and the Middle East is available for delegates.

We congratulate the High Commissioner and the Special Rapporteur for their comprehensive statements and for having highlighted the pursuit of peace based on the full enjoyment of human rights for the peoples and citizens of Palestine and Israel. Such a peace must indeed be our goal.

Much has been said about the need for early warning of conflict. The Special Rapporteur this morning has made reference to the warnings he gave in his last report to the Commission of the rising tensions in the region. He noted the growing impatience of Palestinians with a peace process which has brought them little peace and which stifles their desire to engage in a form of development of their homeland which will threaten no neighbor, but rather give them and their children the essential basis for dignified life. In view of this and many other such warnings, no one in this room can be surprised at the terrible violence in recent days, the genesis of which has been traced skillfully by the High Commissioner.

The churches in the Holy Land have long given a credible and compelling witness for lasting peace built on the foundations of justice. The experience of the past half-century has shown that justice delayed is justice denied. For too long the ministries of these churches have been to the victims of injustice: the displaced, the abjectly poor, and the victims of systematic violation of human rights. The churches have never failed, however, to bring a message of hope, of the longing for peace, and the promise of peace given by God who loves all without distinction.

We bear testimony today of how difficult it has been to hold fast to this message in the face of the consistent defiance of international law and the admonitions of the international community on the part of the occupying power. The roots of the present violence certainly lie there, and in Israel's systematic violation of Palestinians' human rights including collective punishments. The repeated use of excessive military and armed force in the name of a false notion of security has effectively denied both peace and security to both peoples. This force has been

370

turned now upon the Arab population of Israel itself, contributing further to their vulnerability and alienation. It has intensified the polarization of Israeli society and widened the chasm that separates Israelis from Palestinians living in the Occupied Territories.

Peace and security for both peoples does not reside in the accumulation and use of military might, but rather in a will to share: to share the land and its resources equitably, to share the peace and responsibility for maintaining it, and to share the truth. We believe that a shared future is not only possible, but essential.

Christians firmly believe in forgiveness and reconciliation. But for this to be possible it is essential for the truth about past offenses to be revealed publicly, to be acknowledged and shared. For this reason we warmly welcome the call of the Security Council for the establishment of "a mechanism for a speedy and objective inquiry into the tragic events of the last few days with the aim of preventing their repetition". We hope that this Commission will take a lead to put such a mechanism in place without delay. Without such a process there can be little hope for overcoming impunity or for justice, peace or reconciliation between Israeli Jews and Palestinian Christians and Muslims.

However, Mr Chairman, the experience of this Commission through the work of the Special Rapporteur, and of the United Nations General Assembly through its Special Committee to Investigate Israeli Practices affecting the Human Rights of the Palestinian People is not encouraging. There have been efforts to ascertain the truth, but that truth has not been acknowledged and shared by the Occupying Power. Thus we appeal to Israel to cease withholding its cooperation and to use the occasion of the creation of a new mechanism to show its firm will to deal with the past in order to build a new future for themselves and their neighbors.

Mr Chairman, reference has been made to intemperate statements of religious leaders in the course of the recent violence. We grant that some religious figures on both sides have given in to passion and expressed views that demonize the other. Religion can indeed be susceptible to misuse by political forces that aim to divide. But true religion is a resource for peace, harmonious living together, and of hope for a better, more just day.

Christian churches around the world have over the years, and especially now, been constant in prayer for peace with justice in the Holy Land. They have found in the Holy City, Jerusalem, in its Holy Places and its "living stones", and especially in its churches and Christian communities, a source of profound spiritual strength and hope. This strength does not reside in sectarian ideas or exclusivist claims, but rather in the promises shared by those who place their trust in one God. Their Beatitudes and Heads of Christian Communities in Jerusalem gave witness to this in their statement of 26 September in which they expressed their longing for "true peace with true justice and security for the 'two peoples and three religions' of this land - Palestinians and Israelis, Jews, Christians and Muslims alike."

Late last week, at a service of Ecumenical Prayer for Peace organized on the initiative of His Beatitude Diodoros, the Greek Orthodox Patriarch, Latin Patriarch Michael Sabbah spoke on behalf of his fellow Patriarchs and heads of the thirteen churches in Jerusalem who were present. I should like to conclude these remarks by sharing his words with you:

> Although we believe that our land was in the past and is still today a land of hatred and bloodshed, (he said,) we also believe that it was and must be today too a land of forgiveness and redemption. Violence, as long as it lasts, or as imposed by spirits who refuse to listen to the cries of the poor and to the voice of the victims, and to see the core of the question: in other words, a Palestinian people oppressed and deprived of its freedom... Violence as long as it lasts for these reasons, is neither our goal, nor our destiny. Our destiny is freedom in our land, and hence tranquility and security for all, Palestinians and Israelis alike. ...Amidst the hatred and the bloodshed, the word of God (given to us by the Apostle Paul) should dwell in our hearts; we must hear it, meditate upon it, even if it hurts:

> Bless those who persecute you; bless and do not curse them, bless them. Rejoice with others when they rejoice, and be sad with those in sorrow. Give the same consideration to all others alike... Never pay back evil with evil, but bear in mind the ideals that all regard with respect. As much as is possible, and to the utmost of your ability, be at peace with everyone... If your enemy is hungry give him something to eat; if thirsty, something to drink... Do not be overcome by evil, but overcome evil with good. (Rom. 12:14-18, 20-21)

This is a call to conversion of the heart, of the mind and of the spirit. May this message be heard by all, and inspire our common pursuit of peace with justice for all.

Thank you, Mr Chairman and delegates, for your kind attention.

Minute on the situation in the Holy Land after the outbreak of the second Palestinian uprising
Adopted by the Central Committee, Potsdam, Germany, 29 January – 6 February 2001.

In an appeal on November 9, 2000 all thirteen Eastern and Oriental Orthodox, Catholic and Protestant Churches of Jerusalem, expressed their conviction that:

> The Church believes that it is the right as much as duty of an occupied people to struggle against injustice in order to gain freedom, although it also believes that non-violent means of struggle remain stronger and far more efficient. In this sense, both parties must show the necessary fortitude, both in their hearts and in their minds, to look at the core of the conflict so that the Palestinian people can gain at long last its full freedom within its own sustainable state. It is imperative now to implement principles of international legitimacy by

enforcing the binding UN resolutions. Such fortitude is a wise sign of foresight and an indispensable prerequisite for long-lasting peace. (Excerpt from "A Faithful Appeal.")

The Central Committee expresses its deep sadness and grave concern at the new escalation of violence in the Palestinian autonomous and occupied territories as well as Israel over the last four months that has claimed a terrible toll of human life, especially among Palestinian children and youth. It extends its consolation to all the afflicted and the bereaved and assures the Heads of Churches and Christian communities of Jerusalem of its constant prayers and solidarity as they bear in their hearts and minds the pain of their communities and of all those Palestinians and Israelis who are suffering the consequences of this conflict.

We share the frustration and disappointments of our Palestinian sisters and brothers. We are deeply disturbed by and deplore a pattern of discrimination, routine humiliation, segregation and exclusion which restricts Palestinian freedom of movement, including access to the holy sites, and the disproportionate use of military force by Israel, the denial of access to timely medical assistance, the destruction of property, including tens of thousands of olive trees, and which requires special permission for Palestinians to enter areas under Israeli jurisdiction and establishes "cantonization" of the land, so that Palestinian lands are separated from one another – a pattern so very reminiscent of policies that the WCC has condemned in the past.

We therefore urge the member churches of the WCC to increase their efforts to condemn injustice and all forms of discrimination, to end Israeli occupation, to pray for and promote a comprehensive and just peace in the Middle East. To help inform and strengthen those efforts, we commend to the churches the background information presented to this meeting for their study and urgent action.

We call upon the General Secretary and staff of the Council to:
- continue their support of efforts towards a negotiated peace in the Middle East based on international law, paying special attention to the future status of Jerusalem, the right of return of Palestinian refugees, the increasing number of settlements and measures to enforce all relevant United Nations resolutions, including those regarding the withdrawal from all occupied territories – the Palestinian occupied territories, the Golan Heights and Shaba'a;
- continue to analyze and to keep the member churches regularly informed on the evolving situation;
- accompany the churches of the Holy Land and their members, and advocate their rights;
- support local Israeli and Palestinian grassroots peacebuilding efforts; and

- promote and/or cooperate with church, ecumenical and other initiatives, to strengthen broad international support for a comprehensive peace based on justice and security for all the peoples of the region.

Background Document on the Situation in the Middle East

Commended to the churches for their study and urgent action by the Central Committee, Potsdam, Germany, 29 January – 6 February 2001.

Since the Preliminary Report on Public Issues was prepared, the conflict between the Palestinians and Israel has further intensified. As noted in that earlier report, the Commission of the Churches on International Affairs (CCIA) of the WCC sent a delegation comprised of representatives of member churches in Palestine and led by a member of the WCC Executive Committee to the Fifth Special Session of the UN Commission on Human Rights called last October to consider the implications of Israel's disproportionate use of force. In a written submission to that meeting, entitled "Sharing the Land, the Truth and the Peace," the WCC noted that

> events following the provocative visit (of Ariel Sharon) on 28 September to Al-Haram Al-Sharif have again shown that the consequence of (Israel's) repeated defiance of international law, of continuing systematic violations of human rights, including the application of collective punishments, has been to incite to violence and to deny peace and security to both peoples. Israel's particularly harsh response through the use of excessive force against its own Palestinian minority in recent days has contributed to their further vulnerability and alienation and to a deeper polarization of Israeli society.

It went on to say that

> Most Israelis and Palestinians fervently desire peace, but many also despair at the lack of progress towards it. Jerusalem – home to Arabs and Jews, and considered holy by Christians, Jews and Muslims alike – has been regarded as the most complicated and difficult issue and has repeatedly been left to the end of the negotiation process. Believing that a resolution of this question could open the way to agreements on equitable sharing of the land and resources in Palestine, the last WCC Assembly (Harare, 1998) called upon the parties not to postpone further but to include final status negotiations on Jerusalem as an integral part of negotiations on a general settlement of the wider Middle East conflict. In fact an approach along these lines was taken during the most recent talks in Camp David. For the first time, both sides tabled constructive proposals for shared sovereignty in Jerusalem. Recent events have cut short this hopeful process. Once again the exercise of peoples' rights to peace and sovereign development has fallen victim to the enemies of peace.

It was not surprising that these confrontations began in Jerusalem, the nerve center of the conflict. In a resolution adopted on 29 September the WCC Executive Committee nevertheless shared the conviction expressed by Their

Beatitudes the Patriarchs and Heads of Churches and Christian Communities in Jerusalem in their statement of 26 September 2000 that a successful conclusion of final status negotiations on Jerusalem would contribute greatly to "true peace with true justice and security for the 'two peoples and three religions' of this land – Palestinians and Israelis, Jews, Christians and Muslims alike." The WCC is firmly convinced that God intended the Holy City to be a source of peace, stability and coexistence rather than of the division and conflict that destroy human dignity and hope. We hope that the present special session of the Commission on Human Rights will draw on the spiritual resources God offers through Jerusalem and contribute constructively to this end.

Few international conflicts have been so marked by the dominant power's defiance of its obligations under the Charter to abide by decisions of the Security Council and its treaty obligations such as those of the Fourth Geneva Convention. Here as elsewhere self-asserted claims to impunity pose barriers to peace and reconciliation between nations and peoples. Thus the WCC welcomed the important decision of the Security Council in res. 1322 (2000) that stressed "the importance of establishing a mechanism for a speedy and objective inquiry into the tragic events of the last few days with the aim of preventing their repetition". Such an investigation could provide an essential beginning to revealing, sharing and mutual acceptance of the truth about past systematic violations of peoples' rights. Without such a process there can be little hope for justice, peace or reconciliation between Israeli Jews and Palestinian Christians and Muslims within and beyond Israel's legitimate borders.

On 10 October 2000 the General Secretary wrote to Secretary-General Kofi Annan, offering support and prayers for the success of the mission he had undertaken to the region. Dr Raiser said there:

Both sides have suffered from this renewed violent confrontation. But once again it is the Palestinian people, especially Palestinian youth, who pay by far the greater price in God-given life as a result of the disproportionate use of armed force by Israel.

We pray that Prime Minister Barak and President Arafat and all those caught up in the terrible, rising spiral of violence will respond to your initiative and to the appeals of governments and peoples around the world by stepping back from the brink before they and the region as a whole are cast again into the abyss of full-scale war.

This is not a time for ultimatums or threats of more violent acts of retribution, but the hour to join together in declaring a truce and days of public mourning for the victims of the violence on all sides.

WCC initiatives. As noted in the Preliminary Report on Public Issues, the WCC has paid regular visits to Palestine and Israel in light of the VIII Assembly Statement on the Status of Jerusalem. In addition to the steps reported there, the Deputy General Secretary and International Relations staff met in May 2000 with the Vatican State Secretariat to share the WCC's positions on the Status of Jerusalem and discuss common concerns. In June 2000 staff addressed an international human rights conference in Jerusalem on "Freedom of Access to the Holy City of Jerusalem," presenting the WCC principles on the Status of Jerusalem.

As part of its international advocacy efforts, a hearing for the international diplomatic, NGO and ecumenical community and press was held in Geneva on the Geopolitical Situation in Israel-Palestine, where the territorial and water issues at the heart of the final status negotiations were detailed after the breakdown of the Camp David talks.

During Advent, the General Secretary wrote a pastoral letter on behalf of the WCC Officers to the churches and Christian communities in Jerusalem. In that letter Dr Raiser reassured them of WCC's constant prayers, and recalled his Christmas message where he

> ...recalled the centuries-old unwritten rule that at Christmas a cease-fire be observed in all situations of military conflict. In both of these contexts I had particularly in mind our sisters and brothers caught up in the terrible new spiral of violence in Israel and Palestine.

> Clearly a cease-fire is not enough. True peace is our shared goal, a peace built on the foundations of justice, so together with you we long for justice for the Palestinian people. Just peace and an end to the vicious cycle of violence demands a fundamental conversion of the human spirit, a recognition of the God-given dignity and the rights of the other, a change of heart. It was surely this that the Prophet had in mind when he foretold the coming of the Prince of Peace.

The current situation. Two weeks prior to this meeting, a small consultation with experts on and from the region was convened in Geneva by the CCIA to analyze the current situation and assess prospects for peace. In brief summary, participants there concluded the following:

• The present Palestinian Intifadah (uprising) results from the growing frustration of the people with the Oslo Peace Process that after seven years the promises of the Oslo Accords had not borne fruit. The significant compromises made by the Palestinian leadership to meet Israel's demands had not been reciprocated by significant steps on the part of Israel to implement their commitments, but rather by reiterated delays accompanied by ever increasing demands on the Palestine National Authority to provide security, *inter alia*, for illegal Israeli settlers. In the view of many Palestinians, the moribund peace process was dealt a death stroke in Jerusalem with the massive show of armed force at the time of the visit of Ariel Sharon.

- The heart of injustice, and thus the greatest impediment to peace, is the continuing and in fact expanding occupation of Palestinian lands by Israel. Settlements increased rather than decreased during the seven years of Oslo, in violation of both the spirit and the letter of the Accords. Some experts estimate that the number of settlers has grown during this period from 95,000 to over 390,000 today, a growth rate three or four times that of the annual population increase in Israel itself. Rather than decreasing, illegal settlements in the West Bank, Gaza and Jerusalem have also grown rapidly and have in fact accelerated since 1999, together with the construction of even more direct access highways and security roads throughout Palestine. The price continues to be paid by the Palestinians in further displacement, destruction of even more homes, and the alienation of property.

- The last-minute effort of US President Clinton to "make peace" has again revealed that the future status of Jerusalem and the Palestinian refugees' right of return remain still at the center of contention and a motivating factor at the heart of the present Intifadah. The ecumenical positions on Jerusalem are clear and relevant especially in the present context. The WCC also has a long history of involvement with the Palestinian and Jewish peoples, going back to the period even before the Partition and the creation of the State of Israel in 1948. It has reaffirmed the principles embodied in UN General Assembly Resolution 194 of 1948 that held that Palestinian "refugees wishing to return to their homes and live at peace with their neighbors should be permitted to do so at the earliest practicable date, and that compensation should be paid for the property of those choosing not to return and for loss of or damage to property which...should be made good by the government or authorities responsible." The implementation of these provisions is not only a basic human rights concern, but also a necessary precondition for a durable peace.

- The disproportionately violent reaction of Israel to the present Intifadah represents not only a rise in the use of armed force, but seems to respond to a clear strategic plan aimed at strengthening Israeli occupation of land taken by force in 1967, its control over water and other resources in Palestinian lands, and the maintenance of dependency of Palestinians on Israel. That dependency has many facets, but the primary one strengthened in the present strategy is the economic control over Palestine by Israel. A 1997 World Bank report warned that "Since the signing of the Oslo Agreement, the economic situation (of the Palestinians) has continued to deteriorate. The decline in household incomes, a sharp increase in unemployment, and the general broadening of poverty pose serious challenges for economic sustainability." Israel's actions now of blocking Palestinians' access to employment both in the areas under control of the Palestinian National Authority and in Israel has only served to make this lasting situation more acute.

377

- Israel's long-standing practice of sweeping closures of Palestinian areas, curfews and other forms of restrictions of free movement made Palestinians, even those now living under Palestinian control, prisoners in their own land. In recent weeks these practices have been taken to an extreme, blocking access even from one town or neighborhood to another, and thus to schools, medical care and places of worship in an apparent attempt to destroy the very fabric of Palestinian society. Palestinians, through the new Intifadah, signal their unwillingness to continue to live under siege from their powerful neighbor.

- The international community, and particularly the United Nations, has continuing responsibility for the situation in Israel and in Palestine under international law. Israel, often supported by the USA, has managed especially since 1967 to act with virtual impunity, ignoring or openly violating admonitions and resolutions of the UN General Assembly and Security Council. It is clearly time for the international community, and perhaps especially for the European States to assume their responsibilities in a more determined way.

- The violence generated by the present conflict is generally known as a result of massive media coverage of events. The second Intifadah demonstrates that the way to end the violence is not through simplistic appeals for a cease-fire. What is needed is a true change of heart, especially by the occupying power, and the engagement of new negotiations that will take advantage of the undeniable gains achieved by the Oslo Accords. The WCC Executive Committee welcomed the signing of the agreements in Oslo, but at the same time expressed serious reservations about the degree to which they would lead in fact to a just peace. The WCC long expressed the conviction that an effective agreement for the Palestinian-Israeli conflict must be found in the context of an international conference. An urgent task now is to find a new, broader framework of negotiation that builds upon the achievements especially since the Madrid Conference in 1991.

Resolution on ecumenical response to the Palestinian-Israeli conflict
Adopted by the Executive Committee, Geneva, 11-14 September 2001.

The Executive Committee of the World Council of Churches, meeting in Geneva, 11-14 September 2001,

1. *alarmed and dismayed* by the escalation of violence in the Holy Land since the Central Committee adopted its last "Minute on the Situation in the Holy Land After the Outbreak of the Second Palestinian Uprising," in Potsdam, February 2001;

2. *expresses its profound condolences* to all the victims of the conflict, and especially to the families of those who have been killed in both Palestine and Israel;

3. *recalls and reaffirms* the policies of the World Council of Churches on the pursuit of a just peace in the Middle East, and for the status of Jerusalem; and its commitment to active dialogue among Christians, Muslims and Jews;

4. *reiterates* its appeal to the parties directly involved and to the international community to bring an end to aggressive acts and the violence that have again overtaken the Holy Land and threaten international peace and security;

5. *welcomes and affirms* the initiatives undertaken by the General Secretary and staff of the World Council of Churches in implementing the recommendations of the Central Committee in Potsdam by promoting an active, coordinated ecumenical response to end the illegal occupation of Palestine; expressing solidarity with the Churches and Christian Communities most directly affected; and providing auspices for member churches to develop a plan of concerted non-violent ecumenical action to protect vulnerable communities in Palestine and to promote an end to the hostilities;

6. *requests* **the WCC General Secretary and staff** to continue and intensify their facilitating and coordinating role for ecumenical advocacy, networking, communication and active solidarity with the victims of the conflict;

7. *welcomes and endorses* the recommendations of the WCC delegation to Israel and the Occupied Palestinian Territories including Jerusalem in June 2001 as further developed by the International Ecumenical Consultation on the Palestinian - Israeli Conflict held in Geneva, 6-7August 2001:

   7.1. *develop an accompaniment programme* that would include an international ecumenical presence based on the experience of the Christian Peacemakers Team;

   7.2. *call upon the WCC member churches and ecumenical partners,* in the context of the Decade to Overcome Violence: Churches Seeking Reconciliation and Peace, **to focus attention in 2002 on intensive efforts to End the Illegal Occupation of Palestine,** and to participate actively in coordinated ecumenical efforts in this connection;

   7.3. *consider the organization of an International Conference on the Illegal Occupation of Palestine,* bringing together representatives of the churches, ecumenical partner organizations, competent international bodies, scholars and experts in 2002 as part of the special ecumenical focus on efforts to End the Occupation of Palestine;

   7.4. *call for* an international boycott of goods produced in the illegal Israeli settlements in the occupied territories;

   7.5. *call on member churches and Christians* to

7.5.1. *join in non-violent acts of resistance* to the destruction of Palestinian properties and to forced evictions of people from their homes and lands; and

7.5.2. *join in international prayer vigils* to strengthen the "chain of solidarity" with the Palestinian people;

8. *calls upon member churches and ecumenical funding partners* to respond as a matter of urgency to this appeal, and to make available the necessary resources for the WCC to be able to fulfill its tasks and responsibilities in relationship to the proposed coordinated ecumenical action plan;

9. *requests the General Secretary* to bring the present resolution to the attention of member churches, ecumenical partners, competent UN bodies and specialized agencies, regional intergovernmental bodies and to Governments of their member states, and to make a progress report on implementation to the next meeting of the Executive Committee.

Statement on Israel's obligations as occupying power
Issued by the CCIA on the occasion of the Conference of the High Contracting Parties to the Fourth Geneva Convention, Geneva, 5 December 2001.

The Commission of the Churches on International Affairs of the World Council of Churches welcomes today's conference of the High Contracting Parties (hereinafter HCP) to the 1949 Fourth Geneva Convention (hereinafter the Convention) "on measures to enforce the Convention in the Occupied Palestinian Territory, including Jerusalem, and to ensure respect thereof in accordance with common Article 1" (*UNGA RES/ES –10/3, July 1997; 10/4 November 1997; 10/5 March 1998; 10/6 February 1999*).

While the CCIA believes that the reaffirmation by the HCP of the principles defined for the protection of civilian populations under occupation is an important step, the Declaration of 5 December 2001 falls short by failing to recommend concrete measures to ensure the respect of these same principles.

In view of the horrific escalation of the conflict, especially in these last weeks, the CCIA reaffirms once again its endorsement of the conclusions and recommendations of the Human Rights Inquiry Commission of 16 March 2001, which, inter alia, recommended that the reconvened "Conference should establish an effective international mechanism for taking urgent measures needed ... to alleviate the daily suffering of the Palestinian people flowing from the severe breaches of international humanitarian law."

The CCIA notes that the Convention is a cornerstone of international humanitarian law and provides basic legal standards for the treatment of civilians during armed conflict or under occupation. It bans, among other things; indiscriminate use of force against civilians, wanton destruction of property, torture, collective punishment, the annexation of occupied territory, the establishment of settlements on occupied land and requires judicial accountability for those who commit war crimes.

Most importantly CCIA reiterates that the Convention requires that all HCP ensure that the Convention is respected in all circumstances. In this context the CCIA believes that there are immediate moves available to fulfill this obligation, and a meeting of the HCP is the first effective step towards achieving that goal.

The CCIA reaffirms previous statements of its governing bodies, where it highlighted grave breaches of the Convention by Israel against civilians, including repressive forms of collective punishments, restriction of freedom of movement including access to the Holy sites, the bombing and shelling of civilian neighborhoods and the destruction of property including tens of thousands of olive trees and the denial of access to timely medical assistance.

The CCIA once again calls upon Israel to abide scrupulously by its legal obligations and responsibilities as a signatory to the Fourth Geneva Convention to put an end to the ongoing violations in the Occupied Palestinian Territories, including the military occupation itself. In addition, it restates its position that Israel's repeated defiance of international law, its continuing occupation and the impunity it has so long enjoyed are the fundamental causes of the present violence and threaten peace and security of both peoples.

The CCIA appeals to the international community to fulfill its obligations under international humanitarian law. This it should do by ensuring that Israel complies with the requirements of international law so that the international community is not complicit in its violations of human rights but is instrumental in ensuring the protection of all civilians.

As people of faith we uphold and defend the sanctity of all life, both Palestinian and Israeli and cannot remain silent in the face of suffering, insecurity and fear of both peoples.

Therefore we reiterate the WCC Executive Committee resolution of September 14, 2001 which calls the WCC member churches, ecumenical partners and Christians around the world, in the context of the Decade to Overcome Violence: Churches Seeking Reconciliation and Peace (2001-2010), to focus attention in 2002 on intensive efforts to End the Illegal Occupation of Palestine, and to participate actively in coordinated ecumenical efforts, among others, to support the newly established Ecumenical Monitoring Programme in Palestine and Israel (EMPPI); to join in non-violent acts of resistance to the destruction of Palestinian properties and to forced evictions of people from their homes and lands; an international boycott of goods produced in the illegal Israeli settlements in the occupied territories; and in international prayer vigils to strengthen the "chain of solidarity" with the Palestinian people, and for a just peace in the Middle East.

Appeal for urgent action

Open letter to the member churches, regional and national councils of churches and ecumenical partner organizations, 15 March 2002.

Dear sisters and brothers in Christ,

We have all been watching with growing alarm as hour by hour the violent conflict between Palestinians and Israelis intensifies. The killings, bombings and destruction continue to escalate in defiance of the repeated admonitions and appeals of the United Nations, of governments and of people around the world. Israel is rapidly re-occupying Palestinian lands by military force, raiding Palestinian refugee camps and engaging in mass indiscriminate detentions of civilian inhabitants under the most degrading circumstances. Attacks on medical and rescue staff, coupled with the severe new restrictions on access to hospitals and other medical facilities, add to the systematic violations of human rights and international humanitarian law. In his address to the United Nations Security Council on March 12, Secretary General Kofi Annan emphasized the critical need to end the illegal occupation and the violence.

The WCC is receiving regularly eye-witness reports from Palestinian church workers about invasions, occupation and major physical damage or destruction of church-related and internationally supported schools and other facilities. A number of statements and appeals have also come to us from the Middle East Council of Churches Department for Service to Palestinian Refugees (MECC/DSPR) and from other Christian, Muslim and Jewish religious groups and secular Palestinian and Israeli organizations pleading for determined international action, including the deployment of UN monitors, to put a stop to the escalating violence and to address dire humanitarian needs.

The thirteen Patriarchs and Heads of Churches and Christian Communities in Jerusalem issued a statement on March 9 (attached) expressing their deep distress at the increasing bloodshed, joining their voices with every Palestinian and Israeli seeking a just peace. Saying that "Israeli security is dependant on Palestinian freedom and justice", they call upon Israeli citizens and the Israeli government to "stop all kinds of destruction and death caused by the heavy Israeli weaponry [for the] way the present Israeli government is dealing with the situation makes neither for security nor for a just peace". The church leaders also urge the Palestinian people to put "an end to every kind of violent response", reiterating that the way to peace is through negotiations. They appeal too, and in particular, to the churches around the world to contact their respective governments to seek their active involvement in the quest for peace.

The WCC, Action by Churches Together (ACT), APRODEV (WCC-related development organizations in Europe) and the MECC/DSPR are all seeking to respond to the humanitarian crisis, and all need your help and support. Above all, however, an immediate common effort is required to break through the stagnation of the international community and to encourage action that corresponds to words. More than ever we must hear and respond to the cries of the churches and bring them to the urgent attention of Christians, our communities, our media and our governments.

Our united message is clearly stated by the WCC Executive and Central Committees: the violence of the illegal occupation of Palestine must come to an end. The occupation is at the root of the violence. Unless this is addressed, there can be little hope for a just and lasting peace. We therefore urge you to strengthen your efforts related to the 2002 focus of the Decade to Overcome Violence: "End the Illegal Occupation of Palestine".

The WCC has also initiated the Ecumenical Accompaniment Programme in Palestine and Israel (EAPPI). Through this the Council is organizing a continuing international ecumenical presence in Palestine to monitor and report on human rights violations, offer protection of individuals and communities and accompany local Christian and Muslim Palestinians and Israeli peace activists in their efforts of non-violent resistance to occupation, closures, and destruction of Palestinian homes and sources of livelihood. Some Christians and others are already present and have remained through the current violence. It is hoped that others will join soon. We urge you to contact your own national organizing bodies to offer participation or other forms of support.

In the present circumstances, however, this is not enough to provide the immediate protection needed. Thus we urge you to apply pressure on your governments to support proposals that have been brought to the UN Security Council, and encourage the rapid deployment of an intergovernmental monitoring body in Palestine.

The churches of Jerusalem have also asked for prayers for peace. The global fellowship of churches can join together in special prayer vigils and services of worship with the Christians of Palestine. A collection of prayers from the local churches has been published by the WCC for use on such occasions. These prayers and other materials related to the WCC initiatives are available at www.wcc-coe.org or by mail upon request.

We are not alone in our faith commitments to the peoples caught up in this tragic conflict. Thus wherever possible, we encourage you to engage in dialogue and common actions with your Jewish, Muslim and other neighbors who share a common longing for peace and justice.

This terrible tragedy of violence and injustice must end. To be silent now can only be seen as complicity with the violence, the systematic abuses of human rights and the refusal, especially by the State of Israel, to abide by its obligations under international law. Now is the time for each one of us to speak out and act, fulfilling our Christian vocation as peacemakers.

Dwain C. Epps
Director
Commission of the Churches on International Affairs

Appeal to the European Union to take a leading role in seeking a just and sustainable peace in the Middle East

Letter to foreign ministers of EU countries on the eve of their meeting in Luxembourg, 12 April 2002.

Your Excellency,

I write to express appreciation for the efforts you and your European Union counterparts have undertaken recently to bring an end to the Palestinian/Israeli conflict. In particular, we welcome the Joint Statement of the EU, the US, Russia and the UN on the escalating confrontation in the Middle East issued yesterday following their meeting in Madrid. At the same time, we deeply regret the slow progress made by the international community in obliging the two sides, and in particular Israel, to comply with UNSC resolutions 1397 of 12 March, 1402 of 30 March and 1403 of 4 April. As a result, hundreds more Palestinian lives have been lost and untold additional damage done to Palestinian homes, institutions and infrastructure. The cycle of violence has not been halted, claiming an unconscionable number of Israeli lives as well.

The international community bears full, continuing responsibility for the effective implementation of UN resolutions since the adoption by the UNGA of the Plan of Partition in resolution 181 of 1947. Yet it has consistently allowed the State of Israel to ignore or openly violate successive General Assembly and Security Council resolutions with virtual impunity. For the international rule of law to be universally respected, and for the decisions of the United Nations to be credible, their selective application must be avoided at all costs.

In its statement to the current session of the UN Commission on Human Rights, the European Union has made its position on the Palestinian/Israeli conflict and its causes clear in a way that we fully support. Now measures need urgently to be taken that translate declarations into actions to oblige compliance with the expressed will of the international community. This applies particularly to the repeated demand that Israel withdraw all its forces from Palestinian territories immediately and unconditionally. We therefore urge you to take further, decisive steps in this direction at the forthcoming meeting of EU Foreign Ministers along the lines of the resolution adopted by the European Parliament on 10 April. Specifically, we urge you to consider initiatives that take account of Article 2 of the EU-Israel Euro-Mediterranean Association Agreement that conditions "relations between parties, as well as all the provisions of the Agreement itself...on respect for human rights and democratic principles, which guides their internal and international policy and constitutes an essential element of this Agreement" and suspend this agreement until such time that Israel complies with these provisions; review all forms of military cooperation with the State of Israel including instituting a strict arms embargo; affirm the willingness of the European Union to participate in an international mission or third-party mechanism on the ground to oversee Israeli compliance with the Security Council's demand that it withdraw immediately and completely from Palestinian territories, and Palestinian compliance with the demand to cease all further terrorist attacks against the Israeli population.

We believe that the European Union should commit itself to taking a leading role in seeking a just and sustainable peace. This should apply not only to the immediate measures recommended above, but as EU High Representative Javier Solana told the European Parliament early this week, EU states must move rapidly towards addressing and removing the causes of this and future crises by pressing for an end to occupation and the establishment of two states within guaranteed and secure borders; proposing modalities for a new negotiation framework and participating fully in its elaboration and implementation; participating fully in efforts to reconstruct the Palestinian Authority's capacity to administer the territories under its control and to construct the Palestinian State.

We make these appeals for prompt action not as retribution against any party, but rather in the spirit of the WCC's Decade to Overcome Violence, that calls for non-violent means of resolving conflict and the application of restorative justice. In so doing, we echo the appeals and join with the intentions of the Heads of Christian churches and communities in Jerusalem who have consistently called for an end to violence on all sides and have offered their good offices in the interest of a durable, negotiated settlement.

Responding to the churches' urgent appeals, the World Council of Churches has launched a campaign this year "To End the Illegal Occupation of Palestine: Support a Just Peace in the Middle East." In relation to this campaign, we have also established an Ecumenical Accompaniment Programme in Palestine and Israel in order to manifest the active solidarity of Christians around the world with the people living in the Holy Land at this critical time. The churches of Europe have taken a significant lead in these initiatives, seeking to embody our shared hopes and aspirations for peace with justice for all the peoples in these lands where our Lord and Saviour Jesus Christ was received as the Prince of Peace.

The European Community has taken the lead and been generous in its support for Israel and the Palestinian people in the past. In particular, it has supported Palestinian aspirations as they have struggled for their rights, to establish their own independent state, and to rebuild and develop their war-torn lives and land. Much of what they have done with your help has again been destroyed. We sincerely hope that you will face up boldly to this new challenge and prove your willingness to provide badly needed new leadership for peace and a new future. We assure you of our constant prayers and support in your efforts to that end.

Respectfully yours,

Konrad Raiser
General Secretary

385

Statement on the ecumenical response to the Israeli-Palestinian conflict in the Holy Land
Adopted by the Central Committee, Geneva, 26 August - 3 September 2002.

The Central Committee of the World Council of Churches, meeting in Geneva, 26 August to 3 September 2002:

Recalling its "Minute on the Situation in the Holy Land after the Outbreak of the Second Palestinian Uprising", adopted at its last meeting (Potsdam, February 2001) in which the Central Committee expressed
> its deep sadness and grave concern at the new escalation of violence in the Palestinian autonomous and occupied territories as well as Israel over the last four months that has claimed a terrible toll of human life;

Alarmed and dismayed at the escalation of violence over the past twenty-three months that has claimed hundreds of lives in Palestine and Israel, and that has created the worst humanitarian catastrophe for the Palestinian population in recent history;

Expressing once again its grief and profound condolences to all the victims of the conflict, and especially to the families of those who have been killed in both Israel and the occupied Palestinian territories;

Profoundly regretting the inability or unwillingness of the international community, especially the governments most directly concerned, to respond to repeated appeals to establish a presence in the area to bring the parties to the conflict into compliance with the resolutions of the UN Security Council, thus allowing illegal actions to continue and a climate of mistrust, fear and hatred to grow;

Reaffirming its conviction that a just and lasting solution of the Arab and Israeli conflict must be sought through active negotiations based on United Nations Security Council resolutions 242 (1967) and 338 (1973);

Reiterating its appeal that the universally accepted norms of the Fourth Geneva Convention, which is the cornerstone of international humanitarian law and provides basic legal standards for the treatment of civilians during armed conflict or under occupation, be respected in all circumstances;

Reaffirming the right of an occupied people to struggle against injustice by non-violent means in order to gain freedom;

Reiterating its support for Israeli and Palestinian individuals and organizations who reject the logic of violence and occupation and are striving together for justice, peace, security, mutual understanding and reconciliation between their peoples;

Reaffirming the need for full respect of the Holy Places, and *condemning* all actions that violate them;

Condemning the occupation and misuse of church or other religious buildings and sites for military or other purposes inimical to their religious vocation;

386

Reiterating its support for the churches and Christian communities of the Holy Land as guardians of the Holy Places, for their efforts to sustain and serve their communities and their witness as peacemakers;

Reiterating its long-standing commitment to active dialogue and cooperation among Christians, Muslims *and* Jews;

Reiterating its conviction that Jerusalem must remain an open and inclusive city with free access assured for the Palestinian people and shared in terms of sovereignty and citizenship between the State of Israel and the future State of Palestine, and that Jerusalem can be a source of peace, stability and coexistence rather than of division and conflict;

1   *Calls again and insistently for* the immediate withdrawal of the Israeli occupying forces from Palestinian territories, to end its illegal occupation of Palestinian territories;

2   *Calls upon Israel,* the occupying power, to abide scrupulously by its legal obligations and its responsibilities under the Fourth Geneva Convention relative to the Protection of Civilian Persons in Time of War of 12 August 1949;

3   *Receives with appreciation* the report of the actions taken by the Council in pursuing the recommendations of the Potsdam meeting of the Central Committee;

4   *Endorses* the Executive Committee Resolution on Ecumenical Response to the Palestinian-Israeli Conflict of September 2001 and welcomes the considerable efforts of the General Secretary and staff to implement it;

5   *Reaffirms, in the context of the Decade to Overcome Violence,* the belief Christians share with Jews and Muslims that all human life is sacred in the eyes of God, and that the taking of human life is contrary to the moral and ethical teachings of the three monotheistic faiths;

6   *Joins its voice* with those many Christians, Muslims and Jews in the region and around the world who have strongly deplored all acts of violence related to this conflict, including:

   • Israel's military invasion and reoccupation of the Palestinian territories, extra-judicial executions of Palestinian leaders, killing of Palestinian civilians, application of collective punishments, and destruction of Palestinian homes and property in Israel and the occupied territories; and

   • all acts of terror against civilians in Israel and in the occupied territories, including especially the growing and deeply troubling practice of organized and indiscriminate suicide bombings;

7   *Calls upon* all concerned parties, including Israelis and Palestinians, to ensure the safety of all civilians, and to respect the universally accepted norms of international humanitarian law;

8 *Calls upon the High Contracting Parties to the Fourth Geneva Convention* to enforce their declaration of 5 December 2001 in which they

call upon the Occupying Power to fully and effectively respect the (Convention) in the Occupied Palestinian Territory, including East Jerusalem, and to refrain from perpetrating any violation of the Convention, …(and) reaffirm the illegality of the settlements in the said territories and of the extension thereof, and the need to safeguard and guarantee the rights and access of all inhabitants to the Holy Places;

9 *Calls insistently upon the international community*, especially the Quartet (United Nations, European Union, USA and Russian Federation), to take a more active, determined, objective and consistent role in mediating between the two parties based on the relevant UN resolutions and to do its utmost to stop further bloodshed and suffering;

10 *Urges the Government of Israel* to recognize the election of His Beatitude Patriarch Irineos I as the head of the Greek Orthodox Patriarchate of Jerusalem;

11 *Calls on* all authorities concerned not to interfere in the internal affairs of the churches;

12 *Welcomes* **the positive response** of many member churches and ecumenical partners to the call to join together, in the context of the *Decade to Overcome Violence: Churches Seeking Reconciliation and Peace (2001-2010)*, in an action-oriented ecumenical campaign to end the illegal occupation of Palestine, in support of reconciliation between Israelis, Palestinians and others in the Middle East and their coexistence in justice and peace, and **urges others** to join them in:

a. Supporting the *Ecumenical Accompaniment Programme in Palestine and Israel (EAPPI)*, as a concrete manifestation of Christian solidarity through active presence and witness of a non-violent resistance to the occupation of Palestine, working towards public awareness and policy change through advocacy;

b. Calling for the suspension of the EU-Israel Euro-Mediterranean Association Agreement that conditions "relations between parties, as well as the provisions of the Agreement itself on respect for human rights and democratic principles which guides their internal and international policy and constitutes an essential element of this Agreement", until such time that Israel complies with these provisions;

c. Pressuring governments, in particular the USA, to review economic aid to the State of Israel and to halt all forms of military cooperation with the State of Israel including instituting a strict arms embargo, until such time that Israel complies with UN Security Council Resolutions

d. Providing generous financial resources towards the ecumenical humanitarian and human rights efforts that seek to respond to the ever increasing human suffering;

e. Praying together for peace and for all those who work for peace and an end to all forms of violence in the Holy Land, seeking to embody our shared hopes and aspirations for peace with justice for all the peoples in these lands where our Lord and Saviour Jesus Christ was received as the Prince of Peace.

JERUSALEM

Minute on Jerusalem
Adopted by the Central Committee, Geneva, 26 August – 3 September 1999.

The Central Committee of the WCC, meeting in Geneva, 26 August - 3 September 1999, has received with gratitude the (attached) letter signed and sealed by the Patriarchs and Heads of the Christian Communities in Jerusalem, addressed to the General Secretary on August 12, 1999. This letter expresses the appreciation of the Church of Jerusalem for the WCC Statement on the Status of Jerusalem, adopted at the Eighth Assembly in Harare, Zimbabwe, in December 1998, recognizing that it will help strengthen the Christian witness in the Holy Land and promote the achievement of an agreement on the status of Jerusalem which affirms the principle that it should be shared and include two peoples and three religions.

The Central Committee requests the General Secretary to respond to the Patriarchs and Heads of Christian Communities, reaffirming the WCC's conviction that Jerusalem is central to the faith of Christians and Christians' responsibility to pray and work for the peace of Jerusalem.

Letter from Jerusalem

Revd Dr Konrad Raiser
General Secretary
World Council of Churches
Geneva

Jerusalem, 12 August 1999

Dear Dr Raiser,

First and foremost, we would like to express our appreciation to the World Council of Churches for its Statement on the Status of Jerusalem that was adopted during its VIII General Assembly in Harare, Zimbabwe, in December 1998.

Based on the spirit of our Memorandum on the Significance of Jerusalem for Christians, dated 14 November 1994, this statement will help strengthen the Christian witness in this land as much as promote the status of this holy city as being one that includes its two peoples and three religions.

We strongly encourage the World Council of Churches - through its Central Committee and its other clusters and departments - to ensure that the pivotal issue of Jerusalem stays on its agenda. We also trust that the on-going cooperation between the Churches of Jerusalem and the WCC be maintained so that the voice of the Church of Jerusalem could be heard by all church constituencies world-wide.

As the Holy Land prepares itself to usher in a fresh millennium, We all pray and hope that Jerusalem will truly become faithful to its calling as a City of Peace.

Yours in Christ,

+Diodoros I
Greek Orthodox Patriarch

+Michel Sabbah
Latin Patriarch

+Torkom Manoogian
Armenian Patriarch

Giovanni Batistelli
Custos of the Holy Land

+Anba Abraham
Coptic Orthodox Archbishop

+Mar Swerios Malki Murad
Syrian Orthodox Archbishop

+Abba Gabriel
Ethiopian Orthodox Archbishop

+Riah Abu Al-Assal
Anglican Bishop

+Lufti Lahham
Greek Catholic Patriarchal Vicar

+Mounib Younan
Lutheran Bishop

+Boulos Sayyah
Maronite PSatriarchal Vicar

+Boutros Abdel Ahhad
Syrian Catholic Patriarchal Vicar

(Absent due to illness)
+Andre Bedoghlyian
Armenian Catholic Patriarchal Vicar

Resolution on Jerusalem Final Status Negotiations
Adopted by the Executive Committee, Geneva, 26-29 September 2000.

Recalling the appeal of the WCC Eighth Assembly (Harare, 1998) that negotiations on the future status of Jerusalem should "be undertaken without further delay and considered to be part of rather than a product of a comprehensive settlement for the region;"

Noting that negotiations on the final status on Jerusalem have begun; and

Sharing the conviction expressed by Their Beatitudes the Patriarchs and Heads of Churches and Christian Communities in Jerusalem in their statement of 26 September 2000 "that the political negotiators (must) take all necessary steps to (conclude them in a way that would) best ensure true peace with true justice and security for the 'two peoples and three religions' of this land – Palestinians and Israelis, Jews, Christians and Muslims alike."

The Executive Committee, meeting in Geneva, 26-29 September 2000:

Expresses its appreciation for the comprehensive analysis of issues related to the present final status negotiations contained in the document, "Background paper on the Status of Jerusalem – December 1998 to the Present," prepared by International Relations staff, and commends it to the churches and ecumenical bodies for study and appropriate action;

Commends the initiatives taken in follow-up to the Statement on the Status of Jerusalem adopted by the Eighth Assembly;

Firmly believes that Jerusalem can be a source of peace, stability and coexistence rather than of division and conflict that destroy human dignity and hope;

Reaffirms the principles contained in that statement as particularly relevant in the context of the present negotiations;

Remains convinced of the urgency of pursuing negotiations on Jerusalem based on these principles;

Encourages the parties to have the courage to abandon narrow, exclusive claims in favour of efforts to build an open, inclusive and shared city where free access to Holy Places and freedom of worship is assured for people of all faiths;

Reiterates its conviction "that the solution to the question of Jerusalem is in the first place the responsibility of the parties directly involved, but that the Christian churches and the Jewish and Muslim religious communities have a central role to play in relation to (the) negotiations;"

Welcomes in this connection the recent initiatives taken by Heads of Churches of Jerusalem and the supportive steps taken by church leaders in the USA; and

391

Urges all member churches

- to bring the WCC's Eighth Assembly Statement on the Status of Jerusalem to the attention of their governments;
- to speak out boldly and in unison for the application of these principles; and
- to remain constant in prayer and in solidarity with the local churches for a just peace in Jerusalem and for the whole of the Middle East.

Advent message to the churches and Christian communities of Jerusalem

Letter from the General Secretary to the patriarchs and heads of Christian communities in Jerusalem, 12 December 2000.

Your Beatitudes, Graces and Eminences,

The Officers of the World Council of Churches, meeting on the eve of the Advent Season, have once again turned their thoughts to you and all the people of Palestine. They have asked that I write you to assure you of their and the World Council of Churches' constant prayers. I do so with a heavy heart, deeply conscious of your pain and suffering in these days when you mourn the deaths of so many of your children and friends; when Palestinians suffer the destruction of many more of their homes and pass once again through the valley of the shadow of violence and death. Nor can we ignore the victims on the Israeli side of the continuing conflict.

In my Christmas message I have pointed out that the World Council of Churches will soon launch the Decade to Overcome Violence: Churches seeking reconciliation and peace. I also recalled the centuries-old unwritten rule that at Christmas a cease-fire be observed in all situations of military conflict. Here I had particularly in mind our sisters and brothers caught up in the new spiral of violence in Israel and Palestine.

Desirable as it would be, a cease-fire is clearly not enough. Our shared goal must be true peace, a peace built on the foundations of justice. Together with you, therefore, we long for justice for the Palestinian people. Just peace and an end to the vicious cycle of violence is more than an urgent political necessity. It confronts us with the call to repentance and a change of heart, the readiness to recognize the God-given dignity and the rights of the other. It was surely this transformation that the Prophet had in mind when he foretold the coming of the Prince of Peace.

In these days Christians around the world prepare to celebrate the birth of the Christ child, confessing anew our faith in God who humbled himself and took on human flesh in order that we might be reconciled to God and with one another. Many will draw hope once again from the song of the Virgin Mary, praising God who "has regarded the lowly estate of his handmaiden", and saying,

his mercy is on those who fear him from generation to generation.
He has shown strength with his arm, he has scattered the proud in the imagination of their hearts,
he has put down the mighty from their thrones,
and exalted those of low degree;
he has filled the hungry with good things, and the rich he has sent empty away.

For two millennia Christians have turned at this time of year to the Holy Place of the manger, Bethlehem, to celebrate the birth of Jesus. Many have longed once to make the pilgrimage to the manger, there to kneel down before the birthplace of the Christ child. This year especially, millions anticipated making this journey, and you have gone to great lengths to prepare hospitality for them. Tragically, the present circumstances have rendered virtually impossible such pilgrimages and even those of Christians in Palestine itself.

Nevertheless, the bonds of faith and love cannot be broken by violence and war. You are not alone in this tragic time. We and other Christians around the world will be making a pilgrimage of the heart to the manger, surrounding and sustaining you now and always in prayer.

May the hope that abounds in this time of preparations for the Holy Feast of Christmas give birth to a new day of peace and joy and prosperity for you and all who live in the land which has been forever blessed by the coming of Christ.

Yours ever in Emmanuel,

Konrad Raiser
General Secretary

LEBANON

Statement on the Israeli withdrawal from South Lebanon
Issued by the General Secretary in Geneva, 26 May 2000.

The World Council of Churches has closely followed the events in Lebanon since the 1978 Israeli invasion of the country that led to massive loss of human lives and continuing tragedy in the region. The Council on several occasions expressed its concern at these developments and called on the parties in Lebanon to renounce violence and seek harmonious community relations in order to work together for a united and sovereign Lebanon committed to justice, development and peace in the Middle East.

The World Council of Churches shares in the jubilation of the Lebanese people at the withdrawal of the Israeli security forces. The action of the Israeli government is in keeping with the spirit of the United Nations Resolutions 425 and 426, the implementation of which have been a long-standing demand of the Council. We hope and pray that this significant development will enhance internal unity and a

393

spirit of cooperation amongst the people of Lebanon, who have suffered much as a result of the ongoing tensions and conflict in the region.

The Israeli withdrawal from Lebanon by itself will not bring the much needed stability and peace in the region, though it could be a step in that direction. A comprehensive, just and lasting peace can only be achieved through the full implementation of all relevant UN Resolutions. It is our hope that the implementation of UN Resolutions 425 and 426 will result in ensuring progress in the remaining tracks of the Middle East peace process.

The Council appreciates and is supportive of the United Nations' efforts to stabilize the situation and to assist the Government of Lebanon in ensuring the return of its effective authority in the territory from which the Israeli troops have just withdrawn. During the transition period it is essential that the lives and properties of the civilian population on both sides of the international border be duly safeguarded. Towards this end all parties concerned should exercise restraint and avoid recourse to violence that could lead to an escalation of the present tension and conflict.

The World Council of Churches welcomes the release of the Lebanese detained as hostages by the Israeli Security Forces. The Council while welcoming the resettlement of expelled Lebanese families expresses its concern about the ultimate fate of the stateless Palestinian refugees in Lebanon and reiterates their right of return to their homeland.

We are also encouraged by the assurances of the President of Lebanon, H. E. Mr Lahoud that the Lebanese authorities would immediately begin to rebuild this devastated area.

The member churches of the World Council have played a significant role in relation to the conflict in the Middle East. The Council is committed to stand in solidarity with its member churches in the region, especially in Lebanon, in their ministry to rebuild and establish peace and reconciliation in their land. The Council calls on its members to take an active part in the reconstruction and rebuilding of Lebanon as well in peace-building initiatives. The relief and humanitarian assistance arm of the Council, Action by Churches Together (ACT) is in the process of issuing an appeal in this connection.

PALESTINE

Statement of support at the Bethlehem 2000 International Conference
Presentation by the Director of the CCIA to the conference convened at FAO headquarters by the UN Special Committee on Palestine, Rome, 18-19 February 1999.

Mr Chairman, President Arafat, Excellencies, Friends,

I have the honor to bring you the greetings of Dr Konrad Raiser, General Secretary of the World Council of Churches on the important occasion of this Conference organized by the Committee on the Exercise of the Inalienable Rights of the Palestinian People to mobilize international public opinion in pursuit of the aims outlined in Res. 53/27 of the United Nations General Assembly.

The World Council of Churches has warmly endorsed and joined in the appeal for the Bethlehem 2000 Project. In his letter to President Arafat on the occasion of the Brussels Participants Conference, Dr Raiser underscored the attachment to Bethlehem of the WCC and its 330 member churches in some 125 countries around the world, and our commitment to the Palestinian people who call it home.

We have long supported these living stones in affirmation and in deed, Dr Raiser wrote. For fifty years we have been engaged in support to refugees and displaced persons, the building of significant educational, medical and social institutions and facilities. We have made important financial contributions to Palestinian cultural, economic and social development programs.

Thus as the end of a century which has brought so much pain and suffering to the Palestinian people draws near we are acutely aware of the urgent, continuing development needs of Palestine. ... This is undoubtedly the time for the international community to commit itself also through generous multi-lateral support for Palestine, its infrastructure and its people. Development and peace do indeed go hand in hand. The Bethlehem 2000 Project has the potential of being a significant stepping-stone to a new millennium and a new era of peace in the Holy Land.

Responsible tourism

Long ago, the World Council of Churches recognized that while thousands of Christians belonging to our member churches gained spiritual nourishment and renewal from pilgrimages to holy places or visits to biblical sites in Israel and Palestine, very few such visitors were exposed to the daily life of the Palestinian society. Thus, for more than two decades, the WCC has supported, in cooperation with the Middle East Council of Churches, programs of responsible tourism to the Holy Land to remedy this situation wherever possible. Through such visits, very many Christians around the world have gained deeper insights not only into their faith, but also a greater understanding of the socio-political and faith realities of the Holy Land. New, strong bonds of friendship and solidarity have been established between visiting Christians and their Palestinian brothers and sisters. As a result, many have become deeply dedicated to the pursuit of peace with justice.

We are encouraging member churches to build upon this concrete experience, and to participate in the Bethlehem 2000 Project as an opportunity to expand upon and deepen the awareness and relationships which have been established. Recognizing the enormity of the task, churches around the world are seeking ways to assist the local Christian communities in and around Bethlehem to make their own contributions to the success of the Project.

Pilgrimages for Peace

Two thousand years after the birth of Jesus, who, Christians believe, was proclaimed by the prophets as the Prince of Peace, the land of his forebears still longs for the peace Jesus taught, a peace built upon love and forgiveness. Mistrust and fear prevail between Palestine and Israel. Economic disparity, struggles over control of vital land and resources continue to sow the seeds of animosity, violence and insecurity for all.

A just and lasting peace must be built upon the pillars of

- comprehensive economic development based on open borders and free movement of people, goods and capital,
- wide-ranging people-to-people contact at all levels of Israeli and Palestinian society, and
- political agreements answering to the national and strategic interests of both peoples.

We remain convinced that there is a will among people in both Israel and Palestine, among faithful Jews, Muslims and Christians, to strengthen these foundations of peace. Sadly, however, Bethlehem risks on this occasion to become not a universal symbol of peace, but rather a focus of continuing confrontation. Israel's declared intentions to expand the Har Homa settlement, and to exploit the millennium celebrations at the expense of Bethlehem are deeply troubling.

The Bethlehem 2000 Project should not be seen as a threat or as an invitation to competition, but rather as a welcome opportunity to build strong foundations for peace by narrowing the economic gap between Israel and Palestine. The building of a solid, self-sufficient economic infrastructure for Palestine with its promise of well-being and economic equality for Palestinians should be viewed as an opportunity for Israel, a chance for peaceful cooperation.

We therefore hope that tourists, pilgrims, Christian and Muslim Palestinians, Jews, and people of other faiths will have free access to the celebrations in Bethlehem in the year 2000, and that this will be a period in which people from Israel, Palestine and many other lands who love and pursue peace will be able to meet and build upon their shared aspirations.

Concluding remarks

It is, therefore, Mr Chairman, Excellencies, Friends, with these hopes and aspirations in mind that the World Council of Churches again offers its encouragement and support for the Bethlehem 2000 Project. We shall be encouraging Christians from around the world to take this opportunity to visit Bethlehem as peacemakers and bridge-builders, on a pilgrimage of faith, bringing with them a message of love and hope that the message of Jesus the Christ, the Prince of Peace may be realized in our time.

Message of condolences on the death of Faissal Husseini

Letter to H.E. Mr Nabil Ramlawi, Permanent Observer of Palestine to the United Nations in Geneva, 6 June 2001.

Your Excellency,

On behalf of the General Secretary of the World Council of Churches, Rev. Dr Konrad Raiser, I would like to extend our heartfelt condolences to the Palestinian people, the Jerusalemites and Husseini family on the sad occasion of Mr Faissal Husseini's sudden death.

We join the numerous voices from all over the world in our praise and appreciation for what Mr Husseini believed and stood for throughout his lifetime. The WCC benefited immensely from his wisdom and expertise, especially in considering policy positions on the future status of his beloved city of Jerusalem. His commitment to justice and sharing, coexistence and non-violence will always remain with us as his true legacy.

With all peace-loving people of this world we mourn the loss of this great leader and pray that the Palestinian and Israeli people, and the Jerusalemites in particular, will be able to keep his memory alive by following in his courageous steps until Jerusalem really becomes the city of all its inhabitants.

For the writers of the New Testament, Jerusalem represents a symbol for the new creation, for the promise of the fullness of life in community where God will wipe away all tears, and *"there shall be no more death or mourning, crying out or pain, for the former world has passed away."* (Rev. 21:4)

Respectfully Yours,

Salpy Eskidjian
Programme Executive for Middle East
Affairs
International Relations

397

CANADA

Legal claims against the federal government and the churches arising from past practices in residential schools for children of native peoples
Letter from the General Secretary to member churches in Canada: Anglican Church of Canada, Presbyterian Church of Canada, United Church of Canada, 5 July 2000.

Dear Friends,

Aware of the critical consequences for your churches of claims resulting from the past practices in residential schools that have been filed against the federal government and against your churches, we wish to express our ecumenical solidarity with you in your efforts to find just and viable responses that would contribute to healing. We are reassured to see the strength of ecumenism in Canada as we read of your and other churches' efforts to work together in confronting this challenge in a responsible way.

We believe that churches around the world have much to learn from your witness as you explore alternatives to adversarial court proceedings to bring about needed reconciliation, and as you consider the possible consequences for the churches. The fact that you began to confront the painful legacy of the residential schools and showed your willingness early on to confront openly the churches' role in a system which caused significant damage to aboriginal peoples gives credibility to your efforts now. You have publicly admitted and apologized for your part in this tragedy, often as instruments of the Canadian Government's educational system. You have taken a lead in supporting the First Nations' claims for justice. You have taken significant steps to address the discrimination against native peoples in the lives of your own churches. These are necessary first steps towards reconciliation. The next step is compensation for the harm done. You are not alone in having to struggle with the moral, ethical, theological and financial implications of the enormous claims involved in this case. Churches in many parts of the world are likely soon to have to confront similar challenges. We hope to learn from and share your experience as you seek ways to build reconciling communities through mediation and other creative alternatives which favor restorative justice over acts of retribution.

We do not pretend to understand all the complexities of the legal issues involved or to advise you on how to proceed. But we wish to assure you that our thoughts and prayers are with you as you seek faithfully to contribute to healing the wounds of the past and to stand with the Indigenous Peoples of Canada in their continuing struggles for justice. As Paul wrote to the Corinthians, "If one member [of the body] suffers, all suffer together with it; if one member is honored, all rejoice together with it."

Yours in Christ,

Konrad Raiser
General Secretary

UNITED STATES OF AMERICA

Message to the churches after the bombing attacks of September 11th

Sent from the meeting of the Executive Committee, Geneva, 11 September 2001

News of the terrible tragedies in New York and Washington, D.C. has just arrived here in Geneva where the Executive Committee of the World Council of Churches (WCC) is currently meeting.

At their request and on their behalf, and for all our member churches around the world, I wish to express to the people of the United States, their churches and religious bodies, and to the president and other leaders of the nation, our profound shock and our heartfelt sympathy.

You are all in our prayers. We pray especially for the victims of these tragedies and for their families and loved ones. We pray for those providing emergency services. We pray for the leaders of your nation. May God give them courage and wisdom in this terrible hour. We fervently pray that this is the end of terror, and implore those responsible to desist from any further such acts of inhumanity.

Lord, have mercy; Christ, have mercy; Lord, have mercy. Amen.

Rev. Dr Konrad Raiser
General Secretary

Open letter to the member churches in the United States
Geneva, September 20, 2001.

Dear Sisters and Brothers in Christ,

Grace and peace to you in our One Lord and Savior, Jesus Christ.

In the brief message I sent you on behalf of the Executive Committee of the World Council of Churches on that tragic morning of September 11, I assured you of the prayers of your sister churches around the world. That was an affirmation of faith. Now you have had the evidence of those prayers in an almost unprecedented flood of messages of compassion, love and solidarity from churches in East, West, North and South.

This expression of unity in such a time of trial gives flesh to the words Paul wrote to the Church in Corinth: "Blessed be the God and Father of our Lord Jesus Christ, the Father of mercies and God of all comfort, who comforts us in all our affliction, so that we may be able to comfort those who are in any affliction, with the comfort with which we ourselves are comforted by God. For as we share abundantly in Christ's sufferings, so through Christ we share abundantly in comfort too... Our hope for you is unshaken, for we know that as you share in our sufferings, you will also share in our comfort" (II Cor. 1:3-7).

As I write to you now, ten days after the tragedy, the words in the Revelation to John addressed to the angel of the church in Ephesus also come to mind. "I know your works, your toil and your patient endurance... I know you are enduring patiently and bearing up for my name's sake, and you have not grown weary" (Rev. 2:2-7).

In these days, you have sought to respond in faith to many contradictory voices. Some plead for a form of justice that would name the evil and identify those responsible and bring them to trial in appropriate courts of law. Others, however, want decisive military action to show the will of the nation to avenge its losses and deny victory to its enemies. Very many share the deep apprehension you have heard from churches abroad about the prospect of the United States striking out again with its uncontested military might. They fear that this would result in an ever rising spiral of retributive violence and the loss of ever more lives.

Words of condemnation and the language of "war" come so quickly to the fore. Blame is easily assigned to "the enemy." These are reinforced by the images and messages streaming across all our television screens, wherever we live. It is far more difficult to regard ourselves in the mirror of such hatred, and to have the courage to recognize how deeply violence is rooted within ourselves, our communities and even our churches. These are lessons we are all trying to learn in the Decade to Overcome Violence.

Among those who have contributed to the remarkable outpouring of sympathy with the USA have been other communities of faith. They share both your sufferings and your fears. Partly in response to this, but also out of your own sense of justice, you have reached out to those communities in your own nation and with them have spoken out clearly against threats or open acts of violence against Muslims and Arab Americans. This powerful witness must be heard both at home and abroad. No one should be allowed to forget that in the places often mentioned as primary targets of military retaliation, Muslims, Christians, and people of other faiths live side by side. Minority Christian communities and those majority communities with whom their lives are shared stand to suffer severely at the hands of religious extremists if the "Christian" West strikes out yet again.

People in your country and around the world have gathered together during this past week in sanctuaries of the churches for silent reflection, and to invoke the presence of the Holy Spirit, who stands beside us in our time of need and

400

journeys with us through the Valley of the Shadow of Death. In these safe spaces Christians and others have sought to discern the deeper meaning of such thoughtless acts and the suffering they have inflicted. This is indeed a time for quiet discernment of the "signs of the times," for courage and wisdom, and to pray for God's guidance. As the prophet Isaiah says: "In quietness and trust shall be your strength" (Is. 30:15).

The message to the church in Ephesus goes on, however: "But I have this against you, that you have abandoned the love you had at first. Remember then from what you have fallen, repent and do the works you did at first." The United States was one of the early architects of the United Nations and was once among the strongest advocates for the international rule of law. In recent times, however, it has repeatedly ignored its international obligations and declared its intention to ignore the rest of the world in pursuit of its own perceived self-interests. This it does to its own and the world's peril. The events of September 11 have again reminded all nations that all are vulnerable and that the only true security is common security. The United States, so often accused, has now been the beneficiary of the sympathy and solidarity of the whole world. It could respond in kind and with humility by reversing its course now and rejoining the global community in a common pursuit of justice for all. It could set aside its reliance on military might at whatever cost and invest in efforts to find non-violent solutions to conflicts generated by poverty, mistrust, greed and intolerance.

As the writer of the Book of Revelation says, "He who has an ear, let him hear what the Spirit says to the churches."

It is one of the chief marks of the ecumenical movement that the churches understand Jesus's prayer that they all might be one, as he is one with the Father. They are being called to practise mutual love and to extend this love even to the enemy, to become, as our familiar hymn puts it, "one great fellowship of love in all the whole wide earth." No one can live alone, separated from the wider fellowship, for we share one humanity. When one hurts, all suffer together.

As an expression of that fellowship, the WCC Executive Committee has expressed its desire to send to you a delegation of church leaders from around the world as "living letters" of compassion, and to engage with you in a common reflection about how we can shape a shared witness to the world in a time of such great need. I hope that you will welcome and open your hearts to them as they will to you.

I reassure you again of our constant prayers, our love and our appreciation for your ministries of consolation and of prophetic vision. May God bless, guide and continue to strengthen you.

Yours in Christ, the Prince of Peace,

Konrad Raiser
General Secretary

Congratulations to Jimmy Carter on the award of the Nobel Peace Prize

Letter to the former president of the U.S.A., 16 October 2002.

Dear President Carter,

We are delighted to congratulate you for being awarded the Nobel Peace Prize this year. The honor is well-deserved. For decades you have worked to advance the cause of human rights, to bring about an end to suffering, and to work for the peaceful resolution of conflicts. In your capacity as US President, you were instrumental in making the issue of human rights an integral part of US foreign policy and placing it squarely on the international agenda. The Carter Center, which celebrates its twentieth anniversary this year, has become a widely recognized instrument for improving the lives of people throughout the world. We commend you for your steadfast efforts to translate your Christian faith into concrete actions to bring about peace and justice in this troubled world.

At a time when the US government seems to be moving towards war, we are particularly appreciative of your efforts to speak out against the threat of another war against Iraq. We hope that you will continue to use your position to advocate for the peaceful resolution of all conflicts and for the strengthening of multilateral institutions to respond to global needs.

Yours in Christ,

Konrad Raiser
General Secretary

PACIFIC

FEDERATED STATES OF MICRONESIA AND THE MARSHALL ISLANDS

Minute on the renegotiation of the Compacts of Free Association between the U.S.A. and the Federated States of Micronesia and the Republic of the Marshall Islands
Adopted by the Central Committee, Geneva, 26 August - 3 September 2002.

At the end of World War II the USA was given trusteeship of Micronesia and the Marshall Islands by the United Nations, with an obligation to assist the two Pacific nations in becoming self-sufficient and independent. These islands, located in Pacific halfway between Hawaii and Australia, were seen as militarily strategic by US policy-makers, and from 1946 to 1958 the USA conducted 67 nuclear tests in the Marshall Islands.

Since 1986, the US relationship to the Federated States of Micronesia (FSM) and the Republic of the Marshall Islands (RMI) has been defined by Compacts of Free Association, which expired in 2001 and are under re-negotiation until October 2003. In early September 2002, a delegation of church representatives from the RMI, hosted by two US churches, will visit Washington, D.C. to meet with members of Congress concerning the Compacts, which were negotiated by Micronesians and Marshallese unaware of the full consequences of the nuclear testing and of the true costs both of independence and of the clean-up from the testing.

In the year prior to the Vancouver Assembly (1983), the World Council of Churches sent a delegation to Micronesia and the Marshall Islands as part of the pre-Assembly visits and through them learned of the health problems suffered by the people as a result of the nuclear testing, and of the forced relocation of people from some of the atolls of the Marshall Islands to accommodate US military requirements. Several weeks before that Assembly, a four-member delegation, including a nuclear physicist, was sent to the Marshall Islands and Micronesia to assess the health impact of radiation on the people and the social and human costs of the US military presence there. This delegation's report was received in Vancouver, where Ms Darlene Keju-Johnson, a Marshallese woman, gave a powerful personal testimony in which she informed Assembly delegates that the problem of nuclear exposure was far greater than the US had admitted. She pointed out that the US restricted its health care for her people to those of just two atolls. Darlene died in 1996 at age 45 of breast cancer.

While the WCC's comprehensive report laid an excellent foundation, little follow-up has been given in recent years. A University of Hawaii study has now been released that shows that the 67 nuclear detonations carried out in the atolls were roughly the equivalent of ten Hiroshima-sized bombs per week throughout the testing period. Likewise, a recently declassified US government document, "The Solomon Report," reveals an effort to keep both of these Pacific countries permanently tied to the USA through "strategic economic dependency". To all this must now be added the environmental impact of global warming on sea-level islands.

The Central Committee therefore requests the WCC to monitor developments related to the renegotiations of the Compacts of Free Association, to study the issues and concerns of the peoples of Micronesia and the Marshall Islands, and in cooperation with the US churches to explore ways to support their advocacy for just compensation and the removal of unfair provisions of the Compacts. This work should be linked with similar efforts being made by the Council to advocate for just compensation for the damage caused to the lands and peoples of all the peoples in the Pacific, including especially those in and near Tahiti, who have been deeply affected by French nuclear testing.

Fiji

Message on the internal crisis
Message to the member churches in Fiji, 26 May 2000

Dear Sisters and Brothers in Christ,

The recent events that began in Fiji with protest marches in the streets and the take-over of the Parliament complex and government officials as hostages by a group of armed men on 19th May have been a matter of deep concern for us. The situation has plunged the country into a deepening political crisis and the President, Ratu Sir Kamisese Mara, has been constrained to declare a state of emergency. There have been several meetings of the Great Council of Chiefs in their effort to resolve the crisis.

The officials of the United Nations and the Commonwealth have visited the country and met the parties to express the concern of the international community at the developments that have taken place. Despite unanimous condemnation of the armed take-over, the stand-off between the President, Ratu Sir Kamisese Mara, and the leader of the armed group continues. This has brought the country to a virtual standstill with much suffering and uncertainty for the people.

The World Council of Churches strongly condemns the armed intervention to subvert the popular will of the people obtained through the democratic process. The Council supports the commitment of the Churches in Fiji to maintain an egalitarian and tolerant society. It calls on the parties concerned to maintain the sanctity of the Constitution and to respect the rule of law in the country. The long and careful consultative process involved in the drafting of the present constitution should not be lightly set aside.

We appreciate the initiatives taken by the member churches of the Council in their endeavors to seek a peaceful resolution of the conflict through dialogue and prayers. It is through such concrete involvement that the Church is able to provide a living witness. The witness of the Church is strengthened in the process of assisting in the healing of the wounds of discord and conflict.

The World Council of Churches expresses its sympathy for all those who have suffered loss as a result of the breakdown of law and order. Please convey to those aggrieved and affected by these events our sympathy and prayers. We will continue to keep you and the people of Fiji in our prayers and will do whatever is necessary to support the endeavours of the Churches to establish a just and lasting peace through dialogue, cooperation and building of trust and mutual understanding between the concerned parties.

Geneviève Jacques
Acting General Secretary

BY-LAWS OF THE COMMISSION OF THE CHURCHES ON INTERNATIONAL AFFAIRS (CCIA)*

1. Name and Organization

1.1. The Commission shall be called the Commission of the Churches on International Affairs.

1.2. The Commission is an agency of the World Council of Churches, responsible to the Central Committee through its Programme Committee.

2. Aims

2.1. It shall be the task of the Commission to witness to the Lordship of Christ over human beings and history by serving people in the field of international relations and promoting reconciliation and oneness of human beings by creation; to God's gracious and redemptive action in history; and to the assurance of the coming kingdom of God in Jesus Christ. This service is demanded by the continuing ministry of Christ in the world of priestly intercession, prophetic judgement, the arousing of hope and conscience and pastoral care. This task necessitates engagement in immediate and concrete issues as well as the formulation of general Christian aims and purposes.

2.2. In seeking to fulfil this task the Commission shall serve the Council, the member churches, the national and regional ecumenical organisations and Christian world communions with which the Council is related and such other international Christian bodies as may be agreed by the Council, as a source of information and guidance in their approach to international problems, as a medium of counsel and action and as an organ in formulating the Christian mind on world issues and bringing that mind effectively to bear upon such issues.

2.3. The *Commission* will call the attention of churches and councils to problems which are especially claimant upon the Christian conscience at any particular time and suggest ways in which Christians may act effectively upon those problems in their respective countries and internationally and respond to issues raised by churches and national and regional ecumenical organisations.

2.4. Special relations may be negotiated from time to time by the Council with the Christian world communions, other international Christian bodies and with regional and national councils of churches and the Commission shall assist them in their approach to international affairs and be assisted by them.

---

* As revised by the Central Committee, meeting in Geneva, 26 August - 3 September 1999.

2.5. The *Commission* shall encourage:

a) the promotion of peace with justice and freedom;

b) the development of international law and of effective international institutions;

c) the respect for and observance of human rights and fundamental freedoms, special attention being given to the problem of religious liberty;

d) the promotion of the rights and welfare of refugees, migrants and internally displaced people;

e) efforts for disarmament;

f) the furtherance of economic and social justice;

g) acceptance by all nations of the obligation to promote to the utmost the welfare of all peoples and the development of free political institutions;

h) the promotion of the right of self-determination of peoples under alien or colonial domination;

i) the international promotion of social, cultural, educational and humanitarian enterprises.

3. Functions

3.1. To initiate and carry out appropriate actions for the furtherance of the aims.

3.2. To advise and assist in the formulation of the Council's policies on international affairs.

3.3. To assist churches and national and regional ecumenical organisations in the formulation of their policies on international affairs and to consult them.

3.4. To share with the churches information and analysis on critical political issues as part of the educational task.

3.5. To monitor national and international political developments and to analyse and interpret them, especially as they affect the life and witness of the churches.

3.6. To arrange for or promote research on selected problems of international justice, world order and peace and to utilise the results in the furtherance of the work of the Commission.

3.7. To support the efforts of the churches and related groups in their activities in conformity with the aims of the Commission.

3.8. To follow up and support at the international level initiatives taken by churches and ecumenical organisations in the areas of concern of the Commission.

3.9. To be a forum for exchange of information and experience among churches and groups in international affairs, especially related to conflict resolution and the promotion of peace and human rights, including the rights of uprooted people.

3.10. To make representations to governments in accordance with the policies of the Council in matters of concern to the Council or to any of its member churches.

3.11. To develop relationships in study and action with non-member churches and organisations, including those of other faiths, sharing aims similar to those of the Commission.

3.12. To maintain and provide for the maintenance of contacts with international bodies such as the United Nations and its agencies, including regional bodies and other non-governmental organisations, which will assist in the attainment of the aims of the Commission.

3.13. To represent the Council or to provide for its representation and the coordination thereof before these international bodies, as may be specifically arranged. The Commission may also represent, facilitate and help coordinate the representation of member churches, related international Christian organisations and non-member churches before such international bodies.

4. Membership, Officers and Staff of the Commission

4.1. The Commission shall be composed of 30 members and, *ex officio*, the Coordinator of International Relations staff of the Council.

4.2. The Officers of the Commission shall be the Moderator, who shall be elected by the Central Committee, a Vice-Moderator, who shall be elected by the Commission, and, ex officio, the Coordinator, who for the purpose of the external relations of the Council may use the title Director of the Commission.

4.3. Christian knowledge and commitment and technical competence in international affairs and related subjects shall be the chief qualifications sought in all members. There will be an emphasis on laymen and laywomen as members of the Commission and a proper balance of the membership in respect of geography, age, race, culture and confession shall be sought.

4.4. The tasks of a Commissioner shall be:

a) to attend meetings of the Commission and to participate in its work;

b) to correspond with the Officers, drawing their attention to matters which in his or her view should occupy their attention, and to advise them in pursuit of such matters,

c) to cooperate with recognised councils and church agencies and committees in educating public opinion.

4.5. The staff assigned by the Council to work on international relations will be appointed and employed according to the normal procedures of the Council, in consultation with the Moderator and Vice-Moderator with respect to the appointment of executive staff.

5. Panels or Advisory Groups

The Commission may appoint panels or advisory groups on particular aspects of its work in pursuance of its aims and the performance of its functions.

6. Meetings of the Commission

6.1. The Commission shall normally meet every eighteen months at a place and time determined by the Coordinator in consultation with the Moderator.

6.2. Any eight members of the Commission or the General Secretary of the Council may require a meeting to be convened for any purpose within the aims of the Commission and the Moderator shall forthwith convene a meeting giving due notice of its purpose.

6.3. In the case of members who give sufficient notice that they are unable to attend a meeting of the Commission, the Moderator and Coordinator may invite a substitute, who shall have the right to speak and to vote.

6.4. Consultants may be invited by the Moderator and Coordinator to attend meetings of the Commission based on their having special competence on major matters under consideration. They shall have the right to speak, but not to vote.

6.5. The quorum for meetings of the Commission shall be one third of the members.

6.6. The Commission shall determine the general policies to be followed by the Moderator, Vice-Moderator and staff in fulfilment of its aims. The Commission may also approve statements proposed for general publication in the name of the Commission, subject to the relevant rules of the Council.

7. Finance

7.1. The staff shall prepare a budget for the activities of the Commission, to be submitted as part of the unified programme budget to the Finance Committee and the Central Committee.

7.2. The Commission will receive reports on the budget and funding of the work and will provide oversight of the detailed planning and policy in relation to the funding of programmatic activities and projects relating to its work within the overall policies and budget approved by the Central Committee.

7.3. The Commission should assist in developing the financial resources available for the work of international relations.

8. Contacts with Governments and Intergovernmental Bodies

8.1. General principles

    a) The Commission may negotiate directly in its own name and in the name of the Council with the United Nations and other international bodies in conformity with the policies of the Council.

    b) In making representation to national governments or other national entities to advance a Christian view on any problem in accordance with its aims, the Commission shall do so ordinarily in consultation with member churches, national councils and the Commission members in the country or countries. However, in exceptional circumstances the Commission may make such representations without such consultation and even when national or regional bodies do not concur.

7.2. Representations:

a) the Commission, when meeting, may propose representations in keeping with Council policy;

b) the Moderator and Vice-Moderator, in their official capacities, may make such proposals, provided that it is also in agreement with the decisions of the Commission and after consultation with the General Secretary of the Council and the Moderator of the Central Committee and with their concurrence;

c) a member of the Commission may not act in the name of the Commission unless specific authorization has been given;

d) the Commission may, in addition, prepare and recommend statements through the appropriate channels to the governing bodies of the Council for their consideration and to any appropriate assemblies or conferences meeting under the auspices of the Council and to such bodies with which relationships have been agreed under the provisions of by-law 2.4.

7.3. Procedures for contact with the United Nations:

1) In accordance with the arrangements provided by the United Nations and its specialised agencies, the staff in consultation with the General Secretary of the Council are empowered to seek and maintain consultative status with the United Nations, its specialised agencies and other intergovernmental bodies on behalf of the Council.

2) Such contacts with other organs and specialised agencies may be necessary to accomplish the Commission's aims and the programmes of the Council;

3) The Commission shall, with the approval of the General Secretary of the Council, be responsible for facilitating and arranging such direct contact with organs and specialised agencies of the United Nations as may be requested by other programme staff of the Council and by bodies with which special relations have been agreed under the provisions of by-law 2.4.

8. Amendments to the By-Laws

8.1. These by-laws may be amended by the Central Committee on the recommendation of, or in consultation with the Commission.

8.2. Three months' notice shall be given to members of the Commission in respect of any proposal to consider an amendment to the by-laws at a meeting of the Commission.

CCIA MEMBERSHIP

Mr Bethuel KIPLAGAT, Moderator — Anglican Church of Kenya

Dr Dale Bishop — United Church of Christ, USA

Mr Marwan Bishara — Greek Orthodox Patriarchate, Palestine

Sr Patricio Alejandro Castillo Peña — Methodist Church of Chile

Archpriest Vsevolod Chaplin — Russian Orthodox Church

Ms Lois McCullough Dauway — United Methodist Church, USA

Pasteur Jean-Arnold de Clermont (from 2002) — Reformed Church of France

Rev. Shirley C. deWolf — United Methodist Church, Zimbabwe

Dr Annemarie Dupré — Waldensian Church, Italy

Mrs Donnalie Edwards-Cabey — Church of the Province of the West Indies, Antigua

Dr Alison Elliot — Church of Scotland, UK

Dr Rubem Cesar Fernandes — United Presbyterian Church of Brazil

Prof. Cees Flinterman — Reformed Churches in the Netherlands

Rev. Rafael Goto Silva — Methodist Church of Peru

Mr Gabriel Habib — Greek Orthodox Patriarchate of Antioch, Lebanon

Mr Rasmus Hylleberg — Baptist Union of Denmark

Rev. Norbert Kenne — Evangelical Church of the Cameroon

Mr John Langmore — Anglican Church of Australia

Archbishop Nifon of Targoviste — Romanian Orthodox Church

Rev. Kenichi Otsu — United Church of Christ in Japan

Dr Antonios Papantoniou — Church of Greece

Mr Ernie Regehr — Mennonite Church, Canada

Ms Ashley Seaman — Presbyterian Church (U.S.A.)

Rt Rev. Bishop Dinis S. Sengulane — Church of the Province of Southern Africa, Mozambique

Mr Lopeti Senituli — Free Wesleyan Church of Tonga

Rev. Jacques Stewart (to 2001) — Reformed Church of France

Dr Christopher Tremewan — Anglican Church, Aotearoa/New Zealand

Mr Stein Villumstad — Church of Norway

Ms Monica Vincent — Church of South India

Mr Tony Waworuntu — Protestant Church in Indonesia

Ms Glenda Wildschut — Church of the Province of Southern Africa, South Africa

Ms Cristina Zeledon — Evangelical Methodist Church of Costa Rica

411

CCIA MEETINGS

Report of the XLIII Meeting of the Commission of the Churches on International Affairs
La Longeraie, Morges, Switzerland, 22-28 January 2000.

The first meeting of the Commission of the Churches on International Affairs (CCIA) elected by the Central Committee after the Eighth Assembly in Harare was held in Morges, Switzerland, 22-28 January 2000. The meeting was characterized by a deep concern for the well-being of Creation. Despite our sense of inadequacy in the face of many apparently insurmountable threats, as we approached our task we kept in mind Paul's counsel to the Church in Corinth:

> *Not that we are competent of ourselves, but our competence comes from God who has made us ministers of a new covenant, a covenant not of the word but of the Spirit which gives life... Therefore, since it is by God's mercy that we are given this commission, we do not lose heart.* (II Cor.3:5-6, 4:1)

Two-thirds of the Commissioners participated in this meeting which remained regionally balanced despite absences. Ten Commissioners were prevented by illness or unavoidable schedule conflicts from attending, but all were consulted in shaping the agenda and several shared perspectives which were taken into account. The Commission was grateful to Dr Konrad Raiser, WCC General Secretary, Ms Geneviève Jacques, Director of the Cluster on Relations, Ms Joan Geuss, Cluster Finance Officer, Ms Sara Speicher, Cluster Communications Officer, and to staff of the Justice, Peace and Creation, and Regional Relations teams who joined in and contributed to parts of our deliberations.

The **purposes of this first meeting** were to:
- familiarize Commissioners with the mandate given in the CCIA Bylaws, the mandate given to International Relations by the Central Committee, and the directives given by the Harare Assembly and the Program Committee;
- bring the Commissioners' regional, professional and pastoral expertise and experience to bear;
- build a sense of solidarity and team spirit among Commissioners and with staff;
- build consensus and advise the Program Committee with respect to principles, program priorities and policy in the field of International Relations;
- review the budgetary needs and fund-raising concerns related to International Relations program; and
- review the role and functions of Commissioners and organize their involvement with program.

The Commission heard **reports from the Moderator and the Coordinator.** Amb. Bethuel Kiplagat addressed the "Challenges to the Ecumenical movement in International Affairs in an Age of Globalization." The Rev. Dwain Epps reviewed the development of the new WCC integrated staff structure and the place of International Relations within it. He described how the concerns of the two streams which flowed together in this programmatic team – International Affairs (CCIA) and Uprooted People (RMS) – were being integrated into a single, interrelated team approach in a way which kept the two components visible in the life of the WCC. He traced briefly the history of the CCIA Commission and described the roles of Commissioners.

The Commission received and reviewed **program reports** on:
- Peace and conflict resolution
- Peacebuilding and disarmament
- Impunity, truth and reconciliation
- Uprooted people
- Human rights and religious liberty
- United Nations relations

It reviewed plans to create a new **ecumenical mechanism for advocacy**, and forwarded its comments to the General Secretary for consideration in the further discussions on this matter between the WCC and its partners in the following months.

The Commission also reviewed a staff proposal for a study requested by the Central Committee on the ethics of **"humanitarian intervention"**. This study to be done in consultation with church-related and other humanitarian agencies, and in cooperation with competent research institutes, should lead to the development of a set of applicable ecumenical criteria. The Commission made recommendations on the issues to be taken into account in the study and consultation process. Several Commissioners will remain closely involved in the study and the resulting policy proposal will be sent to the full Commission for comment, amendment and adoption before it is forwarded to the Central Committee at its next meeting.

Election of the Vice-Moderator

Ms Lois Dauway, a Central Committee member from the United Methodist Church in the USA, was elected vice-moderator of the Commission by acclamation.

Recommendations on program directions and priorities

The Commission welcomed the progress being made in integrating concerns for International Affairs and for Uprooted People (Refugees, Migrants and Internally Displaced Persons) in the program, work and approach of the International Relations staff team. While appreciating the holistic approach taken, it stressed the need for the specificity of the concerns of these two important streams of ecumenical work to be visible. It took particular note of the continuing role of the Global Ecumenical Network on Uprooted People (GEN) in policy and strategy development on behalf of the Commission.

413

The Commission discussed in detail various aspects of **International Relations program** in working groups, a summary whose conclusions is appended to this report. It considered policy formation to guide the churches in their efforts and to advise staff in the shaping and implementation of WCC programs which will support the churches' engagement. Commissioners were appointed to reference groups to guide the implementation of action plans in the mentioned program areas.

It considered that the present direction of program planning generally corresponds to the mandate of International Relations, to the needs of the churches, and to the ecumenical vision of the Commission which was briefly summarized as follows:

- Religion, including Christianity, is being used increasingly to fuel conflict. We have a special responsibility to demonstrate that our faith is committed to and a source of peace.
- The alarming and increasing racial dimension to conflict and choices of engagement for conflict resolution must be acknowledged and systematically addressed. The indivisibility and cultural inclusiveness of the concept of the universality of human rights is essential to narrowing rapidly widening religious, racial, ethnic, national and cultural divides.
- Victims of injustice and violence are essential to the search for solutions, and deserve a place table where response strategies and actions are being considered and decided.
- Economic injustice under conditions of globalization, and the social disorders to which it gives rise are at the root of many conflicts and of many of the concerns mandated to this Commission and the staff of International Relations.
- The increasing militarization of conflict management, the continuing proliferation of conventional weaponry and small arms, and the continuing threat posed by nuclear weapons combine to pose a major threat to life.
- "Humanitarian intervention" has become a common rationale for response to complex emergencies. For such actions to be responsible and effective clear criteria need to be established to ensure that they protect life, and promote the re-establishment of the rule of law and the resolution of the underlying conflict.
- The protection of human rights is a priority for the churches, especially the rights of the most vulnerable groups in situations of conflict: women and youth, people displaced by conflicts within their own countries, uprooted people subjected to trafficking, and others.
- Better systems of bridge building between potential protagonists need to be developed and put in place at the earliest stages of identification of conflict.
- Africa is a special region of concern both to the WCC and to this Commission, given the combined and incremental effects of underdevelopment, poor governance, the spread of the AIDS virus, militarization and war which hinder the protection and promotion of abundant life on that continent.

- There is a strong commitment by the CCIA to search for innovative processes, mechanisms and methods to pool and coordinate the various human and material resources within the ecumenical family which are required for the work of the churches in international affairs. The Commission expressed appreciation for funding partners who are assisting and hopes that they will increasingly support programs that emphasise long-term process development in addition to their ongoing support for short-term projects and emergencies.

Some of the implications of the above for this Commission, the WCC and the programmatic work of International Relations are:

1. Frequent interchange and joint vision building is necessary between the various Commissions of the WCC, particularly between the CCIA Commission and the Justice, Peace and Creation Advisory Group. The Commission has noted with appreciation that at the staff level the new structure and creative practices are allowing this to happen. Mechanisms need to be enabled for the same to take place at the level of advisory bodies.

2. The connections between uprootedness and its causes – poverty, the breakdown of community stability, armed conflict and war, and human rights violations – are now part of the revised mandate of the CCIA. The Commission drew attention to the need for the Global Ecumenical Network on Uprooted People (GEN) to contribute to the building of the agenda.

Report of the XLIV Meeting of the Commission of the Churches on International Affairs
Crans-Montana, Switzerland, 14-18 May 2001.

1. Reports of the Moderator and Coordinator were presented and discussed.

2. The agenda was presented and adopted as revised.

3. Panel presentations by Commissioners and staff were made on the following topics and discussed in plenary:

    The political economy of ecumenism
    Churches witnessing to power
    The shifting bases of power: Implications for ecumenical witness and action
    The impact of globalization in areas of the CCIA mandate
    Youth perspectives on the uses of power in an age of globalization

4. The WCC General Secretary presented a paper on "Theological and ethical considerations on the uses of power in the ecumenical movement today."

5. *Program Budget and Finance Report.* Joan Geuss, Finance Officer for the Cluster on Relations, presented the International Relations finance report for

2000, indicating that operating expenses had been under budget. The following minute was adopted:

Minute on Fundraising

The Commission recognizes the need to increase secure financial support for the Council's work on International Relations.

In this regard, the Commission

welcomes the General Secretary's affirmation of a renewed emphasis on fund development;

affirms the role of program staff in these efforts; and

expresses appreciation to staff for their work in this area.

The Commission affirms its own role in interpreting WCC programs and in suggesting and pursuing possible sources of additional funding in their own regions and churches.

6. ***Future meeting dates.*** The proposed dates for meetings of the Commission through the next WCC Assembly were confirmed as follows:

3-8 June 2002
27-31 October 2003
21-25 February 2005

Staff was requested to plan the agendas for future meetings to include no more than three or four full working days, exclusive of travel, and to seek meeting venues easily accessible from an international airport.

7. ***Approval of minutes of the forty-third meeting of the Commission.*** The minutes of the last meeting, held in Morges, Switzerland were adopted as amended. Staff was requested to circulate texts of decisions taken as soon as possible after meetings for more effective follow-up and interpretation in the churches and regions.

8. ***Findings from discussions on the uses of power in the age of globalization.*** In the plenary review of the panels it was generally agreed that:

8.1. Some kind of global consultation or consultative process is needed to review and assess the role and approach of the WCC and its member churches to international relations in the changing world environment.

8.2. This is an appropriate role for the Commission to play in the light of its By-Laws.

8.3. The focus should be on global trends in the areas of the mandate of the CCIA, and on the uses or misuses of power rather than on the topic of globalization *per se.*

Some suggestions made were:

- The process should link the global and the local, and move from the experience of churches and church-related partners at local, national, regional and world levels.
- The process should not be "top-down," but rather one of identifying "generating themes" derived from people's existential experiences and working on them in a way that identifies and stimulates work around centers of dynamism in the present ecumenical movement.
- Ways should be explored to make the process inter-generational, and discussions should be held with other faith communities along the way.
- Various methodologies were suggested to achieve this. The General Secretary could circulate a study paper highlighting trends and problems, and asking churches and national and regional ecumenical bodies to place it on their agendas for discussion. Teams composed of members of the Commission and staff could take opportunities of meetings or assemblies of these bodies, or of interregional gatherings, to interpret these concerns and see to what extent there is complementarity among the regions on the issues.
- Reference groups of the Commission should pursue these questions in the areas of their advisory work on program.
- A small consultation including Commissioners and other experts to work out a detailed agenda and to shape the agenda and the methodology of such a process.

Some cautions were expressed:
- This process should not lead to a further restructuring of the WCC's program or of the place of International Relations within it. The current structure provides an adequate framework for pursuing these concerns and no more time, energy or resources should be devoted to restructuring.
- To have the required impact, the process should be engaged soon and be of such a character as to dramatize the impact of present trends on peoples' lives, the churches and international institutions. The interactive use of the Internet would be an essential element of the process.
- The focus of the process should not be on "globalization." Other teams of the WCC are working on this in their respective mandated areas, especially the teams on Justice, Peace and Creation and on Regional Relations with respect to the global economy. This process should focus most particularly on the impact of global trends on the churches and their ministries in the areas of the International Relations mandate.

- Given the ambitious aims of such a process, assurances of adequate funding, including the possible engagement of short-term staff before it is undertaken.
- The process should not replace, but complement and give dynamism to program work underway.
- Specific concerns were expressed about the discussion paper and proposed project on "Globalization, Civil Society and the Churches," urging that it be reformulated in the light of the discussion during this meeting, and that it be seen not as a separate process, but rather in close relationship to it.

9. *Global consultation process on the changing role of power and its impact on the churches.* These ideas were submitted to program reference groups for further discussion with respect to whether a consultation process should be undertaken or if another means should be found for following up the findings of the plenary discussions. On the basis of reference group reports it was **agreed** that:

9.1. A global consultation process should be undertaken.

9.2. It should be a *process* that would build on the history of ecumenical thinking, including *inter alia* the report of the 1937 Oxford Conference, the 1966 Church and Society Conference, the 1981 Consultation on Political Ethics, the statement of the Common Understanding and Vision of the WCC adopted by the Eighth Assembly in Harare, take into account the findings of the Special Commission on relations with the Orthodox Churches, and that it would involve continuing follow-up after a consultation.

9.3. The process should not focus on the concept of "globalization," but rather on current global trends in international relations and the changing configurations of power, particularly those related to the mandate of the CCIA, and on their impact on the churches' common witness in society.

9.4. Staff should prepare a detailed proposal on the basis of the discussion during this meeting and of the reports of the reference groups and share it with Commissioners for comment and refinement.

9.5. A preparatory committee comprised of Commissioners and other experts identified in discussion with other WCC teams be formed to elaborate the agenda and process of consultation.

It was also noted that the process followed during the Year of the Uprooted in preparing the ecumenical policy statement provided a good model of building from the local to the global and as a reminder of the need for follow-up of the conclusions of the process of consultation. The proposed study on Globalization, Civil Society the Churches presented to this meeting for discussion should be pursued within the context of the wider consultation process. Given the broad nature of the process envisaged, the General Secretary should be encouraged to bring other WCC programmatic teams and their advisory groups into discussion with regard to their participation. A key aim of the process should be to renew the vision and stimulate new dynamism in the ecumenical movement. It should be linked closely to other activities being undertaken in the WCC, the churches and the wider ecumenical movement in the context of the Decade to Overcome Violence

10. **Commission report.** It was agreed to ask staff, in consultation with the Moderator, to draft a report of this meeting of the Commission to the Program Committee that would describe the process of reflection undertaken, and indicate decisions that had been taken. This draft is to be sent to the Commission if possible within one month of the meeting for comment and refinement, and a revised draft sent back to Commissioners for final adoption.

11. **Review of reference groups.** It was agreed that

11.1. The practice of having reference groups to work with staff in the various programmatic areas has been useful and such groups should be continued for Human Rights, Peace-building and Disarmament, Uprooted People, Impunity, Truth and Reconciliation, and UN Relations. The work of the previous reference group on Peace and Conflict Resolution will be incorporated in the agenda of these groups.

11.2. The membership of the groups should be revised, expanding on the distribution used at this meeting, incorporating one member each from the other reference groups in the one to be formed on UN Relations.

11.3. Provisions for meetings of the reference groups should be taken into account in program planning and budget building.

11.4. Consideration should also be given to the possibility of regional meetings of Commissioners, perhaps in relation to another scheduled activity.

12. **UN Relations.** The Commission adopted the following:

Resolution on United Nations Relations

At its meeting in Crans-Montana, Switzerland, 14-18 May 2001, the Commission of the Churches on International Affairs (CCIA) of the World Council of Churches:

- *recalling and reaffirming* the "Memorandum and Recommendations on the Occasion of the Fiftieth Anniversary of the United Nations," adopted by the Central Committee in September 1995, that states the policy of the WCC on UN relations;

- *recalling the mandate of the CCIA* and the team on International Relations
  - ✦ to maintain and provide for the maintenance of contacts with international bodies and the coordination thereof before these international bodies, as may be specifically arranged;
  - ✦ to represent, facilitate and help coordinate the representation of member churches, related international Christian organizations and non-member churches before such bodies;
  - ✦ to seek and maintain on behalf of the World Council of Churches consultative status with the United Nations, its Specialized Agencies and other inter-governmental organizations;
  - ✦ to be responsible for facilitating and arranging such direct contact with organs and specialized agencies of the United Nations as may be requested by other teams of the World Council or churches and related ecumenical organizations.
- *noting with appreciation the innovative work done in recent years* by the UN Headquarters Liaison Office in New York that has enhanced the visibility and effectiveness of the WCC, the member churches and other partners in bringing ecumenical perspectives to bear on key policy debates;
- *noting with appreciation the work of the International Relations staff* with the UN in Geneva, especially in relation to the UNHCR and the Commission on Human Rights, and in coordinating, facilitating and assisting other teams' direct relations with various UN bodies and agencies in the areas of their mandates;
- *notes that both opportunities for and expectations of the WCC* in the field of UN relations have risen considerably in recent years, but that the capacity of the WCC to respond has not kept pace;
- *conveys to the Central Committee through the Program Committee* its conviction that his capacity must be strengthened as a matter of urgency;
- *requests the staff of International Relations* to develop immediately a proposal for designated funding for a minimum period of three years to allow for the addition of an experienced program staff person and a technical staff person to the staff of the UN Liaison Office in New York;
- *encourages funding partners* to provide sufficient resources in time to engage the program staff person by 1 January 2002 in order to assure continuity and a smooth transition in that office in view of the retirement of the current staff person in late 2002; and
- *expresses the hope* that the strengthening of the staff in the UN Headquarters Liaison Office in New York be done in a way that tightens the programmatic link of this office with Geneva headquarters and assures general oversight of UN relations, including maintenance of consultative status, and cooperation with NGO partners in promoting effective NGO relations with the UN and its related agencies.

13. **Reference Group Reports** on Peacebuilding and Disarmament, Human Rights, Impunity, Truth and Reconciliation, and on Uprooted People were presented, discussed and received.

14. **Small Arms and Light Weapons.** On the recommendation of the reference group, the Commission adopted the statement attached.

15. **Meeting Evaluation.** Commissioners expressed appreciation for the meeting, but agreed that the agenda of this meeting, like the previous one, had been too complex and dense. Meeting process should be more dialogical, and decisions should be made along the way rather than being dealt with at the end of the meeting. The meeting should be shortened, experience having shown that this poses a particular burden on very busy commissioners to set aside a full week. Optimum length of the meeting should be a maximum of 3-4 working days. Gatherings of Commissioners in reference groups between meetings could build on relationships established among commissioners and with staff during the first two meetings. Future meeting agendas should focus more on issues arising in relation to program and from reference group work.

16. **Closing actions.** The Moderator expressed thanks to Commissioners for having contributed to a meeting with important substance in a way that had strengthened our feeling of being together in an engaged and committed ecumenical family. He also thanked the Coordinator and International Relations staff. Special recognition was paid to Lore Hyatt who would retire within a few months. The Commission expressed sincere thanks for her contributions over the years she had worked in the WCC, and particularly for her work as administrative assistant to the Coordinator in the crucial formative years of the new International Relations team.

The Moderator also conveyed thanks to the General Secretary, Konrad Raiser, for having made an uplifting contribution to the reflections of the Commission during this meeting.

The Commission, in turn, thanked the Moderator for his skillful and congenial moderation of the sessions and for the spirit he brought to his task.

The Moderator adjourned the meeting with an appeal to Commissioners to stay in contact with one another and with staff during the coming period.

Report of the XLV meeting of the Commission of the Churches on International Affairs
La Tour-de-Peilz, Switzerland, 3-7 June 2002.

The Commission of the Churches on International Affairs (CCIA), the advisory group to the team on International Relations, has met twice since the Potsdam meeting of the Central Committee, 14-18 May 2001 and 3-7 June 2002, both times in Switzerland. The report of the first meeting was provided earlier to the Core Group of the Program Committee.

The conceptual and theological basis

According to its by-laws: "It shall be the task of the Commission to witness to the Lordship of Christ over human beings and history by serving people in the field of international relations and promoting reconciliation and oneness of human beings by creation; to God's gracious and redemptive action in history; and to the assurance of the coming kingdom of God in Jesus Christ. This service is demanded by the continuing ministry of Christ in the world of priestly intercession, prophetic judgement, the arousing of hope and conscience and pastoral care. This task necessitates engagement in immediate and concrete issues as well as the formulation of general Christian aims and purposes.

The Commission shall encourage:
a) the promotion of peace with justice and freedom;
b) the development of international law and of effective international institutions;
c) the respect for and observance of human rights and fundamental freedoms, special attention being given to the problem of religious liberty;
d) the promotion of the rights and welfare of refugees, migrants and internally-displaced people;
e) efforts for disarmament;
f) the furtherance of economic and social justice;
g) acceptance by all nations of the obligation to promote to the utmost the welfare of all peoples and the development of free political institutions;
h) the promotion of the right of self-determination of peoples under alien or colonial domination;
i) the international promotion of social, cultural, educational and humanitarian enterprises."

A Global Ecumenical Network on Uprooted People (GEN) guides the work of the team in this specialized area and seeks to coordinate the global ecumenical response to the needs of the most vulnerable of our sisters and brothers on all continents.

September 11 and its impact on international relations

Through its regular reports on Public Issues to the WCC Officers and the Executive and Central Committees, the International Relations Team gives an accounting of its work in addressing urgent issues on the world agenda, and their impact on people and the lives and witness of the churches. At its 2001 meeting the Commission decided to undertake a global consultation process on the changing role of power in the world and its impact on the churches. The tragic events of September 11th underscored and accelerated global trends that led to this undertaking. In this meeting we have reviewed their implications for the ecumenical movement as follows:

1. The global situation has become more complex, making a coherent and effective ecumenical response more difficult to shape. The proliferation of internal and international conflicts has posed unprecedented challenges to the churches at all levels.

2. There has been an accelerated attack on the framework of global governance, the rule of law and the institutions painstakingly built over the past fifty years to apply it. Treaties have been abrogated for the first time in many decades, and a systematic effort is being made from several quarters to weaken the system of obligations freely entered into by states and to erode international protections. The USA has led this trend, withdrawing its signature from the Rome Statutes of the International Criminal Court and giving notice that it would no longer abide by the terms of the Anti-Ballistic Missile Treaty.

3. Taking advantage of the climate created by the "War on Terrorism," a number of states have resorted to "states of emergency," undermining due process of law with respect to dissidents, minority groups and persons suspected of involvement in terrorism. This has resulted in grave violations of human rights and threatens a return to national security doctrines.

4. Major increases in military budgets have been made in a number of countries, further limiting resources available for economic, social and environmental needs.

5. Efforts to control the production, transfer and use of weapons, has been slowed in the conventional sphere, and despite the new agreement between the USA and Russia on decommissioning nuclear weapons, for the first time in decades a new generation of nuclear weapons is being developed and new threats of the use of such weapons in regional wars have arisen.

6. The process of globalization and economic neoliberalism has reduced the capacity of many nation-states to determine and implement strategies to meet the needs of their own people, strengthening the powers of the major industrialized nations and weakening those of most developing nations, widening the gap between rich and poor.

7. The blatant unilateralism of the USA and its attempts to impose its own will and standards on the entire world have severely weakened the project of world order provided by the UN Charter which foresaw a form of governance in which all nations, small and large, rich and poor would have a say.

8. Religion has been pushed back into the center of world affairs and that of the peoples, reversing the trends of secularization that dominated in previous

decades and calling into question many of our previous assumptions based on the secular society. It has become a central factor in many open conflicts, making them more resistant to peaceful resolution.

9. There has been a political backlash in many countries of the North that is deeply troubling. It has a particular impact on human rights, particularly those of the uprooted. It also has had serious implications for the churches.

10. At the same time, the churches, the ecumenical movement and its institutions, including the WCC have seen their resources dwindling to an extent unprecedented since the WCC was formed. The resultant weakening of ecumenical structures has been accompanied by trends toward uncoordinated and sometimes competing responses to crises by churches and related agencies.

In the view of the Commission it is more important than at almost any time since 1946, when the CCIA was created, to reaffirm the aims and principles included in its by-laws cited above. There are growing imperatives expressed by the churches and secular partners for the WCC to provide information and analysis and to engage in advocacy to confront these trends. In light of this and of the WCC's seriously diminishing financial resources, the Commission has reviewed international relations program plans, seeking to provide clearer priorities and focus, new styles of work and collective approaches to its mandated tasks in collaboration with other teams and with other parts of the ecumenical movement.

It has done so recognizing that there are significant signs of hope. Global civil society movements are being formed to resist the negative impacts of economic and financial globalization. In its work in UN arenas, the WCC has been an important actor in such fields as sustainable development, social development and financing for development. Headway has been made in the arms field with a global accord to ban landmines and rapid progress in building awareness of the analogous need to control small arms and light weapons. Again here the WCC and the wider ecumenical movement has been a significant actor. The statutes of the International Criminal Court will come into force on 1 July 2002, providing an important new instrument to reverse the trend to give impunity against prosecution to persons responsible for massive crimes against humanity. Awareness of and action on critical global agendas too often ignored in the past, like the HIV/AIDS pandemic, is growing.

In the light of both the negative trends present in the world today, and these new signs of hope, the Commission has taken account of the WCC's privileged position as a body that links local, national, regional and global human realities more than almost any other; and as a religious body in dialogue and cooperation with people of other faiths. The following recommendations with regard to future priorities seek to combine these strengths and to take into account the present financial limitations in a way that will allow the Council to continue to contribute to unity of the churches in doctrine and witness, to respond to present crises in a coherent way, and to take a long-range view of social and political change in a world where such change often becomes visible only after years or decades of patient, principled and continuous witness and action.

United Nations Relations

During its 2001 meeting, the Commission stressed the importance of the role of the WCC at the United Nations. It recalled the mandate of the CCIA to maintain consultative relations with the UN and its specialized agencies on behalf of the Council; to represent, facilitate and help coordinate the representation of member churches and related ecumenical councils and partners; and to coordinate the work of other teams in order to bring the Council's perspectives effectively to bear in global discussions. The Commission forwarded to the Program Committee its recommendation that this function of the Council that is lodged in the International Relations team be strengthened. Subsequently, the Staff Leadership Group (SLG) engaged a highly-qualified external consultant to perform an external review of the WCC's work in UN relations, and this review was undertaken in close collaboration with the CCIA's reference group on UN relations. The consultant presented her findings to this meeting of the Commission where the report and recommendations were discussed. The Commission strongly endorses and commends both, with the following remarks:

1. The Commission reaffirms the central importance of the UN as the heart of the international community and of its role in continuing to shape and strengthen global governance.

2. The UN relations work of the Council should not be seen as a program in itself, but rather as an important instrument to advance the WCC's global agenda. In this connection, the Commission underscores the importance of the recommendation that

   A cross-team UN Coordination Forum should be established (in the WCC) in order to facilitate coordination, prioritization and strategic planning. It should be convened by the CCIA Director and be responsible for producing a draft rolling three-year strategic plan with annual action plans.

   This coordination among International Relations with other relevant teams should develop a more detailed working methodology and should be done in a way that would continue to involve the CCIA reference group on a regular basis.

3. In pursuing the strengthened relationship with the UN care should be taken to involve wherever possible members of the CCIA Commission and of other relevant Council Advisory Groups in ecumenical teams or delegations to UN meetings and conferences.

4. More intentional work with member churches and related Councils is needed to address concerns on the UN agenda not just at UN meetings, but also at

national government levels from the earliest stages of policy development through the implementation of agreed plans of action.

5. Implementation of the recommendations contained in the review report will require priority setting among and within WCC programs.

6. UN relations work should not be limited to follow-up of UN decisions, but rather keep in mind the 1995 Central Committee policy statement that makes engagement with selected UN World Conference processes from the earliest stages of their preparatory processes a condition for WCC involvement.

7. Means must be found to communicate more effectively concerns addressed at the UN and the results of WCC and ecumenical work there to the churches and the wider public.

8. The successor to the present UN Representative in the UN Headquarters Liaison Office in New York, who retires at the end of 2002, should be a person deeply rooted in his or her church tradition; with wide experience of the WCC, its history and its programs; with considerable knowledge of the UN system; and with highly developed diplomatic skills.

Program priorities in the field of international relations

The Commission has also reviewed the three-year budget plan developed for presentation to the Central Committee, especially those parts that correspond to the programs mandated to the International Relations Team. It expressed appreciation for the effort to develop a comprehensive presentation of budget and program within the limits of projected income while maintaining a viable core program for the Council. It endorses this presentation, stressing the importance of special priority to be given to the changing character and role of religion in the world and the importance of dialogue and cooperation with other faith communities in this critical period of history. It makes the following comments on program priorities for International relations:

1. **Human Rights.** Priority should be given to:

   1.1. Training and capacity-building for local churches in human rights and their defense.

   1.2. Engaging CCIA commissioners more fully in the Council's efforts to monitor and respond to human rights violations in their respective countries and regions.

   1.3. Identifying and addressing emerging trends in the field of human rights.

   1.4. Survey and develop information for the churches on particular violations of human rights arising in the context of September 11th and its aftermath.

   1.5. Paying particular attention to the rise of religious intolerance.

1.6. Seeking inter-religious cooperation for the fulfillment of human rights as a basis for peace and justice.

1.7. Strengthening cooperation with churches, agencies, concerned individuals and others with respect to funding for the Specific Expression on Public Witness – Human Rights, Impunity, Justice and Reconciliation.

1.8. The following situations were identified as requiring priority response: the Balkans, Colombia, Indonesia, Israel/Palestine, Solomon Islands, Sri Lanka and Zimbabwe.

2. **Impunity.** Recalling the priority given to impunity, truth and reconciliation in the context of the DOV, the Commission stressed the linkage between impunity and conflict prevention, the need further to strengthen international law in this area, the need for continuing theological and ethical reflection as a specific WCC contribution in international forums, and the need to further deepen reflection on justice and restorative justice. Priorities were recommended as follows:

2.1. At least one regional workshop or seminar per year must be held, the next in Asia (possibly Indonesia or Sri Lanka).

2.2. Promotion of ratification of the Statutes of the International Criminal Court through work with national churches in cooperation with other teams.

2.3. Strengthening of work with UN bodies like the High Commissioner for Human Rights and the Commission and Subcommission on Human Rights.

2.4. Monitoring opportunities to address questions of impunity for crimes against humanity in relation to the current Palestinian/Israeli conflict.

3. **Uprooted People.** Given the trends described above that often directly affect uprooted people in the first instance, the Commission believes that this is a high priority program of the Council, and that advocacy at the UN for uprooted people's rights and protection needs to be continued and strengthened. The WCC also has an important role to play in sensitizing and encouraging churches to keep migration and refugee issues as priorities in their own programs at a time when the general tendency is for them to cope with their own financial difficulties by cutting these back or eliminating them. This is particularly important in Europe in view of the growing climate of xenophobia and the resulting political changes. Migration counseling should be given special attention as a pastoral task. The following steps are proposed for establishment of priorities in light of shortfalls in income:

3.1. Strengthening advocacy work on uprooted people by developing new ways of working, especially through increased collaboration with members of GEN, asking them to take the lead on particular issues like work on international and regional protocols on trafficking and smuggling.

3.2. Urging church and church-related agencies to give increased priority to uprooted concerns.

3.3. Experimenting with a new model of producing the *Uprooted People Newsletter*, urging partners to share information with one another directly via a common electronic mailing list, maximizing the time available to staff to provide analyses of global developments.

3.4. Exploring possibilities of handing over some of the present project administration work to those regional groups with the capacity to do direct fund-raising, oversee the proposal process, monitor reporting and transferring funds.

3.5. Pursuing discussions that would allow support for regional uprooted working groups to be supported through bi-lateral relationships, round tables or by local churches in view of the importance of the role of such groups and the projected declining support for them through the WCC.

3.6. Pursuing efforts underway to approach foundations and other non-traditional funding sources for funding a consultation on detention, an interfaith consultation on theological reflection on uprootedness, and for further work on trafficking.

3.7. Continuing discussions with the Conference of European Churches and the Churches' Commission on Migrants in Europe (CCME) with respect to more effective cooperation on European uprooted concerns.

3.8. Developing a pilot project on African victims of trafficking in Europe in connection with the Council's Africa Focus.

3.9. Welcoming the secondment of an International Relations team member to the AACC as its interim General Secretary, recognizing that this will place additional pressures on other staff, and urging staff to turn to members of the Commission for assistance when the burden on staff becomes too onerous.

4. *Peace and Conflict Resolution.* The Commission reviewed and strongly endorsed the work done by the International Relations team and the Council in the field of peace and conflict resolution during the past year and the centrality of this work to the life of the WCC and the ecumenical movement. With regard to working styles and priority setting, the Commission:

4.1. Stressed the need to broaden and strengthen ecumenical networks in a way that will make possible better coordination of efforts and sharing of human and financial resources.

4.2. Stressed the need for wide and timely dissemination of information, analysis and actions on public issues in the working languages of the Council in a way to reach the actors addressed and groups within and beyond the churches who need to be involved in strengthening advocacy on situations and the issues.

4.3. Noted and reaffirmed the interrelated dimensions in this area of the Council's work that include advocacy, mediation, engagement in post-crisis situations and the development of effective public policies.

4.4. Expressed concern about the decline in income designated by donors to this work of the Council that is highly visible, central to the agendas of its governing bodies and for which appreciation has been expressed by the churches, and urged funding partners and churches who are not now contributing but who benefit directly from this work to consider their own priorities in this light.

4.5. Strongly reaffirmed the importance of ecumenical team visits, pastoral visits and teams to assist in mediation and reconciliation efforts of churches in situations of conflict, and to make fuller use of Commissioners in establishing the membership of such teams and delegations.

5. **Peacebuilding and disarmament.** The Commission revised the program planning document presentation, and recommends renaming this program **Demilitarization, Disarmament and Prevention of Armed Conflict.** The following priorities were identified for 2003:

5.1. The Peace to the City Network should be strengthened through continuing communication efforts including further publications, additional language translations and videos. Network partners' advocacy work should be strengthened by further inter-regional exchanges. New partners' capacities to advocate for community policing and security sector reform should be built along the lines of the Boston and Rio "peace to the city" partners models through a regional training workshop. Partners should be drawn more fully into international campaign efforts related to the 2003 UN Review Conference on Small Arms.

5.2. A global ecumenical review consultation should be organized to develop further policy and action on small arms control and demand reduction for adoption by the Central Committee and presentation to the 2003 UN Review Conference on Small Arms by a WCC /CCIA delegation. Two meetings of ecumenical partners and members of the CCIA Reference group on Demilitarization, Disarmament and Prevention of Armed Violence should be held to prepare for the global consultation process and identify post-conference follow-up. The Ecumenical Network on Small Arms should be strengthened through provision of seed funding to selected faith-based grassroots initiatives on practical disarmament.

5.3. In the field of nuclear disarmament, follow-up should be given to the 2002 ecumenical visit to capitals of non-nuclear member states of NATO. Building on the proposed Southern Asia policy statement of the Central Committee, a regional consultation should be organized on the threat of nuclear weapons and to assist the churches in their advocacy efforts to encourage the governments of India and Pakistan to ratify the Nuclear Non-Proliferation Treaty and the Comprehensive Test Ban Treaty and to declare the sub-region a nuclear weapons free zone.

CCIA STAFF

Coordinator

Dwain C. Epps, Presbyterian Church (U.S.A.) (to August 2002)
Peter Weiderud, Church of Sweden (from September 2002)

Executive Secretaries

Salpy Eskidjian, Armenian Apostolic Church of Cyprus
Elizabeth Ferris, Religious Society of Friends, U.S.A.
Geneviève Jacques, Eglise Réformée de France
Clement John, Church of Pakistan
Melaku Kifle, Ethiopian Orthodox Tewahedo Church

Consultant

Guillermo Kerber, Roman Catholic Church, Uruguay

Technical Staff

Mariette Grange (France), UN Representative in Geneva
Gail Lerner, UN Representative in New York

Administrative Assistants

Patricia Brüschweiler
Diana Chabloz
Beth Godfrey
Christiane Hoeffel
Lore Hyatt
Beatrice Merahi

Interns*

Sarah Woodside, October 1998 - March 1999
Holly McNamara, July 1999 - February 2000
Glenys Stevenson, September 1999 - February 2000
Sarah Estabrooks, Canada, September 2000 - September 2001
Heather Exner, September 2002 - April 2003
Sarah Davies, Australia, March - September 2002
Denise Garcia, Brazil, April 2000 - March 2001
Alexandros Karides, Cyprus, July 2000 -

STAFF CHANGES

Dwain Epps retired in August 2002.

Mariette Grange departed in January 2001.

---

* Interns who served for six months or more.

Christiane Hoeffel departed in January 1999.

Lore Hyatt transferred from Refugee and Migrant Services in January 1999 and retired in August 2001.

Geneviève Jacques left the CCIA in November 1999 to become Director of the Cluster on Relations.

Guillermo Kerber joined the staff in February 2001.

Melaku Kifle transferred from Refugee and Migrant Services in January 1999.

Peter Weiderud was elected Director of the CCIA and Coordinator for International Affairs and assumed his responsibilities in September 2002.

Appreciation to the Rev. Dwain Epps
Minute adopted by the Central Committee, Geneva, 26 August – 3 September 2002.

As Dwain Epps now retires from his long and committed service with the Commission of the Churches on International Affairs of the World Council of Churches, the Public Issues Committee on behalf of the Central Committee of the WCC, would like to express its deep appreciation for Dwain's contribution to its deliberations and wish him all the best in his retirement. We have drawn on his extensive knowledge. We have been gifted with his excellent ability to formulate texts which are precise and have created consensus among us, guiding the Council in the area of international affairs. We have benefited tremendously from his theological insights and political analysis. Most of all we have appreciated his sense of humour, his company, his friendship and his deep loyalty for the ecumenical movement. In short: we shall miss him immensely.